of Politics

FRED R. DALLMAYR

The University of Massachusetts Press   Amherst

309845

Library of Congress Cataloging in Publication Data
Dallmayr, Winfried Reinhard, 1928–
Twilight of subjectivity.
Includes bibliographical references and index.
1. Individualism.   2. Subjectivity.   3. Inter-
subjectivity.   4. Political psychology.   5. Social
evolution.   I. Title.
HM136.D27   302.5   80–23433
ISBN 0–87023–314–9
ISBN 0–87023–315–7 (pbk.)

The publisher gratefully acknowledges the support
of the National Endowment for the Humanities
toward the publication of this book.

FOR MY MOTHER

In paradisum deducant te angeli
et perducant te in civitatem sanctam

CONTENTS

PREFACE

THE PRESENT VOLUME probes the decline or twilight of *subjectivity,* which has served as cornerstone of modern philosophy since the Renaissance, together with the repercussions of this decline on social and political thought. In the latter domain, modern subjectivity has tended to foster a distinctive type of individualism: one which treats the ego as the center not only of theoretical cognition but of social-political action and interaction. In trying to pave the way toward a "post-individualist theory of politics," the volume does not simply reject individualism, but seeks to divest it of its anthropocentric, "egological," and "possessive" connotations. The motivation animating the study, in any case, is not an anti-individualist, and even less an "anti-modernist," sentiment. The rise of modern subjectivity and man-centered individualism is seen here not merely as an avoidable mistake, but as a phase in the course of human emancipation and maturation— though a phase whose intrinsic shortcomings have now become obvious.

Pondering reflectively the decline of subjectivity may seem incongruous, especially in a scientific age. Yet, in my view, reflection is not necessarily tied to egological premises; at least on occasion, it is able to scrutinize its own non-subjective and even non-reflective underpinnings. The incongruence appears heightened by the intellectual climate of our era—a time when science and technology dominate Western culture and social discourse. To question the role and status of subjectivity at this juncture may seem to buttress "scientism," or scientific objectivism, and to hasten the defeat of human autonomy. In an earlier volume, entitled *Beyond Dogma and Despair,* these concerns were paramount in my mind: while distancing itself from a subjectivist idealism, the argument of that volume found in "philosophical anthropology"—revolving around a concretely embodied subjectivity—an antidote to the objectivist peril. In the intervening period my thoughts on autonomy have not changed, but I have come to see more clearly that subjectivity and objectivity, like subjectivism and objectivism, are two sides of the same coin. Thus, to challenge the preeminence of science and technology may require more than a renewed Cartesian meditation. The change in outlook is reflected in the group of mentors invoked in the present study, a parentage outlined in the introduction.

To be sure, the list of intellectual influences could have been expanded, especially by taking into account broader affinities or more oblique sources of inspiration. Space limitations, apart from limitations of expertise, militated against such an endeavor. In retrospect I regret esepcially the relative neglect of two major authors. The discussion of intersubjectivity could have benefited from greater attention to Max Scheler's writings; his study on *The Nature of Sympathy* in particular is noteworthy, both because of the outline of different modes of interpersonal relations and because of the effort to balance intentional empathy against the need to recognize the "otherness" of fellow beings. In all chapters a distant but not specifically mentioned reference point is Gabriel Marcel; his notion of creative fidelity is a benchmark which for some time I have tried to emulate (though mostly unsuccessfully). Sometimes the affinity has been subterranean or subconscious; this is especially true with regard to the idea of recollection. After having completed this volume I read (or perhaps reread) a statement which appears in his *Philosophy of Existence* and which deserves citation: "It should be noted that recollection which has received little enough attention from pure philosophers, is very difficult to define—if only because it transcends the dualism of being and action or, more correctly, because it reconciles in itself these two aspects of the antinomy. The word means what it says—the act whereby I re-collect myself as a unity; but this hold, this grasp upon myself, is also relaxation and abandon."

Apart from focusing on a limited set of mentors, the study is also circumscribed in its thematic range. Given the pervasive character of the twilight noted in the title, no attempt is made here to offer an exhaustive treatment of all the relevant issues. While the first chapter sets the stage for the volume by delineating the controversy surrounding the status of individualism and the "thinking subject" in contemporary philosophy and social-political thought, subsequent chapters examine the repercussions of this controversy in four main thematic areas: the domain of intersubjectivity or *sociality;* the relationship between man and nature; the theory of social and individual development or maturation; and the ethical or metaethical infrastructure of social-political obligations. In all instances, specific implications for political theory are explored after a discussion of broader philosophical arguments. Sometimes these implications are left in a tentative state, awaiting more detailed scrutiny on later occasions.

The volume as it stands is a work for which I take full responsibility and blame, but not full credit; "post-individualism" certainly has a direct bearing on authorship. My gratitude goes first of all to the intellectual mentors who charted a course on which I proceeded sometimes very haltingly. In addition there are friends and colleagues, too numerous to recite, whose comments and correspondence have sustained me in my undertaking; in random sequence these include Bill Connolly, Hwa Yol Jung, Ted Bluhm, Cal Schrag, Bill McBride, Dick Bernstein, and Tom McCarthy. A major debt of gratitude is owed to the National Endowment for the Humanities. Most of the work on this study was done during 1978–1979 when I held a Fellowship for Independent Study and Research from the Endowment; the fellowship gave me the freedom and leisure to collect my thoughts and write, unburdened by the normal routine of academic duties (a freedom which was particularly appreciated after several years of service as departmental chairperson). The National Endowment for the Humanities has also provided support for the publication of this work. All these forms of intellectual and financial assistance would have been of little avail without the more intimate support given me over the years by my wife, Ilse, who also typed initial versions of some chapters. The entire manuscript was typed competently and expeditiously by Ms. Ann Steppe. Special thanks are due to Ms. Deborah Robson for her labors invested in copyediting the volume and readying it for publication.

South Bend, August 1980

INTRODUCTION

REFLECTING ON THE Cartesian legacy of the "thinking substance" or "thinking subject," Ortega y Gasset wrote: "Suppose that this idea of subjectivity which is the root of modernity should be superseded, suppose it should be invalidated in whole or in part by another idea, deeper and firmer. This would mean that a new climate, a new era, was beginning." The present volume explores this assumption and its ramifications, especially in the area of social and political theory. Actually, the thoughts in this volume are based on more than a mere supposition; it seems to me that the idea of subjectivity has been losing strength for some time, due both to concrete experiences of our age and to the probings of leading philosophers. Yet the claim of a weakened condition should not be misconstrued in the sense of a complete reversal. Regardless of his own philosophical leanings, Ortega was quite correct when, in the same context, he depicted the idea as "so enormous, so firm, so solid, that we cannot create for ourselves an illusion that it will be easily overthrown."[1] In fact, nothing would be more ill-conceived in my view than to imagine a total rejection of subjectivity. For intrinsic reasons—which should become more obvious in the course of the study—the passage beyond modernity cannot take the form of a deliberate invalidation. If, as I suspect, we are slowly entering a new era, our entry will probably occur without intention—which does not mean that it must happen without awareness or reflection.

The preceding comments on subjectivity or the idea of subjectivity might suggest that the subtitle of the study should refer more appropriately to a post-subjectivist than to a post-individualist theory of politics. However, there are several motives for clinging to the notion of post-individualism. First of all, the term *post-subjectivist* might denote that the core or "root" of modernity (in Ortega's sense) resided in its "subjectivism"—which is plainly false. Actually, as inaugurated by Descartes, the stress on subjectivity reflected an endeavor to discover an indubitable starting point and thus to arrive more securely at "objective" knowledge. The same stress, one might add, entailed a division between "thinking substance" and "extended matter" or between "subject" and "object" of knowledge—a division which in due course formed the backbone of both rationalist and empiricist perspectives. More importantly, even when disassociated from subjectivism, the term *post-subjectivist* has distinct drawbacks, owing mainly to its narrowly epistemological connotations. In modern philosophical usage, "subjectivity" or "thinking substance" tends to stand primarily as a synonym for theoretical consciousness (and even "transcendental consciousness") construed as a premise of cognition. However, at least from the vantage point of social and political theory, "modernity" appears characterized not only by its reliance on the cognitive-epistemological ego but by its concern with the practical, or acting, human subject. Precisely this aspect of the practical ego tends to be highlighted in the notion of individualism as traditionally employed. It was by accentuating this aspect that Elie Halévy was able to write: "In the whole of modern Europe it is a fact that individuals have assumed consciousness of their autonomy, and that every one demands the respect of all the others, whom he considers as his fellows, or equals: society appears, and perhaps appears more and more, as issuing from the considered will of the individuals which make it up. The very appearance and success of individualistic doctrines would alone be enough to prove that, in Western society, individualism is the true philosophy."[2]

The same emphasis can still be found in recent writings on the topic. In his informative and insightful study on *Individualism,* Steven Lukes locates the essence of the concept in four basic unit-ideas or principles: namely, respect for human dignity, autonomy (or self-direction), privacy, and self-development; these principles, which are also termed "core values of individualism," are said to be actually variants of the "ideas of equality and liberty," in the sense that "the idea of human dignity or respect for persons lies at the heart of the idea of equality, while autonomy, privacy and self-development represent the three faces of liberty or freedom." Little effort is required to show that, in modern times, equality and liberty are the key concerns of practical reason or the practical ego, to the extent that they pinpoint the individual's status and role in relation to other human beings and to society. Apart from the mentioned principles, Lukes also lists a number of other "elements" or "doctrines"—mostly of a cognitive character— traditionally affiliated with individualism, especially the notion of the "abstract individual" referring to a creature endowed with theoretically presupposed "interests, wants, purposes, needs"; the latter notion, in his view, was closely akin to modern "epistemological individualism" and exerted a crucial impact on prevalent versions of "political" and "economic individualism." A central thesis advanced in the study is that it may be possible to preserve the "core values" while abandoning the more cognitive elements and, in fact, that a serious "commitment to equality and liberty" requires the rejection of the "abstract individual" in favor of the conception of "individuals in their concrete specificity."[3] Couched in this manner, the argument strikes me as hazardous and beset with several quandaries. The segregation of practical-moral from cognitive components tends to reduce individualism to a "commitment" or choice devoid of adequate justification; in addition, the argument leaves unclarified the philosophical status of concrete persons in comparison with abstract egos and the reasons for preferring one view to the other.

A chief motivation behind the notion of post-individualism, as invoked in this volume, is exactly the philosophical elusiveness of individualism, considered in both its practical and its cognitive-epistemological dimensions, and particularly with reference to the former. What is at issue, in my view, is not so much the substance of individualism or its positive assertions, as the manner of accounting for them; as it seems to me, individualism can no longer (or can only with greatest difficulty) be justified or buttressed on "individualist" premises, mainly because these premises—revolving around the practical and the cognitive ego—have become tenuous or implausible. Seen in this light, the concern with post-individualism does not simply imply a dismissal of individualism and its concrete social and political acquisitions; actually, by ceasing to cling to the individual as an ultimate foundation or primary possession, such a concern is prone to make room for a richer and more diversified notion of individuality than has been traditionally contemplated.[4] To some extent, the "end of the individual" (to use a somewhat dramatic phrase) may perhaps be fruitfully compared to the "end of metaphysics" as portrayed by Martin Heidegger—where *post-metaphysical thinking* denotes not so much a denial or negation of metaphysics as the endeavor to reflect on the subterranean underpinnings hidden from its own view. "Metaphysics cannot simply be discarded like an opinion," he observes in an essay dealing with the issue; "one can by no means leave it behind as a no longer cherished or defended doctrine." As he adds: "What the incipient completion of metaphysics signals is the unrecognized—and from the vantage point of metaphysics basically inaccessible—preparation of a first emergence of the difference and reciprocal envelopment of Being and ontic reality."[5]

The perspective delineated in this volume is not presented as an "individual" accomplishment or possession. On the contrary, the volume is in large measure intended as a tribute to several recent or contemporary thinkers to whose writings I am deeply indebted (although, to be sure, they are in no way accountable for my shortcomings). As the reader will quickly discover, the volume relies extensively on the insights of some four or five thinkers, and principally on those of two or three. During the past decade I have been chiefly influenced by two intellectual mentors: Maurice Merleau-Ponty and Theodor Adorno. Merleau-Ponty has taught me the need to be attentive to pre-reflective experience, and also the importance of patience and sobriety in following the intimations of "perceptual faith." Adorno, in a similar vein, exemplifies critical reflectiveness, understood as the endeavor to preserve the integrity of thought while simultaneously pursuing reflection to its limits—to the point where the "utopia of knowledge" comes into view, consisting in the ability to gain access to non-thought (or the other side of thought) through reflective means "without levelling it into the latter." To a lesser extent I have learned from the teachings of Paul Ricoeur, especially from his proclivity to expose the "antinomies" of traditional philosophy, thereby paving the way toward their tentative transgression. More recently I have also benefited strongly from the writings of Jacques Derrida, although my focus in his case has been restricted almost entirely to his exegetic efforts in the domains of structuralism and phenomenological ontology; in terms of overall orientation, I take seriously his statement that "the step 'beyond or outside philosophy' is much more difficult to conceive than is commonly imagined by those who pretend to have made it long ago with cavalier ease and who in general remain tied to metaphysics together with the entire body of discourse which they claim to have disengaged from it."[6] Last but certainly not least there is Heidegger's influence; his thought, like a *basso continuo,* underscores and permeates all the themes and arguments of this volume, even where his name is not specifically mentioned.[7]

The volume also contains references (sometimes repeated references) to several other present-day thinkers to whose teachings I am indebted, although their views are subjected in many respects to critical commentary. This is true especially of Jean-Paul Sartre, Jürgen Habermas, and Karl-Otto Apel. Using a shorthand formula, all three may be said to follow a transcendental or quasi-transcendental philosophical approach; despite the difficulties inherent (in my judgment) in this approach, I consider their position greatly preferable to positivist empiricism in its various forms, including functionalism, linguistic descriptivism, and positivist versions of structuralism. In dealing with these and other writers, and also in my treatment of the cited mentors, I have tended to give ample room to an exposition or recapitulation of their arguments. The reader may sometimes feel that I almost disappear behind the exposition; however, in my view the procedure is entirely congruent with a non-individualist or post-individualist outlook. The volume is not meant to offer a rehearsal of personal opinions or beliefs, but an introduction to a transpersonal problematic. In such an endeavor, "my" thought has a chance of finding its way only in closest contact with the views of others and only by being constantly ready to transgress its boundaries in their direction. While not adhering to the dialogue form in its strict sense, the adopted procedure seeks to capture the advantages of a dialogical presentation, without courting the risk of artificiality involved in a literary dialogue written by one author.

Considering its various mentors, the theoretical perspective animating this volume might be labeled *critical post-phenomenology;* but it might also (and perhaps better) be described as a *practical ontology*—provided *ontology* is not confused with an ontic objectivism and the term *practical* is not narrowly or exclusively identified with subjective-intentional activity. Given the peculiar or oblique character of ontology (especially in the Heideggerian sense)—its irreducibility to either logical axioms or empirical findings—the volume does not advance a systematic doctrine or a set of analytical or inductive propositions; rather, an effort is made to grapple successively with a series of distinct though related issues which are likely to be encountered in any attempted move beyond the confines both of traditional (metaphysical) epistemology and of traditional individualism. The parts of the volume thus form a mosaic of themes and motifs, with each part representing a variation on the central topic and being internally refracted into a number of contrasting vantage points. Although concerned in the end with the clarification of longstanding questions beleaguering social and political thought, the study does not pretend to be a political treatise in the sense of advocating a cluster of political ideas or policy programs— an undertaking which appears predicated on a prior understanding of politics and its proper ramifications; instead of proceeding from this assumption, the study regularly probes implications for political theory only as a sequel to broader philosophical considerations.

The first three chapters are probably most crucial to the volume's overall endeavor. The opening chapter addresses itself to the troubled condition of individualism in our time, especially as it reflects the legacy of possessivism deriving from the modern focus on individual enterprise and initiative; steering a course between recent reaffirmations of individualism (on both empiricist and transcendental-humanist premises) and radical countercurrents proclaiming the "end of the individual" or "end of man," the discussion seeks to clear a path pointing toward a post-individualist *reductio hominis*. The next two chapters deal with two major dimensions of human existence or of man's *being-in-the-world:* the dimensions of his interaction with other humans and of his relationship to nature. Given its importance for the very notion of society or political community, the second chapter, devoted to *intersubjectivity,* is not only the lengthiest but also thematically the centerpiece of the volume. In accordance with traditional epistemology, social interaction or aggregation has tended to be treated either as a factual-empirical occurrence or structure or else, more commonly, as an outgrowth of converging individual initiatives (along the lines of modern "state-of-nature" and "social contract" theories). To show the virtues and difficulties of this legacy, the chapter focuses first of all on prominent recent restatements of the individualist or *egological* approach to intersubjectivity—those of Edmund Husserl and Sartre; their formulations are then juxtaposed to non-egological treatments of the topic as found in Heidegger's discussion of sociality and in Merleau-Ponty's and Derrida's notion of human reversibility. After a brief comparison of these views with conceptions prevalent in critical (Marxist) theory, the concluding portion of the chapter delineates a typology of possible modes of sociality, stressing the categories of *communalism, association, movement,* and *community* (or *"polis,"* properly speaking).

The issue of the man-nature relationship seems particularly urgent and controversial in view of the expanding role of technology and man's claim to mastery over nature. Following a critical review (inspired by Ricoeur) of the conflict between nature and human freedom, the third chapter examines phenomenological and structuralist endeavors to bridge the gulf, and also the repercussions of such endeavors on contemporary "ideological politics" and the role of the "state." While the initial chapters probe the general character of post-individualism and its dimensions in terms of human *space,* the fourth chapter draws attention to the *temporal or genetic* aspect of the theme. A recapitulation of Habermas' major arguments relating to individual development and social evolution is followed by an extended critical commentary, and finally by a synopsis of Adorno's "negatively dialectical" (and post-individualist) views on the same topics and especially on the idea of *natural history.* The fifth chapter concentrates on a problem which has always been a main facet of practical philosophy and which is bound to preoccupy political theorists seeking to transcend the positivist fact-value dichotomy: the problem of ethics and of the "meta-ethical" justification of norms. In this case, a critical discussion of recent attempts to overcome the "naturalistic fallacy"—especially of John Searle's linguistic descriptivism and Alan Gewirth's axiomatic-analytical strategy—leads to the delineation of a *recollective* ethics bypassing both inductive and deductive procedures.

The appendix expands on a number of points only briefly treated in the volume: the philosophical status of Vico's *New Science* (a work cited in the chapter on social evolution); Ricoeur's social and political philosophy; and the orientation and aims of critical theory, especially as manifest in Habermas' publications during the past two decades. Two major issues directly pertinent to a post-individualist perspective are not specifically discussed in the present study, mainly for reasons of space (but also because I have dealt with them tentatively elsewhere). One issue is chiefly epistemological in character and revolves around the meaning of truth or validity claims in the context of a practical ontology. Taking my bearings from Merleau-Ponty's later works, I tend to approach this issue basically as a problem of translation, involving the task of adequately transposing the lessons of pre-reflective perception or discovery into the idiom of veridical statements (a transposition which is not synonymous with inductive verification, nor with a priori certitude, nor with the congruence of constitutive subjectivities). The second issue arises from the constellation of mentors outlined above, and especially from the juxtaposition of Adorno's critical Marxism and Heideggerian ontology. As is well known, several of Adorno's writings have the form of an extensive critical commentary on Heidegger's philosophical posture. One of the central criticisms frequently reiterated in these writings concerns the alleged particularism and earthbound (or "folkish") quality of that posture, as distinguished from the universalist aspirations of critical reflection. Apart from pointing to the emptiness of a free-floating universalism, I am inclined on this issue to agree with Derrida's comments that the preoccupation with locality and earth in Heidegger's thought "has nothing in common with a passionate-emotional attachment to a territory or region and thus with provincialism or particularism; it is as little linked to an empirical 'nationalism' as the Hebraic nostalgia for the homeland—a nostalgia which is not governed by an empirical passion but rather *provoked* by the incursion of a speech and a promise." As he adds: "The thinking of Being, therefore, is not a pagan cult of a locality, since locality here means not a given but a promised proximity."[8]

CHAPTER ONE

Beyond Possessive Individualism

What there is to be grasped

is a dispossession

MERLEAU-PONTY

WESTERN CIVILIZATION BEARS deeply the imprint of individualism; perhaps the two are so closely linked as to be inseparable. Successive stages or developmental thrusts in Western history testify to the steady strengthening of this linkage. The rise of philosophy in ancient Greece was tied to the efforts of individual thinkers dissatisfied with traditional cosmologies. In the midst of the rigid structures of the Roman Empire, Christianity preached the value of the human soul, holding out the promise of individual salvation. At the dawn of modernity, the Reformation freed individual conscience from clerical control—just as the Enlightenment, in subsequent centuries, freed individual reason or the "thinking subject" (*ego cogitans*) from unexamined beliefs. To a large extent, Western history can thus be read as a story of liberation—involving the progressive emancipation of man from all kinds of external tutelage or spurious constraints.[1] Much of the significance of Western civilization is tied up with this story. Clearly, advances in knowledge are inconceivable without the possibility of free individual scrutiny; similarly, actions cannot properly be called moral in the absence of autonomous judgment.

Despite these merits, however, individualism has been a mixed blessing; and Western history is not simply synonymous with growing freedom. From the beginning, individualism carried overtones of segregation and willful arrogance. In its relation to nature, in particular, the story of emancipation has tended to be pervaded by a domineering impulse—an impulse which found overt expression in Francis Bacon's *instauratio magna* of modern science as an instrument of human mastery. Through their implication in the mastery of nature, individual reason and the thinking subject were part and parcel of *anthropocentrism*, construed as the quest for general-human supremacy or *species* liberation. In the long run, however, the goal of domination was incompatible with the species character of the enterprise; if, in Bacon's terms, knowledge equals power, modern science was bound to reinforce not only the gulf between man and universe but also the differentiation between the powerful and the powerless. As Max Horkheimer has observed: "In the course of emancipation man shares the fate of his world; domination of nature implies social domination."[2]

The rise of experimental science, one must add, was paralleled in the social and economic domain by the decline of feudal hierarchy and its progressive replacement by competitive market relations—relations which relied essentially on a conception of man as a possessive and acquisitive creature. In the words of Crawford Macpherson, the "roots of the [modern] liberal tradition" must be found in the premise of possessive and dissociated individuals, a premise treating man "as essentially the proprietor of his own person or capacities, owing nothing to society for them." As in the case of science, modern market society was initially permeated by general-human or species aspirations. Early liberal doctrine—Macpherson suggested—had at least a tinge of plausibility as long as it was accompanied by the prevalence of fairly equal life chances and by a widespread consensus among property owners.[3] To phrase matters differently (and more broadly): the virtue of nascent bourgeois thought—both in its empiricist and its rationalist manifestations—resided in its non-restrictive, utopian quality; the concrete-economic interests of early entrepreneurs were as little compatible with a hierarchical or stratified structure of society as was the notion of a universally shared reason.

Whatever mitigating qualities may have been attached to this tradition in the past have dissipated in our time. Various developments, of both a social and an intellectual character, have collaborated to produce this outcome. Industrialization and the replacement of small-scale enterprises by corporate business have reinvigorated social hierarchy and placed a premium on economic privilege, undermining the equality of life chances and dimming utopian prospects. Simultaneously, the progressive fusion (or collusion) of government and business has tended to substitute for social consensus the increasingly efficient management of public opinion. In the intellectual domain, the rise of positivist empiricism has encouraged the identification of man with his physical traits or empirical possessions, while promoting his congruity with environmental conditions through the process of adaptation. At the same time, losing or abandoning its linkage with general-human purposes, reason has come to be equated with an abstract calculus—a set of instrumental rules designed to maximize preferences of any sort. As a result of these and related trends, the possessive and manipulative traits of traditional individualism—traits which in more subdued form were present at least since early modernity—have gained preeminence. If Horkheimer's comments above are correct, however, the strengthening of possessivism has as a consequence that the individual himself is increasingly possessed—due to the adaptive mechanism and the internalization of manipulation. Contemporary technology illustrates this nexus of control. While supposedly expanding human mastery, technological advances have tightened the network of causal and managerial constraints enveloping social life.

The role and meaning of individualism and the status of the thinking subject are today surrounded by intense controversy. The present chapter seeks to elucidate a number of prominent contemporary perspectives on the issue. According to one perspective—which may be described as *possessive neo-individualism*—the dilemmas and (1) shifting fortunes of liberalism are not so much sources of embarrassment as motives for reaffirmation. Far from deploring possessivism, the perspective counsels its candid acknowledgment, by insisting that contingent individual interests and possessions be treated as legitimate "by nature" (provided they are pursued or acquired in conformity with a set of formal, procedural rules). In the words of Robert Nozick, whose writings exemplify this approach: *"From each as they choose, to each as they are chosen."*[4] A second perspective—labelled here *transcenden-* (2) *tal humanism* and exemplified in Sartre's early writings—is repelled by the conception of man as a robust empirical entity linked with empirical possessions; harking back to the general-human (or humanist) aspirations of early liberalism and rationalism, the perspective accentuates the emancipatory quality of individualism and man's ability to transcend prevailing conditions—but without abandoning the notion of an (inner) human self maintaining control and possession of itself. To defenders of a third view, the present condition of individualism— in both its robust-affirmative and its transcendental formulations—is evidence of its bankruptcy. Seen from this vantage point, the malaise (3) of modern and contemporary life can be traced, either directly or indirectly, to its anthropocentric and subjectivist thrust or its focus on the thinking subject; according to some, the malaise has already reached a crisis stage with the result that the "end" or "death of man" is imminent (if not an accomplished fact). Spokesmen differ as to the nature of proposed antidotes or substitutes for modern subjectivity and individualism; but a preferred (though not uniformly endorsed) remedy consists in a radical shift of attention, aimed at dislocating or "decentering" man in favor of overarching structures or systemic relationships. Deviating from both supporters and opponents of traditional individualism, a last perspective sketched in this chapter seeks to maintain the concern for human autonomy while reinterpreting individualism in a non-subjectivist and non-anthropocentric direction. Although nurtured by somewhat different philosophical concerns, the writings of Heidegger, Merleau-Ponty, and Adorno adumbrate the contours of an open-ended, non-possessive individuality enmeshed in, but not entirely congruous with, its surroundings; shunning both mastery and blind submission, the conception favors partnership and attentive care for nature and fellow humans.

Possessive Neo-Individualism

Recent decades have seen a strong revival of traditional liberalism *cum* individualism, at least in the North American context. To a considerable degree, this revival can be ascribed to the steady expansion of bureaucratic and managerial controls and the corresponding shrinkage of the realm of privacy and individual initiative; despite the overt or subterranean connections between such controls and the possessive-individualist heritage, the latter heritage is invoked by many as a viable corrective for the ills of post-industrial society. For present purposes I intend to concentrate briefly on one recent work which has widely been heralded as a bulwark of neo-individualism: Robert Nozick's *Anarchy, State, and Utopia*. As it seems to me, the book deserves attention because of its philosophical forthrightness and because of its relevance to social and political scientists: by and large, its arguments articulate the theoretical and moral underpinnings of contemporary choice or decision models which derive social phenomena from the exchange of individual utilities. Despite some unusual facets, the work is not basically idiosyncratic, nor does it advocate an eccentric position. Nozick is careful to differentiate his stance from a simple defence of selfishness or selfish survival needs and also from a radical version of anarchism. Challenging the perspective favored by "individualist anarchists," he seeks to demonstrate the inevitability and moral legitimacy of a "minimal state" or a set of public arrangements designed to protect individual life and property.[5]

The chief ambition of *Anarchy, State, and Utopia* is to recapture and reinvigorate the Lockean theory of natural rights and individual liberties. This goal is reflected in Nozick's vindication of the state-of-nature doctrine and in his primary concern with individual life and possessions. Yet the book is not merely a restorative exercise. At several important junctures, the author attempts to correct or improve on Lockean teachings, regularly with an eye toward sharpening their "libertarian" message; a prominent example can be found in the replacement of the "social contract" by an "invisible-hand" process governing the emergence of the (minimal) state. Nozick starts his argument from what he considers a solid, empirical premise: the factual separateness of individuals. Rejecting the notion of a "social good" attaching to a "social entity," he asserts that "there are only individual people, different individual people, with their own individual lives." The premise is reiterated in emphatic terms. Thus, one reads of "the existence of distinct individuals who are not resources for others" and even of "sovereign individuals" who should be viewed in analogy with sovereign nations. According to Nozick, the moral framework—called *entitlement theory*—delineated in the book ultimately reflects "the fact of our separate existence." Individual separateness entails that "no moral balancing act can take place among us" and that "there is no moral outweighing of one of our lives by others so as to lead to a greater overall *social* good." The same "root idea," he adds, "namely, that there are different individuals with separate lives and so no one may be sacrificed for others, underlies the existence of moral side constraints, but it also, I believe, leads to a libertarian side constraint that prohibits aggression against another."[6]

Taken at face value, these assertions are puzzling and questionable in many respects. First of all, in the absence of empirical or philosophical demonstration, the thesis of the factual separateness of individuals is simply one view among others—a weak foundation for a theoretical edifice. Even assuming conclusive proof, it is unclear how factual separateness can serve as adequate support for an argument in favor of individuality and moral obligations. Supposing that human beings are simply bundles of empirical traits differentiated from one another by a contingent mixture of traits, how could one detect a locus of individuality and personal identity? Moreover, in demonstrating the existence of separate traits, would empirical science not also uncover the underlying causes of these traits and thus submerge separateness again in a uniform mechanism of natural causation? Similar questions apply to ethics and moral obligations. Why, one may ask at the very start, should a specified factual condition—here: human separateness and distinctness of traits—give rise to any moral considerations or justify any kind of moral obligation? In particular: why should the fact that "there are different individuals with separate lives" entail—as Nozick claims—a prohibition against mutual aggression? Does separateness of existence imply a guarantee of continued undisturbed existence and inviolability?[7] More importantly, does complete individual segregation not also carry over into moral views—with the result that the maxim *from each as they choose* applies to moral principles as well? Differently phrased: does separateness not necessarily nullify any *general* moral argument, including the entitlement theory?

Apparently sensing the dilemma implicit in his starting point, Nozick in subsequent passages moves to a more qualitative, quasi-Kantian level of discourse. There is a problem, he realizes, in linking particular individual traits with moral considerations. To render this linkage feasible, he writes, it would appear that human traits "must themselves be valuable characteristics." Nozick examines at this point some "traditional" conceptions identifying qualitative human endowments—conceptions presenting man as "sensient and self-conscious; rational (capable of using abstract concepts, not tied to responses to immediate stimuli); possessing free will; being a moral agent capable of guiding its behavior by moral principles and capable of engaging in mutual limitation of conduct; having a soul." Although acknowledging their partial merits, he finds these specifications "insufficient to forge the requisite connection" between human traits and moral constraints. An "intervening variable" is needed, he asserts, "for which the listed traits are individually necessary, *perhaps* jointly sufficient" and "which has a perspicuous and convincing connection to moral constraints on behavior" toward someone endowed with this variable. On reflection, Nozick locates this required variable in the "ability to form a picture of one's whole life" and "to act in terms of some overall conception of the life one wishes to lead." The moral relevance or importance of this ability, he suggests, resides in its connection with "that elusive and difficult notion," the meaningfulness of life: "A person's shaping his life in accordance with some overall plan is his way of giving meaning to his life: only a being with the capacity to so shape his life can have or strive for meaningful life."[8]

Nozick, it is true, is not entirely comfortable with his argument—noting that it does not resolve all quandaries, including the question: Why shouldn't my life be meaningless? He proposes to "grapple with these and related issues on another occasion."[9] Actually, there is ample reason for the author to be uneasy: far from merely raising interesting side issues, his qualitative or quasi-Kantian turn threatens to undermine his atomistic starting point and his preeminent concern with possessions. Clearly, moral growth and ownership of possessions are not necessarily symmetrical; some Kantian philosophers have relied on moral autonomy as a lever to challenge prevailing property and status arrangements. What is more important in the present context: the notion of meaning or meaningfulness militates against individual separateness. The formulation of an overall conception designed to give meaning to one's life implies the ability to articulate this conception at least in one's own thought; such articulation, however, involves recourse to concepts and types of argumentation which are intersubjectively available and intelligible. The notion of a strictly private meaning accessible to only one individual is incongruous. Drawing both on language theory and on Kantian teachings, Karl-Otto Apel in some of his writings has traced the ethical implications of the intersubjective structure of meaning; as he endeavors to show, every individual choice or act pretending to be meaningful is subject to the (categorical) standard of universal justification.[10] From this perspective, the query *Why shouldn't my life be meaningless?* is inherently paradoxical—since it is expressed in a sentence aspiring to convey meaning.

Nozick's avoidance or postponement of such issues is hardly fortuitous or surprising: on closer inspection his qualitative propositions are at best a thin veneer adorning a basically non-qualitative and naturalistic perspective. In unfolding his theoretical approach, Nozick refuses to draw any concrete inferences from *meaning* or related normative terms—especially inferences which might sustain social or intersubjective responsibilities.[11] According to his entitlement theory, an individual has a right to any possessions which have been acquired or transferred in conformity with general procedural principles or side constraints (principles which, one may note, are not spelled out in great detail, except for the postulate of non-aggression); any distribution of possessions consistent with procedural rules is viewed as just and legitimate. Regarding the establishment of rules legitimating acquisitions, the author (as previously mentioned) relies on an invisible-hand process, that is, a process in which property rights and other normative titles are presumed to emerge directly or automatically from conditions in the "state of nature."[12] In adopting this stance, his argument is bound to become embroiled in the so-called naturalistic fallacy—the fallacy of deriving immediately "ought" from "is," normative yardsticks from factual premises. Nozick is aware of this hazard. His temporary foray into qualitative terrain and especially his speculation about meaningfulness are prompted at least in part by the desire—as he writes—"to bridge an 'is-ought' gap." The bulk of the work, however, seems untroubled by such concerns; repeatedly he feigns complete ignorance of the issue (as when he challenges John Rawls to show why natural endowments and conditions should not directly give rise to rights and duties).[13] Given the basic tenor of the book, the naturalistic fallacy becomes in fact inescapable.

As outlined in *Anarchy, State, and Utopia,* the entitlement theory places a premium on instrumental or strategic human behavior, that is, on behavior designed to maximize utilities within the parameters of strategic rules. As is well known, success in games of strategy does not regularly depend on moral desert, certainly not on such quasi-Kantian criteria as being "sentient and self-conscious" or being endowed with moral autonomy. Nozick acknowledges as much when he asserts that entitlement to holdings does not follow a particular design, including the pattern of merit. The human characteristics favored by strategic rules include cleverness, cunning, adaptive dexterity, and manipulative skill—features which do not figure prominently in moral teachings; discouraged or disadvantaged by such rules are people of a contemplative, meek, or morally scrupulous disposition as well as the physically handicapped. It is not quite clear how a philosopher can endorse a rank order of this kind; it is inconceivable—as Nozick candidly admits—that a majority of people would adopt it if placed in a deliberative context (Rawls' "original position").[14] In the absence of such consensus, however, the entitlement doctrine falls short of "universalizability"—the capacity, normally required of any ethical theory, to justify claims or interests in a rational, non-discriminatory manner. With the collapse of its ethical scaffolding, the naturalistic underpinning of the doctrine comes to the fore, revealing it as a new version of Social Darwinism or else as a variation on the age-old adage that might (here: private might) makes right.

Transcendental Humanism

Irrespective of its normative pretensions, Nozick's version of neo-individualism seems farfetched and implausible on experiential or mundane-pragmatic grounds. Given the longstanding erosion of bourgeois lifestyles and the interpenetration of politics and economics, his assertion of private initiative and concrete-empirical autonomy is bound to have a hollow ring—not to speak of its moral and general philosophical shortcomings. Against the background of social and economic stratification, the preservation of the liberal-individualist heritage would seem to require a retrenchment of its mundane claims—more specifically, a trimming-back of the notion of individualism or individual "man" to its non-contingent and non-empirical core ingredients. One obvious (though relatively minor) advantage of such retrenchment resides in the avoidance of immediate pragmatic falsification; more importantly, however, the focus on core features seems conducive to the

potential recovery of some of the broadly humanist and utopian qualities inherent in earlier formulations of the liberal heritage. In line with
the internal complexity of this legacy, several types of retrenchment
appear feasible—and have actually been proposed in our century. Following certain traditional religious teachings, one version identifies
man's core with his *spirit* or *soul,* as distinguished from bodily-material
or biological components. Deriving its inspiration chiefly from classical
antiquity, another version concentrates on man's *essence* or *nature,*
which is said to reside in his rational faculty or else in a composite
mental structure. Both types of humanism leave the non-empirical status of the chosen core somewhat in doubt—since *spirit* and *mind* may
still be interpreted in an ontic-psychological sense. The most radical
break with empiricism occurs in transcendental-philosophical arguments; drawing in part on Cartesian and Kantian notions of subjectivity, these arguments depict man as basically a fugitive or intangible
creature capable through his *consciousness* to negate and transcend contingent conditions. A prominent and eloquent formulation of this view
can be found in one of Jean-Paul Sartre's early writings: his essay entitled "Existentialism is a Humanism."

The central purpose of the essay—as Sartre states in its opening
passages—is "to offer a defense of existentialism against several re-
proaches that have been laid against it," a defense which above all requires a definition of terms. Regarding the term *existentialism,* he
observes that it "can easily be defined" once popular misconceptions
are cleared away: the thesis or premise shared by its rigorous (and especially non-religious) proponents concerns the absence of a substantive human essence and the incongruence between human initiative
and ontic delimitations. What these existentialists "have in common,"
he writes, "is simply the fact that they believe that *existence* comes before *essence*—or, if you will, that we must begin from the subjective."
As Sartre adds, this thesis is in conflict with a longstanding and pres-
tigious philosophical tradition which stresses the primacy of substantive or essential criteria, a tradition which was still influential in Enlightenment thought and "in the philosophic atheism of the eighteenth
century." According to that tradition, man "possesses a human nature," that is, a nature which "is found in every man; which means
that each man is a particular example of a universal conception, the
conception of man." In contrast to this legacy, existentialist thinkers
assert that "there is at least one being whose existence comes before its
essence, a being which exists before it can be defined by any conception
of it." The stipulated precedence of existence, Sartre elaborates, im-

plies that "man first of all exists, encounters himself, surges up in the world—and defines himself afterwards"; or, phrased more sharply, that "to begin with he is nothing" and "will not be anything until later," when he designs himself in his projects. "Man," we read, "is nothing else but that which he makes of himself. That is the first principle of existentialism. And this is what people call its 'subjectivity', using the word as a reproach against us."[15]

In Sartre's view, the reproach is entirely misguided—not because the chosen label is itself inappropriate, but because it designates an unavoidable and unassailable philosophical assumption. "Our point of departure," he affirms, "is indeed the subjectivity of the individual, and that for strictly philosophic reasons. It is not because we are bourgeois, but because we seek to base our teaching upon the truth, and not upon a collection of fine theories, full of hope but lacking real foundations." Invoking the legacy of the thinking subject (*ego cogitans*), the essay insists that the Cartesian formula—properly understood—still provides the crucial yardstick for assessing the validity of theoretical assertions: "At the point of departure there cannot be any other truth than this, *I think, therefore I am,* which is the absolute truth of consciousness as it attains to itself." Any theory or doctrine, the essay continues, which relies on some factor other than "this moment of self-attainment" or self-consciousness, "is a theory which thereby suppresses the truth, for outside the Cartesian *cogito,* all objects are no more than probable, and any doctrine of probabilities which is not attached to a truth will crumble into nothing." Even more urgently than scientific findings and commonsense maxims, philosophical reflection requires as a touchstone the notion of an "absolute truth," a notion which is by no means an esoteric or cryptic speculation: "There is such a truth which is simple, easily attained and within the reach of everybody: it consists in one's immediate sense of one's self."[16]

Apart from reasserting and clarifying the status of selfhood and subjectivity, existentialism—according to Sartre—places into relief the inescapable character of freedom and human responsibility. "If indeed existence precedes essence," he writes, "one will never be able to explain one's action by reference to a given and specific human nature; in other words, there is no determinism—man is free, man *is* freedom." The identification of man (or subjectivity) and freedom entails that human behavior cannot be derived from external circumstances or nonhuman sources. Absence of determinism in Sartre's view also signifies the absence or unavailability of extrinsic justifications—whether they be sought in divine precepts, social customs, or instinctual promptings:

"We are left alone, without excuse. That is what I mean when I say that man is condemned to be free." Due to the lack of external warrants, man shoulders the full burden of responsibility for his deeds and for his entire life; moreover, given the general-human character of subjectivity and freedom, responsibility likewise has a universal thrust. In the words of the essay: "Thus, the first effect of existentialism is that it puts every man in possession of himself as he is, and places the entire responsibility for his existence squarely upon his shoulders. And when we say that man is responsible for himself, we do not mean that he is responsible only for his own individuality, but that he is responsible for all men." As Sartre explains, the broad sway of responsibility is linked with the universal impact of human choice, that is, with the fact that man chooses not in private seclusion but in the face of others and that his actions thus fashion not only his own life but a general image of human existence. In "choosing for himself" an individual can be said to choose "for all men: for in effect, of all the actions a man may take in order to create himself as he wills to be, there is not one which is not creative, at the same time, of an image of man as he believes he ought to be." Since "in fashioning myself I fashion man," it follows that "our responsibility is much greater than we had supposed, for it concerns mankind as a whole."[17]

Given the stress on subjectivity and self-creation, the essay inevitably conjures up the spectre of solipsism or at least the peril of human self-centeredness. Sartre takes considerable pains to counteract the impression of solipsistic enclosure, arguing that on this point "again people badly misunderstand us." His vindication proceeds chiefly along two lines. First of all, from an existentialist vantage point, man is said to be a creature not divorced from, but inescapably inserted in the world; existentialism is expressly defined as a perspective "which affirms that every truth and every action imply both an environment and a human subjectivity." Man's placement in an environment, the essay emphasizes, can be described as a basic human *situation* and even as a manifestation of a "human universality of *condition*"—where *condition* refers to "all the *limitations* which *a priori* define man's fundamental situation in the universe." Despite its reiteration, however, the man-environment theme appears unable (or at least highly unlikely) to jeopardize the primacy of subjectivity in Sartre's outlook. As the use of the term *limitations* indicates, man in his presentation does not derive his cues from, or owe his self-conception to, environmental settings; rather, the latter function merely as challenges or obstacles in relation to subjective-individual initiative.[18] A second barrier to solipsism men-

tioned in the essay—one even more precarious on Sartrean premises—
resides in the dimension of *intersubjectivity,* construed as a general network of subjectivities. As the essay insists (moving on this score beyond the Cartesian formula), consciousness is not the prerogative of
one person, but a general-human endowment shared by all individuals.
The subjectivity postulated as the "standard of truth," we are told, is
"no narrowly individual subjectivism," for "it is not only one's own
self that one discovers in the *cogito,* but those of others too. Contrary
to the philosophy of Descartes, contrary to that of Kant, when we say
'I think' we are attaining to ourselves in the presence of the other, and
we are just as certain of the other as we are of ourselves." While intriguing as an attempt to revive the universalist promise of liberalism,
the preceding statements are scarcely free of ambiguity, for it remains
unclear how "others" or the "self" of others can be discovered "in the
cogito" without thereby being reduced to projections of subjective experience.[19]

Whatever the resolution of these and related quandaries may be,
in my view Sartre's position—although not synonymous with solipsism
—cannot (and does not mean to) offer a reprieve from subjectivity;
even assuming, for the sake of argument, a successful settlement of the
issues surrounding interpersonal relations, the outcome would at best
be a "noumenal community" of subjects or a "subjectivity writ large."
Actually, despite his rejection of ontic-empirical criteria, Sartre's perspective may be said to carry overtones of possessive individualism—by
portraying the *cogito* as a self-controlling agency or, to use a previously
cited passage, by presenting existentialism as a doctrine which "puts
every man in possession of himself as he is." The possessive-individualist aspect, it is true, seems to be contradicted in the discussed essay
by the stress on self-transcendence. "Man," we read, "is all the time
outside of himself: it is in projecting and losing himself beyond himself that he makes man to exist; and, on the other hand, it is by pursuing
transcendent aims that he himself is able to exist." Yet by propelling
himself in ever new directions and abandoning himself in changing
projects, man is not necessarily a fugitive from himself; his openness
toward "transcendent aims" does not imply a breach of selfhood. Sartre
acknowledges as much when he adds in the same context: "Since man
is thus self-surpassing, and can grasp objects only in relation to his
self-surpassing, he is himself the heart and center of his transcendence.
There is no other universe except the human universe, the universe of
human subjectivity." Returning to the theme announced in its title, the
essay concludes by depicting humanism as the underpinning of a hu-

man universe designed and fashioned by man's self-surpassing existence. The relation of "transcendence as constitutive of man" with "subjectivity," Sartre notes, "is this that we call existential humanism."[20]

"Egophany" and the "End of Man"

Although eloquently expressed, Sartre's arguments appear dated to the present-day reader. After enjoying a brief vogue during the postwar period, existentialism and existentialist humanism have been swept aside in Sartre's home country by the structuralist tide—a broad, interdisciplinary movement whose heterogeneous components are held together chiefly by their common opposition to subjectivity and to the conception of man as a self-centered and self-directing agency. Actually, structuralism itself is only one recent and particularly emphatic manifestation of a broader and more amorphous intellectual trend in Western society, a trend whose antecedents reach back at least to the middle of the last century and whose common denominator consists in a steadily deepening dissatisfaction with basic premises of Western thought as they are evident in traditional philosophy (with its reliance on consciousness and the thinking subject) as well as in traditional social theory and practice (with a focus, shared equally by empiricists and transcendental rationalists, on individual initiative and human autonomy). In our own time, anti-subjectivist and anti-humanist leanings can be detected among proponents of such widely divergent enterprises as religious historiography, linguistic analysis, systems theory, and structuralism—to mention only a few orientations. To be sure, formulations of such leanings vary in terms of cogency, perceptiveness, and intellectual ambition. In some instances, the chief issue seems to be simply a readjustment of the relative weights assigned to *part* and *whole,* individual and society; in other instances, by contrast, the critique of subjectivity assumes the proportions of a full-fledged indictment of modern anthropocentrism. In the eyes of some thinkers, self-centered humanism is a raging virus whose effects are still spreading through Western life, while others stress the availability of antidotes and their (at least locally) successful application; according to still others, the humanist legacy is already moribund if not defunct—and only seems to thrive, due to culture lag and ideological artifacts. In the present context I can only hope to convey a glimpse of this range of arguments.

The notion of a spreading virus can be gleaned chiefly from the writings of Eric Voegelin, a political thinker and historian animated by Christian religious insights. According to his multi-volume study entitled *Order and History,* the modern age—at least since the Enlightenment era—is characterized by the progressive accentuation of human self-centeredness and self-development or, in his terms, by the growing infatuation with *egophany* at the expense of the *theophanic* and *hierophanic* events which permeated Biblical accounts and also some types of classical philosophy. In Voegelin's view, this infatuation is particularly obvious in modern historical interpretations. In the wake of the deepening "revolution of egophany," he writes, the conception of a divinely guided history becomes "eclipsed by an imaginary egophanic history which is devised to culminate in the apocalyptic self-realization of the thinker, as in the 'philosophies of history' of Condorcet, Comte, or Hegel." Such egophanic interpretations, he adds, are designed not as a sequel to a (meaningful) theophanic past, but rather as its supersession and replacement. "In order to create this imaginary history, the theophanic events must be reconstructed as egophanic events." In other words, "the symbols engendered by theophanic events must be understood as projections of an imperfectly evolved self-reflective consciousness," with the result that "no room" is left for "theophanic experiences and their symbolization." Among modern thinkers, Hegel is singled out as "the philosophically most competent and historically most knowledgeable" spokesman of egophany or—less politely —as "the egophanic manipulator *par excellence.*" In the notion of the absolute idea and the "Logos of Hegel's 'absolute knowledge'," we read, the theophanic "parousia" was absorbed "in the egophany of the speculative thinker."[21]

From the perspective of contemporary systems theory and structuralist analysis, individual subjectivity and ego-centered humanism are no longer viable theoretical guideposts. In the writings of Niklas Luhmann—a defender of functionalist systems theory—individuals (and the notion of purposive *meaning*) are not entirely shunned, but subordinated and adjusted to systemic relationships and imperatives. Adapting and refining concepts derived from cybernetics, Luhmann sees the central task of systems, including social systems, in the reduction and management of environmental complexity through processes of selection and steering, processes which in turn enhance the systems' internal diversity and flexibility. As he insists, the systemic outlook is no longer indebted to subjective intention and, more generally, to traditional subject-object distinctions. "The term 'system,' " he writes, "is not designed as a synonym for subjectivity, or for a subjective construction, or for an aggregate of individual subjects." At least since Talcott Parsons, he adds, "the irreversible gain of systems theory consists in its

ability to derive the need of system formation no longer from the vantage point of the (intentional) actor, but rather from the situated character of action"—in other words: from the network of social interaction. The basic thesis connected with this insight is that interaction is
possible and conceivable only "as a system," and, "to go one step further," that the actor himself must be construed in systemic terms or as
"a system in interaction." Far from being a constitutive agent, the individual in Luhmann's view is "constituted" by social interaction as a
"contingent actor," that is, as a system engaged in the reduction of
complexity through selection. In his words: "The individual subject
must be seen first of all as a process of contingent selectivity."[22]

In a still more radical and emphatic manner, the role of subjective agency is expunged in the writings of Louis Althusser—who is
sometimes described as spokesman of a structuralist Marxism (although
his links with structuralism are somewhat tenuous). According to
Althusser, the debunking of the traditional "image of man" as a "human subject" was inaugurated during the last century in the works of
Marx and Freud—an accomplishment comparable to the "upheavals
of the Copernican Revolution" in its long-range effects. "Since Coper-
nicus," he states in *Lenin and Philosophy*, "we have known that the
earth is not the 'center' of the universe. Since Marx, we have known
that the human subject, the economic, political or philosophical ego is
not the 'center' of history—and even, in opposition to the philosophers
of the Enlightenment and to Hegel, that history has no 'center' except
in ideological misrecognition." Marx's discoveries on the plane of epistemology and political economy were paralleled by the findings of
Freudian psychoanalysis, for Freud's investigations demonstrated that
the "real subject" or concrete human being "has not the form of an
ego, centered on the 'ego,' on 'consciousness' or on 'existence'—whether
this is the existence of the for-itself, of the body-proper or of 'behavior'—that the human subject is de-centered, constituted by a structure
which has no 'center' either, except in the imaginary misrecognition of
the 'ego,' that is, in the ideological formations in which it 'recognizes'
itself."[23]

According to Althusser, subjectivity and self-centered humanism
are entirely the outgrowth of ideology, in particular of bourgeois ideology, while science—above all Marxist science or historical materialism—is devoid of subjective self-reference. The notion of "a subject
endowed with a consciousness," who "freely forms or recognizes ideas
in which he believes" and acts in conformity with those ideas, must, in
his view, be seen as an "absolutely ideological 'conceptual' device." As

he insists: "There is no ideology except by the subject and for subjects." The "category of the subject" is said to be "constitutive of all ideology" chiefly by virtue of the fact that ideology, in turn, has the specific function of transforming human beings and "constituting" them "as subjects." In Althusser's presentation, this transformation is effected through the procedure of *hailing* or *interpellation,* through which human beings are located in the cultural matrix and able to recognize themselves and others as subjects. Actually, in view of the ineluctable predominance of the ruling ideology, interpellation does not involve a temporal sequence or alteration; rather, human beings are "always-already interpellated by ideology as subjects," with the result that *"individuals are always-already subjects."* In contrast to the subjective-humanist implications of ideology, scientific inquiry is claimed to operate on an objective-rational plane. The author of a treatise "which claims to be scientific," we read, "is completely absent as a 'subject' from 'his' scientific discourse," for "all scientific discourse is by definition a subject-less discourse" and "there is no 'subject of science' except in an ideology of science."[24]

The subject-less character of science, *Lenin and Philosophy* affirms, is particularly manifest in historical materialism conceived as a science of history and social development. Although experimenting in some early writings with the issue of human alienation and recovery, Marx in his later analyses—especially in *Capital*—thoroughly "exploded" the thesis of a subject-centered history: "The result of this explosion was the evaporation of the notions of subject, human essence, and alienation, which disappear, completely atomized," and the emergence of the conception of history as *"a process without a subject"*— that is, of the insight "that the dialectic at work in history is not the work of any subject whatsoever, whether absolute (God) or merely human, but that the origin of history is always already thrust back before history, and therefore that there is neither a philosophical origin nor a philosophical subject to history." According to Althusser, this insight forms the backbone of the "Marxist-Leninist concept of the materialist dialectic," with its stress on "the absoluteness of movement" or process. In its basic thrust, he adds, the insight can be traced back to Hegelian philosophy and especially to the notion of the absolute idea, provided the latter is viewed through materialist lenses—as it was done by Lenin. In studying Hegel's *Logic,* we read, Lenin found "a confirmation of the fact that it is absolutely essential (as he had learned simply from a thorough-going reading of *Capital*) *to suppress every origin and every subject,* and to say: what is absolute is the *process without a sub-*

ject, both in reality and in scientific knowledge." Instead of revealing the culmination of egophany (as claimed by Voegelin), Hegel's *Logic* in Althusser's view thus shows the reverse, for "a process without a subject is precisely what can be found in the chapter on the 'absolute idea.' "[25]

In present-day French thought, opposition to subjectivity and self-centered humanism is not restricted to the confines of Althusserian scientism or scientific Marxism. On a less doctrinaire level, anti-humanist views are shared by numerous philosophers not closely tied to partisan platforms or circumscribed schools of thought. At this point, at least two thinkers deserve brief mention because of their influence and the perspicacity of their arguments: Michel Foucault and Jacques Derrida. Although at one time sympathetic to the structuralist perspective, both have moved in the meantime in their own directions; one of the main links between their works is their common treatment of anthropocentrism as a defunct legacy. Both the character of this legacy and its disintegration are compellingly delineated in Foucault's *The Order of Things.* Subtitled *An Archaeology of the Human Sciences,* the study tries to uncover the hidden underpinnings of Western humanism and to show how successive "archaeological" endeavors have in fact unhinged its epistemological and ontological moorings. As presented by Foucault, the human sciences comprise chiefly the three disciplines of psychology, sociology, and philology—disciplines which are loosely tied to three basic dimensions of experience: life, labor, and language. Traditionally, the mentioned disciplines were wedded to a basic "humanist" purpose: the task of furthering the knowledge of "human nature." Practitioners of the human sciences were expected to explore in ever greater detail the substantive characteristics and accomplishments of the human species. According to Foucault, however, the human disciplines had barely managed to gain academic recognition when they began to be challenged by critical and even antithetical trends. Since the end of the last century, he notes, new types of inquiry or counter-sciences have come to the fore which have succeeded in carrying a "perpetual principle of dissatisfaction" into the study of humanity. Instead of dwelling on the positive features of man's physiognomy, these inquiries have shifted the focus to the outer limits of human experience—to those parameters and preconditions which lie beyond the reach of human intentionality and conscious design. The general labels of the new counter-sciences are psychoanalysis, ethnology, and linguistics.

In Foucault's treatment, psychoanalysis is not merely a version of positive psychology, but rather a science preoccupied with the boundaries of psychic life; far from simply expanding the range of man's psychic capacities, the Freudian perspective injects into the human disciplines the "analytic of finitude," an analytic operating at the limits of psychic space. "In setting itself the task of making the discourse of the unconscious speak through consciousness," we read, "psychoanalysis is advancing in the direction of that fundamental region in which the relations of representation and finitude come into play." Whereas the traditional human sciences "advance towards the unconscious only with their back to it," psychoanalysis "points directly towards it, with a deliberate purpose—not towards that which must be rendered gradually more explicit by the progressive illumination of the implicit, but towards what is there and yet is hidden, towards what exists with the mute solidity of a thing." Similarly, in Foucault's view ethnology is not simply a discipline investigating more primitive or exotic types of societies; rather, functioning as a corrective to positive sociology, ethnological studies focus on the preconditions of social life, on the domain where cultural ambitions intersect with the dictates of nature. "Ethnology, like psychoanalysis," he observes, "examines not man himself, as he appears in the human sciences, but the region that makes possible knowledge about man in general; like psychoanalysis, it spans the whole field of that knowledge in a movement that tends to reach its boundaries." In a sense, both psychoanalysis and ethnology can be viewed as "sciences of the unconscious"—not because they open up new dimensions of man, but "because they are directed towards that which, outside man, makes it possible to know, with a positive knowledge, that which is given to or eludes his consciousness." The third and most recently developed counter-science is linguistics, a discipline designed to unearth the structural premises and a priori principles of all knowledge; given its proclivity to "traverse, animate, and disturb the whole constituted field of the human sciences," the discipline forms "the most general contestation of that field."[26]

According to Foucault, the research aims of the counter-sciences are not only at odds with the cognitive goals of the humanities: their inquiries are predicated on the obsolescence and irrelevance of the humanist legacy. This irrelevance is evident in the case of psychoanalysis and ethnology. "The idea of a 'psychoanalytic anthropology,' and the idea of a 'human nature' reconstituted by ethnology," he notes, "are no more than pious wishes. Not only are they able to do without the concept of man, they are also unable to pass through it, for they always address themselves to that which constitutes his outer limits. One may say of both of them what Lévi-Strauss said of ethnology: that they dissolve man." As a science dealing with the a priori structures of signification, linguistics is equally unconcerned with human agency or experience; once linguistic or symbolic structures are seen as underlying all types of human cognition and behavior, the study of language emerges as an enterprise which lays "siege on every side to the figure of man." In their combined impact the three counter-sciences thus manage progressively to annihilate the subject matter of the human studies: "From within language experienced and traversed as language, in the play of its possibilities extended to their furthest point, what emerges is that man has 'come to an end,' and that, by reaching the summit of all possible speech, he arrives not at the very heart of himself but at the brink of that which limits him; in that region where death prowls, where thought is extinguished, where the promise of the origin interminably recedes."[27]

As Foucault adds, the struggle between the counter-sciences and the humanities is not merely an academic skirmish: extending beyond narrowly epistemological and methodological concerns the contest touches at the basic fabric and significance of the modern era. In pursuing their strategy, the counter-sciences of our century not only challenge the status of epistemological subjectivity, but call into question the anthropocentric pillars of modern thought, thus paving the way to a post-humanist life-form. Regarding the overall assessment of this epochal transformation, Foucault pays tribute chiefly to Nietzschean insights as marking the watershed between two ages. While, sensing a profound cultural and social crisis, other thinkers in the last century (including Marx) concentrated their efforts on rendering humanism or the future of man more secure, Nietzsche alone ventured to proclaim the impending disappearance of man, as a corollary of the eclipse of God: "In our day, and once again Nietzsche indicated the turning-point from a long way off, it is not so much the absence or the death of God that is affirmed as the end of man." In Nietzsche's view, the vanishing of humanism is a more radical and far-reaching change than the abolition of God: having vanquished God, the "last man" himself cannot savor his triumph but is swallowed up in the vortex of annihilation. "Man will disappear," *The Order of Things* asserts. "Rather than the death of God—or rather, in the wake of that death and in profound correlation with it—what Nietzsche's thought heralds is the end of his murderer; it is the explosion of man's face in laughter, and the return of masks; it is the scattering of the profound stream of time by which he felt himself carried along and whose pressure he suspected in the very being of things; it is the identity of the Return of the Same with the absolute dispersion of man."[28]

A few years after the publication of Foucault's work, a similar perspective was articulated by Jacques Derrida in a paper called "The Ends of Man" (delivered at a conference devoted to the contemporary role of philosophical anthropology). The title of the paper was indicative of the argument's general thrust. In Derrida's usage, the expression *ends of man* referred to two different meanings or aspects of finality: the dimension of ultimate purpose and fulfillment, and the aspect of human mortality and finitude. In Western thought, the two connotations have tended to be intimately linked. "The Greek conception of 'telos,' " he noted, "comprises the unity of the two *ends* of man: the unity of his mortality and of his completion or fulfillment." Despite their close relationship, the two meanings were given different weight in traditional metaphysics, where mortality was treated as subsidiary to final purpose; on the whole, teleology prevailed over eschatology: "Metaphysics—committed to the search for the true essence of man—contained implicitly the notion of human finitude." According to Derrida, what is needed in our time is an effort to shift the weight of the two connotations—which involves a struggle against the metaphysical legacy: "What is difficult to conceive today is an end of man which is not dominated in advance by the dialectic of truth and purposive negativity and which does not rely on a teleology in the first person plural."[29]

Like Foucault's study, Derrida's essay combined cognitive-epistemological considerations with broader, quasi-ontological assessments of our age. While in *The Order of Things* epistemological issues were profiled in the context of the traditional human sciences, Derrida concentrated on more recent intellectual trends, especially on the vogue of humanist existentialism in post-war France. As he readily conceded, existentialism as propounded in that period was by no means synonymous with traditional or metaphysical humanism; actually a major effort was made by existentialist writers to strip man of substantive connotations and to replace human nature with the notion of the human condition or human reality. "The fact," we read, "that the concept of man's nature—with all its metaphysical overtones and its inherent substantialist motives and temptations—was transformed into the neutral and indefinite phrase 'human reality' is evidence of the desire to cut loose from all those premises and suppositions which traditionally have been associated with the unity or compactness of man." Despite these changes, however, post-war existentialism in Derrida's view was still deeply attached to the humanist legacy; this was true especially of the

Sartrean variety. Irrespective of his assault on human essence, Sartre's perspective was according to his own account a humanism; to the extent that it depicted the "structures of human reality," his phenomenological ontology (outlined in *Being and Nothingness*) remained a *philosophical anthropology*. What existentialists assiduously neglected was the evanescence and finite character of man; despite frequent appeals to history, they failed to ask about the "history or genesis of the concept of man. Everything happened as if 'man' had no origins and was devoid of historical, cultural, and linguistic boundaries."[30]

In Derrida's presentation, post-war existentialism was at most a belated flurry, an epilogue to a vanishing heritage. For some time, Western humanism had been eroded by subterranean tremors—which now have reached cataclysmic proportions. A major manifestation of the contemporary cataclysm consists in the fact that, for the first time in history, "Western civilization as a whole" is challenged by the insurgency of the non-Western world—a circumstance corroborating (in Derrida's view) the thesis that any genuine change can only "originate from the *outside*." Two major strategies of responding to the challenge are sketched in the essay: first, an attempt to embrace and assimilate the external perspective without leaving the original position; and second, a leap beyond tradition coupled with "the affirmation of a radical rupture and absolute discontinuity." While weighing the advantages and risks of both strategies, the paper on the whole favors the second. As a central guide on the road toward discontinuity, Derrida—like Foucault—invokes Nietzsche's philosophy, especially the distinction between the *last man* and *overman*. Whereas the last man is still wedded to the celebration of humanism and human dignity, overman leaves behind his past without looking back: "He burns his texts and erases the imprints of his steps; his laughter erupts toward a Return of the Same which is no longer a metaphysical repetition of humanism." Outside the confines of human ecology and habitation, overman prepares "to practice that 'active forgetfulness' and to dance that 'cruel feast' about which we read in the *Genealogy of Morals*."[31]

Reductio Hominis

As presented by Derrida and Foucault, contemporary anti-humanism has a powerful appeal. Their arguments, it seems to me, point to a strong undercurrent in Western thought which, though buried for some time, can no longer be ignored: an undercurrent testifying to a deep-seated dissatisfaction with, and estrangement from, traditional views of humanity and of a man-centered universe. Juxtaposed to this sense of dissatisfaction, the strutting self-confidence of neo-individualism appears hollow and quixotic; the same juxtaposition renders implausible even the notion of a transcendental subjectivity, construed as central agency or origin of human designs. Yet, despite the prima-facie merits of anti-subjectivist teachings, it seems advisable to proceed cautiously on this terrain: the abolition of man, as counseled or intimated by end-of-man arguments, may carry a price which outweighs its benefits. In the absence of diligent safeguards, the chief casualties of anti-humanism are likely to be self-reflection and moral responsibility. On the cognitive-epistemological level, the main peril of anti-subjectivist positions—a peril evident in Althusser's case and, to some extent, in Luhmann's writings—is the proclivity toward objectivism: by downgrading individual reason and consciousness they tend to curtail the reflective capacity needed for the critique of knowledge claims. Similarly, in the moral domain, the stress on preconscious or extra-human structures or contexts is prone to obscure the dimension of human autonomy and responsibility.

Apart from the problematic character of its cognitive and normative implications, one may doubt the feasibility of anti-humanism as a strategy aiming at radical change. Is it reasonable, one may ask, to expect a radical transformation of (Western) man from purely "external" or "exogenous" sources or from a leap beyond tradition? Does reliance on external forces not necessarily presuppose a domain of human *internality,* and is a challenge from the outside not liable to strengthen and rigidify internal dispositions—with the result that anti-humanism becomes the harbinger of a heightened humanism?[32] This result is all the more probable given the entrenched status of individual subjectivity in Western thought and culture—an entrenchment, one might add, which has yielded significant gains in the field of individual rights and constitutional guarantees. Moreover, even if feasible (and not simply the consequence of external compulsion), a sudden and complete departure from this heritage would likely be an empty gesture, for if anti-humanism is indeed meant to be a corrective to traditional conceptions and life patterns, it can maintain its function only through intimate contact and struggle with these patterns. For these and related reasons, abolitionism may not be the most suitable means for human transformation. Perhaps change is more likely to result from a patient endurance of contemporary challenges and dilemmas than a sudden withdrawal—from a willingness to be stretched beyond one's present limits rather than an obliteration of all (traditional) limits.

The alternative to anthropocentrism may not be anti-humanism but a deflated notion of man. Stripped of claims to superiority, man in this view would be less the master than the servant of his world; loath to accept praise, he would readily assume responsibility for any detrimental effects of his behavior on his environment. As it seems to me, hints of such a deflated and non-possessive conception can be found in phenomenological and neo-Marxist literature, especially in the writings of Heidegger, Merleau-Ponty, and Adorno.

Heidegger is sometimes described as a founder of existentialism or existential phenomenology—where the latter terms stand as synonyms for anthropocentrism. Formulated in this manner, the description is erroneous or at least greatly misleading. Undeniably, Heidegger's early publications contained voluntaristic arguments which, removed from their philosophical context, might encourage anthropocentric leanings. Thus, *Being and Time* portrayed human life as a sequence of intentional projects and society as a largely anonymous dimension obstructing authentic human experience. Notions of this kind, however, were tempered from the beginning by ontological qualifications and, above all, by the non-subjectivist thrust of Heidegger's study. Deviating from the egological perspective of Husserlian phenomenology, *Being and Time* characterized man as a being-in-the-world—a hyphenated creature enmeshed (though not completely submerged) in a preexisting life-world which is not the result of either individual or intersubjective design. The crucial experiential trait of this creature, in Heidegger's treatment, was neither rationality nor will power but *care*—a term denoting both the anxiety deriving from the lack of a fixed behavioral structure and the capacity for genuine attentiveness reaching beyond subjective-instrumental pursuits. The deepest expression of care resided in man's concern for the meaning and ultimate foundation of existence; as the study indicated, this concern could be viewed as the source of emancipation and human autonomy since it catapulted man both beyond factual contingencies and beyond the range of subjective or egocentric dispositions.[33]

Two decades after the first appearance of *Being and Time,* Heidegger addressed himself again extensively to the theme of human existence and of man's status in the world. By that time, whatever subjective or anthropocentric motives may still have been operative in the earlier study had receded into the background or been placed into a completely new frame of reference. The philosophical ambition of the *Letter on Humanism* was far-reaching: the goal was not merely to correct the excesses of existentialist arguments but to attempt a radical revision of Western anthropological conceptions since antiquity. As presented in the *Letter,* man was no longer the lord of the universe, entitled to mastery by his capacity for reason and voluntary action; rather, the emphasis was now entirely on human attentiveness—on man as the "shepherd of Being." The term *existence* itself was now specifically interpreted in such a manner as to highlight its non-subjective and non-possessive quality. Relying on the etymological roots of the term, Heidegger defined man as an *ek-static* creature, capable of reaching beyond the confines of subjective, manipulative pursuits. *Being-in-the-world* as a synonym for *Dasein* was said to imply man's openness to the *world*—a term denoting not simply an empirical environment, but the arena in which meaning and ultimate Being become manifest. Thrust into this open arena, *Dasein* revealed itself as a *project*—but not in the sense of a human fabrication. Man is human, the *Letter* stated, "insofar as he exists, that is, insofar as he stands out into the openness of Being which has cast or projected man in the modality of 'care'. . . . 'World' designates the clearing of Being into which man reaches out by virtue of his thrown or projected nature. 'Being-in-the-world' describes the nature of existence with reference to that cleared dimension which nurtures the ek-static character of existence."[34]

The view of man delineated in the *Letter* stood in marked contrast to traditional conceptions of human nature—all of which could be (and usually were) subsumed under the heading of *humanism.* According to Heidegger, humanism in its customary meaning was an outgrowth of Western philosophy and more specifically of Western metaphysics; metaphysical thinking, in turn, was marked by the predominance of the subject-object polarity: in other words, by the proclivity to treat the entire world as an assembly of objects or phenomena amenable to inspection by a detached mind or consciousness. In order to overcome traditional humanism, it was first necessary to escape the stranglehold of metaphysical antinomies; a path had to be found pointing past doctrines which pictured man either as a reified substance or as constitutive mind or as a combination of the two. "Man," the *Letter* affirms, "is never simply or primarily juxtaposed to the world as a concrete subject, be it in the singular or plural. Nor is he principally or only an (epistemological) subject intentionally directed to objects in such a manner that his nature resides in the subject-object relationship. Rather, man by nature exists first of all in the openness of Being—a clearing which alone sustains that 'in-between' zone in which a subject-object relationship can emerge."[35] The move beyond customary antinomies was not meant to suggest that past definitions of man were simply erroneous or obsolete, nor was the critique of traditional humanism prompted by an anti-human impulse—by the desire (as Heidegger writes) "to vindicate inhumanity and to debase human dignity." Far from trying to stifle human development or to muffle independent judgment, the intent of the *Letter on Humanism* was to rescue man from his excessive self-entanglement, from his bondage to egocentrism and metaphysical subjectivism.

To the extent that the traditional label was to be retained, Heidegger's *Letter* delineated a new version of humanism—a version in which man, without being repressed or abolished, was removed from the limelight of philosophical attention and placed in a broader context. "If we decide to keep the label," Heidegger observes, "the term 'humanism' signifies that human nature is crucial for the truth of Being— but crucial precisely in a way where everything does not depend on man as such." Conceived as a creature reaching out for Being, man occupies a much more modest status than metaphysical doctrines had assigned him; according to Heidegger, however, the loss of mastery entails an enormous benefit: the liberation from anthropocentric delusion and the improved ability to find fulfillment in the proximity of Being. "Man as the ek-static project of Being," he writes, "is more than *animal rationale* precisely to the degree that he is less in comparison with man construed in terms of subjectivity. Man is not the master of reality; he is the shepherd of Being. In this 'lesser' status man does not suffer any actual loss but rather gains by coming closer to the truth of Being; he gains the essential poverty of the shepherd whose dignity consists in his calling to guard carefully the truth of Being." By acting as the guardian of Being, man also remains attentive to his own nature, bringing into focus the *"humanitas of the homo humanus"*—a humanity "in the service of the truth of Being but freed from the shackles of a metaphysical humanism."[36]

In a sense, Heidegger's later thought can be viewed as an elaboration on the *Letter on Humanism*. His writings published during the last few decades of his life witness a steadily intensifying aversion to anthropocentrism; progressively man recedes into the role of supporting agent in a complex web of relationships whose axis revolves around Being. Occasionally, Heidegger's later arguments have a structuralist flavor—provided the term *structure* is not used as a synonym for a reified set of elements. A prominent recurring term in these arguments is *Ereignis,* frequently translated as "appropriation" or as "appropriating" or "gathering event." *World,* previously portrayed as the clearing of Being, is now presented as the arena of a complex gathering bringing together four major constitutive factors: earth, heaven, mortals, and immortals. The term *appropriation* in this context signifies that, by virtue of such a gathering, the four elements are able to come into their own and to assume their "proper" status and autonomy—an autonomy which, far from denoting segregation or indifference, nurtures the bond of mutual care through reciprocal recognition or the willingness to let each other "be." As he writes at one point: "Each of the four reflects in its own way the nature of the others; in doing so it establishes its own sphere within the fourfold correlation. Reflection in this case is not the representation of an external image; rather, it is an occurrence which, promoting reciprocal transparency, allows each of the elements to find its place in the common fabric."[37]

At least with regard to his views on man or man's status in the world, Merleau-Ponty's thought parallels Heidegger's intellectual development. As in the case of *Being and Time,* it is possible to detect in Merleau-Ponty's early writings subjectivist or voluntaristic overtones— although these aspects were counterbalanced from the beginning by the stress on embodiment or bodily perception as evidence of man's concrete insertion in the world, an insertion superseding egological designs. Undeniably, early definitions of social action or *praxis* tended to accentuate (and perhaps overaccentuate) the role of human initiative and intentionality. Thus, pleading for a reinstatement of man as the "subject of history," an article written at the end of the war referred to the "real humanity which *creates* itself through work and through praxis rather than seeking to define itself once and for all." One should note, however, that the plea did not convey the full tenor of the argument. In the same essay, existentialism was portrayed as a new perspective according to which "the relationship between subject and object is no longer that *relationship of knowing* postulated by classical idealism, wherein the object always seems the construction of the subject, but a *relationship of being* in which, paradoxically, the subject *is* his body, his world, and his situation, by a sort of exchange." Similarly the *Phenomenology of Perception,* published during the same period, asserted that "the world is not an object such that I have in my possession the law of its making; it is the natural setting of, and field for, all my thoughts and all my explicit perceptions. Truth does not 'inhabit' only 'the inner man,' or more accurately, there is no inner man, man is in the world, and only in the world does he know himself."[38]

In his subsequent writings, Merleau-Ponty endeavored with growing intensity to divest himself of subjectivist and anthropocentric leanings—without lapsing into reification or an anti-human objectivism. Returning to the theme of perception, his last major work—published posthumously under the title *The Visible and the Invisible*—portrayed perceptual experience not as confrontation between a self-contained subject and external reality, but as a complex interlocking relationship, a reciprocal incursion of "seer" and "visible" world. As he pointed out, the juxtaposition of subject and object, of *cogito* and *cogitatum,* "contains neither the whole nor even the essential of our commerce with the world" but rests on "a more muted relationship with the world" which is "always already accomplished when the reflective return intervenes." Once the focus was placed on the precognitive domain, perception could not be equated with an empirical occurrence or with a subjective initiative: "If the 'world' upon which it opens, the ambiguous field of horizons and distances, is not a region of the objective world, it resists as much being ranked on the side of 'facts of consciousness' or 'spiritual acts.' " The deemphasis of cognitive subjectivity, the study noted, was not meant to encourage a conception which merges the "seer" with perceived phenomena; such an identification on the contrary rendered perception unintelligible: "The visible about us seems to rest in itself. It is as though our vision were formed in the heart of the visible, or as though there were between it and us an intimacy as close as between the sea and the strand. And yet it is not possible that we blend into it, nor that it passes into us, for then the vision would vanish at the moment of formation, by disappearance of the seer or of the visible."[39]

The major concern of the study was the dismantling of egological pretensions. In Merleau-Ponty's presentation, vision was not simply a subjective act or achievement. "What is this talisman of color," he asked, "this singular virtue of the visible that makes it, held at the end of the gaze, nonetheless much more than a correlative of my vision, such that it imposes my vision upon me as a continuation of its own sovereign existence?" Although impossible without a perceiving agent, vision—according to Merleau-Ponty—was marked by the inherent tendency to push beyond subjective boundaries, a movement which was not the result of subjective intentionality; visual experience thus belied "the solipsist illusion that consists in thinking that every going beyond is a surpassing accomplished by oneself." As an experience, vision inevitably had a human connotation, or referred to something "given to us"; however, this connotation did not entail a possessive or anthropocentric enclosure: "We are not implicating in *'our experience'* any reference to an *ego* or to a certain type of intellectual relations with being, such as the Spinozist *'experiri.'* We are interrogating our experience precisely in order to know how it opens up to what is not ourselves. *This does not even exclude the possibility that we find in our experience a movement toward what could not in any event be present to us*

*in the original and whose irremediable absence would thus count among
our originating experiences.*"[40]

Given the non-subjective or transpersonal thrust of perception, the
nexus between vision and visible phenomena emerged as an interlocking relationship; once experience was seen as an excursion into the
world, the relationship acquired reversibility. "He who sees," the study
noted, "cannot possess the visible unless he is possessed by it, unless
he *is of it,* unless, by principle, according to what is required by the
articulation of the look with the things, he is one of the visibles, capable, by a singular reversal, of seeing them." In Merleau-Ponty's view,
this conception could be extended from the domain of vision to philosophical thought and to the general interaction between man and the
world; such an extension could serve as a corrective to traditional theoretical postures. "We do not have to choose," he asserted in *The Visible and the Invisible,* "between a philosophy that installs itself in the
world itself or in the other and a philosophy that installs itself 'in us,' "
that is, between an internal and an external perspective: "these alternatives are not imperative, since perhaps the self and the non-self are like
the obverse and the reverse and since perhaps our own experience *is* this
turning round that installs us far indeed from 'ourselves,' in the other,
in the things."[41]

Although generally critical of phenomenology, Adorno's thoughts
on the topic were compatible with the preceding arguments. His *Negative Dialectics* in particular was pervaded by a strong anti-subjectivist
bent—which did not coincide with anti-humanism or even with a rejection of individualism. As the study tried to show, Western philosophy or metaphysics has been marked from the beginning by a fascination with subjectivity, a fascination which carried a price: as a "penalty
for its glorification" the epistemological subject was "incarcerated permanently in its selfhood," condemned to gaze at the world like a knight
"through the casemate of a fortress." In modern thought since Descartes and especially since Kant, subjectivity moved progressively into
the limelight of philosophical attention, just as self-centered individualism—anchored in property rights—emerged during the same period
as the centerpiece of social life. In Adorno's view, the philosophical
movement reached its apex in recent existentialism. In the writings of
leading existentialists, he notes, subjectivity "congeals into an absolutely solid premise," a development which "had been implicit as a
tendency in Kant's notion of transcendental synthesis." As a result of
this hardening process, however, subjectivity loses its linkage with
"truth" which presupposes the "constellation of subject and object":
"The truth-element of the subject unfolds only in its relation to what it

is not—by no means through a self-centered affirmation of its existence or givenness." As Adorno adds, the modern attachment to subjectivity and anthropocentrism has been accompanied by a steady accentuation of its costs. Implementing the thrust of Western metaphysics, modern science has paved the way to man's subjugation of nature: "The primacy of subjectivity replicates in spiritual guise the Darwinian struggle for survival." While designed initially as a counterpoise to natural bondage, human rationality in our time has spawned a new and more complete type of bondage and even a new mythology. Under these circumstances, further advances in emancipation and "enlightenment" can no longer be expected from the simple invocation of subjective humanism: the traditional *reductio ad hominem* has to be replaced by or at least coupled with a *reductio hominis*—the debunking of anthropocentric pretensions (which is not synonymous with the elimination of reflection in favor of objectivism).

According to *Negative Dialectics,* such debunking involves an effort to break open subjectivity in the direction of non-subjective reality, an effort guided not by the desire to control or manipulate the world, but by an attitude of attentive care and a willingness to respect diversity. "Things," we read, "are reified as targets of a long-standing oppression." Their recovery requires expiatory measures: measures which, contrary to "the imperialist impulse to annex the otherness of the world," would tend to "recognize the element of distance and strangeness even in proximate surroundings." As Adorno emphasizes, recovery and recognition of this kind are incompatible with possessive self-enclosure. "Nothing on earth or in an emptied heaven can be salvaged through stubborn defense," he affirms, adding: "Nothing can be saved without transformation, nothing which has not passed through the portals of its death. While salvaging is the innermost impulse of mind, there is no hope outside of unconditional surrender: a surrender of both the target of salvation and of the searching mind guided by hope." In a passage reminiscent of Merleau-Ponty's posthumous work, Adorno refers to the "intelligible sphere" or *mundus intelligibilis* as the transcendence of finite-factual experience—a transcendence which, though not identical with finitude, is not simply its denial but rather its reverse side (or, in Merleau-Ponty's terms, the "invisible of the visible"). "The concept of intelligibility," he writes, "denotes the transgression of finite thought. In thought every factual givenness discovers its insufficiency; departure from self-possessed existence is the source of that element in mind which overcomes its impulse toward domination of nature."[42]

CHAPTER TWO

Intersubjectivity and Political Community

CONTEMPORARY SOCIAL SCIENCES exhibit a striking mixture of vitality and infirmity. Recent decades have seen vigorous strides to enhance the methodological capabilities of these sciences; the upsurge of behavioristic and economic models is frequently portrayed as having catapulted them from infancy to analytical maturity. Unfortunately, these advances are offset by the weakness of underlying premises, and especially by the fragility of the small and seemingly unobtrusive building-blocks out of which analytical frameworks are constructed. The literature of social and political science is filled with observations about human action or behavior, and also about the salient features of societies, cultures, and political communities. But the meanings of these terms are rarely explored and, for the most part, remain obscure.[1] Sample questions arising on this level are: What is the significance of *action* or *practice* and what is its relationship to *behavior?* To what extent is social or political practice an outgrowth of human agency or a human subject, and what is the meaning of *subjectivity?* In what sense can social and political life be said to emerge from human interaction or *intersubjectivity?* Does intersubjectivity denote an aggregation of human actors, and how is such aggregation intelligible?

In my view, this obscurity is only in small part due to the inattentiveness of practitioners. It results instead from inherent complexities in the issues—complexities which have been greatly aggravated in our century. For a long time, the questions surrounding human agency and interaction seemed to be relatively settled; at least since the dawn of the modern age, individual man was assumed to be the bedrock on which social and political life was founded. In the philosophy of Hobbes, the natural state of man was depicted as a solitary and atomistic condition, with political organization deriving from contractual agreement. While, in Hobbes' case, the meaning of *nature* or *natural* remained ambivalent, subsequent theories typically chose either a rationalist or an empiricist interpretation, locating man's core respectively in a "thinking substance" or in concrete-empirical traits. Despite differences of accent, the two interpretations concur in one crucial

point: they see the human condition as involving a confrontation between man (typically individual man) and his natural and social environment. The precise character of this juxtaposition can in turn be
construed from diverse perspectives, two of which have been particularly prominent. In the first view, man's relationship to the world can
be defined in a basically theoretical or cognitive sense, with man functioning both as recipient of environmental stimuli and, more importantly, as detached spectator of natural and social processes. From the
second perspective, the relationship may be cast in a more practical or
even an activist mold, so that man appears either as determining factor
in a causal chain or as the vital center of plans designed to shape the
environment.

In our century, the sketched assumptions of the modern era—
problematical from the beginning—have tended to be undermined by
intellectual and social-political developments. In the intellectual sphere,
an important trend has been the change in focus from individual consciousness to language and linguistic communication, a turn which is
prominent in both Anglo-Saxon and Continental European philosophy.
While opening up a number of new vistas, philosophical argument in
our time has not produced a neat resolution of the theoretical predicaments which afflict social and political life. On the contrary, new quandaries have been stirred up, for example: What is the meaning of *intersubjectivity* once the human subject is removed as cornerstone of
social analysis? Does the community's function as the context of linguistic communication imply an individualism of a higher order—a
"subjectivity writ large"—or does it envelop the subject like an external destiny? Is communication a practice incapable of correction or
does it make room for normative standards—and if so, how? Queries
of this kind, one should add, are not (or are no longer) purely theoretical concerns. Social and political developments of our age have
thrown into sharp relief the concrete implications of individualism and
the hazards of a non- or anti-individualist approach to politics. Global
events during recent decades have been overshadowed by the confrontation between liberal-democratic and socialist or communist regimes,
with the two sides extolling—respectively—the virtues of individual
freedom and the collective needs of society. In either camp the stri-
dency of ideological pleas seems inversely related to the clarity of the
proclaimed goals.[2]

The present chapter seeks to clarify the festering issues surrounding intersubjectivity or social interaction. Admittedly, *intersubjectivity*
is a rough approximation of the topic of these explorations, since the

term prejudges the intended theme as a relationship between *individuals*. Perhaps terms like *sociality* or *co-being* would be more fitting labels. The advantage of *intersubjectivity* is its customary usage; cautiously employed, the term serves as a handy launching-pad for excursions into less familiar terrain. Instead of offering a panoramic survey of contemporary literature, the presentation concentrates on two major intellectual trends of our age: phenomenology and critical Marxism. Within the broader confines of the phenomenological movement, the study will focus on two successive phases: first, the period of the founders, covering the first several decades of this century; and second, the period of the so-called French School, whose beginning coincides roughly with the Second World War. As is well known, the "founding" period was characterized by the successive emergence of two contrasting philosophical perspectives: Edmund Husserl's version of transcendental phenomenology, anchored in the constitutive functions of subjectivity (and secondarily in the experiences of the *life-world*), and Martin Heidegger's phenomenological-existential ontology, stressing human *Dasein* as a key to the question of Being. In terms of social interaction, the contrast involved, first, the attempt to elaborate on egological premises a conception of transcendental intersubjectivity and, second, the delineation of co-being (*Mitsein*) as an ontological dimension of existence. Following a portrayal of these two perspectives, I intend to show, in a second section, that a similar distinction between a transcendental and a more ontological or quasi-ontological viewpoint can be found in French phenomenology, with Jean-Paul Sartre exemplifying the first alternative and Merleau-Ponty and Jacques Derrida the second. Turning to critical Marxism, the third part of this chapter depicts a broadly comparable transition from an idealist-Hegelian conception of social action and interaction, as articulated in Georg Lukács' *History and Class Consciousness*, to a non-subjectivist and non-idealist view of intersubjectivity, as found in Adorno's later writings. Linking together the preceding arguments, the concluding section sketches a typology of modes of human sociality.

HUSSERL AND HEIDEGGER

The founding period of the phenomenological movement deserves close attention both for general philosophical reasons and because of its decisive contributions to the elucidation of intersubjectivity. In general terms, the thinking of the founders—above all, Husserl and

Heidegger—was marked by an intensity of reflective commitment unmatched since the time of Kant and Hegel. Regardless of their disagreements, both philosophers were uncompromising in their rejection of positivist complacency—the positivists' acceptance of the world as simply given—and in their endeavor to return philosophy to a renewed preoccupation with first issues. As Derrida has correctly stated: "In our proximity and in the aftermath of Hegel or in his mighty shadow, the two great voices which have dictated to us this renewed and complete rehearsal—recalling us to it and revealing it as of utmost philosophical urgency—are unquestionably those of Husserl and Heidegger."[1] Even when their differences are taken into account, the perspectives of the two founders are instructive for their boldness and incisiveness. To a considerable extent, Husserl's opus can be viewed as the culmination—and perhaps incipient turning point—of the modern philosophy of subjectivity and of its cognitive-theoretical as well as practical-purposive ambitions. While linked with his teacher through a common tradition of discourse, Heidegger undertook a determined effort—probably the most resolute in our time—to remove the human subject from the center without lapsing into an anti-human objectivism. Both the radicalness of their common philosophical quest and the distinctiveness of their individual formulations throw the problem of intersubjectivity and human interaction into sharp relief.

Life-world and Monadology: Husserl

Husserl's thought is sometimes accused, especially by non-phenomenologists, of being entirely unconcerned with intersubjectivity; his outlook, in this view, is sharply segregated from perspectives which stress communicative interaction. This assessment is at least misleading. Undeniably, his philosophy was intimately wedded to subjectivity, construed as the meaning-giving and confirming agency of last resort. Husserl's study on *Formal and Transcendental Logic* depicted the "ego" as existing "primordially and prior to any conceivable object" and as "the intentional foundation of my world."[2] This ego-focus remained a central ingredient of Husserl's thought, despite his much-belabored stress on the *life-world* during his later years. His last major work, *The Crisis of European Sciences and Transcendental Phenomenology,* still adhered firmly to the tripartite structure of phenomenological inquiry, summarized by the labels *ego—cogito—cogitatum.* The same work spoke of the "singular philosophical solitude" engendered by rigorous reflection and especially by the phenomenological "bracketing" of the world; it also insisted—"for the profoundest philosophical reasons"—on the need to depart from the "absolute uniqueness of the ego."[3] Nevertheless, *egology* in the phenomenological sense should not simply be equated with a defense of subjectivism. Throughout his life, Husserl struggled valiantly against the pitfalls of solipsism and intellectual self-enclosure. What was at stake in this endeavor was major—the objectivity of cognition and the possibility of arriving at a generally shared notion of reality. As he untiringly emphasized, only a solidly grounded intersubjective framework could provide a reliable basis for the universal validation of propositions.

The importance of intersubjectivity in Husserl's thought is demonstrated by his repeated attempts to give a proper account of the topic.[4] Only the major highlights of this intellectual journey can be sketched here. Assumptions about intersubjectivity can be found in his early formulations of *eidetic* analysis; clearly the idea of general structures of consciousness which grant access to universal essences implies a shared world of phenomena. A first outline of the theme was presented in Husserl's *Ideas Concerning a Pure Phenomenological Philosophy,* a comprehensive study conceived on the eve of the First World War (with only the first volume, however, published at that time). The study introduced and developed phenomenological *bracketing* or *reduction* as a gateway to transcendental consciousness and as the dividing line between *pure* and *mundane* types of cognition. Regarding intersubjectivity, the first volume of *Ideas* made an important distinction between different levels of experience, especially between the mundane level of the *natural attitude* and the level of rigorous phenomenological reflection. On the first level, according to Husserl, the intersubjective character of experience was taken for granted. Defined as "the world in which I find myself and which is also my world-about-me," the *natural world* was said to include from the beginning other *ego-subjects* related to their surroundings in a similar manner—with the result that "I apprehend the world-about-them and the world-about-me objectively as one and the same world." The problem was how this naive belief could be cognitively explored and phenomenologically validated. The suggested solution involved the perception of other human beings first as physical bodies and next as psychophysical creatures. In a cognitive framework, Husserl stressed, only bodies are immediately present, while the mental life of others—manifest in their bodily expressions—is accessible only indirectly, through empathy. Raised to a reflectively refined level, reciprocal acts of empathy could lead to a "possible community consciousness," that is, to an "essentially possible plurality of personal centers of consciousness and streams of consciousness enjoying mutual intercourse."[5]

Tentative notions of this kind were fleshed out in the second (posthumously published) volume of *Ideas*. Adopting a cognitive perspective, Husserl in this volume started with a delineation of different domains of empirical reality and corresponding modes of perception. The first region discussed was that of material inanimate objects, a domain whose real features and causal linkages could only be perceived through the senses. The second major region was that of the animalia, that is, of animate creatures—including human beings—endowed with psyches or souls. In this domain, Husserl argued, one's own mental life was accessible to inner perception as a stream of experiences. Fellow creatures, on the other hand, were encountered as the combination of a directly perceived material object and a conjectured internal life. More precisely stated: material objects resembling my own body are construed as living bodies which belong to other ego-subjects to whom mental activities are transferred by empathy. The Other's mental life, in this context, is available only in the form of a transferred *co-presence* or *compresence,* not by direct inspection; in phenomenological terms, it is not present to perception but merely *appresented*. Despite this restriction, empathy in Husserl's view served as bridge to the other ego-subject and to his range of perceptions and experiences—a range including my own body or myself as the Other's *alter ego.* In this manner, intersubjectivity emerged as a relationship of animate, psychophysical creatures. The last region treated in the volume was that of spirit or subjectivity proper, a domain transcending empirical nature. To gain access to this region, Husserl urged that the cognitive-sensorial (or *naturalistic*) attitude be replaced by a *personalistic* one. From this vantage point, I am first of all the subjective center of a surrounding world to which I am tied through intentional acts; as the matrix of everyday experience, this world also contains fellow-men who are immediately seen as *consociates* or *counter-subjects* in a common communicative environment (although each retains an individual aura of subjective perceptions). Genuine communication, according to Husserl, may lead to the formation of subjectivities or personal entities of a higher order, existing in the environment of a common culture.[6]

Although intriguing, the arguments presented in *Ideas* were in many respects disjointed; thus, the postulated compresence remained opaque and the relationship between different attitudes elusive. Husserl himself was dissatisfied enough with the second volume to postpone publication. On a limited scale, clarification of the outstanding issues was undertaken in studies written during the twenties. Apart from depicting phenomenology as *prima philosophia,* the manuscript on *First Philosophy* tried to establish a link between communicative experience and the natural attitude outlined at an earlier point; in the natural context of everyday life, one reads there, we always speak and act "in the communicative plural"—although the meaning of this plurality requires phenomenological scrutiny. The next study, on *Formal and Transcendental Logic,* sought to establish transcendental consciousness as the constitutive source of all the meaning-contents of the world. At the same time, Husserl endeavored to confront the dilemma of subjectivism—or, as he phrased it, "the dark corner haunted by the ghosts of solipsism and, perhaps, of psychologism, of relativism." In this task several "painfully puzzling" questions had to be resolved. It was desirable to elucidate the distinction between the experience of my own internal life and the experience of the mind of other psychophysical egos. On the transcendental level, there was a crucial need to show how my own consciousness was able to constitute another subjectivity, which was simultaneously an ego and different from my ego, and how such constitution could even present myself as the Other's *alter ego* and ultimately entail a transcendental community.[7]

The most thorough attempt to deal with these quandaries was contained in Husserl's famous *Cartesian Meditations* (first published in French in 1931), specifically in the Fifth Meditation devoted to the portrayal of transcendental reflection as foundation of a monadological intersubjectivity. Again, the barest outline must suffice here. As a first prerequisite for a rigorous account of intersubjective life, Husserl introduced a new type of reduction or *epoché* which has to be performed in the domain of transcendental consciousness: a reduction entailing the bracketing or screening out of all *alien* features of the world, including all social or cultural meaning-patterns referring to other human beings. What is left after this reduction is the ego's own *proper* or *primordial* sphere, containing both the ego's actual or potential intentionalities and the intended features of the world or "nature as experienced by me." Within this primordial and radically private context, I find my own body to be distinct from all other things because it is the carrier of my perceptions and the functioning organ of my movements; in other words, I encounter myself as a unity of mind and body or as an integral *monad.* Viewed from this angle, fellow-men first appear as mere corporeal objects in the outer world; however, due to an intrinsic similarity, I am able to bestow on these objects the sense *living body* and even *other human being*—a bestowal predicated not simply on inference, but on a complex process of analogical perception or associative pairing, where two phenomena are experienced as *co-present* (although, strictly speaking, only my own living body is immediately given while the Other's humanity is appresented). Analogical perception yields access to the Other's monadic existence and to his primordial sphere with its range of perceptions; rigorously pursued, appresentation in the end leads to a fusion of primordial spheres and the emergence of a shared or objective world. According to Husserl, other types of intersubjective communities can be derived from this common framework. Thus, once it is realized that the Other's primordial sphere is, like mine, the outgrowth of a transcendental constitution, empathy opens the door to a transcendental community of monads or a transcendental intersubjectivity which, however, in a strict sense is nurtured only from sources of my own intentionality.[8]

Husserl's last years show him deeply preoccupied with the same set of problems. On the whole his later manuscripts and publications tended to elaborate on the arguments presented in *Cartesian Meditations* and earlier studies; they did not involve a basic change of perspective. Despite a wealth of new insights and numerous modifications of detail, this continuity is still manifest in the *Crisis of European Sciences*—a study sometimes used as evidence of a complete reversal. For present purposes, Husserl's later writings are significant chiefly for their subtle portrayal of different types of intersubjectivity: especially the transcendental community of monads and the mundane life-world, or world of everyday experience. The *Crisis* contains a number of eloquent and captivating passages on the community of monads. Thus, in a fragment appended to the study, it is depicted as the "absolutely functioning community of subjects through whose communicative-intentional acts the objective world is constituted." At other points, the same community is portrayed as the result of an intersubjective merger or a constitutive "we-synthesis," which entails an "intentional interpenetration of ego-subjects and of their transcendental life." As in the pages of *Cartesian Meditations,* Husserl in the *Crisis* does not simply presuppose such an interpenetration of subjects; on the contrary, he insists strongly on the need to elucidate the genesis of intersubjectivity. Other human beings are perceived initially as *implications* of my primordial world—but in such a manner that the appresented fellow-men experience me as their implicit *alter ego.* "Every ego-subject," Husserl writes, "has his horizon of empathy, that of his co-subjects, which can be opened up through direct and indirect commerce with the chain of others, who are all others for one another."

Consequently, "within the vitally flowing intentionality in which the life of an ego-subject consists, every other ego is already intentionally implied in advance by way of empathy and the empathy-horizon." Transcendental phenomenology, the concluding section of the *Crisis* notes, ultimately yields "the discovery of an absolute intersubjectivity (objectified in the world as mankind)"—a community in which reason through constant efforts at self-clarification is "in infinite progress."[9]

The notion of the life-world is often treated as the crucial innovation in Husserl's later thought, yet aspects of the idea were clearly anticipated in earlier discussions of the natural and personalistic attitudes. In the *Crisis,* the life-world is a "surrounding world of life" which is initially taken for granted; from the beginning this world includes not only inanimate and animate phenomena but also fellow-men with whom we are linked in an unquestioned community: "Each ego-subject and all of us belong together as living with one another in a common world; and the world is our world, valid for our consciousness as existing precisely through this 'living together.'" "Two possible fundamental ways" of approaching the life-world are distinguished by Husserl: a "naive and natural straightforward attitude"—which he describes as "the naturally normal one which absolutely must precede" the other—and a "consistently reflective attitude," which explores the meaning and validity of experiences. Despite its obvious significance, the relationship between life-world and reflection is not entirely clear in the *Crisis.* On the one hand, the life-world is said to function as a pre-reflective matrix underlying and nurturing reflective endeavors; on the other hand, the intelligibility of the life-world seems to depend on its origin in transcendental reflection.

However this question may be resolved, the important point for our present purposes is the implicit egological character of the life-world viewed as a mundane habitat. This was evident in *Ideas,* where the domain of the natural attitude was defined as the world "in which I find myself and which is also my world-about-me." In a similar manner, the personalistic perspective was said to reveal me as the personal center of a surrounding world whose phenomena are arranged about me in varying degrees of spatial and temporal distance. In the *Crisis* the life-world is likewise depicted as "a realm of subjective phenomena" whose sense initially remains "anonymous" or unthematized; the "general structures" of the life-world are said to embrace two poles: "thing and world on the one side, thing-consciousness on the other." Despite a perceptive historical account of the emergence of reflective consciousness from primitive ways of life, Husserl treats subjectivity, at least in incipient form, and attendant subject-object relationships as natural human condition: "The pre-given world is the horizon which includes all our goals, all our ends, whether fleeting or lasting, in a flowing but constant manner, just as an intentional horizon-consciousness implicitly 'encompasses' everything in advance. We, the subjects, in our normal unbroken, coherent life, know no goals which extend beyond this."[10]

Some Post-Husserlian Views

Husserl's theory of intersubjectivity, to the extent that one can speak of an integral theory, has been the target of numerous detailed critiques. I wish to draw attention briefly to three critical assessments which seem to me particularly instructive because of their differences of accent, and in part because of the light they shed on Heidegger's approach. The three reviewers are, in the chronological sequence in which their comments appeared: the Spanish philosopher José Ortega y Gasset, the Husserl student and sociological phenomenologist Alfred Schutz, and the German philosopher Michael Theunissen. Despite the noted differences, all three critics are opposed to central facets of Husserl's conception of intersubjectivity; read in conjunction, their appraisals reveal important weaknesses of that conception—without necessarily vindicating their own counter-proposals. Of the three, Ortega follows Husserl's account most closely, although he manages to infuse the ego with a dramatic, quasi-existentialist vitality. His critique focuses on Husserl's notion of appresentative empathy as foundation of a transcendental community—which, in his judgment, jeopardizes the uniqueness of the ego. While generally respectful of Husserl's transcendental perspective, Schutz finds it incapable of escaping the bounds of solipsism; only a mundane phenomenology operating on the level of the natural attitude, he concludes, can give access to social and intersubjective life. Comparatively speaking, Theunissen's review contains the most far-reaching critique since it attacks the egological structure of Husserl's thought, questioning the propriety of approaching human interaction from either a transcendental or a mundane-egological viewpoint.

Ortega's discussion of intersubjectivity occurs in his last major book, called *Man and People,* which he completed shortly before his death in 1955. As indicated, the study carried an existentialist flavor, particularly evident in the stark confrontation between genuine subjectivity and social anonymity.[11] Toward the beginning of the book, Ortega invites the reader to perform a quasi-phenomenological reduction: namely, "to an order of ultimate reality, to an order or area of reality which because it is *radical* (that is, of the root) admits of no other reality beneath it"—an order which he identifies as "our life, human life" and more particularly as "my" own life, since "human life as radical reality is only the life of each person, is only *my* life." Due to its basically untransferable character, human life is said to be "essentially *solitude, radical solitude*"—which does not mean the absence of an environment; rather, man is alone precisely in relation to his surroundings.

The outside world—an "immense thing, with shadowy frontiers and full to bursting with smaller things"—is initially encountered as a pragmatic context or vital field (one might call it a milieu) whose contents are experienced as instruments or obstacles. The philosophical problem consists in rendering intelligible the sense and manner of appearance of these contents. The first step along this road is a realization that I perceive the world through my body (since man is "shut up in his body for life"); consequently, other contents of the world appear to me primarily as bodies or as related to bodies. After having sketched the sense of inanimate and animate phenomena, Ortega queries how the "other man" emerges in "my vital world" and he answers with Husserl: "As a sensible presence, all that I have of him is a body"—although it is a body which "is constantly sending us the most various signals or indications or suggestions as to what is going on in the within that is the other man. This within, this inwardness or intimacy, is never present, but is compresent, like the side of the apple that we do not see." Actually, in contrast to the sides of the apple, "the inwardness that the other man *is* has never made itself, nor can ever make itself, present to me." More emphatically yet: "The life of another is not patent reality to me as my own life is"; rather, it is "only a presumption or a presumed or assumed reality, as likely as you please, but not radically, unquestionably, primordially 'reality.' "[12]

At this point Ortega's objections to Husserl's theory come into view. Although praising Husserl's normally "exact, careful work" and crediting him with having "most accurately formulated" the question of intersubjectivity, Ortega finds in Husserl's approach a "colossal error"—one particularly grievous "because of the carelessness that it reveals." At issue is the process of appresentation or analogical transposition through which the Other's body is assumed to reveal "another I" or an *alter ego*. "The colossal error," Ortega writes, "consists in supposing that the difference between my body and the Other's is only a difference in perspective—the difference between what is seen here and what is seen *from here, hinc*—there, *illic.*" In truth, he adds, "this thing that I call 'my body' is very little like the Other's body." The reason for the difference is that my body is the direct instrument of my activities, the universal *"organon* on which I can count," while the Other's body is given to me "only through my body, my seeing, my touching, my hearing, its resisting, and so on." Differently phrased: "my body is felt principally from within it, it is also my 'within,' it is the intra-body—whereas all that I observe of the Other's body is its exteriority, its alien form, its without." The perceptual difference, in Ortega's view, is so pronounced that the body of the Other acquires a status akin to the bodies of animals "that are also present to me outwardly."[13] Given this contrast, Husserl's attempt to link egos through bodily transposition is doomed to failure. What the theory of appresentative empathy can generate, he asserts, is at most an abstract cognitive identification which is irrelevant to human life: *"Ego,* strictly, is something that I alone am, and if I refer it to an Other, I have to change its meaning. *Alter ego* has to be understood analogically: there is in the abstract Other *something* that is in him what the *Ego* is in me. The two *Egos,* mine and the analogical one, have in common only certain abstract components, which, being abstract, are unreal."[14]

Ortega's critique of appresentation does not imply a rejection of all kinds of human interaction; on the contrary, in his opinion intersubjective encounters are a basic feature of the human condition but tend to occur on a mundane level, without involving a convergence of egos. The "first social theorem" articulated in *Man and People* is that "man is *a nativitate* open to the Other, to the alien being; or, in other words: *before each one of us became aware of himself,* he had already had the basic experience that there are others who are not 'I,' the Others." Prior to self-reflection, "all men live in one and the same world," so that *living* means essentially "co-living, *living together.*" This, Ortega comments, "is what we may call the natural, normal, and everyday attitude in which we live."[15] Although the Other's ego and internal life are not accessible, in daily life "we live [with] these presumptions or second-degree realities as if they were radical realities." Only through a reflective turn—too arduous to be widely practiced—are we able to grasp the illusory character of these presumptions: "We habitually pretend to live, but we do not actually live our genuine life, the life that we should have to live if, freeing ourselves from all these interpretations accepted by the other people among whom we find ourselves and who are commonly called 'society,' we from time to time made energetic and clear contact with our life as radical reality"—that is, with our radical solitude. Genuine existence, according to Ortega, can only be accomplished through a frequent withdrawal to this primordial domain: "In solitude, man is his truth; in society, he tends to be his mere conventionality or falsification." From a reflective stance, the Other is revealed as an *essential stranger,* while society appears as a *pseudo-reality,* a fabric of anonymous *opinions,* a *gigantic architecture of usages.* Actually, as a collective entity, society is not so much a synonym for interhuman or inter-individual relations as for an anti-individual and almost non-human structure: *"Collectivity* is indeed something human, but it is the human without man, the human without spirit, the human without soul, the human dehumanized."[16]

Two years after the completion of *Man and People* Alfred Schutz published a detailed appraisal of Husserl's concept of *transcendental intersubjectivity.*[17] The study recapitulated Husserl's arguments and offered a lengthy catalogue of their main weaknesses. Focusing on the successive theoretical steps outlined in the Fifth Cartesian Meditation, Schutz found the first step, the *primordial reduction,* flawed on several counts. Does not the definition of the ego's "proper" sphere, he asked, presuppose knowledge of the excluded world? Moreover, is it possible to differentiate between our thematic experience of others and their actual subjectivity, and does the former not already include reference to "a possible Us and We"? In the second step of analogical perception, Schutz, with Ortega, pointed to the essential disparity of the paired bodies. My own body, he noted, "is present as inner perception of its boundaries and through the kinaesthetic experience of its functioning. It is thus present precisely in a way which is as dissimilar as possible from the external perception of an animate body other than mine." Empathy likewise seems implausible, given the prior reduction to the primordial sphere; for, "what sense can it make within this sphere to refer to congruent psychic events pertaining to the Other?" The same quandary applies even more strongly to the next theoretical step, the appresentation of the Other's primordial world and the emergence of an objective universe, based on a convergence of perspectives: "Does not the constitution of an objective nature presuppose as warranted the systematic unity of identity of the natural object given *to the Other* in primordial originarity with the same natural object as appresented by him as it might be given to me? Does not, therefore, the instituting of a common and objective nature presuppose a we-relationship, and is it not founded upon the possibility of communication?"[18]

With this question Schutz arrived at the culminating point of Husserl's theory: the notion of a transcendental community of monads, or transcendental intersubjectivity. As Schutz tried to show, the conception of a transcendentally founded community is basically incongruent. First of all, assuming the process of reciprocal appresentation, it is unintelligible how the constitutive activities of transcendental egos can penetrate to the dimension of a "transcendental we-relationship": all that each ego can accomplish is the constitution of his world and his fellow-men *"just for himself and not for all other transcendental egos as well."* In this case the constituted fellow-men are at best projections of myself, rather than *alter egos.* The entire argument is further weakened by the presumed plurality of monads. In Schutz's words: "Is not the concept of the transcendental ego conceivable only in the singular? Can it also be 'declined' in the plural, or is it, as the Latin grammarians call it, a *singulare tantum?"* The latter view gains support from Husserl's concept of the *eidos ego,* or transcendental ego at large, containing the possible variations of egos and *alter egos;* but "what sense would it make to speak of intersubjectivity with reference to the one and unitary Eidos 'transcendental ego at large'?" The entire critical analysis led to the conclusion that "Husserl's attempt to account for the constitution of transcendental intersubjectivity in terms of operations of the consciousness of the transcendental ego has not succeeded." This conclusion, in Schutz's view, warranted the inference that "intersubjectivity is not a problem of constitution which can be solved within the transcendental sphere, but is rather a datum of the life-world. It is the fundamental ontological category of human existence in the world and therefore of all philosophical anthropology."[19]

Schutz's critique, unlike Ortega's book, was not prompted by concern for the solitary ego and its falsification by mundane, social life. On the contrary, the notion of a radical monadic solitude or absolute subjectivity, in Schutz's opinion, was a synonym for solipsism and the outgrowth of philosophical abstraction from the life-world.[20] His perspective betrayed none of the intense drama implicit in Ortega's confrontation of genuine life and social anonymity—a tension also present, though in less emphatic form, in Husserl's distinction between the natural and the reflective attitudes and in his portrayal of human history as a process of reflective self-emancipation. While not rejecting entirely Husserl's transcendental philosophical ambitions, Schutz preferred to redefine them in the direction of phenomenological description. In his own work, Schutz tended to confine himself to descriptive analyses of the commonsense world of everyday life as seen from the perspective of the natural attitude—analyses which frequently were distinguished by a painstaking attention to detail. Despite these advantages, his mundane phenomenology was purchased at a price: the loss not only of the mentioned tension but also of normative standards applicable both to the validation of cognitive claims and to the justification of social practices. Having put aside, for whatever plausible reasons, the benchmark of absolute subjectivity, he neglected to articulate yardsticks operative in the context of intersubjective life. Although differentiating astutely between degrees of intimacy in social relations, his studies did not venture beyond the descriptive domain; none of the outlined types of interaction carries overtones of the good life—such as can be detected in Husserl's transcendental intersubjectivity.[21]

Schutz's rejection of transcendental constitution, incidentally, did not signify the complete abandonment of subjectivity. His explorations of the commonsense world and its taken-for-granted features invariably took one premise without question: the essentially subjective character of mundane experience in both a private and a social frame of reference. Following in Husserl's footsteps (but less cautiously) his writings depicted man's natural condition as incipiently egological, and the life-world as an environmental context surrounding individual human designs. In a passage reminiscent of the distinction between subject and object poles in the *Crisis,* Schutz noted that "the individual living in the world always experiences himself as being within a certain situation which he has to define" and that closer analysis of this circumstance reveals "two principal components": one consisting in "the ontological structure of the pregiven world," the other deriving from "the actual biographical state of the individual, a state which includes his stock of knowledge in its actual articulation."[22] The same study delineated the "stratification of the life-world" by differentiating between various zones of experience—all of which centered on the individual's biographical situation. Proceeding outward from this center in both spatial and temporal directions, the first zone encountered was the domain of direct social experience, where individuals (sometimes called *consociates*) interact in a common span of time and typically in face-to-face relationships. The next or *surrounding* layer was the "world of my contemporaries whose subjects coexist with me in time without, however, being with me in reciprocal spatial reach." Further zones were inhabited by *predecessors* and *successors*—groups with whom reciprocal interaction is impossible. Despite differences between individual biographical situations, everyday experience was inherently intersubjective due to the prevalence of *typifications* or typical role patterns and a generally presumed reciprocity of perspectives—factors which, however, were merely commonsense constructs and did not contravene the subjective motivation of social action.[23]

A decade after Ortega's death Michael Theunissen published a lengthy study entitled *Der Andere* ("The Other"), which dealt with a wide range of recent views on intersubjectivity. The first part of this study—devoted to a review of the transcendental-philosophical conception of intersubjectivity—contains a most penetrating (albeit somewhat exaggerated) critique of Husserl's theory. In contrast to Ortega's radical and Schutz's mundane individualism, Theunissen's analysis aimed to dislodge the egological moorings of Husserl's argument; in fact, it found the central shortcoming of Husserl's approach in his attachment to subjectivity on both the reflective and the mundane-experiential levels, an attachment which was claimed to shortchange the transcendent status or the otherness of fellow-men. According to *Der Andere,* Husserl's effort to escape the confines of solipsism was ultimately unsuccessful due to the inherent inability of subjectivity to transgress its own boundaries and to make room for genuine interaction: the diverse procedures outlined by Husserl in his articulation of an intersubjective framework presuppose the constitutive functions of an ego whose "proper" domain is taken for granted and seemingly immune to external challenge. Even the estrangement experienced as a result of my self-perception as the Other's *alter ego,* Theunissen argued, is basically a self-inflicted and thus readily manageable trauma. Despite the dislocating effect of my integration into the Other's perspective— he wrote—"Husserl presents me as the executive organ of my own self-estrangement"; in the end intersubjectivity remains an outgrowth of the *ego cogitans,* a phenomenon locked into the immanence of consciousness.[24]

Theunissen noted an occasional ambivalence in Husserl's account of the mundane level of the natural attitude, although this ambivalence was finally resolved in favor of subjectivity. The notion of the life-world seemed to point to a layer of precognitive experience which undercuts traditional subject-object distinctions, and in which fellow-men are encountered as integral creatures rather than as synthetic amalgams of body and (appresented) mind. Seen in this light, everyday interaction—instead of denoting a juxtaposition of embryonic subjectivities— emerges as a communal matrix predicated on a common presubjective bond; chief manifestations of this unifying bond are a shared language, shared communication patterns and, most importantly, joint involvement in ongoing practices, especially in the tasks of daily work.[25] As

Theunissen added, however, the sketched perspective was only intermittently voiced and was ultimately overshadowed by Husserl's dominant egological commitment. A clear example of this commitment was his persistent identification of the natural and personalistic attitudes, with the latter defined as a subject- or person-centered outlook; from a personalistic vantage point, fellow-men could only be encountered as ingredients of the surrounding world and, in a strict sense, were accessible only through a process of empathy. Given the subjective structure of the life-world, incidentally, the natural character of everyday experience appeared questionable. According to Theunissen, Husserl's natural attitude was not so much a non-prejudicial starting point as a (less reflective) derivative of transcendental reflection: "The notion of everyday interaction which is meant to serve as guide for transcendental theory is itself preshaped by a transcendental-cognitive interpretation of the life-world."[26]

The dominant role of subjectivity was indisputable in phenomenological analysis; so, in Theunissen's view, was its corrosive effect on the conception of intersubjectivity. As he pointed out, the procedures of appresentation and empathy denote at best an outward projection of subjectivity, and not a pathway to reciprocal encounter. In Husserl's treatment, one's fellow-man appears typically as "another I" or an *alter ego*—with emphasis on the ego-component; the Other's ego, however, is derived through analogical projection from my own subjectivity. The process of self-duplication is particularly pronounced in *Cartesian Meditations,* where the Other's "proper" sphere is presented as an *analogue* of my *primordial* world; just as my own body functions as primary reference in the perception of others, my own subjectivity is described as *basic norm* in the constitution of intersubjectivity. Actually, according to Theunissen, Husserl's account of the relationship between ego and *alter ego* pointed beyond analogy in the direction of identity—although the identity was restricted to the dimension of pure subjectivity (as opposed to the bodily insertion of individuals in the natural universe). This restriction did not negate the aspect of self-duplication; its effect was to reduce the difference between individuals to the level of mundane, corporeal diversity. In Theunissen's words: "The identification of the *alter ego* with my own ego is not affected by this qualification; for the Other's ego signifies the selfhood of the Other, the Other in his basic 'primordial' core." Although acknowledging bodily differentiation, Husserl's approach ultimately failed to make room for the otherness of *alter egos* conceived as integral fellow-men, with the result that "the Other can never surprise me and transform me in the course of an encounter; he can never happen to me or approach me from the horizon of an unknown future."[27]

Egology and *Being and Time*

At first glance, the step from Husserl to Heidegger seems relatively uncomplicated, especially with regard to the topic under discussion. Despite their epistemological differences, the arguments of the two thinkers concerning human interaction appear to be broadly congruent—or at least reconcilable given various adaptations. Some of these adaptations have surfaced in the preceding discussion; in particular, the post-Husserlian perspectives advanced by Ortega and Schutz may be held to encapsulate the essence of Heidegger's outlook. There is, in fact, a widespread tendency to interpret Heidegger's work through Ortega's or Schutz's, or through a combination of the two. Thus, in contrast to Husserl's transcendental approach, Heidegger's *Being and Time*—with its focus on man's being-in-the-world—inaugurated the analysis of concrete, worldly experience, loosely akin to Schutz's mundane-phenomenological inquiry; as a corollary of this change, pure egology is assumed to have been replaced by *Dasein,* construed as concrete, bodily existence. The latter aspect concurs with Ortega's notion of the man of flesh and bone—although Ortega insists on the tension between mundane and genuine-individual experience. This dualism finds a parallel in *Being and Time,* where the distinction between authentic and inauthentic life is equated with the contrast between radical solitude and social anonymity. In summary, worldliness with a tragic flavor seems to be the core of Heidegger's existentialism.

One of the ambitions of these pages will be to show that this assessment is mistaken or at least lopsided. It seems to me that Heidegger's outlook cannot be identified with either a worldly or a tragically strained individualism, despite occasional ambivalent passages in *Being and Time.* Above all, the focus on *Dasein* does not simply vouchsafe the abandonment of the *ego cogitans* in favor of embodied subjectivity. Although gaining a measure of concreteness, Heidegger's argument in the latter case would be in danger of lapsing into a subjectivism devoid of the cognitive merits of Husserl's egology, especially with regard to the validation of knowledge claims. The equation of the analysis of *Dasein* with mundane inquiry in the Schutzian vein is ill-advised for a number of reasons. First, the interpretation of being-in-the-world as a mode of subjective experience seems dubious; also implausible is the restriction of *Dasein* to a worldly domain in the sense of a surrounding (ontic) environment. Among other things, this restriction shortens the ontological reach of Heidegger's thought: his insistence on the open-ended character of *Dasein* and his portrayal of human *existence* as a gateway to *Being*.[28] Although more difficult to disentangle, Heidegger's and Ortega's views in my judgment are by no means congruent: the notions of authentic and inauthentic existence do not coincide with Ortega's experiential alternatives, chiefly because of Ortega's egological premises.

Treatment of Heidegger as an existentialist commonly ignores his break with these premises or, more cautiously phrased, his effort to move beyond the confines of subjectivity. This endeavor characterizes his later work, but is already clearly manifest in *Being and Time,* first published in 1927.[29] The central theme of this study was neither consciousness and its constitutive functions nor any other strictly human competence or aptitude, but rather the question of *Being,* or of the *meaning of Being.* According to the prologue to *Being and Time,* the work aimed "to elaborate concretely the question of the meaning of 'Being' "; similarly, the first chapter stressed the "primacy of the question of Being" and insisted on the "need for a renewed explicit focus" on that issue. Human existence was only indirectly a topic of investigation, to the extent that man is the inquirer or questioning agent in the mentioned theme (which does not mean he is able to constitute or grasp Being in a definitive manner). As Heidegger writes: "Elaboration of the question of Being means thus: rendering transparent one entity—the inquirer—in his Being. As a mode of being, the very asking of this question is essentially marked or shaped by the target of the question or inquiry: Being. That entity which each one of us is or represents and which includes inquiry among its possibilities of being, we denote by the term *'Dasein.'* "[30]

As presented in *Being and Time,* human existence is not self-contained or autonomous; it is shaped by Being. For the same reason, *Dasein* cannot be a synonym for *ego, selfhood,* or *subjectivity,* as these terms have traditionally been employed. Etymologically, *subjectivity* in particular denotes an underlying foundation or pre-given substance in which human experiences are rooted; the terms *ego* and *self* are customarily viewed in the same light. Commenting on the question of the coherence of *Dasein,* Heidegger observes that the "I" or the ego "seems to 'hold together' the totality of the structural complex. In the 'ontological' treatment of man, the 'I' or the 'self' have from time immemorial been construed as the supporting ground (that is, as substance or subject)." Due to their habitual usage, the meanings of the mentioned terms seem not to be problematical. In everyday life, human *Dasein* tends to refer to itself as "I" or *ego:* "The content of this expression is assumed to be utterly simple; it designates me and nothing further. In this simple reference, the 'I' is neither an attribute of other things nor itself a predicate, but rather the absolute 'subject.' " According to Heidegger, however, traditional linguistic practice is not a reliable guide and may actually be an obstacle to human self-understanding. Regarding the philosophical analysis of *Dasein,* he writes that "one of its first tasks will be to demonstrate that any approach which starts from a pre-given I or subject completely misses the phenomenal content of *Dasein.* Ontologically speaking, every notion of subjectivity— unless it is refined through a prior ontological clarification—continues and replicates the approach relying on the *subjectum* (or *hypokeimenon*), no matter how strenuously one may protest on an ontic level against the concept of 'psychic substance' or against the 'reification of consciousness.' "[31]

In moving away from subjectivity, *Being and Time* departs from a longstanding philosophical tradition which dates back at least to the dawn of modernity. Heidegger in his study elaborates repeatedly on this contrast, in particular with reference to modern thought from Descartes to Husserl. Despite his radical ambitions Descartes—Heidegger notes—failed to question the bedrock foundation (*fundamentum inconcussum*) of his argument: the ego construed as thinking substance: "With the principle *'cogito sum'* Descartes claimed that he was putting philosophy on a new and secure footing; but what he left undetermined in this 'radical' departure was the mode of being of the *res cogitans* or—more precisely—the *meaning of being of the 'sum.'* " Actually, Descartes' vagueness on this score was not simply a gap; it concealed a persistent traditionalism, since the thinking substance remained dependent on medieval ontology, with its focus on *created* substances. In Heidegger's view, a similar traditionalism was at work in Kantian philosophy, notwithstanding its comparative refinement of critical reflection. While exposing ontic misconceptions, Kant also neglected a "prior ontological analysis of the subjectivity of the subject"; although he demonstrated the "untenability of the ontic theses concerning a psychic substance," he refrained from undertaking an "ontological interpretation of selfhood." A major advantage of Kantian thought resided in the replacement of the thinking substance by a transcendental or logical subjectivity, by a "pure consciousness which accompanies all conceptions" or substantive representations. This reformulation, however, did not clarify subjectivity itself: while sharpening the notion of the "I think," Kant "persisted in treating the 'I' as a subject and thus in an ontologically inappropriate manner"; for, "to define the 'I' ontologically as a 'subject' means to regard it as a pre-given entity."[32]

Post-Kantian thought has brought advances in self-reflection and in the struggle against human reification, without eroding traditional conceptions of subjectivity. In fact, the indeterminacy of the ego, which results from the removal of all substantive connotations, tends to serve as a warrant for bypassing its ontological scrutiny. *Being and Time* points primarily to the work of Husserl and Scheler as examples of this tendency. For both thinkers man's essence—his consciousness, spirit, or personality—was completely transempirical, that is, purged of all ontic or objectivistic traces. As formulated by Scheler, the term *person* designated the source of intentionality or the performer of intentional acts, not an empirical-psychological phenomenon. Scheler's *person* was not far removed from Husserl's transcendental constitution. In Scheler's view, Heidegger comments, "the person is not a thing, not a substance, not an object. What is emphasized here is the same kind of demarcation which Husserl employs when he postulates for the unity of the person an essentially different constitution from that required for natural objects." Despite its stringency, however, this distinction did not necessarily disturb traditional premises; for, Heidegger asks, what might be the ontological meaning of *intentionality, constitution,* and—more generally—of the *mode of being of the person?* Without an exploration of such questions, *person* and *consciousness* were liable to be taken as pre-given entities—a consequence illustrated by early phenomenology. Although "more radical and transparent" than previous approaches, "phenomenological interpretations of personality do not penetrate to the question of the being of *Dasein.* No matter how much Husserl and Scheler may differ in their respective inquiries, methods and worldviews, they concur negatively in their treatment of personality: they no longer raise the question of the 'being of a person.' "[33]

Unlike traditional subjectivity, *Dasein* as presented in *Being and Time* is marked by a porous, centrifugal character. As previously indicated, the study focuses on the question of Being, while *Dasein* indicates the locus or inquiring agency of that question. Correspondingly, human existence—far from simply denoting a mundane, commonsense entity—is endowed with the ek-static capacity of searching and *caring* for Being. To the extent that ego and selfhood are ascribed to existence, these terms have to be reinterpreted in the same light: as attributes of *care.* In Heidegger's words: "If selfhood belongs to the central traits of *Dasein*—whose 'essence,' however, resides in its *existence*—

then ego and selfhood must be construed in an *existential* sense." As he adds, selfhood is not merely a byproduct but is virtually a synonym of existential care; care, in fact, "contains within itself already the phenomenon of the self," with the result that "the expression 'self-care' or 'care for self' appears as a *tautology." Dasein's* care, one should note, is directed not only at Being in general, but at the meaning and being of all ontic phenomena—first and foremost at the meaning of existence itself. Since ontic phenomena, however, are embedded in the context of a *world,* care for their being presupposes a basic attentiveness to this context, not merely through a juxtaposition of care and world, but through an intrinsic worldliness or world-involvement of *Dasein.* This intimate permeation of self and world is reflected in the term *being-in-the-world.* "The term 'I' actually points to that entity which one is in 'being-in-the-world,' " Heidegger observes. "Being-already-in-a-world, however, means being-close-to-ready-to-hand-things-in-the-world which in turn signifies being-ahead-of-oneself. The word 'I' designates that entity for which the Being of its own being is at issue. The 'I' is an expression of care—although an expression which initially and commonly tends to take the form of the 'fugitive' I-talk of busy daily concerns."[34]

Heidegger's departure from subjectivity is evident also in the portion of *Being and Time* which is most directly relevant to our study: the chapter dealing with "being-in-the-world as co-being and self-being." The opening section of that chapter focuses on the "existential question regarding the 'who' of *Dasein.*" This question, Heidegger notes, is commonly resolved in an egological manner, largely due to the pervasiveness of everyday "I-talk": "The 'who' seems to point to an ego, a 'subject,' or a 'self.' The 'who' in this sense designates that entity which maintains its identity in the flux of experiences and modes of behavior and which relates and orients itself to this flux." To deviate from this conception, he adds, seems to violate common sense and the "rules of sound methodology"; for, "what is more indubitable than the givenness of the ego? And does this givenness not suggest the proper procedure to be followed in its primordial elaboration: namely, to bracket or disregard everything else that may be given—not only the givenness of the 'world' but also the existence of other egos?" According to *Being and Time,* commonsense notions about ontic phenomena, including the ego, cannot be viewed as self-evident; ontological analysis has to treat such notions warily and at best as "short-hand labels for something which in the actual phenomenal context may emerge as the very opposite." Instead of proceeding from egological premises, the question of "who" in Heidegger's judgment needs to be approached from the vantage point of *Dasein,* which yields an initial sense of co-being or being-with-others: "The elucidation of being-in-the-world has shown that we do not find as a starting point nor as a given entity a mere subject without a world. Likewise, we cannot treat as principally given an isolated ego without others."[35]

Notwithstanding its prominence and repeated articulation, Heidegger's critique of subjectivity has tended to be deemphasized by reviewers of *Being and Time.* Despite the stress on care and co-presence as intrinsic attributes of being-in-the-world, most commentators have construed *Dasein* egologically and have seen Heidegger's entire argument as an existentialist adaptation of Husserl's phenomenology, and in particular of his theory of intersubjectivity. This mode of interpretation arose at the first appearance of *Being and Time.* In a study entitled *Gegenwart* ("The Present Age"), published in 1928, the German philosopher Eberhard Grisebach detailed the affinities between Husserl's and Heidegger's arguments. Both thinkers, he affirmed, were ultimately concerned with subjectivity or selfhood, although Husserl's thought focused on the general-logical self and Heidegger relied on an "ontologically and existentially construed self"; in both cases, the stress on selfhood entailed a fascination with subjective human design—couched in one instance as *intentional constitution* and in the other as existential *project.* The move from phenomenology to existential analysis thus involved only a slight reformulation: "Despite a methodological change everything remains basically the same: the self is lodged in the center of his world which he relates to himself and molds in his image." Grisebach did not entirely neglect the central place accorded in *Being and Time* to the question of Being. Yet, interpreting Being in the sense of a purified essence intuited or fashioned by thought, he viewed the question as a corroboration—not a rebuttal—of the book's subjectivist thrust. Intent on capturing "reality in the infinite circle of pure essence," Heidegger's ontology was said to be an offshoot of eidetic phenomenology and ultimately of subjective idealism; confined to the "sphere dominated by selfhood and its categories," his analysis of *Dasein* could not penetrate to non-subjective Being and reality, including the domain of genuine co-being or interaction with fellow-men.[36]

In the year of Grisebach's study, the specific issue of co-being was scrutinized by Heidegger's one-time student and collaborator, Karl Löwith. Although proceeding from different premises, Löwith's treatise—dealing with "The Individual in the Role of Fellow-Man"—concurred with Grisebach's argument regarding the basically egological and ego-centric outlook of *Being and Time*. One of Löwith's central criticisms concerned the alleged subordinate status of co-being in Heidegger's overall presentation: the aspect that human interaction played a relatively insignificant part in *Dasein*'s relations with the world (a charge which, in my view, misses the ontological character of the term *world*). According to Löwith, Heidegger's cursory treatment of the topic was not accidental, but proceeded directly from his conception of human existence, especially from the postulated "mineness" of *Dasein* —a concept which, in Löwith's view, was a synonym for egocentrism and atomistic individualism. Only by lapsing into inauthenticity was the individual able to escape his isolation; human existence in this mode had as a corollary an inauthentic type of co-being or togetherness: the togetherness of "the They" (*das Man*), where the individual was submerged in social anonymity and the sway of public opinion. Authentic *Dasein,* by contrast, signified a deliberately cultivated solitude and non-involvement. Löwith found the idea of *emancipatory solicitude*—used by Heidegger to characterize authentic existence and co-being—to be doubly defective. Given the "mineness" of *Dasein,* he argued, emancipation of others merely denoted the imposition of one's own view of freedom, and thus a subtle form of manipulation; at the same time, due to the self-enclosure of freedom, liberating efforts simply segregated one's life *from* others. Manipulation and segregation, however, were incompatible with genuine human interaction, especially with an intimate "I-thou" relationship.[37]

With slight alterations, Grisebach's and Löwith's arguments were subsequently reformulated by numerous writers.[38] In his previously mentioned study, Theunissen presented Heidegger's social ontology or conception of co-being as a "modified restatement of Husserl's theory of transcendental intersubjectivity." The major differentiation between the two thinkers, in his judgment, derives from Heidegger's notion of being-in-the-world, and thus from his focus on mundane existence and on the "concrete human being," in contrast to Husserl's emphasis on epistemological subjectivity. Other distinguishing traits can be found in the close connection between *Dasein* and co-being, as compared to Husserl's systematic egology, and in the practical rather than strictly cognitive-theoretical connotations of Heidegger's perspective. "Probing beneath the cognitive truth of perception," Theunissen observes, "Heidegger explores the discovery or disclosure of worldly entities through practical involvement."[39] Despite such differences, Theunissen insists on the essential continuity of the two approaches; although couched in less abstract terms, Heidegger's analysis of co-being in his view "merely repeats Husserl's theory of intersubjectivity on a new—namely, an existential—level." This basic congruence is underscored, not challenged, by the primacy of the question of Being in *Being and Time*. Like Grisebach, Theunissen treats this question as a variant of eidetic phenomenology, and the characterization of *Dasein* as inquiring agency as a reformulation of the constitutive role of consciousness. The linkage is said to be particularly evident in the "ontological structure of *Dasein* as 'project'": that the examination of co-being does not "move beyond" Husserl's outlook, he writes, is explained "by its transcendental-philosophical conception, by its reliance on 'project' understood as transcendental constitution of the world."[40]

Theunissen's commentary corroborates the thesis of philosophical convergence by exploring the various presumed parallels between the respective accounts of human interaction. A major piece of evidence cited in support of the thesis concerns the affinity between Heidegger's conception of existential encounter—that is, the encounter of *Dasein* and co-*Dasein*—and Husserl's view of the relationship between ego and *alter ego*. Following Löwith, Theunissen criticizes Heidegger's neglect of direct interpersonal contact and his stress on the worldly and quasi-external presuppositions of co-being—a stress which is claimed to replicate Husserl's theory of appresentation. Just as, in Husserl's case, intersubjective empathy was dependent on the process of bodily appresentation and associative pairing—he notes—*Being and Time* presents existential encounters as adjuncts of impersonal affairs, especially of practical, everyday dealings with "ready-to-hand" things or "equipment." Apart from this common rejection of immediacy—"among all the affinities one of the most crucial"—Heidegger's thought is said to replicate the steps of Husserl's analysis: from the notions of the natural attitude and the natural we-community to the level of the transcendental ego and the community to monads. In particular, Heidegger's distinction between authenticity and inauthenticity is portrayed as a modified implementation of the phenomenological method of bracketing or reduction. "The division of *Dasein* into authentic and inauthentic 'modes of being,'" one reads, "repeats on an existential-ontological plane the transcendental-egological bifurcation between primordial and natural ego. Like the natural ego (or the ego of the natural attitude), inauthentic selfhood is marked—in Husserl's terminology—by its 'lostness in the world.' For, while authentic *Dasein* genuinely grasps and fashions the self, the self of everyday existence is called 'inauthentic' because everyday *Dasein* views itself not autonomously but from the vantage point of the 'world.'"[41]

In Theunissen's presentation, intersubjectivity and being-with others are restricted to the domain of natural or inauthentic experience, while self-reflection and authentic *Dasein* are solitary ventures. As delineated in *Being and Time,* he writes, inauthenticity is an attribute not so much of an independent though embryonic self, but of an undifferentiated plurality or collective fabric called "the They" (*das Man*); leveled into this fabric, everyday existence emerges as interchangeable or "one among others." Although detecting a certain ambivalence in Heidegger's treatment of *everyday life*—the term sometimes seems to denote inauthenticity and sometimes a neutral (but pre-reflective) mode of being-in-the-world—Theunissen firmly opts for the first alternative, thereby solidifying the dichotomous scheme of his interpretation. By contrast to the anonymous character of "the They," cultivation of authenticity in his view involves a process of individualization or isolation and "in a certain sense a transcendental reduction." As he writes: "Since inauthenticity means submergence in collectivity, *Dasein* can become authentic only through self-emancipation from the dominion of others or through 'individualization.'" The egological structure of authenticity, he adds, is reinforced by *emancipatory solicitude,* defined as the recognition of the *being* of others or as willingness to *let* the *Dasein* of others *be* (*Seinlassen*). Construed as an outgrowth of such solicitude, *authentic co-being*—to the extent that this term makes sense in Heidegger's analysis—signifies at best the juxtaposition of atomistic monads, reminiscent of Husserl's transcendental community: "While implying positively the recognition of the others' autonomy, the 'let-be' attitude means negatively the dissolution of all direct linkages between the others and me. Such solicitude can emancipate the *selfhood* of others only by liberating them *from me.*"[42]

Heidegger and Co-being

At this point it seems desirable to take a closer look at *Being and Time* to see whether the study sustains—perhaps even demands—a different, non-egological interpretation. This effort is complicated by ambivalent passages and the occasional use of quasi-egological terms—such as *mineness,* as structural attribute of *Dasein,* or *unrelatedness* and *individualization,* as trademarks of authentic existence. Yet, given Heidegger's critique of subjectivity, such terms probably need to be understood in a sense which diverges from habitual "I-talk." In the light of Theunissen's critical commentary, the first point which needs to be examined is the presumed parallel between bodily appresentation and

Heidegger's description of existential encounter—a parallel which, if valid, would make co-being ultimately dependent on empathy and the transfer of experiences from ego to *alter ego*. Although proceeding from a correct observation, Theunissen's argument on this score seems to me mistaken. Undeniably, Heidegger's portrayal of encounter has a strongly worldly and practical character, since human contact is presented as enmeshed in, and arising from, everyday affairs and practical dealings with equipment. This aspect emerges very clearly in the section dealing with the "co-presence of others and everyday co-being." Heidegger observes that the analysis of the immediate life-context, such as the work-world of the artisan, reveals that others are first encountered in conjunction with work; more precisely, "that simultaneously with the equipment handled in work others are encountered for whom the 'work' is destined. The mode of being or significance of ready-to-hand equipment implies a basic reference to possible users or wearers whom it is meant to 'fit like a glove.' " As he adds: *"Dasein* finds itself first of all in *what* it does, needs, expects, uses—that is, in the ready-to-hand things of the life-context which are the immediate target of attention and 'concerns.' " Similarly, "the others who are 'encountered' in the context of ready-to-hand equipment are not somehow appresented or added in thought to empirically given objects; rather 'things' are found in a world in which they are handled by others—a world which from the beginning is also mine."[43]

Theunissen's assertion of the worldly or mediated character of encounter is thus clearly valid; mediation in this case, however, is entirely incongruent with Husserl's notion of intersubjectivity. As emerges from the preceding citations, the life-context as presented by Heidegger does not denote an array of objects facing a *subject,* or to which human subjects are *added in thought.* Unlike Husserl's concept of the body, *ready-to-hand equipment* is not the external enclosure of an ego or a mental substance; as a corollary, fellow-men are not initially perceived as bodily objects on which mental life is imposed through analogical transference. Unlike the traditional bifurcations of subject and object, mind and body, Heidegger's *Dasein* is intrinsically permeated by *world* and by others. Differently phrased, *Dasein* is pre-egological in the sense that it precedes and bypasses customary dichotomies; it is also precognitive since it primarily signifies practical attentiveness. This aspect is forcefully reiterated: "The worldly structure of the world entails that others are not first of all given as free-floating subjects or egos juxtaposed to other objects, but that in their distinct worldly status they emerge in the ready-to-hand life-context." Heidegger's account of

Dasein has some additional corollaries which should briefly be mentioned. First, the stress on worldliness implies that encounter is not an internal process or spiritual merger (a connotation present in Scheler's and Löwith's views); by tying co-being to practical work, *Being and Time* takes a stand against idealism—and also against a speculative materialism. Next, given the pre-egological character of existence, involvement with ready-to-hand equipment is not synonymous with instrumental labor, or with an activity which fashions the world in accordance with egocentric (or human-centered) designs; instead, man and equipment are both ingredients of a larger life-context which molds users and utensils alike.[44]

The divergence between Husserl's and Heidegger's accounts is not restricted to the dimension of everyday work situations; it persists when fellow-beings are considered more for their own sake, that is, when co-being is explicitly studied. At this point, the importance and even primacy of appresentation and empathy appear at a first glance incontestible; as Heidegger concedes, a proper understanding of fellow-men seems to presuppose such procedures. The *thematized* preoccupation with others, he writes, "emerges readily as the central and primary issue in theoretical discussions regarding the understanding of the 'psychic life of others.' Moreover, this particular mode of attuned interaction tends to be construed as the very source which constitutes co-being (or being-toward-others) and renders it possible. Designated (not very aptly) as 'empathy,' this preoccupation is then expected to provide an ontological bridge, as it were, from one's own subjectivity—which at first alone is given or available—to the initially concealed *alter ego.*" Such bridge-building, to be sure, would be impossible if one's ego were not destined to relate to another ego, by virtue of the process of egological self-reflection and self-reference. Empathy thus emerges as an extension of the ego's relation to itself: "Access to others coincides with the projection of the ego's self-reference onto an *alter ego:* the Other is a duplicate of the self." According to Heidegger, the entire argument—though apparently plausible—is basically misconstrued. In his view, the ego's self-reference is not a replica of or substitute for *Dasein's* relation to others. More importantly, the stress on empathy involves a reversal of priorities: instead of functioning as a *source,* understanding is predicated on *Dasein's* being-in-the-world and its structural quality of *care.* In Heidegger's words: "Empathy does not constitute co-being; rather it arises on its basis and is rendered particularly urgent by the predominance of deficient modes of co-being."[45]

The reference to "deficient modes of co-being" points to a domain repeatedly touched upon in the preceding discussion, that of inauthentic experience or "the They" (*das Man*). Theunissen's comments are again descriptively accurate, but misleading in their conclusions. As presented in *Being and Time*, inauthenticity denotes the prevalence of an undifferentiated, quasi-collective life-form, where *Dasein* appears as interchangeable and "one among others"; the notion of "the They" is said to answer "the question regarding the 'who' of everyday existence." Yet what needs to be considered is the ontological, more than the ontic or empirical, status of "the They." The term implies an onto-logical-existential condition, a mode of *Dasein's* being-in-the-world, not an outgrowth of subjects (in the sense of an aggregate of individuals, or a "subject-writ-large") or an empirical collectivity into which individuals are leveled. As an existential condition, inauthentic co-being is characterized by its own type or types of human care or *solicitude*. Since fellow-men are initially encountered in the context of ready-to-hand affairs, and since attention to ready-to-hand equipment is the hallmark of *concern*, everyday co-being is marked primarily by *solicitous concern* or *concerned solicitude*. Between this type of con-textual care and the more genuine versions of solicitude, Heidegger sketches a broad range of forms of attentiveness, most of which are described as deficient modes of solicitude prevalent in everyday exis-tence. As he writes: "Being for, against, or without one another, pass-ing one another by, not 'mattering' for one another—these are possible ways of solicitude; and it is precisely these latter modes of deficiency and indifference which characterize everyday or average co-being." Even on the level of properly interhuman, *Dasein*-focused care, *Being and Time* mentions a type with deficient connotations, namely, "man-agerial solicitude," through which *Dasein* takes over and manipulates the cares of others, which commonly entails domination.[46]

What Theunissen and other commentators neglect is that care and solicitude in their different forms are not synonyms for intentionality or "states of mind," but rather are structural attributes of *Dasein* and diverse modes of human interaction. Inauthentic existence is not simply the outlook of a muffled or embryonic subjectivity; similarly, the "defi-cient modes" of care do not merely point to a defective individuality, but to a deficient manner of being-in-the-world. In Heidegger's words, inauthentic existence tends to view itself "from the vantage point of the world," that is, from the perspective of ready-to-hand affairs and of others perceived as "the They." What is lacking in this state is not simply consciousness but the question of Being: that is, the exploration of *Dasein's* proper relationship to the world and to others. This lack, incidentally, should not be construed as a complete gap. Everyday existence, Heidegger observes, "does not signify a diminution or deprecation of the facticity of *Dasein,* just as little as 'the They' defined as 'no-man' is equivalent to nothingness"; instead, " 'the They' is an existential attribute and belongs as primordial phenomenon to the positive structure of *Dasein."* Paraphrasing this statement, one might say that everyday existence, although regularly inauthentic, is not only a defect to be remedied, but a mode of being-in-the-world. As such it is implicitly open to Being and thus contains at least the anticipation of authentic co-being. In any case, the move toward authenticity does not imply the birth of egological solitude from anonymity: "Authentic *self-hood* does not consist in an exceptional condition of subjectivity detached from 'the They'; rather it is an *existential modification of 'the They' considered as a basic existential structure.* The selfhood of the authentically existing self is consequently separated by a gulf from the identity of an ego maintaining itself in the flux of its experiences."[47]

It seems to me that Heidegger's entire argument relating to authenticity can and should be viewed in the light of these maxims. This applies to the remarks on emancipatory solicitude and even to the comments on being-toward-death, probably one of the most difficult portions of *Being and Time.* Emancipatory solicitude—also called anticipative-emancipatory solicitude—is introduced in the section delineating different types of care, especially as a counterpoint to managerial solicitude. In contradistinction to the latter's manipulative thrust, Heidegger writes, "there is the possibility of a kind of solicitude which does not so much displace the Other as anticipate him in his existential potentiality for Being—not in order to take 'care' away from him but in order to restore it to him in a genuine fashion. Involving the dimension of authentic care, that is, the very existence of the Other and not merely the affairs with which he is concerned, this type of solicitude helps the Other to become transparent to himself in his care and to become *free for* it." While other forms of solicitude characterize deficient or exploitative modes of human interaction, the emancipatory variety is linked with genuine co-being devoid of egocentric jealousies and oppression: "Such an *authentic* community renders possible the proper realism or respect for Being ('*Sachlichkeit*') which frees the Other in his freedom for himself."[48] As is apparent, Heidegger's observations carry important normative implications; in fact, his conception of authentic existence and co-being can in my view be seen as a reformulation of the traditional notion of the good life and in particular of the Kantian postulate of the kingdom of ends. Compared to the latter principle, Heidegger's conception has the advantage not only of increased realism or concreteness but also of greater moral adequacy. Despite its anti-utilitarian intent, the postulate to treat others as ends rather than means contains instrumentalist traces, in the sense that the ego tends to function as a means for others who, in turn, appear as values "for me" or as "my" ends. Authentic co-being, on the contrary, is distinguished by respect for others in their *Dasein* and their "potentiality for Being," rather than in their role as moral goals.

The theme of authenticity and genuine co-being is discussed in greater detail in later parts of *Being and Time,* especially in the sections dealing with being-toward-death. Some of the language in these sections provides ammunition for Heidegger's critics. The following passage in particular has repeatedly been cited as evidence of an incipient solipsism: "As the end of *Dasein,* death is *Dasein's* innermost possibility—a possibility which is non-relational, certain and at the same time indefinite and unsurpassable." Critical attention has focused on the terms *innermost* (or *ownmost*) and *non-relational.* Heidegger's elaborations on these terms help to clarify their meaning, but at times add fuel to the controversy. Commenting on death as innermost possibility, he writes: "Poised toward this possibility *Dasein* discovers its *innermost* potentiality for Being in which the very Being of *Dasein* is at stake; at this point it becomes manifest that, in its distinctive and intrinsic possibility, *Dasein* escapes the confines of 'the They.'" Regarding the non-relational quality of death as existential possibility Heidegger adds: "The anticipation of death"—which is implied in being-toward-death—"teaches *Dasein* that the potentiality for Being in which its own intrinsic Being is at stake must be shouldered by *Dasein* alone. Death does not just vaguely 'belong' to one's *Dasein* but *lays claim to it* in an *individual* manner. The non-relational character of death—experienced in anticipation—individualizes *Dasein* and throws it back upon itself. This individualization is a mode of disclosing the locus of existence (that is, the *'Da'* of *Dasein*)—making it clear that all involvement in daily concerns and every co-being with others is bound to fail us where our innermost potentiality for Being is at stake."[49]

Although difficult to disentangle, the preceding statements in my judgment do not strengthen the critics' case; as presented by Heidegger, the individuality of *Dasein* is far removed from an egocentric individualism. What needs primarily to be taken into account is the significance of being-toward-death for authenticity. Although described as a *possibility,* death is not simply a theoretical option which consciousness (or a cognitive subjectivity) could contemplate among other alternatives. Nor is death a practical possibility in the sense of an intentional design or a project which an individual could actively implement. Rather, death is an extreme invasion which, in Heidegger's words, "lays claim" to human existence and which brings into view the ultimate possibility of *Dasein*'s cessation and "self-surrender." Thus being-toward-death is conducive to authenticity—not by enhancing self-assertiveness or self-enclosure, but by prying existence open for the sake of a genuine care for Being and a proper attentiveness to *Dasein's* "potentiality for Being." As Heidegger insists, anticipation of death has a humbling and sobering effect; confronting its ultimate possibility *Dasein* faces a domain which completely eludes human management, manipulation, and domination. "Death as possibility," we read, "offers to *Dasein* nothing which could be 'actualized' or implemented and nothing which, once implemented, *Dasein* actually could *be*. Rather, death is the possibility of the impossibility of every type of human comportment or attitude and of every mode of existence."[50]

Individuality, against this background, simply means that every *Dasein* has to face its own death (and live its own life accordingly), since death is not transferable. This circumstance does not preclude genuine interaction and care. Just as being-toward-death is not a warrant for solipsism, human interaction on the same level is not an aggregation of monads. Far from reinforcing individual isolation, the non-relational character of death guards against spurious shortcuts or oversimplifications—such as the view that *potentiality for Being* is somehow derived from daily concerns or is the product of subjective or intersubjective designs. Differently phrased: authentic *Dasein* does not rule out co-being, but only efforts of interhuman management. Forsaking manipulation and mastery, genuine solicitude manifests itself in *letting be,* in the willingness to let others live their lives and anticipate their deaths—an attitude which is far removed from indifference. The link between authenticity and co-being is stressed by Heidegger in the passage which elaborates on the term *non-relational.* "The insufficiency of daily concerns and human solicitude," he writes, "signifies by no means a removal of these modes of *Dasein* from authentic selfhood. As essential structures of *Dasein,* these modes are among the basic conditions of possibility of existence. *Dasein* is authentic only to the extent that it orients itself in the modes of concern and interhuman solicitude centrally toward its potentiality for Being, rather than toward the possibility of 'the They.' "[51]

The authenticity of *Dasein,* as portrayed by Heidegger, implies a distinct mode of sociality which differs both from deficient types of interaction and from social aggregates predicated on subjective designs (including the designs of a plurality of subjects). Under the auspices of emancipatory solicitude, others are not approached through egological constitution, nor are they presupposed as intrinsic components of an "ego in general"; differently phrased, co-being on this level denotes neither a fusion of subjectivities nor a monadological isolation of *Dasein* from *Dasein,* but rather a reciprocal willingness to confront the question of Being. Reflecting on the relationship between authenticity and sociality, a later passage in *Being and Time* observes that being-toward-death "does not isolate *Dasein* from its world or transform it into a free-floating ego"; such anticipation "first provides *Dasein* with the possibility to 'let' co-present others 'be' in their innermost potentiality for Being and to assist in the disclosure of this potentiality through anticipative-emancipatory solicitude."[52]

FRENCH PHENOMENOLOGY

The turn from the founding period to the French school of phenomenology involves more than a change of locale; although linked with their predecessors through a continuity of central preoccupations, the members of the French movement were separated from them by different historical experiences and intellectual influences. In comparison with the relatively strong theoretical bent and social-political reticence of most spokesmen of the early phase, French phenomenology from the beginning was characterized by considerable intellectual diversity and by greater worldliness (in the sense of a greater willingness to tackle social and political issues). Its leading representatives managed to blend Husserlian teachings with existentialist and Hegelian conceptions, as well as the powerful indigenous legacy of Cartesianism. This confluence was not fortuitous. During the interbellum period, French philosophers attentive to German thought often encountered Husserl's writings in conjunction with Heidegger's *Being and Time,* a circumstance which encouraged an uneasy symbiosis of the two perspectives. In addition, these philosophers could hardly avoid being affected by the strong Hegelian revival which occurred in France during the same time—especially since Hegelianism seemed to provide an antidote to solipsistic dangers inherent in the phenomenological concern with subjectivity.[1] As a result, French phenomenology as it emerged before and during World War II can generally be described as a mixed transcendental, ontological, and dialectical enterprise.

The sketched pattern of thought does not represent an indistinct amalgam uniformly shared by phenomenological thinkers; against its background it is possible to identify diverse accents and perhaps even an internal tendency bent on rearranging its ingredients. As it seems to me, French phenomenology and post-phenomenology can be construed as exhibiting a development roughly parallel to the movement in German philosophy from transcendental to existential-ontological analysis: that is, a trend leading from a preoccupation with the constitutive functions of transcendental consciousness, via a progressive decentering of subjectivity, to a quasi-ontological stance reminiscent of Heidegger's "destruction of Western metaphysics." This discussion will focus on three figures: Jean-Paul Sartre, Maurice Merleau-Ponty, and Jacques Derrida. Since Derrida's pertinent views have been articulated mainly by way of a critical rejoinder to his compatriot, one-time phenomenologist Emmanuel Levinas, brief attention will also be given to the latter's arguments. In light of the preceding comments, the three thinkers can be arrayed along an intellectual spectrum, with Sartre marking the opening and Derrida the culminating phase of the decentering development. To be sure, the divergence of perspectives should not be exaggerated; as will become obvious, the theme of intersubjectivity imposes a common problematic on the individual philosophers which overshadows their different approaches—a problematic which centers on the relationship between *sameness* and *otherness* or between *interiority* and *exteriority*. The basic question faced by any treatment of the *alter ego* is how the Other can be both *alter* and *ego*—in other words, how the fellow-man can be different from, and thus external to, and yet comparable to, and thus internally linked with, the ego. French phenomenological and post-phenomenological writings are instructive because of their steady radicalization of this problematic, leading to a progressive exposure of its implicit antinomies.

The Look and Interpersonal Conflict: Sartre

The confluence of diverse inspirations is best illustrated in Sartrean philosophy. Sartre's early writings, especially his treatise on phenomenological ontology entitled *Being and Nothingness*, blended Husserlian, Hegelian, and Heideggerian motifs, in a conjunction which escaped eclecticism through the integrative force of Sartre's theoretical initiative. During the postwar period, Sartre was increasingly preoccupied with Marxist dialectics. However, as has been frequently observed (and as I intend to corroborate), his turn toward Marxism—while producing significant readjustments—did not entail the abandonment of earlier influences, only their absorption into a new intellectual symbiosis. The various ingredients of his outlook were never equal in stature and impact. During his early phase—to which primary attention will be given in these pages—the dominant role of transcendental phenomenology cannot be overlooked. Sartre at that time fully accepted Husserl's premise of a constitutive consciousness, although he hesitated to embrace some of the traditional tools of phenomenological inquiry, such as bracketing or categorial intuition. In the domain of intersubjectivity, his chief departure from Husserl consisted in the substitution of an *existential encounter* (or an encounter on the level of *being*) for the Husserl's cognitive or noetic-noematic approach; however, as will become clear, the change was less crucial than supposed since existence remained moored in subjectivity. This kind of existentialism was bound to overshadow Sartre's relation to Heidegger: despite frequent references to the vocabulary of *Being and Time,* Sartre (together with numerous other interpreters) construed *existential categories* as a priori structures of consciousness and *Dasein* as basically a subjective-individual project. A similar contraction can be seen in the adaptation of Hegelian teachings: while invoked as a corrective to egological self-enclosure, Hegelian dialectics was stripped of the power of synthesis and the capacity of absolute knowledge, so that intersubjectivity emerged as a collision between for-itselfs, or between for-itself and in-itself. On the whole, Sartre's outlook during this phase presents an "ontology with a phenomenological foundation," or, if one will, as a Husserlianism with ontological and dialectical overtones.[2]

The relationship between Sartre's early position and that of his intellectual mentors is not simply a matter of conjecture; in *Being and Nothingness,* the chapter devoted to being-for-others, and especially to the question of the existence of others, offers a probing review of the legacy of his predecessors. With regard to Husserl, Sartre acknowledges important advances over classical-idealist, and particularly Kantian, conceptions on the level of mundane analysis, in the assumption of an intermonadic parallelism or pluralism of mundane egos and in the thesis that reference to others is "the indispensible condition for the constitution of a world." For all practical purposes, however, these advances were canceled by Husserl's separation of mundane and transcendental inquiry and by his adoption of a strictly cognitive approach in the latter domain, an approach which was not "perceptibly different from Kant's." The touchstone of intersubjectivity, Sartre wrote, does not reside in the joining of mundane-empirical egos; rather, "the true problem is that of the connection of transcendental subjects who are beyond experience." By relying on purely noetic-noematic procedures, Husserl effectively barred himself from access to the *alter ego;* by defining *"being* as the simple indication of an infinite series of (noetic) operations to be effected," he "removed the very possibility of understanding what can be meant by the extra-mundane *being* of the Other." To render these operations successful, one would have to understand the *alter ego* "not as I obtain knowledge of him, but as he obtains knowledge of himself"—which is impossible in cognitive terms since it would require "the internal identification of myself with the Other." As a result, what transcendental inquiry yielded was the Other as "the object of empty intentions," as one who "on principle refuses himself to us and flees," a circumstance recognized by Husserl when he noted that " 'the Other' as he is revealed to our concrete experience is an *absence.*" Having reduced "being to a series of meanings," the chapter concludes, "Husserl cannot escape solipsism any more than Kant could."[3]

In comparison with Husserlian phenomenology, Hegelian dialectics in Sartre's view had the merit of posing the issue of intersubjectivity on an ontological plane and of postulating an intrinsic interdependence of human beings. As presented in his *Phenomenology of Mind,* the appearance of the *alter ego* was "indispensable not to the constitution of the world and of my empirical 'ego' but to the very existence of my consciousness as self-consciousness." In order to gain self-awareness, human consciousness according to Hegel had to manifest and objectify itself externally, a process which necessarily involves intersubjective mediation, specifically reciprocal negation: "The Other appears along with myself since self-consciousness is identical with itself by means of the exclusion of every Other." Hegel's "brilliant intuition" thus consisted in making "me depend on the Other in my *being*" and in assuming that "the Other penetrates me to the heart." Despite these and similar advantages, however, Sartre found Hegel's dialectics marred by its abstract-conceptual character and by the identification of being and knowledge. His argument neglected the fact that "the *very being* of consciousness" is "independent of knowledge" and that "consciousness *was there* before it was known"—an insight which had been articulated long ago by Kierkegaard, with his stress on the claims of the concrete individual. Broadening his criticism, Sartre leveled against Hegel a charge of twofold *optimism,* in both the epistemological and the ontological spheres. Epistemologically, Hegel failed to perceive the conflict between the being of consciousness *for itself* and its appearance as an object of knowledge for the *alter ego* or as a *being-for-others:* "Between the Other-as-object and Me-as-subject there is no common measure, no more than between self-consciousness and consciousness *of* the Other. I cannot know myself *in* the Other if the Other is first an object for me; neither can I apprehend the Other in his true being—that is, in his subjectivity." Hegel failed to see this ontological separation of individuals because of his more basic ontological optimism, that is, his belief that he could surpass the plurality of consciousnesses by adopting the viewpoint of totality or of absolute knowledge: "But if Hegel can assert the reality of this surpassing, it is because he has already given it to himself at the outset."[4]

Heidegger's *Being and Time,* in Sartre's interpretation, undertook a more resolute step toward ontology and toward a conception of human interaction in terms of a "relation of being." In Heidegger's treatment, intersubjectivity was a basic structural correlate of human *Dasein,* construed as being-in-the-world; moreover, the relation between *Dasein* and *alter ego* involved an intrinsic reciprocity and interdependence— an interdependence which this time was "not established from outside and from a totalitarian point of view as it was with Hegel." However, while acknowledging the innovative boldness of *Being and Time,* Sartre detects in the study several peculiarities which ultimately cancel its virtues. A major deficiency in his view consists in the stress on co-being or being-with, in lieu of frontal encounter. "Being-with," we read, "does not intend the reciprocal relation of recognition and of conflict which would result from the appearance of a human-reality other than mine *in the midst* of the world; it expresses rather a sort of ontological solidarity for the exploitation of this world." The aspect of solidarity is said to be particularly prominent on the inauthentic level of existence, where it manifests itself in the indiscriminate merger of subjects and in their absorption in the "social unity of the They"; it can also be detected in the authentic mode, where being-unto-death joins individuals in a common solitude.[5] According to Sartre, the emphasis on togetherness and the neglect of interhuman confrontation can be attributed to a pervasive epistemological slant of Heidegger's ontology: namely, to his presentation of *Dasein* and its existential correlates as an a priori structure of awareness. Instead of explaining co-existence, Heidegger is accused of offering simply a categorial definition—a procedure which approximates his ontology to the "abstract view of the Kantian subject" and its universal faculties: "To say that human reality (even if it is my human reality) 'is-with' by means of its ontological structure is to say that it 'is-with' by nature, that is, in an essential and universal capacity." More importantly, the treatment of co-existence as a categorial structure of *Dasein* obliterates the otherness of the *alter ego* and the distinctive uniqueness of concretely experienced fellow-men: "Thus the existence of an ontological and hence *a priori* 'being-with' renders impossible all ontic connection with a concrete human reality which would arise *for-itself* as an absolute transcendent. The 'being-with,' conceived as a structure of my being, isolates me as surely as the arguments for solipsism."[6]

In an effort to learn from his precedessors' mistakes, Sartre outlined a few general guideposts which must inform an adequate theory of human co-existence. In contrast to the holistic or totalitarian outlook adopted by Hegel, he insists that "the only point of departure possible is the Cartesian *cogito*" or "the interiority of the *cogito*," provided the *cogito* is existentially construed so that the question of co-existence is posed "in terms of my being": "Each one must be able, by starting out from his own interiority, to rediscover the Other's being as a transcendence which conditions the very being of that interiority." This starting point has as a necessary corollary the separateness and incommensurable "multiplicity of consciousnesses," a separation which "no logical or epistemological optimism" can disguise. Yet co-existence cannot be reduced to an external juxtaposition of substances or sealed-off interiorities; the *alter ego* must not only be different from, but also internally linked with, the *cogito*: "Thus we must ask the For-itself to deliver to us the For-others; we must ask absolute immanence to throw us into absolute transcendence." Delivery in this case, however, cannot mean the submergence of the *alter ego* in noetic procedures of cognition nor his derivation from the a priori structures of *Dasein*; rather, access must take the form of an existential encounter which leaves to the Other's existence the character of a "contingent and irreducible fact." In order to be significant to our lives, the *alter ego*—despite his transcendent otherness—must be "one who 'interests' our being," that is, one who affects it "concretely and 'ontically' in the empirical circumstances of our facticity."[7] Taken in conjunction, these guideposts lend to Sartre's approach the air of a radicalized Husserlianism: existential encounter replicates—at least in part—Husserl's "phenomenology of non-phenomena" or "phenomenology of absence"—although *absence* now refers to the Other's *Dasein* as being-in-the-world. In addition to the reformulation of absence, one should note, radicalization involves a novel linkage of *immanence* and *transcendence*, or of transcendental and mundane levels of inquiry.

The postulated features of human encounter are illustrated and implemented in Sartre's analysis of "the Look." As he notes, when I meet and see a fellow-man in a given context, he initially appears to me simply as an object among other objects in "my" world. Yet, the "object-ness" of the fellow-man is unusual. If I wish to assert that the Other is not merely a thing or a figment of my imagination but a "man," I have to accord him a peculiar status: I must make room for "a fundamental apprehension of the Other in which he will not be revealed to me as an object but as a 'presence in person.'" This apprehension first gains tentative support from a certain convergence of objects around the Other (still seen as man-object), a convergence coinciding with a certain decentralization of "my" world: "The appearance among the objects of *my* universe of an element of disintegration in that universe is what I mean by the appearance of a man in my universe." I discover at this point that "suddenly an object has appeared which has stolen the world from me"; although everything is "in place" and "still exists for me," I find the world "traversed by an invisible flight and fixed in the direction of a new object." To be sure, since I am still looking at the Other, disintegration is not complete; it simply "appears that the world has a kind of drain hole in the middle of its being and that it is perpetually flowing off through the hole"—although the flow and the drain hole are "all once again recovered, reapprehended, and fixed as an object." In order to penetrate fully to the humanness of the Other, a new element has to be taken into account, namely, the Other's "look" as it is directed at me: "If the Other-as-object is defined in connection with the world as the object which sees what I see, then my fundamental connection with the Other-as-subject must be able to be referred back to my permanent possibility of *being seen* by the Other." This focus on the look, which implies a "radical conversion of the Other," reveals an entirely new dimension of human encounter. "This relation which I call 'being-seen-by-another,'" Sartre writes, "far from being merely one of the relations signified by the word *man,* represents an irreducible fact which cannot be deduced either from the essence of the Other-as-object, or from my being-as-subject. On the contrary, if the concept of the Other-as-object is to have any meaning, this can be only as the result of the conversion and degradation of that original relation." As he adds: " 'Being-seen-by-the-Other' is the truth of 'seeing-the-Other.' "[8]

The Other's look, as delineated by Sartre, establishes not merely a cognitive but an existential linkage between human beings, a linkage which—without voiding the transcendental quality of subjectivity—exerts concrete worldly effects. In looking at me, the Other manifests a direct worldly presence—although, while being under the impact of his gaze, I cannot perceive him as a mundane object endowed with empirical traits: "The Other's look hides his eyes; he seems to go *in front of them.*" At the same time, my exposure to the Other's gaze is not simply a marginal experience, but an event which involves my *Dasein* or being-in-the-world. If "moved by jealousy, curiosity, or vice," Sartre observes, I happen to peep through a keyhole and am surprised in the act by another's glance, I am bound to be affected to the point that "essential modifications appear in my structure." First of all, while I previously existed only as a non-thetic or unreflective consciousness, I now suddenly notice and see myself; more precisely, "I see myself because somebody sees me." Moreover, I perceive myself at this point not in a random fashion but essentially as I appear to the Other's gaze or as I am *"an object for the Other":* "This means that all of a sudden I am conscious of myself as escaping myself, not in that I am the foundation of my own nothingness but in that I have my foundation outside myself. I am for myself only as I am a pure reference to the Other." Furthermore, far from rejecting the Other's image of myself, I readily accept it; in the cited instance, I identify with it to the degree that I am ashamed of myself. This experience of shame, in Sartre's words, is "the *recognition* of the fact that I *am* indeed that object which the Other is looking at and judging"; my feeling ashamed is "a confession." In identifying myself through shame with the Other's image of myself, I acquire solid features, in contrast to my original freedom and unpredictability; under the Other's gaze my "transcendence" turns into a mere "transcendence transcended," exhibiting aspects of an objective "nature": "My original fall is the existence of the Other. Shame—like pride—is the apprehension of myself as a nature although that very nature escapes me and is unknowable as such."[9]

As a result of the Other's look, I acquire the status of a being-for-others, a transformation which I experience as a "solidification and alienation of my own possibilities" or of my original indeterminacy. In Sartre's presentation, *being-for-itself* designates a nihilating transcendence or (in Heideggerian terms) a type of being "which is what it is not and which is not what it is." Under the impact of the look, my transcendence is not eliminated; it is integrated and absorbed into the Other's overarching designs: "Of course I still *am* my possibilities in the mode of non-thetic consciousness of these possibilities. But at the same time the look alienates them from me." While prior to (or in abstraction from) the encounter I was an open-ended and nondescript potentiality, the Other's gaze confers on me a distinct character and physiognomy: "Thus I, who insofar as I am my possibles, am what I am not and am not what I am—behold now I *am* somebody."

Moreover, this somebody that I have become, "I am he *in the midst of the world* insofar as he escapes me," that is, insofar as he is appropriated by the Other's designs and possibilities. Integration into the Other's world means that I am placed in a context of spatial-temporal coordinates or into a mundane situation whose order and purposes I do not define. "With the Other's look," Sartre writes, "the 'situation' escapes me"; more dramatically phrased, "I am *no longer master of the situation.*" In effect, mastery devolves upon the Other to whose judgment I submit: "As a temporal-spatial object in the world, as an essential structure of a temporal-spatial situation in the world, I offer myself to the Other's appraisal." Since I not only submit to but accept and endorse the Other's judgment, subjugation appears complete: "Thus being-seen constitutes me as a defenseless being for a freedom which is not my freedom. It is in this sense that we can consider ourselves as 'slaves' insofar as we appear to the Other."[10]

While through the encounter I am alienated and objectified, the Other emerges as a trans-mundane freedom which I am unable to grasp or objectify: "In the phenomenon of the look, the Other is on principle that which cannot be an object." The non-worldly character of the Other's gaze does not reduce the strength of its impact; on the contrary, my inability to pinpoint the Other testifies to the immediacy of his presence. "Insofar as I experience myself as looked-at," Sartre notes, "there is realized for me a trans-mundane presence of the Other. The Other looks at me not as he is 'in the midst of' *my* world but as he comes toward the world and toward me from all his transcendence." Being under the spell of the look, "I experience the inapprehensible subjectivity of the Other directly and with my being." As one should notice, however, this experience concerns a freedom *"which is not mine,"* that is, which is neither mediated through my body nor the result of a noetic-cognitive constitution on my part. Exposure to the Other's look is not an outgrowth of my faculties, but rather an inflicted event which is incontestible because of its effects. In Sartre's words, "the Other is given to me as a concrete evident presence which I can in no way derive from myself and which can in no way be placed in doubt nor made the object of a phenomenological reduction or of any other 'epoché.' " The disintegration of my world which derives from the Other's look involves also a "dissolution of my knowledge" since it is an occurrence which I cannot cognitively apprehend but can only endure: "The presence to me of the Other-as-a-look is therefore neither a knowledge nor a projection of my being nor a form of unification nor a category. It *is* and I cannot derive it from me."[11]

Bondage to the Other's gaze, however, is not absolute or irremediable. To the extent that the *otherness* of the Other presupposes not only his ability to differentiate himself from me by surpassing me but also my (latent) ability to elude him, I retain the faculty of recapturing my freedom by casting my look on him: "I can obtain an explicit self-consciousness inasmuch as I am also responsible for a negation of the Other which is my own responsibility." As Sartre emphasizes, the recovery of my freedom is not an abstract decision, but rather an outgrowth of the shame and fear experienced during my previous subjugation; termination of bondage thus involves a flight from fear: "It is by thrusting myself toward my possibles that I shall escape fear to the extent that I shall consider my object-ness as non-essential." To the degree that I contribute to the uniqueness of the Other through my refusal to identify myself with him, he comes to depend on my refusal and is integrated into my designs: "The Other becomes then *that which I make myself not-be,* and his possibilities are possibilities which I refuse and which I can simply contemplate—hence dead possibilities." Transformed into an ingredient of my world, the Other's transcendence no longer surpasses me, but is a "purely contemplated" or "transcended transcendence," just as his worldly status is a "degraded presence." This degradation ensnarls even his basic subjectivity, turning it from a trans-mundane freedom into a worldly possession: "From the moment that the Other appears to me as an object, his subjectivity becomes a simple *property* of the object considered." Once objectified the Other " 'has' a subjectivity as this hollow box has 'an inside'; in this way I recover myself, for I cannot be *an object for an object."* As a consequence of these changes, my subjugation not only ceases but gives way to mastery; for the Other is now "an order of *my* instruments which is included in the order which I impose on these instruments."[12]

Sartre's theory of coexistence, as delineated in his analysis of the look, has a number of implications and invites several critical comments. One important implication is that human encounter is essentially antagonistic and synonymous with a struggle for power. The recovery of my freedom—with which the description of the look concludes—does not designate a final settlement; it produces only a temporary interlude which may at any moment be "unsettled." While treating the Other as an object, my perception of him includes an apprehension of his elusiveness: "The Other is at present what I make myself not-be; but although for the instant I am rid of him and escape him, there remains around him the permanent possibility that he may *make himself* other"; in other words, he still possesses a freedom which surpasses me. "Thus," Sartre writes, "the Other-as-object is an explosive instrument which I handle with care because I foresee around him the permanent possibility" that circumstances may "make it explode and that with this explosion I shall suddenly experience the flight of the world away from me and the alienation of my being." In view of this danger, "my constant concern is to contain the Other within his objectivity," and my relations with him are "essentially made up of ruses" designed to accomplish this goal; but "one look on the part of the Other is sufficient to make all these schemes collapse and to make me experience once more the transfiguration of the Other." As a result, "I am referred from transfiguration to degradation and from degradation to transfiguration without ever being able either to get a total view of the ensemble of these two modes of being on the part of the Other" or to "hold firmly to one of them, for each has its own instability and collapses in order for the other to rise from its ruins." As we are told in another context: "Conflict is the original meaning of being-for-others."[13]

Intimately connected with this essential conflict is the relative insignificance of solidarity or communal modes of coexistence. In Sartre's account, *being-with* interpreted as a type of togetherness is relegated to a subsidiary status. As he insists, the "experience of the 'we' " cannot constitute "an ontological structure of human-reality" or serve as a key to human encounter. On the contrary, "the 'we' is a certain particular experience which is produced in special cases on the foundation of being-for-others in general"; in other words, being-with-others presupposes being-for-others as exemplified in the interplay of the look. Due to its derivative status the "we," according to Sartre, can manifest itself in two ways: namely, in the active and passive senses of We-as-subject and Us-as-object. To explicate the passive mode, an additional ingredient is introduced into the model of the look: the *appearance of a third person* or the role of the *Third*. If, during an encounter with the Other, the Third comes on the scene and "embraces both of us with his look," we find ourselves both transcended and objectified; our possibilities are "equally dead possibilities *for the Third.*" At this point I discover the "existence of an objective situation-form in the world of the Third," in which the Other and I "figure as *equivalent* structures in *solidarity* with each other." Through his look the Third transforms me and the Other into integral parts of the "Them": "And this 'Them' which is assumed by a subjectivity as its meaning-for-others becomes the 'Us.' " In Sartre's view, the emergence of the Us-object involves a particularly grievous experience of "humiliation and impotence": "The one who experiences himself as constituting an *Us* with other men feels himself trapped among an infinity of strange existences; he is alienated radically and without recourse." To illustrate this condition he points to the situation of industrial labor, where "several persons experience themselves as apprehended by the Third while they work in solidarity to produce the same object" and where "the very meaning of the manufactured object refers to the working collectivity as to an 'Us.' " The same situation, in his opinion, can engender "class consciousness," especially when the relations between oppressing and oppressed classes are sharply antagonistic. What gives rise to such consciousness is not so much economic deprivation but the position of the oppressors *"as Thirds":* "It is therefore *for* them and *in their freedom* that the reality of the oppressed class is going to exist; they cause it to be born by their look."[14]

While according moderate importance and cohesiveness to the Us-object, *Being and Nothingness* reduces its correlate—the We-subject—to a marginal role. When I use a manufactured product or a means of transportation in the same fashion as a multitude of other consumers or passengers, I feel myself integrated into an "undifferentiated" and "unnumbered transcendence" which may be described as an active mode of the They or as a We-subject. If this undifferentiated transcendence, we read, "projects its projects, whatever they are, in connection with other transcendences experienced as real presences similarly absorbed in projects identical with my projects," then I have the sense of "a common transcendence directed toward a unique end of which I am only an ephemeral particularization." As Sartre insists, however, this sense is limited. First, the experience in his view is purely "of the psychological order and not ontological"; arising as a "subjective event" in my consciousness, it does not correspond to "a real unification of the for-itselfs" or to the implementation of "any *Mitsein.*" Psychologically, participation with others "in a common rhythm which I contribute to creating" is most likely to induce the feeling of being involved in a We-subject: "This is the meaning of the cadenced march of soldiers; it is the meaning also of the rhythmic work of a crew." The real motive for the feeling in these cases is simply *"our rhythm."* Furthermore, the experience of the We-subject is not "an original attitude toward others," but presupposes a prior "recognition of the existence of others." Arguing against Heidegger's notion of inauthentic co-being, where others are encountered initially in connection with things at-hand, Sartre stresses that "in order for the object to appear as manufactured it is necessary that the Other be first given in some other way." The subsidiary character of the We-subject, in his judgment, is manifest even in the context of industrial class struggle, since the "bourgeoisie" as oppressing class is inherently atomized and "anarchistic" while the oppressed class seems unable to move beyond crowd behavior or mob psychology. Thus, neither the experience of the We nor that of the Us can modify the results obtained in the analysis of the look: "The essence of the relations between consciousness is not the *Mitsein;* it is conflict."[15]

In a critical vein one may first observe that Sartre's emphasis on conflict appears linked to his deep-seated attachment to traditional philosophical antinomies. Even a cursory reading of *Being and Nothingness* discloses the pervasive impact of inherited (metaphysical) dichotomies between subject and object, or consciousness and its ontic correlate. Despite his effort to substitute an existential-ontological perspective for a noetic-cognitive one, Sartre's account of encounter is permeated by cognitive-epistemological categories and conceptions; even when he takes recourse to an existential-practical vocabulary, the active and passive modes of experience still reflect the opposition between knower and the known. The impact of the epistemological legacy is evident in the distinction between *cogito* or for-itself and in-itself, and especially in that between being-for-itself, as the being "which is what it is not and which is not what it is," and being-for-others as a mundane somebody; it is equally obvious in the bifurcation between the Other-as-object and the Other-as-subject and between the Us-object and the We-subject. Given the persistent influence of traditional epistemology, Sartre's presentation cannot evade the quandary which earlier beset Husserl's theory of intersubjectivity: namely, how I can experience and give an account of the Other as a phenomenon which on principle escapes me. This dilemma has been noticed by critics. As one commentator stated: "By and large, Sartre's descriptions may be regarded as refinements of Husserl's theory of 'appresentation,' with the difference that Sartre is not dealing with successive stages of interpersonal meaning-constructs but with the factual upsurge of the Other, if only of a presumed one. However, the fact that the event of such an upsurge is *understood* in its meaning seems to presuppose the constitution of interpersonal meaning, ranging from objective space and nature to the comprehension of the possibilities of other persons."[16]

Sartre's attachment to epistemological dichotomies is also manifest in his treatment of coexistence as a relation of reciprocal negation and mutual exclusion. This relation, to be sure, is not simply synonymous with an external segregation of substances. Commenting on the intrinsic problematic of the *alter ego*—that the Other is a "self which is *not* myself"—Sartre noted that traditional versions of idealism and realism were content to construe being-for-others as an external negation or a relation of exteriority, a construction which precluded the possibility of my being existentially "affected by either the upsurge or the abolition of the Other." To correct this defect, he resorted to *internal negation,* according to which "the original distinction between the Other and myself" is "such that it determines me by means of the Other and determines the Other by means of me." Yet the stress on interiority does not obviate the negative character of encounter—although the negation is effected not cognitively but through existential choice. "In order for a consciousness to be able to not-be the Other and therefore in order that *there may be an Other,*" we read, two things are required: "consciousness must have to be itself and must spontaneously have to be this non-being; consciousness must freely disengage itself from the Other and wrench itself away by choosing itself as a nothingness which is simply other than the Other and thereby must be reunited in 'itself.' " My disengagement has as its corollary the Other's reciprocal act; for, "I make myself not-be a being who is making himself not-be me." Thus, in the encounter between consciousness and *alter ego,* each of the two terms "constitutes itself by denying that it is the other." This negative reciprocity, however, is inherently unstable or, as Sartre concedes, self-destructive, for the two parties are never able to recognize each other in their mutual acts. The emergence of the Other-as-subject engenders my alienation while the recovery of my transcendence inflicts the same fate on the Other: "If the Other is to be at the start the Other, then on principle he cannot be revealed in the same upsurge by which I deny being him." What I can deny in our reciprocal choices is not so much the Other as the object-me, through which he asserts his otherness: "Thus this Me which has been alienated and refused is simultaneously my bond with the Other and the symbol of our absolute separation."[17]

Apart from the antinomial character of reciprocal negation, the aspect of absolute separation casts doubt on the claimed interiority of encounter. The theme of separation occurs repeatedly in *Being and Nothingness.* Thus, as previously mentioned, the critique of Hegel's optimism is predicated on his presumed neglect of the ontological separation of existences. The theme also looms large in Sartre's discussion of the "metaphysical" question regarding the origin of the plurality of for-itselfs. As he points out, in the case of the reciprocal negations involved in human encounter "each is an internal negation, but they are nevertheless separated from one another by an inapprehensible external nothingness." The facticity of multiple existences is said to arise not as a substantive constellation on the level of "being-in-itself but as a sort of phantom of exteriority which neither of the negations has to be and which yet separates them." As a result of this complication, encounter in Sartre's treatment assumes a mixed internal-external character. On the one hand, we read, "since the negations are effected in interiority, the Other and myself cannot come to one another from the outside"; rather, it seems necessary "that there be a *being* 'I-and-the-Other' which has to be the reciprocal negation of the for-others." On the other hand, unless interiority is to coincide with a Hegelian synthesis or totality, the multiplicity of existences has to be accepted as a "pure, irreducible contingency"; in this respect, being-for-others "can exist only if it involves an inapprehensible and external non-being which no totality, not even the mind, can produce or found."[18] The mixed character of encounter is manifest also in the juxtaposition of inside and outside modes of experience. Under the impact of the Other's look, I am presumed to acquire *an outside* or *a nature,* in contrast to the *inside* of my transcendence; similarly, the object-Me produced by the same look is presented as "my *being-outside"* which must be "assumed and recognized as *my outside*," again in differentiation from the interiority of consciousness.[19]

Sartre's theory of coexistence was modified in subsequent writings, although the reliance on individual subjectivity—and also on the active-passive and inside-outside dichotomies—was never abandoned. As developed in *Critique of Dialectical Reason,* his later position exhibits both significant innovations and a pervasive continuity of views. In comparison with *Being and Nothingness,* the new study places the central focus on human praxis rather than on existence or on an existentially construed *cogito;* moreover, praxis is defined as the intimate dialectical interchange between human purpose and matter, an exchange anchored first of all in the dimension of human need. "The crucial discovery of dialectical investigation," we read, "is that man is 'mediated' by things to the same extent as things are 'mediated' by man"; in this linkage, "need is the first totalizing relation between the material being, man, and the material ensemble of which he is a part."[20] In a further departure from the earlier work, the *Critique* gives more room to the examination of social aggregates or *practical ensembles*—although the starting point of the inquiry (in an analytical and not necessarily historical sense) remains the individual and his projects. The study aims to establish the *intelligibility* of social life by tracing human interaction from the stage of individual praxis to the stage of social or *common* praxis, or from the dialectic of nature to the dialectic of culture; the transition from the first to the second stage occurs when individual action finds its limit in scarcity and in the *anti-dialectic* of the *practico-inert* (or the dialectic of passivity).[21] On the level of individual praxis, the chief advance of the more recent analysis consists in its greater concreteness and in the closer connection between reciprocal negation and the role of the Third. On the properly social level, Sartre—reformulating in a sense Toennies' distinction between *society* and *community*—offered a detailed description of two major aggregates, collectives and groups, with the difference between the two types residing in the degree of their passivity or practical initiative; moving beyond his earlier discussion of being-with-others, he acknowledged, at least in the case of fused groups, the possibility of a genuine We-subject.

The discussion of primary human relations (or relations on the level of individual interaction) in the *Critique* can be read as a variant of the model of the look, in which looking is translated into individual work and praxis. As before, human encounter is defined as reciprocal negation—more precisely, as a double *internal* negation, although each party is seen as mediated in his actions through matter. "Every negation," Sartre writes, "is a relation of interiority. By this I mean that the reality of the Other affects me in the depths of my being to the extent that it *is not* my reality." Due to this reciprocal negation and exclusion, human coexistence is first of all marked by conflict: "It is impossible to exist among men without their becoming objects both for me and for themselves through me, without my being an object for them, and without my subjectivity getting its objective reality through them as the interiorization of my human objectivity." When encountering other individuals in my field of perception, I initially experience them as *holes* in the universe, as "centrifugal and divergent 'slips' within the same world," with the result that I am "robbed of an aspect of the real." Similarly, when I am approached by another, he represents "a point of hemorrhage of the world and makes me a living object within his subjectivity"; by interiorizing his image of me, I become part of the "objective milieu." Despite the interiority of reciprocal negation, one should note, human encounter on the primary level is not simply an internal but rather a mixed occurrence, since individual projects are implemented against the backdrop of both multiple agents and material constraints. Dialectics on this level, we are told, involves "the contradiction between the unifying unity of praxis and the exteriorizing plurality of human organisms. This relation becomes inverted in that the exteriority of multiplicity is a condition of the synthetic unification of the field."[22]

The dialectic of individual projects is further complicated, in the *Critique,* by the original interdependence between reciprocity and the role of the Third, or between *binary* and *ternary* (or triadic) relations. According to Sartre's new account, reciprocal negation can be grasped as a human bond or synthetic nexus only through the mediation of a third party; however, from the vantage point of reciprocity, this synthesis is bound to be perceived as an intervention which jeopardizes the integrity of encounter. While the triad is required "in the extreme case of a relation stranded in the universe or for *actually* linking two individuals ignorant of each other," we read, "it is broken up by the exclusion of the third party as soon as people or groups either assist or fight one another deliberately and self-consciously. The human mediator cannot help transforming the elementary relation—whose essence is to be lived with no other mediation than matter—into *something else.*" In the duality of encounter, each party "lives within the absolute interiority of a relation which lacks unity" or in a "two-centered relation which he can never grasp in its totality"; at this point, the only possible unity comes from a "transcendent hyper-center" or through a "totalization performed from outside by a third party." Yet this totalization is liable to be rejected as falsification by the constituent parties of reciprocity. Thus, in Sartre's view, human coexistence involves a constant alternation between binary and ternary formations; in contrast to Hegelian dialectics, this alternation only aims at synthesis or totality, without ever reaching this goal: "The dualistic ordering is based on an ever ongoing totalization and negates this totalization as soon as it is established." Social life against this background oscillates between an emerging and a vanishing unity: "Neither reciprocity nor the ternary relation accomplish totality; they are multiple adhesions between men which keep society in a colloid state."[23]

As previously indicated, individual interaction reaches its limit where the anti-dialectic of scarcity imposes on individual praxis the constraint of material necessity or ontic determination, thus submerging it in the domain of the practico-inert; in Sartre's view, this point also marks the beginning of social life. "At an elementary level of the social," he writes, everyone "must become conscious of *his being* as the inorganic materiality of the outside interiorizing itself in the form of a bond linking him to everyone else."[24] Social aggregates originally emerge as structures or "beings of the practico-inert field," in the sense that they are rooted in "inorganic materiality"; however, not all aggregates remain tied to this field, since some succeed in exploiting inertia for joint goals and thereby establish a *common* praxis. From this vantage point, the social arena appears populated by diverse types of aggregates, some more active and some more inert (or passive)—the former termed *groups,* the latter *collectives*—and also by many intermediary formations, although all social life remains ultimately subject to the pull of inertia. "Insofar as the group constitutes itself as a negation of the collective which engenders and sustains it," we read, "and insofar as the collective reappears when a complex of historical circumstances negates the group as an undertaking without liquidating it as a constellation, we can identify, at the extremes, groups in which passivity tends to disappear entirely (for example, a very small 'combat unit,' all of whose members live and struggle together and never leave each other) and collectives which have almost entirely reabsorbed their group." Both types of ensembles involve some kind of totalization of individual interaction, but only groups pursue it as an active goal; in both instances the social character of aggregation presupposes the concurrent presence of a third party, although in the case of collectives this role may coincide with an external-material imperative.[25]

As can be seen, collectives in the *Critique* occupy the position previously assigned to the Us-object, with a difference in the source of objectification. In contrast to the self-motivated action of groups, collective ensembles are presented as the result of a *passive synthesis* effected by material constraints. In Sartre's words, a collective is "defined *by its being"* in the sense that it constitutes "a material, inorganic object in the practico-inert field" in which "a discrete multiplicity of active individuals is produced, under the sign of the Other, as a *real unity within being,* that is, as a passive synthesis" and where "inertia penetrates *every individual praxis* as its fundamental determination." One major variant of such passive synthesis discussed in the *Critique* is the *series,* or the juxtaposition of individuals under the unifying impact of "practico-inert matter." In the series, the social bond is established purely on the level of otherness in the sense that everyone is linked with others only in the aspect in which he is *outside* or *other than* himself; on this level, moreover, everyone merges with everyone else in an indiscriminate sameness. "Since all the lived characteristics which might allow some interior differentiation lie outside this determination," we read, "everyone's identity with every Other is their unity elsewhere, as other-being"; everyone "is the same as the others insofar as he is other than himself." Like every form of coexistence, seriality is a mixed external-internal relation—but with the accent on external separation; while not completely eliminating internal negation, human contact "in the mode of identity becomes a false reciprocity of relations" or an "interiority lived in the milieu of exteriority." The synthesis effected through serial ordering is the "passive unity of the multiplicity insofar as it exists in-itself" or the "being-one of the organisms unified through their being-in-themselves in the object," together with the "re-interiorization of exteriority by the human ensemble." Due to the absence of genuine reciprocity, such synthesis is anchored simply in "otherness" and thus *"always elsewhere"*; its unity is a "totalization of flight."[26]

In particularly stratified contexts, passive synthesis may assume the structure of a social class. In line with the discussion of class consciousness in *Being and Nothingness*, the *Critique* presents *class* first of all as a collective ensemble inserted in the practico-inert field. In Sartre's words, class-being can be defined as "practico-inert being mediated by the passive syntheses of worked matter" or as "the practico-inert statute of individual or common praxis." As he adds, the dominance of inorganic materiality does not eliminate the social (or interpersonal) character of this collectivity. Class-being, he notes, "comes to men through men; for each of us it is our being-outside-ourselves in matter, insofar as this condition produces us and awaits us from birth and insofar as it constitutes itself through us as a future fate." Although class membership may "not prevent us from realizing an individual destiny (each life is individual)," this same "realization of our experience until death is only one of several possible ways (determined by the structured field of possibilities) of producing our class-being." Only in situations of intensive struggle can class-being overcome its inert passivity and "lack of solidarity." In such instances, "the organized praxis of a militant group originates in the very heart of the practico-inert, in the opaque materiality of impotence and inertia as the transcendence of *this* materiality." At this point, "the other form of class, that is, the group which totalizes through praxis, emerges at the core of passivity and as its negation." Yet "a *wholly active class*, all of whose members are integrated into a single praxis and whose organizational structures coalesce in unity rather than conflicting with one another, is realized only in very rare (and revolutionary) moments of working-class history."[27]

In its active mode, social class thus approximates—and at times even coincides with—the second major type of social aggregate, the group. Leaving behind the mere "unity of flight" found in collectives, the *group* is defined in the *Critique* as a "moving totality" or as a common undertaking characterized by a "constant movement of integration which tends to turn it into pure praxis by trying to eliminate all forms of inertia." Group members, we are told, perceive themselves "as a common relation to a transcendent aim rather than each apprehending his own ends in a reciprocity of separations." The most intensive integration occurs in *fused groups*—whose opposition to passive sociality is said to assume apocalyptic proportions—since unity in this instance is no longer "elsewhere" but "always *here*." Like every aggregate, group-being also relies on the role of a third party (which is basically everyone in relation to everyone else). Instead of being submerged in otherness, the third party now becomes an integral participant in the common undertaking; differently phrased, the ternary relation emerges as a "free inter-individual reality, as an immediate human relation." As a member, I do not perceive the group as a collective object, nor am I confronted by a group-subject which objectifies me; rather, "I come to the group as its group activity, constituting it as an activity insofar as the group comes to me as my group activity, as my own *group existence*." In Sartre's account, each individual praxis "places itself at the service of a common dialectic"; the latter, in turn, is "modelled on the synthetic action" of individual work—but with the difference that common praxis has been filtered through the counter-dialectic of material necessity and forms its antidote. "In this sense," he writes, "we might be said to be passing here from the nature-dialectic, as an original relation of interiority between the organism and its milieu, to the culture-dialectic, as an apparatus constructed against the power of the practico-inert. In other words, individual dialectics, after having engendered anti-physis as the power of (individual) man over nature and, in the same act, anti-humanity as the power of inorganic matter over man, create their own anti-physis through unification so as to construct human power (that is, free relations among men)."[28]

Interworld and Reversibility: Merleau-Ponty

In descriptive detail and breadth of coverage, Sartre's examination of intersubjectivity is unmatched among French phenomenologists; certainly no one in the latter movement has given equal attention to social aggregates and communal types of experience.[29] This does not mean that his analysis has gone unchallenged or that some of his fellow-phenomenologists have not moved beyond his basic position in significant respects. Merleau-Ponty's treatment of the topic appears both less comprehensive and more subtle and probing than Sartre's account. While sufficiently close—especially in his early phase—to Sartrean existentialism to permit ready comparison, Merleau-Ponty's arguments are ultimately incompatible with existentialist categories. Undoubtedly, Merleau-Ponty's formative years bore the imprint of Husserlian phenomenology and Hegelian idealism with their common focus on subjectivity. Yet his writings also testify to his persistent efforts to decenter the *cogito* and thus to overcome traditional epistemological antinomies, including the subject-object and internal-external bifurcations. These efforts were bound to have an impact on all issues relating to intersubjectivity. Despite the relative restriction of his focus, in my opinion his comments have implications even in the sociological (or sociopolitical) domain: they permit a reformulation of some of the mentioned aggregates and also bring into view modes of social formation not covered in Sartre's typology.

Merleau-Ponty first discussed intersubjectivity in his *Phenomenology of Perception,* a study which appeared shortly after *Being and Nothingness.* A comparative reading of the two works reveals several parallels, but also some striking contrasts. Like Sartre, Merleau-Ponty presented human interaction as an existential encounter, thus advancing beyond a purely noetic-cognitive perspective; to accomplish this aim, both thinkers relied on the Heideggerian notion of being-in-the-world. However, where Sartre's view of existence continued to depend on epistemological categories, Merleau-Ponty from the beginning accentuated the ontological implications of Heidegger's term (although his early writings oscillated between egological and ontological components). For both phenomenologists, being-in-the-world implied a connection between transcendental and mundane types of inquiry; moreover, in both cases an important corollary of being-in-the-world was human embodiment, or man's concrete insertion in the world. While in Sartre's treatment the *body* functioned as a primary instrument or attachment which—like subjectivity—was subject to the antinomies of the look, Merleau-Ponty (in some of his formulations) construed embodiment as evidence of man's embeddedness in, or openness toward, Being.[30] To the extent that man's relation to Being is neither internal nor external—and thus cannot properly be grasped through the categories of identity or negation—Merleau-Ponty transposed the theme of otherness from the level of intermonadic coexistence to the very heart of existence. On the whole, Sartre's early position was characterized as an ontology grounded in (transcendental) phenomenology while Merleau-Ponty's outlook during the same period may be described as a mixture of the two vistas, or as a phenomenology straining in the direction of ontology.

Some general indications of Merleau-Ponty's early approach can be gleaned from the preface to *Phenomenology of Perception,* entitled "What is Phenomenology?" Referring to the Cartesian (and Kantian) legacy of the *ego cogitans,* the preface takes issue with the stress on a completely transparent consciousness and unsituated subjectivity. Pure reflection, we read, "knows nothing of the problem of other minds or of that of the world, because it insists that with the first glimmer of consciousness there appears in me theoretically the power of reaching some universal truth and that—other persons being equally without thisness, location or body—the *alter* and the ego are one and the same in the true world which is the unifier of minds." For intersubjectivity to gain meaning, Merleau-Ponty observes, the abstract *cogito* must be replaced by an embodied and situated being-in-the-world; only when existence is not reduced to the "bare awareness of existence," but construed as including "my incarnation in some nature," does the *alter ego* emerge as a serious philosophical puzzle: "Both he and I must have an outer appearance, and there must be besides the perspective of the For-Oneself—my view of myself and the Other's of himself—a perspective of For-Others—my view of others and theirs of me." He emphasizes that being-for-oneself and being-for-others cannot merely be placed alongside each other, just as inner and outer appearance cannot neatly be segregated: "These two perspectives, in each one of us, cannot simply be juxtaposed, *for in that case it is not I that the Other would see, nor he that I would see.* I must be the exterior that I present to others, and the Other's body must be the Other himself." Against this background, intersubjectivity presupposes a view of human existence as deficiency rather than plenitude: "The paradox and dialectic of the ego and the *alter* are possible only provided that ego and *alter ego* are defined by their situation and not freed from all inherence"; in other words, "provided that at the very moment when I experience my existence (at the ultimate extremity of reflection) I fall short of the final compactness which would place me outside time, and that I discover within myself a kind of internal weakness standing in the way of my being totally individualized: a weakness which exposes me to the gaze of others as man among men or at least as a consciousness among consciousnesses."[31]

Intersubjectivity is explored more fully in later portions of the study, especially in the chapter on "Other People and the Human

World." Following in Heidegger's footsteps, Merleau-Ponty approaches the theme initially on the prereflective level, rather than concentrating immediately on reflective or deliberate forms of interaction; on that level, "other people" are first encountered obliquely, through cultural sedimentations. Prior to cognitive inquiry, he writes, I experientially discover behavior patterns "being deposited in the form of a cultural world. Not only do I have a physical universe or live in the midst of earth, air and water, I have around me roads, plantations, villages, streets, churches, implements, a bell, a spoon, a pipe." These cultural sediments are perceived not merely as mute objects; rather, "I feel the close presence of others beneath a veil of anonymity: *someone* uses the pipe for smoking, the spoon for eating, the bell for summoning." The question which arises is how this anonymous reference and relation to others is conceivable; in other words, how a human act or thought can be "grasped in the mode of the 'one' (or the 'They')" since, by its nature, it appears as "a first person operation, inseparable from an *I*." The customary response to this query, Merleau-Ponty notes, relies on analogical inference; typically, the reply will be "that I see a certain use made by other men of the implements which surround me, that I interpret their behavior by analogy with my own and through my inner experience," and that ultimately the actions of others are "always understood through my own, the 'one' or the 'we' through the 'I.' " But, he adds, "this is precisely the question: how can the word 'I' be put into the plural, how can a general idea of the *I* be formed, how can I speak of an *I* other than my own, how can I know that there are other *I*'s, how can consciousness which, by its nature and as self-knowledge, is in the mode of the *I*, be grasped in the mode of Thou and, through this, in the mode of the 'one'?"[32]

In disentangling this problem one can expect little help, in Merleau-Ponty's view, from traditional epistemology, in both its rationalist and its empiricist versions; "the existence of other people is a difficulty and an outrage" for this legacy, with its subject-object and consciousness-reality dichotomies. In terms of this tradition, my experience of the world and of others is simply an encounter "between bare consciousness and the system of objective correlations which it conceives"; as a consequence, "the body of another, like my own, is not properly inhabited, but is an object standing before the consciousness which thinks about or constitutes it." Seen through the subject-object bifurcation, the *alter ego* remains an insoluble enigma: "My consciousness, being co-extensive with what can exist for me and corresponding to the whole field of experience, cannot encounter, in that field, another consciousness capable of bringing immediately to light in the world the background, unknown to me, of its own phenomena." Basically, Merleau-Ponty states, traditional epistemology knows "two modes of being and only two: being-in-itself, which is that of objects arrayed in space, and being-for-itself, which is that of consciousness." However, "another person would seem to stand before me as an *in-itself* and yet to exist *for-himself,* thus requiring of me, in order to be perceived, a contradictory operation: since I ought both to distinguish him from myself and therefore place him in the world of objects, and think of him as a consciousness, that is, the sort of being with no outside and no parts, to which I have access merely because that being is myself."[33]

Difficulties of this kind seem less formidable once the focus shifts from epistemological categories to prereflective experience and anonymous-cultural encounters. As key guidepost in this domain, Merleau-Ponty relies on being-in-the-world—a notion explicated, at least at this point, not so much in terms of man's openness to Being (or in light of an "ontic-ontological difference") but rather in terms of a situated consciousness and a particularly intimate nexus between perception and world. In order to bypass traditional cognitive dilemmas, he suggests, we must construe individual experience as a manifestation of "our insertion into the world" and perception "no longer as a constitution of the true object, but as our inherence in things." This implies a revision of customary subject-object correlations, and especially a "profound transformation of the notions of body and consciousness" as they are commonly used: "As far as the body is concerned, even the body of another, we must learn to distinguish it from the objective body as set forth in works on physiology," since the objective body is not "capable of being inhabited by a consciousness." Presented as a "chemical structure," we read, the body of physiological textbooks is "formed by a process of impoverishment from a primordial phenomenon of the body-for-us, the body of human experience or the perceived body, round which objective (scientific) thought works, but without being called upon to postulate its completed analysis." A corresponding change is involved on the side of consciousness, one particularly significant for the question of coexistence: "As for consciousness, it has to be conceived, no longer as a constituting consciousness and, as it were, a pure being-for-itself, but as a perceptual consciousness, as the subject of a concrete pattern of behavior, as being-in-the-world or existence; for only thus can another appear at the top of his phenomenal body and be endowed likewise with a sort of 'locality.' " These transformations push the antinomies of epistemology into the background, making room for an experiential, primarily visual-perceptual, encounter with fellow-men: "Through phenomenological inquiry I discover vision, not as a 'thinking about seeing,' to use Descartes' phrase, but as a gaze at grips with a visible world; and that is why for me there can be another's gaze, why that expressive instrument called a face can carry an existence, just as my own existence is carried by my body seen as a learning or knowledge-gathering facility."[34]

According to *Phenomenology of Perception*, human encounter first involves not a confrontation of egos, but a lateral juncture of existences linked through their common inherence in the world. Rejecting implicitly Sartre's contention that anonymous coexistence presupposes a prior experience of the Other's subjectivity (or of the *alter* as an ego), Merleau-Ponty insists on the subsidiary status of analogical inferences about the Other's subjectivity or consciousness. "The perception of others," he writes, "is anterior to, and the condition of, such observations; the observations do not constitute the perception." What is revealed through perception is not a correlation of physical behaviors or of psychic (egocentric) conditions but a reciprocal being-in-the-world, an aspect which sustains a quasi-internal connection, in the sense that ego and *alter* are both inserted into Being: "Between my consciousness and my body as I experience it, between this phenomenal body of mine and that of another as I see it from the outside, there exists an internal relation which causes the Other to appear as the completion of the system. The possibility of another person's being self-evident is owed to the fact that I am not transparent for myself, and that my subjectivity draws its body in its wake." Their joint insertion into Being also entails a lateral inherence of ego and *alter* in each other, a circumstance which legitimates their subsumption under the designation of the *one* (or the *They*): "It is precisely my body which perceives the body of another person and discovers in that other body a miraculous prolongation of my own intentions, a familiar way of dealing with the world. Henceforth, as the parts of my body together comprise a system, so my body and the other person's are one whole, two sides of one and the same phenomenon, and the anonymous existence of which my body is the ever-renewed trace henceforth inhabits both bodies simultaneously."[35]

Due to the absence of an ego-focus, human coexistence in the mode of the *one* does not initially imply mutual objectification. As the study asserts: "If another's body is not an object for me nor mine an object for him, but if both are manifestations of behavior, the emergence of the Other does not reduce me to the status of an object in his field, nor does my perception of the Other reduce him to the status of an object in mine." Far from impeding encounter, prereflective (or non-egological) experience in Merleau-Ponty's view facilitates access to fellow-men: "The Other would never be quite a personal being if I myself were totally one and if I grasped myself as apodictically self-evident; but if I find in myself, through probing, along with the perceiving subject a pre-personal subject given to itself, and if my perceptions are centered outside me as sources of initiative and judgment—if, differently put, the perceived world remains in a state of balance, being neither verified as an object nor projected as a dream, then it is not the case that everything that appears in the world is arrayed or spread out before me, and so the behavior of other people can have its place there." Approached in the milieu of the *one,* individuals are not *"cogitationes* shut up in their own immanence" but rather "beings which are outrun by their world and which consequently may well be outrun by each other." According to Merleau-Ponty, ordinary language provides a crucial demonstration of mutual existential inherence. In the experience of discourse, he comments, "there is constituted between the Other and myself a common ground: my thought and his are interwoven into a single fabric, my words and those of my interlocutor are called forth by the state of the discussion and are inserted into a shared operation of which neither of us is the creator." What arises here is an *interworld* or "dual being where the Other is for me no longer a mere bit of behavior in my transcendental field nor I in his; rather, we are collaborators for each other in consummate reciprocity." Against this background, the primary mode of coexistence is not so much conflict (at least not self-motivated conflict) as partnership: "Other people are not enclosed in my perspective of the world because this perspective itself has no definite limits, because it slips spontaneously into the Other's, and because both are brought together in the one single world in which we all participate as anonymous subjects of perception."[36]

Merleau-Ponty's discussion of intersubjectivity, however, is not restricted to the level of anonymity or to what Heidegger called inauthentic co-being. Reflective endeavor, in Merleau-Ponty's view, carries in its wake the rise of subjective self-consciousness—which, in turn, conjures up the specter of solipsism. The approach followed so far, he concedes, may be claimed to "iron out the I and the Thou in an experience shared by a plurality, thus introducing the impersonal into the heart of subjectivity and eliminating the individuality of perspectives.

But have we not, in this general confusion, done away with the *alter ego* as well as the ego?" The avoidance of an egological focus seems to have precluded the possibility of grasping the difference between ego and *alter ego* and of understanding the multiplicity and diversity of existence: "If the perceiving subject is anonymous, the perceived Other is equally so; so when, within this collective consciousness, we try to bring out the plurality of consciousnesses, we shall find ourselves back with the difficulties which we thought we had left behind." As Merleau-Ponty notes, coexistence must be anchored in the individual experiences of at least two people, although this grounding is elusive: "If neither of us is a constituting consciousness at the moment when we are about to communicate and discover a common world, the question then is: who communicates and for whom does this world exist? And if someone does communicate with someone else, if the 'inter-world' is not an inconceivable in-itself but exists individually for each of us, then again communication breaks down and each of us operates in his own private world like two players playing on two chessboards a hundred miles apart." Traditional philosophy was not altogether mis-guided in linking this premise of individual-subjective experience with the notion of the *cogito;* for "every assertion, every commitment, and even every negation and doubt takes its place in an experiential field posited in advance and testifies to a 'self' contiguous with itself prior to those particular acts in which it loses contact with itself." Thus, we read, "there is here a solipsism rooted in living experience and quite insurmountable"; differently phrased, epistemology and the conception of the *cogito* are not merely fictions but are "firmly grounded phenom-ena of which we shall have to seek the basis."[37]

The study insists that the problem of solipsism—confronted "in all its difficulty"—cannot be banished with a magic wand; neither can the question of the *alter ego,* however, be abandoned as an unintelli-gible riddle: "Consciousnesses present themselves with the absurd spec-tacle of a multiple solipsism: such is the situation which has to be un-derstood; since we live through this situation, there must be some way of making it explicit. Solitude and communication cannot be the two horns of a dilemma, but should be two 'moments' of one phenomenon since, in fact, other people do exist for me." Together with Sartre, Merleau-Ponty refuses to seek refuge from this dilemma in a totali-tarian perspective, from which ego and *alter ego* would be reconciled in an a priori fashion. Arguing against Hegel's transfiguration of sub-jectivity into an absolute spirit in possession of absolute knowledge, he comments: "If reflection should reveal myself to me as an infinite sub-

ject, we must recognize—at least at the phenomenal level—my ignorance of this self which presumably is even more myself than I." The
claim that perception of ego and *alter ego* necessarily presupposes absolute cognition is, in his view, spurious: "If I already had this knowledge, then all the books of philosophy would be useless; in fact,
however, truth needs to be uncovered." The notion of an infinite
subjectivity functioning as *world spirit* appears to him equally unconvincing: "I can never *recognize myself* as God without necessarily
denying what I am trying in fact to assert. Assuming I might know
and love others as myself *in* God, my love in this case would not properly come from me, but would rather be, in Spinoza's expression, the
love which God has for himself through me."[38]

According to Merleau-Ponty, the mutual recognition of ego and
alter ego hinges on the fluid and open-ended character of reflective subjectivity and not so much on a spectator's view. In order to fulfill its
role, he notes, reflection must be able to reach out toward "otherness,"
that is, toward its other, unreflected side: "Reflection must in some
way present the unreflective; for otherwise we should have nothing to
set over against it and it would not become a problem for us." Similarly, subjective awareness must be a gateway to fellow-men if it is to
qualify as *my* awareness. Even solipsism—to be an intelligible proposition—contains a reference to human interaction: "My experience must
in some way present me with other people, since otherwise I should
have no occasion to speak of solitude and could not begin to pro-
nounce other people inaccessible." While I may be able to "evolve a
solipsist philosophy," in doing so I implicitly "assume the existence
of a community of men endowed with speech and address myself to
it." Thus, the premise from which we need to start, in Merleau-
Ponty's view, is not a self-enclosed subjectivity, but rather "a reflection
open to the unreflective, the reflective assumption of the unreflective,"
which implies "the tension of my experience towards another whose
existence on the horizon of my life is beyond doubt, even when my
knowledge of him is imperfect." Returning to being-in-the-world, he
emphasizes the intimate connection between individuality and situation
and especially the aspect of the givenness of subjectivity, seen as a
manifestation of an ontological "there is" (*es gibt*). "The central phenomenon at the root of both my subjectivity and my transcendence toward others," he writes, "consists in my being given to myself: *I am
given,* that is, I find myself already situated and involved in a physical
and social world; *I am given to myself,* which means that this situation
is never hidden from me, it is never round about as an alien necessity,

and I am never in effect enclosed in it like an object in a box." My reflective transcendence and subjectivity—the "power which I enjoy of
being the subject of all my experiences"—does not remove but rather
presupposes my "insertion into the world"; although in exercising my
freedom I "can deny each thing," this is always done "by asserting that
there is something in general—which is why we describe thought as
a 'thinking nature,' an assertion of being over and above the negation
of beings."[39]

The linkage of subjectivity and givenness, Merleau-Ponty adds,
throws doubt on the model of the look as it has been developed by
Sartre (although its author is not specifically mentioned at this point).
The process of reciprocal objectification, in particular, presupposes a
mutual solipsism which the model is meant to overcome: "The other
person transforms me into an object and denies me, I transform him
into an object and deny him, it is asserted. In fact, however, the Other's
gaze transforms me into an object, and mine him, only if both of us
withdraw into the core of our thinking nature, if we both make ourselves into an inhuman gaze, and if each of us feels his actions to be
not taken up and understood, but observed as if they were an insect's."
Such a relative alienation may occur "when I fall under the gaze of a
stranger"; even in this case, the objectification is "felt as unbearable
only because it takes the place of possible communication," whereas a
dog's gaze "causes me no embarrassment." The strangeness of the
stranger—his appearance as "an inhabitant of another world"—can
be maintained as long as he "has as yet not uttered a word"; with the
first word or gesture he becomes accessible and "ceases to transcend
me." Generally speaking, each existence eludes others "only when it
remains inactive and rests upon its natural difference"—which is not
consistently possible "since existing is being in and of the world."[40]
The critique of objectification extends to the Sartrean juxtaposition of
being-for-itself and being-for-others. If one could separate these "two
sorts of categories," Merleau-Ponty asks, "how could I have the experience of another, that is, of an *alter ego?* This experience presupposes
that already my view of myself is half-way to having the quality of a
possible 'other' (or *alter*), and that in my view of the Other is implied
his quality as *ego."* If my subjectivity, however, contains traces of
otherness and the Other contains traces of subjectivity, the categories
of the Other-as-object and Me-as-subject (and vice versa) cannot be
neatly segregated: "The Other-as-object is nothing but an indistinct
modality of others, just as absolute subjectivity is nothing but an abstract notion of myself. I must, therefore, in the most radical reflection,

apprehend around my absolute individuality a kind of halo of generality or a kind of atmosphere of 'sociality.' "[41]

Once the focus is placed on this matrix of *sociality*, society and the various forms of social aggregates cease to be strictly subsumable under customary epistemological antinomies. Our "relationship to the social," Merleau-Ponty emphasizes, is different from any theoretical "judgment." Relying on the interdependence of subjectivity and otherness, *Phenomenology of Perception* distances itself (again implicitly) from Sartre's theory of social aggregation; the notions of the Us-object and the We-subject, in particular, appear as an outgrowth of the *inhuman gaze* and dialectic of objectification mentioned above. According to the study, society and its aggregates can neither be comprehended as an external environment nor as emanations of subjective-internal designs (including designs of a plurality of subjects). "It is as false to place ourselves in society as an object among objects as it is to place society within ourselves as a projection of thought"; in both cases the mistake lies in adhering to the subject-object polarity and especially "in treating the social as an object." Instead of positing it or accepting it as a destiny, Merleau-Ponty suggests, "we must return to the social with which we are in contact by the mere fact of existing and which we carry about inseparably with us before any objectification"; prior to deliberate affirmation or negation, "the social exists obscurely and as a summons"—a summons which is merely implemented in various forms of aggregation. Just as it bypasses the Us-object and the We-subject, social life in his view is not the outcome of a third party intervention. In Sartrean terms, the linkage of binary reciprocity is not solely due to a ternary relation: "Primarily the social does not exist as a third party object. It is the mistake of the investigator, the 'great man' and the historian to try to treat it as such an object."[42]

In Merleau-Ponty's judgment, the reliance on third party constructions is particularly misleading in the case of such social aggregates as *nation* or *class;* outsider definitions in this domain are notoriously unreliable. "The historian and the philosopher," he notes, "are in search of an objective definition of class or nation: Is the nation based on common language or on conceptions of life; is class based on income statistics or on its place in the process of production? It is well known that none of these criteria enables us to decide whether an individual belongs to a nation or a class." To make headway in these matters, he adds, one must realize that aggregates of this kind are neither external determinations nor spontaneous human inventions but rather manifestations of a lived sociality: "Nation and class are neither versions of fate which hold the individual in subjection from the outside nor values which he posits from within; they are modes of coexistence which are a call upon him." Class consciousness, in particular, cannot be derived causally from external conditions; nor does it coincide with a deliberate project. "Class is a matter neither for observation nor decree," we read. "Like the appointed order of the capitalistic system, like revolution, before being thought it is lived through as an obsessive presence, as possibility, enigma and myth. To make class-consciousness the outcome of a decision and a choice is to say that problems are solved on the day they are posed, and that every question already contains the reply that it awaits." Instead of juxtaposing class-being (as an inert-passive collective) and class action (as pure praxis of a group), Merleau-Ponty prefers to differentiate between latent and overt, or explicit, types of aggregates: "Under conditions of calm, the nation and the class are there as stimuli to which I respond only absent-mindedly or confusedly; they are merely latent. A revolutionary situation, or one of national danger, transforms those preconscious relationships with class and nation, hitherto merely lived through, into the definite taking of a stand. Thus, the tacit commitment becomes explicit; but it is nurtured prior to decision."[43]

In refusing to treat social aggregates as deliberate human designs, Merleau-Ponty takes a position against interpersonal manipulation and managerial planning. Sociality or social awareness, from his perspective, implicitly points toward "otherness" and thus toward a domain which inherently resists human control and management. In this sense, his account—at least in some passages—approximates Heidegger's notion of authentic co-being, seen as a mode of coexistence animated by emancipatory solicitude or by the willingness to let others be. *Phenomenology of Perception* compares coexistence to man's relation to death (a relation which was a dominant theme in *Being and Time*). "Whether we are concerned with my body, the natural world, the past, birth or death," we read, "the question is always how I can be open to phenomena which transcend me" and *"how the presence to myself (Urpräsenz) which establishes my own limits and conditions every alien presence is at the same time de-presentation (Entgegenwärtigung) and throws me outside myself."* While being "established in my life" I seem to enjoy "a sort of ubiquity and theoretical eternity"; however, this "flow of endless life" also outlines an otherness which I cannot encompass: together with the apparent "superabundance of being" there arises "the feeling of my contingency, the dread of being outstripped, so that, although I do not manage to incorporate my death into thought, I nevertheless live in an atmosphere of death in general, and there is a kind of essence of death always on the horizon of my thinking." To this extent, death and the otherness of fellow-men converge: "Just as the instant of my death is a future to which I have no access, so I am necessarily destined never to experience the presence of the Other to himself. And yet, each other person does exist for me as an unchallengeable style or setting of co-existence, and my life has a social atmosphere just as it has a flavor of mortality."[44]

Once coexistence is perceived in the light of the correlation between life and death, the tension between subjective experience and otherness is carried into the core of existence (without on this count turning into an a priori category). Differently phrased: the subject-object conflict which, on the epistemological level, appeared as an insoluble antinomy, reemerges as an intrinsic contradiction—or better, difference—on the ontological plane. In concentrating on being-in-the-world, Merleau-Ponty writes, we encounter "that ambiguous life in which the forms of transcendence have their *Ursprung* and which, through a fundamental contradiction, puts me in communication with them, thereby rendering knowledge possible." Given the previous strictures against cognitive dichotomies, he adds, "it will perhaps be maintained that a philosophy cannot be centered around a contradiction and that all our descriptions, since they ultimately defy thought, are quite meaningless." As he concedes, the objection would be valid if the focus on being-in-the-world were content to lay bare "a layer of prelogical or magical experiences" which can be invoked but are entirely recalcitrant to insight. However, this view is predicated on the very epistemology which has been criticized and it fails to take seriously the challenge of a non-cognitive reflection. The descriptions of existence should be an invitation to explore "a variety of comprehension and reflection altogether more radical than objectivist thought" (deriving from traditional epistemology): "To phenomenology understood as direct description needs to be added a phenomenology of phenomenology. We must return to the *cogito* in search of a more fundamental *logos* than that of objectivist thought, one which endows the latter with its relative validity and at the same time assigns to it its place."[45]

The preceding comments—with which the chapter on "Other People" concludes—clearly point beyond a purely descriptive and constitutive phenomenology; in uncovering a tension at the heart of man's relation to Being, they even diverge from the uneasy blend of phenomenology and ontology which otherwise characterizes *Phenomenology of Perception*. In his subsequent writings, Merleau-Ponty did not immediately pursue the implications of these ontological findings. His next sustained examination of intersubjectivity occurred in *The Prose of the World,* a manuscript composed some five or six years after the war and published posthumously. In its discussion, the manuscript departed only slightly from the previous treatment, although the role of language received more attention. Regarding prereflective (or silent) coexistence, Merleau-Ponty again stressed the lateral inherence of ego and *alter ego* which forms the basis of sociality: "Myself and the Other are like two *nearly* concentric circles which can be distinguished only by a slight and mysterious slippage. This alliance is perhaps what will enable us to understand the relation to the Other which is inconceivable if I try to approach him directly, like a sheer cliff." As before, embodiment was seen as necessary to intersubjective encounter; another's behavior was said to be accessible primarily "because the world I perceive still trails with it my corporeality." The new text claimed that language forms the crucial matrix rendering encounter intelligible. Through language, it stated, the *alter ego* "can emerge as both other and myself in a more radical sense." Speech was singled out as the faculty which "endlessly renews the mediation between sameness and otherness." The perception of the *alter ego* "presupposes that his speech, at the point where we understand him and especially at the moment he withdraws from us and threatens to fall into non-sense, be capable of remaking us in his image and to open us to another meaning." In speech we come to "realize the impossible agreement between two rival totalities," for the simple reason that "speech concerns us, catches us indirectly, seduces us, trails us along, transforms us into the Other and him into us, abolishes the limit between mine and not-mine, and ends the alternative between what has sense for me and what is non-sense for me, between me as subject and the Other as object."[46]

Only the later years of Merleau-Ponty's life brought a rigorous unfolding of the insights contained in some of his earlier comments. His final manuscript—published posthumously as *The Visible and the Invisible*—explored the contours of an anti-egological (but non-objectivist) ontology—although the word *ontology* needs to be used cautiously since, as Merleau-Ponty emphasized, Being cannot be approached directly (*intentione recta*), but only laterally through immersion in the world. As presented in the manuscript, being-in-the-world was still intimately linked with corporeality; however, embodiment clearly was no longer seen as the concrete manifestation of a (latent) *cogito,* but rather as evidence of man's participation in *visibility* or of his inherence in the *flesh* of the world. The notion of a tension at the heart of being-in-the-world emerged as a cornerstone of Merleau-Ponty's later thought. Drawing some of its inspiration from the Heideggerian conception of an ontological difference, *The Visible and the Invisible* probed the ramifications of a basic *chiasm* in the relation of visibility and invisibility—an intersection actually involving a dual intertwining or a doubling up, namely, "the insertion of the world between the two leaves of my body" and "the insertion of my body between the two leaves of each thing and of the world."[47] As a corollary of this chiasm, coexistence of ego and *alter ego* denoted not only lateral interdependence, but an ontological intertwining and reversibility.

Taking up more forcefully a theme of earlier writings, the manuscript criticized traditional epistemology with its antinomies in favor of precognitive perception and experience. A central purpose of the study was not to oppose to the "facts" of scientific inquiry "a group of facts that 'escape' it," but rather "to show that the being-object and the being-subject construed as antithetical to each other do not constitute the basic alternatives," since "the perceived world is beneath or beyond this antinomy." The attack on "scientism" or objectivism, the study stressed, was not meant to vindicate subjectivism or a subject-focus concentrating on internal faculties. "Psychological or transcendental immanence," we read, "cannot account for what a horizon or a 'remoteness' is any better than can 'objectivist' thought; for whether it be identified with 'introspection' or with a consciousness constitutive of the perceived, perception would have to be, in actuality and on principle, knowledge and possession of itself—thus it could not open upon horizons and distances, that is, upon a world which is there for it from the first and from which alone it knows itself as the anonymous incumbent toward which the perspectives of the landscape travel." Arguments of this kind were intended to expose the inadequacy not only of "psychologism" but also of the modern "philosophy of reflection" (dating back to Descartes), with its proclivity to treat perception as "the thought of perceiving" and the perceived world as "a thing thought." According to this reflective legacy, Merleau-Ponty noted, "I am forever subjected to the centrifugal movement that makes a cognitive object exist for a thought, and there is no question of my quitting this position and examining what Being might be before being thought by me or (what amounts to the same thing) by another, or what the 'interworld' (*l'intermonde*) might be like where our gazes cross and our perceptions overlap: there is no brute world, there is only an elaborated world; there is no intermundane space but only a signification 'world.' "[48]

The critique of the reflective legacy also applied to the perspective of a radically reflective "dialectics," as it can be found in Sartre's writings (with some indebtedness to Hegelian philosophy). Although claiming to uphold alterity or otherness through its separation of for-itself and in-itself and through its emphasis on reciprocal negation, Sartrean dialectics in Merleau-Ponty's view defaulted on this claim and, more generally, was marred by an intrinsic incoherence. If, in the Sartrean scheme, the Other is to be "really the Other," he noted, *"he must never be so before my eyes,"* that means, there could be no direct perception of him and it was necessary "that the Other be my negation or my destruction"; every concrete linkage would ruin the alterity of the Other and mark "the triumph of a disguised solipsism." Yet the model of the look only apparently confined itself to self-experience; it ascribed the same transcendental quality to the Other as to myself, thus encompassing him in its perspective. The empty space reserved "at the horizon of my universe," the manuscript stated, was not really "a void," nor was it "the simple or immediate negation of myself and of my universe": "From the sole fact that I circumscribe it, be it with dotted lines, it is cut out in my universe; there is an intersection of my universe with that of another." Although rightly emphasizing the "inevitable asymmetry of the I-Other relation," Sartre's model was permeated by a profound dogmatism: "In spite of appearances, it is the philosophy of vision which installs itself dogmatically in all the situations at the same time, by declaring them impenetrable, and by presenting each of them as the absolute negation of the others"; its negativity was "a dogmatism secretly harboring the absolute affirmation of the opposites." Strictly speaking, the Sartrean notion of internal negation—in Merleau-Ponty's judgment—was incoherent; for existential encounter implied contact while negation was synonymous with exclusion.[49]

According to *The Visible and the Invisible,* the relation between ego and *alter ego*—or better, between ego and all the others—was neither a purely internal or immanent linkage, nor could it be construed in terms of complete negation or exteriority; both stipulations were infringements on otherness. Opposing the premise of a dogmatic negativity the study observed: "It is necessary that there be transition from the Other to me and from me to the Other precisely in order that I and the others not be posed dogmatically as universes equivalent on principle, and in order that the privilege of the 'For-Itself' for itself be recognized." Similarly, again in the interest of differentiation, ego and *alter ego* could not be identified uniformly with absolute interiority or a *constitutive nothingness:* "Instead of the Other and me being two parallel for-itselfs each stricken with the same mortal evil—the Other's

presence which crushes us each in turn into the in-itself of our world—
it is necessary that all of us form for one another a 'system' or constellation of for-itselfs sensitive to one another, such that the one knows the
Other not only in what he suffers from him, but more generally as a
witness who can be challenged because he is also himself accused, and
because he is not a pure gaze upon pure being any more than I am."
Respect for the alterity of fellow-men thus was predicated neither on
reciprocal identification nor on complete inaccessibility, but on common
participation in the world: "For the Other to be truly other, it does not
suffice nor is it necessary that he be a scourge, the continued threat of
an absolute reversal of pro and con, a judge himself elevated above all
contestation, without place, without relativities, faceless like an obses-
sion, and capable of crushing me with a glance into the dust of my
world. It is necessary and it suffices that he have the power to decenter
me, to oppose his centering to my own; and he can do so only because
we are not two nihilations installed in two universes of the in-itself,
incomparable, but two entries in the same Being, each accessible to but
one of us, but appearing to the Other as *practicable by right,* because
they both belong to the same Being."[50]

In lieu of negativity, Merleau-Ponty's account stressed the differentiation between ego and fellow-men, a difference growing out of the
tension implicit in being-in-the-world and reflected in the oblique connections between visibility and invisibility and between presence and
absence. The Other's body and his concrete manifestations, he wrote,
"do present to me in their own fashion what I will never be present to,
what will always be invisible to me, what I will never directly witness—an absence therefore, but not just any absence, a certain absence
and a certain difference in terms of dimensions which are from the first
common to us and which predestine the Other to be a mirror of me as
I am of him." Instead of representing a logical antithesis, ego and *alter
ego* in this view were both linked and distinguished by a concrete reversibility: "My consciousness of myself and my myth of the Other are
not two contradictories, but rather each the reverse of the other." With
its emphasis on difference, *The Visible and the Invisible* moved beyond the reflective-idealist dialectics anchored in absolute negation—a
dialectic, in Merleau-Ponty's words, "which thinks it recomposes Being by a thetic thought, by an assemblage of statements, by thesis, antithesis, and synthesis," without realizing "that every thesis is an idealization, that Being is not made up of idealizations or of things said, as
the old logic believed, but of bound wholes where signification never
is except in tendency."[51] Together with the dialectics of antithesis, the

manuscript left behind other dichotomies embraced by dialectical thinkers (including Sartre), such as the antinomies of inside and outside
and of activity and inertia: "There is not identity, nor non-identity or
non-coincidence; there is inside and outside turning about one another." Alluding to the "essential narcissism of all vision," another
passage noted that "as many painters have said, I feel myself looked
at by the things, my activity is equally passivity."[52]

On intersubjectivity, the study emphasized immersion in Being as
the common matrix sustaining human encounter. Once the *ego cogitans*
and reflective dialectics were put aside, coexistence emerged as a "reciprocal insertion and intertwining of one in the other"—or rather,
when "thinking by planes and perspectives" was abandoned, what came
to the fore were "two circles, or two vortexes, or two spheres, concentric when I live naively, and as soon as I question myself, the one
slightly decentered with respect to the other." From the same perspective, social life as a whole had to be seen not in terms of an "Us-
object" or "We-subject," but as a complex intertwining or *"Ineinander*
which nobody sees and which is not a group-soul either, neither object
nor subject, but their connective tissue."[53] Basically, the I-Other relation in Merleau-Ponty's view could be traced to the chiasm operative
in being-in-the-world and ultimately in Being itself. On the prereflective level, he wrote, "like the natural man, we situate ourselves in ourselves *and* in the things, in ourselves *and* in the Other, at the point
where, by a sort of *chiasm,* we become the others and we become the
world." Instead of entailing merger or complete divorce, ontological
differentiation implied a lateral reversibility of self and non-self: "The
chiasm is that: the reversibility. It is through it alone that there is passage from the for-itself to the for-the-Other. In reality there is neither
me nor the Other as positive, positing subjectivities; there are two cav-
erns, two opennesses, two stages where something will take place—
and which both belong to the same world, to the stage of Being. There
is not the for-itself and the for-the-Other; they are each the other side
of the other."[54]

Language and Difference: Derrida

Despite its unfinished and torso-like character, Merleau-Ponty's *The
Visible and the Invisible* has exerted a pervasive influence on phenomenological and post-phenomenological thought in France; French philosophy since the time of its publication has progressively moved into
the terrain tentatively mapped out in the manuscript. Broadly speaking,

the last decade in France has witnessed a profound disenchantment with the Cartesian *ego cogitans* and, more generally, with the legacy of Western metaphysics founded on the preeminence of a cognitive or pragmatic subjectivity; correspondingly, attention has tended to shift from epistemology to an archaeology of knowledge, preoccupied with prereflective and presubjective modes of experience. To be sure, various factors have collaborated in producing this trend, including the rise of structuralism and the reinterpretation of Freudian teachings. However, for a number of thinkers, phenomenology—especially in its postwar manifestations—has been a crucial formative influence; Jacques Derrida is probably the leading representative of this group. Although drawing inspiration from diverse sources (all of them marked by strong anti-idealist impulses), Derrida's outlook has been decisively shaped by the phenomenological movement and particularly by the ontological variant articulated initially by Heidegger and subsequently by Merleau-Ponty. In comparison with his predecessors, Derrida appears relentless in his attack on traditional epistemology and in his attempt to *deconstruct* metaphysics by eroding its egological moorings. Moreover, in exploring the prereflective matrix of thought, his perspective from the beginning accentuated a dimension hinted at in his mentors' works: the dimension of language (above all, *written language,* as contrasted to subjective-intentional *speech*). In a boldly suggestive initiative, some of his writings actually propose a reformulation of the Heideggerian ontic-ontological difference in terms of a difference lodged in the *grammatological* and *graphological* underpinnings of language.[55]

Since Derrida's views on intersubjectivity are outlined chiefly in a critical review devoted to Levinas' philosophical opus, it seems desirable to recapitulate briefly some of Levinas' arguments. This appears particularly appropriate since Levinas' posture reflects an intriguing combination of previously discussed approaches. His notion of coexistence betrays a close affinity with existential-ontological formulations of lateral encounter. In line with the central thrust of French existential phenomenology and especially with Merleau-Ponty's orientation, his presentation of interhuman contact stresses embodiment and visibility—an emphasis which operates as a corrective to traditional epistemological antinomies. Again in conformity with broader existentialist preferences, his publications reject the totalitarian overview, that is, the Hegelian conception of a final synthesis of ego and *alter ego.* As in the case of *The Visible and the Invisible,* this critique of Hegelianism extends to the scheme of thesis-antithesis as applied to the ego-*alter ego* relationship. Despite his basically transcendental status, the Other in Levinas' opinion cannot simply be identified with negativity or complete absence, but only with a partial absence or, better, an intertwining of absence and presence. In some passages, this conception of a non-antithetical differentiation leads to a vision of human community vaguely reminiscent of Heideggerian comments on co-being, in particular, to the adumbration of a community of *non-presence* where love and respect for fellow-men are joined with the renunciation of reciprocal manipulation or "managerial solicitude."[56]

While thus endorsing some central tenets of ontological phenomenology, Levinas, concerned with completely immunizing alterity from egological designs, seeks to rescue the *alter ego* from the domain of ontology (and even from the reach of ontological difference); in pursuing this aim, his writings, up to a point, implicitly replicate Sartrean motifs. Together with the author of *Being and Nothingness*, Levinas, at least in his later writings, depicts ontology as a *logic* of ontic and anonymous mundanity—which means, as a philosophy preoccupied with an ontically compact and self-enclosed universe. In opposing totalitarian fusion, his account in a Sartrean vein emphasizes the ineradicable separation, distinctness, and even mutual exteriority of individuals (although his concern focuses chiefly on the Other's distinctness, rather than the ego's). In dealing with the origin of this multiplicity of existences, Levinas—again like Sartre—takes recourse to *metaphysics,* construed as a speculative enterprise transcending the sphere of descriptive ontology and ontic finitude. A further similarity resides in the portrayal of coexistence as a visual encounter or, in Levinas' terminology, as a *face-to-face situation*—although the two thinkers part company in important details; above all, face-to-face meetings are said to imply neither fusion or communion nor an inevitable conflict. The chief difference between the two perspectives consists in Levinas' refusal (mentioned above) to identify alterity with negation or nothingness; actually, on this score his arguments chart a course not envisaged by existential phenomenology. In an effort to bypass both ontic finitude and Sartrean negativity, his commitment to absolute otherness leads him to embrace a view of transcendence approximating a non-negative or positive infinity. The same commitment carries over to his conception of the Other as a stranger who, in some passages, is depicted as "not-I" or as *alter non-ego*. "The interpersonal situation," we read in one of his works, "is not the of itself indifferent and reciprocal relationship of two interchangeable terms. The Other as Other is not only an *alter ego;* he is what I am not."[57]

In his critical rejoinder, Derrida cogently pinpoints the dilemmas inherent in the notions of an absolute otherness and a non-negative infinity. Regarding otherness, he first challenges the postulate of a transcendence completely unrelated and external to the domain of Being, construed as a set of mundane relationships. While on the whole opposed to traditional dichotomies, including the inside-outside bifurcation, Levinas repeatedly (and with growing insistence) invokes the concept of a social or non-spatial *exteriority* in order to characterize a non-manipulative mode of coexistence.[58] "Why," Derrida asks, "is it still necessary to use the word 'exteriority' which, if it has any meaning and is not simply an algebraic *x,* points obstinately toward space and light—in order to signify a non-spatial relationship?" How sensible or intelligible is it to claim "that *true* exteriority is non-spatial, and thus not (really) exteriority"? As he makes clear, transcendence or otherness cannot coherently be placed *outside* of Being, since outside belongs as much to the dimension of spatiality as inside—a dimension which seems so indelibly implanted in Being as to prevent its successful elimination in discourse. Although it may be possible to use words indiscriminately and to write or speak by employing a process of partial deletion, even such crossing out "is still a form of writing and still makes its mark in space": "One cannot erase the syntax of locality whose archaic inscription on the metal of language may have become illegible; for it is this metal itself, its somber solidity and its overly shining luster." It would be in vain, Derrida adds, in an effort "to wean language from exteriority and interiority," simply "to obliterate the words 'inside,' 'outside,' 'exterior,' 'interior,' or to banish them by decree from the vocabulary," for in doing so "one would not gain access to a language immune from the inroads of space." The ultimate reason for this impossibility, in his view, resides in the not purely cognitive or conceptual status of the mentioned terms; in other words, although they are unsatisfying and confining if approached on the level of conceptual-epistemological antinomies, the terms in the end allude to a non-cognitive (or ontological) matrix. "The meanings conveyed by the word pairs 'inside-outside' or 'light-night,' " he observes, "do not merely inhabit the proscribed terms." This is because "they do not strictly occupy a spatial location. The structure of inside-outside or day-night does not gain its significance *within* an ontically circumscribed and disoriented space; rather, it arises from an (ontologically) *inserted* origin and an *inscribed* horizon which itself is located neither inside nor outside of space."[59]

The critique of exteriority extends to the conception of fellow-man as absolutely Other or as *alter non-ego*. On a purely logical level, Derrida notes, the conception gives rise to insoluble paradoxes—which indicate that "the phrase 'infinitely other' or 'absolutely other' cannot be coherently thought or stated." Undoubtedly, otherness contains a reference beyond itself: the absolutely Other "can be what he is only if he is other, that is, other *than* (something); but *other than* must mean *other than* myself. From this point on, however, he is no longer divorced from the relation to an ego; thus he is no longer infinitely or absolutely Other." Furthermore, unless stabilized by a referential point, otherness has a vertiginous quality: "The infinitely Other can be what he is—infinitely other—only by being absolutely not the self-same, more particularly: by being other than himself (or *non-ego*). Yet, in being other than himself, he is not what he is, and thus not infinitely other." Derrida's point here is not simply to delight in logical puzzles but rather to penetrate these puzzles and discover their detrimental effects on interpersonal encounter. As long as intersubjectivity is viewed as an I-Other relation, he insists, the treatment of the Other as absolute stranger or *alter non-ego* deprives him of his equality as an ego and ultimately destroys his alterity itself. "The Other as *alter ego*," he writes, "signifies the Other as another who is irreducible to *my* ego, precisely because he is himself an ego or has the form of an ego. The ego-quality of the Other permits him to say 'I' in the same manner as myself; and this is why he is Other, and not a stone or a speechless entity *in my concrete economy*," that is, in the arrangement of my world. If the Other were not recognized strictly as another ego, he adds, "he would be completely submerged in mundanity and could not, like an ego, function as origin of the world"; as a result, "his entire alterity would collapse." Conversely, just as the Other's ego-quality sustains his alterity, my ego-status cannot be construed as absolute "self-sameness" untouched by otherness. If "the Other cannot be absolutely exterior to the self-same without ceasing to be other," we read, this implies that "the self-same is not a self-enclosed totality, an identity playing with itself or with the mere appearance of alterity"; for "how could there be a 'play of sameness' if alterity were not already *in* sameness in the sense of an incursion or inherence?"[60]

As Derrida observes, the notion of absolute otherness as formulated by Levinas tends to have as a corollary the assumption of a completely non-negative and therefore positive infinity—an assumption beset by the same quandaries. Given the paradoxes attached to the identification of alterity with complete strangeness, he states, infinity cannot be approached directly (*intentione recta*): "The infinitely

Other or the infinity of the Other cannot mean the Other as positive infinity, that is, as God or mirror-image of God. The infinitely Other would not be what he is—other—if he were a positive infinity and if he did not contain within himself the negativity of the indefinite (or non-positive), of the *apeiron.*" The quandary, according to Derrida, prevails inescapably as long as one remains within the context of (intelligible) language—a context in which, as previously suggested, Being reverberates at least in an indirect or *inscribed* fashion. "Positive infinity (God)—provided these terms have any sense—cannot be infinitely other," we read. "If one thinks, as Levinas does, that positive infinity tolerates and even requires or entails infinite alterity, then one must renounce all language, and first of all the words 'infinite' and 'other.'" From this vantage point, Levinas' philosophy alludes to a basically "nameless" sphere—but by relying on language which cannot possibly be nameless: "From the moment that one attempts to envisage infinity as a positive plenitude (as in the case of Levinas' non-negative transcendence), the Other becomes unthinkable, impossible, and unutterable. Perhaps Levinas calls or beckons us to this unthinkable-impossible-unutterable region beyond Being and (traditional) Logos; but then this call must in turn be unthinkable and unutterable."[61]

Once positive infinity or plenitude is put aside, otherness needs to be articulated in the language of finitude—including the terminology of the in-finite (as the reverse side of the finite): "If I cannot designate the irreducible (infinite) alterity of the Other except through the negation of spatial (finite) exteriority this may be due to the circumstance that the meaning of alterity is finite or not positively infinite." Viewed on the level of finitude, however, otherness appears intimately linked with mortality and being-unto-death—themes familiar from Heidegger's discussion of co-being. "The Other cannot be what he is—in-finitely other—except in the milieu of finitude and mortality (mine *and* his)." According to Derrida, the stress on finitude is particularly appropriate in view of Levinas' reliance on face-to-face encounter; for how can embodiment be conceived outside of concrete spatiality? "To neutralize space in the description of the Other in order to make room for positive infinity," he notes, "does this not mean to bracket the essential finitude of the face (its visual language), a face which, as Levinas himself insists, is *'body'* and not simply the corporeal metaphor of abstract thought?" Against this background, positive infinity and intersubjective encounter emerge as incompatible. At least "within philosophy and within language," Derrida comments, "one cannot simultaneously vindicate the themes of positive infinity and of the 'face' construed as non-metaphorical unity of body, glance, speech, and thought." For "if the face is *body,* then it is mortal; but the in-finite otherness of death cannot be reconciled with infinite otherness seen as positivity and plenary presence (God)." The reason for this incompatibility is that finitude and infinity are not two positive domains and not even two absolutely antithetical regions which might be neatly juxtaposed; rather, both are reflections of an oblique and elementary *difference* which carries Being's inscription: "If therefore God is *nothing* (definite), if he is no living thing because he is *everything,* does this not mean that he is simultaneously all and nothing, life and death? Which in turn means that God is, appears or is *nameable* only in the difference of all and nothing, life and death—in the difference, and ultimately as the difference itself."[62]

In his comments on difference, Derrida refers to Heideggerian teachings, and especially to the notion of ontic-ontological difference expressing the oblique linkage between Being and ontic phenomena. According to Heidegger, he observes, "only the difference is fundamental" in the sense that "being is nothing outside the existent (or ontic beings)." Instead of securing an ontically self-enclosed universe, Heideggerian ontology in his view carries an open-ended, emancipatory thrust: "Far from foreclosing difference, Being which is other than the other and other than the self-same" on the contrary "liberates or makes room for difference and is itself what it is only in and through this emancipation." Taken in its Heideggerian sense, incidentally, difference is not synonymous with logical antithesis: "In reality there is not even a *distinction* in the usual sense of the word, between Being and existent. For fundamental reasons—and especially because Being is nothing outside the existent and because its disclosure hinges on the ontic-ontological difference—it is impossible to avoid ontic metaphors in order to articulate Being and let it circulate in language; this is why Heidegger depicts language as the 'revealing-concealing advent of Being itself.' " Seen in this light, Levinas' resort to metaphysics, establishing it as a separate domain taking precedence over ontology, merely resuscitates the speculative treatment of ontic relations whose quandaries have been exposed by Heidegger. By refusing "to accord any place or dignity to the ontic-ontological difference (viewing it merely as a ruse) and by extolling *metaphysics* as the intra-ontic dynamics of ethical transcendence (meaning: the dynamics of the respectful approach of one existent toward another), Levinas confirms Heidegger's argument: for does not the latter view metaphysics (or metaphysical ontology) as the oblivion of Being and as obfuscation of the ontic-ontological difference?"[63]

Although trying to bypass ontology, metaphysical speculation in

Derrida's opinion presupposes what it denies; above all, the cultivation of ethical respect—so strongly accentuated in Levinas' notion of face-to-face encounter—seems inconceivable without an ontological reference point. "Eyes and mouth," Derrida writes, "form a face only if, beyond the level of need, they are able to 'let be,' that is, if they see and say what is such as it is, and if they thus reach the Being of what is." Just as vision relies on a context of visibility, thought and language are possible only as "the thinking and saying *of* Being" (in the double sense of the genitive); therefore, "the metaphysics of the face *incorporates* the thought of Being and thus presupposes the difference between Being and existent which it simultaneously disavows." According to Derrida, the ontological reference contained in the notion of the face has implications for intersubjectivity, for only the posture of *letting be* can preserve the integrity of the Other's alterity. "If to comprehend Being means to be able to 'let be' (that is, to respect Being in its essence and reality and to assume responsibility for one's respect)," he states, "then comprehension of Being always concerns or relates to alterity, and above all, to the alterity of the Other in all his originality: one can only let be that which one is not. If therefore one always has to let Being be, and if to think implies letting be, then Being is indeed the other (or otherness) of thought."[64]

In delineating the pertinence of ontology for social life, Derrida's account fleshes out the Heideggerian vision of authentic co-being—a mode of collaboration characterized by respect and emancipatory care rather than by indifference, amalgamation, or deliberate manipulation. Levinas' ethical concerns are in this regard maintained, although on a different basis. "The thought—or at least the precomprehension—of Being," we read, *"conditions* (in its own way which excludes every ontic determination through principles, causes, or premises) the recognition of the essence of existents, for example, of someone *as* Other or other self; it conditions the *respect* for the Other *as what he is:* Other. Without this recognition which is not a mere cognition, or let us say: without this 'letting-be' of other beings existing apart from me in their own essence (first of all in their alterity), no ethics would be possible." In supporting interpersonal respect, ontologically motivated *recognition* also makes room for the acceptance of individual freedom and uncoerced human development: "To let the Other be in his reality and essence as Other means that what gains access to thought, and (or) what thought gains access to, is the domain of essence and reality; and also what is presupposed by both: Being. Without the latter no 'letting-be' would be possible, especially not the letting-be manifest in respect and in ethical imperatives addressed to a human freedom." In terms of social aggregation, ontology and ontological difference point to a non-manipulative type of community which coincides neither with an Us-object nor with a fully integrated We-subject. Reference to Being or "ontological anticipation," he affirms, "inhabits and founds language and along with it the possibility of all co-being or being-with; what it renders possible above all is a much more original or genuine form of co-being (*Mitsein*) than any of the modes or variants with which it has often been confused: such as solidarity, team work, or companionship." In permitting "to *let* others *be* in their truth," he adds, "in freeing dialog and sustaining face-to-face situations, the thought of Being is thus as close as possible to non-violence."[65]

CRITICAL MARXISM

The issue of intersubjectivity in our century has not been a monopoly of the phenomenological movement, although its members have probably given the subject its most thoroughgoing treatment. The issue has also been considered by spokesmen of such intellectual trends as symbolic interactionism, role theory, ordinary language philosophy, and communications analysis.[1] I want to draw attention briefly to developments within the confines of Marxist thought, because of Marxism's social-political prominence and because of its overtly non-individualistic premises. Given its strong critique of bourgeois individualism and its emphasis on the social-economic infrastructures of private initiatives, Marxism (and socialism in general) might be expected to be particularly concerned with, and to offer fertile insights into, the problematic of intersubjectivity and social interaction; on the whole, however, this expectation is disappointed. At least in its official version (that epitomized in Stalinism), dialectical materialism has tended to construe social formations of various types as empirical collectivities enveloping their individual participants—a conception which obviously remains predicated on traditional empiricist epistemology. It seems to me that deviations from this approach can be found chiefly among proponents of critical Marxism, and especially among the intellectual architects of the so-called Frankfurt school and its program of critical theory; due to his assault on orthodox determinism and his pervasive influence on Frankfurt theorists, some of Georg Lukács' early writings can also usefully be included in this deviant category.[2]

My aim here is not to offer a comprehensive survey of critical

Marxist literature, but to highlight some parallels between facets of this literature and the phenomenological arguments, especially those advanced by the French school. As I intend to show, critical Marxism (broadly defined) was initially wedded, in the domain of social interaction, to the conception of a homogeneous proletarian class bent on remolding social reality through revolutionary action, a conception akin to Sartre's notions of the We-subject and of the fused group. In Lukács' *History and Class Consciousness* (first published in 1923), the proletariat was portrayed, in quasi-Hegelian fashion, as the incarnation of absolute self-reflection or of a completely self-transparent subjectivity—a subjectivity which, by gaining insight into its own intentionality through contact with the world, was capable of transforming that world in its own image. Regarding other modes of social relations not reducible to this type of group subjectivity, the study discussed mainly pre-modern, semi-organic life patterns and individualistic-atomistic interactions (structured basically in a *serial* manner) prevalent in bourgeois-industrial societies. In large measure, Lukács' views were echoed in initial formulations of the Frankfurt perspective, including Max Horkheimer's programmatic essay (of 1937) differentiating *critical* from *traditional* theory. Only some of Adorno's later writings seriously depart from these precedents and, moving beyond Hegelian and general-metaphysical premises, adumbrate a mode of co-being diverging from both empirical aggregation and the fusion of self-transparent egos.

History and Class Consciousness: Lukács

As presented in *History and Class Consciousness,* social development signifies growing human self-awareness and autonomy, that is, a story of man's slow awakening from the slumber of a prerational or pre-reflective existence. Pinpointing a central motif of the study, the chapter on "Reification and the Consciousness of the Proletariat" asserts that "the historical process in its uniqueness, in its dialectical advances as well as its dialectical reversals is nothing but an incessant struggle to reach higher levels of truth and of the (social) *self-knowledge of man.*" According to Lukács, moreover, genuine human self-knowledge is not merely a cognitive achievement, but carries distinct practical-purposive connotations; at least since the dawn of the modern era, successful self-understanding is predicated on man's ability to see himself not merely as spectator but as the constitutive source of the targets of knowledge, including social and historical phenomena. "Modern philosophy sets itself this problem or task," the same chapter notes: "refusing to accept it as something that has arisen independently of the knowing subject (e.g., through God's creation), it seeks to grasp the world as *its own product.*" Running through the different schools of modern thought, "from the systematic doubt and the *cogito ergo sum* of Descartes, over Hobbes, Spinoza and Leibniz," we read, "there is a direct developmental thrust whose decisive strand, rich in variations, is the conception that the object of cognition can be known by us only because and to the extent in which it has been created or produced by ourselves."[3] Applied to the domain of self-knowledge, the passage suggests that the goal can only be reached once man emerges as the determining agent of his own life and concrete living patterns.

In tracing this emergence, the study delineates a number of successive stages of social interaction. As Lukács points out, the preconditions of self-knowledge were entirely lacking during pre-modern or "pre-capitalist" times; engulfed by the forces and constraints of nature, man was unable to adopt a reflective stance which would allow him to understand himself and his society. "In feudal society," he writes, "man could not become aware of himself as a social being because his social relations were still mainly natural in character. Society in its entirety was still far too unorganized and had far too little control over the entire range of relations between men to be able to appear to consciousness as *the* reality of man." The unorganized condition of society, according to the study, was reflected chiefly in the profuse array of castes, estates, and corporations; in the *particularism* of social customs and economic practices; and in the non-deliberate or *ascriptive* basis of individual roles in society. "The most striking distinction, and the one which primarily concerns us," we read, "is that pre-capitalist societies are economically much less *cohesive* than capitalism, and that their various sectors are much more self-sufficient and economically less closely interdependent than in the capitalist case." Due to the absence of interdependence and cohesiveness, pre-modern societies in Lukács' view were basically resistant to reflection. The "stratified order of estates," he asserts, concealed the connection between the "life of the estate" and the "total fabric of society": "Consciousness is fixated either directly or immediately on privileges (as in the case of the knights during the Reformation) or else—no less directly—on the particular element of society to which the privileges are attached (as in the case of the guilds)."[4]

According to *History and Class Consciousness,* the disjointed character of pre-modern social existence was not affected by the presence of a state organization and its bureaucratic apparatus. On the one hand, those in control of state power did not generally use that power to mold society in conformity with their social-economic principles; rather, they were preoccupied with the possession of political dominion or the ability to wield *"directly this authority itself."* On the other hand, a large part of society remained virtually untouched by the state organization, managing to live out "its 'natural' existence in almost complete independence from the fortunes of the state." To the degree that social conditions were regulated by legal norms and sanctions, these norms usually were tailored to particular circumstances, rather than extending their influence through society as a whole in the fashion of the modern "rule of law." "The division of society into estates, castes, and similar orders," we read, "means in effect that the organizational as well as conceptual status of these 'natural' positions remains economically and socially non-transparent, differently phrased: that the pure traditionalism of naturally grown conditions must be translated directly into legal institutions." The intimate link between legal institutions and concrete life patterns erected a further barrier to the reflective penetration of the structure of society, thereby also blocking the path to human self-cognition. "Economic and legal categories are in their content or *substantively so interwoven as to be inseparable,"* Lukács observes. "In Hegelian terms, political economy has objectively not yet reached the level of 'being-for-itself'; thus, such a society cannot offer a vantage point from which the economic basis of all social relations could be made conscious and recognized."[5]

The opacity characterizing pre-modern life forms was removed at least in part with the rise of bourgeois or capitalist society. The emergence of capitalism, *History and Class Consciousness* notes, shifted the accent from naturally grown conditions to modes of economic production and productive relations, thereby tightening the connection between social life and human motivations, and implementing the long-range *socialization of society* (as distinguished from the realm of nature). "Capitalism destroyed both the spatial-temporal barriers between different countries and regions and also the legal partitions between stratified estates; the formal equality among men inaugurated under its auspices erased progressively those economic patterns which controlled the metabolism between man and nature in earlier periods. As a result, man turns into a social being in the proper sense of the term, while society becomes *the* reality for man." The mentioned process of socialization, according to Lukács, was a precondition for the intelligibility of social relations; it also was the essential prerequisite for man's ability to recognize himself as autonomous social agent. Whereas in pre-modern times the determining forces of existence operated entirely "behind the back of the motivation of historical actors," and thus beyond the pale of their consciousness, motivations and social structure began to converge in the modern era. The difference between the two epochs, he writes, is that in the modern era "economic factors are no longer concealed 'behind' consciousness but are operative *in* consciousness itself (albeit in unconscious or repressed fashion). With the development of capitalism—that is, with the abolition of feudal estates and the formation of a *purely economically* structured society— class consciousness enters the stage of *potential awareness;* social conflict from now on is reflected in the ideological contest over consciousness and over the concealment or disclosure of the class character of society."[6]

Despite its progressive and liberating role, capitalism in Lukács' view was unable to bring to full fruition the socialization of human life; while pointing the way toward complete rationality, the social agents heralding the new age were bound to perform their role in partial ignorance. The class, we read, "which implemented this basic transformation—that is, the bourgeoisie—executed its function largely without awareness; the social forces unleashed by it and which in turn catapulted it into the limelight tend to confront it like a 'second nature,' a nature more inhuman and impenetrable than the structure of feudalism ever was." In contrast to preceding periods—and also in contrast to the situation of marginal modern groups—the factors conditioning bourgeois behavior are not simply an "external" destiny rigidly segregated from human purposes; rather, they manifest themselves as a dialectical conflict within class consciousness, simultaneously animating and obstructing human motivations. "On the one hand, capitalism is the first system of production capable, at least potentially, of permeating and reshaping the entire fabric of society, with the result that, in theory, the bourgeoisie should be able to acquire from this central vantage point an (imputed) awareness of the totality of productive processes. On the other hand, the position of the capitalist class in the economy and the interests governing its actions prevent this class from obtaining a full grasp of its own productive system even in theoretical terms." The limits of capitalism, Lukács notes, thus reside in restrictions of economic productivity *and* in intrinsic limitations of intelligibility: the fact that the bourgeoisie "must necessarily remain ignorant of the objective economic barriers of its system expresses itself as an internal, dialectical contradiction in its class consciousness."[7]

This contradiction results from the individualistic and quasi-atomistic structure of capitalism—in Sartrean terms, from the serial character of bourgeois social relations. The antagonism in awareness, *History and Class Consciousness* states, is intimately linked with the "insoluble dialectical conflict running through the capitalist system between the 'individual' and the 'social' principle, that is, between the function of capital as private property and its objective economic function." Although, in the words of the "Communist Manifesto," capital is a "social rather than personal force," it is a force "whose movements are guided by the interests of individual owners of capital, individuals who cannot perceive and are necessarily indifferent to the social ramifications of their actions; as a consequence, the social principle or the social function of capital can prevail only without their knowledge and, as it were, against their will and behind their backs." In Lukács' account, this conflict between individual initiative and social-economic structure forms "one of the most decisive features characterizing bourgeois class consciousness." Although the bourgeoisie "behaves as a class in the objective-economic evolution of society," he writes, "it can comprehend the unfolding of this self-instigated development only as an external, passively endured process governed by inexorable laws." Viewing economic life "consistently and necessarily from the vantage point of the individual capitalist," bourgeois existence is indelibly marked by the "sharp confrontation between the individual and the overpowering supra-personal 'law of nature' controlling society"—or, to use Sartrean vocabulary again, by the juxtaposition of individual praxis and the passivity of the practico-inert field. In terms of traditional Marxist analysis, the dichotomy can be formulated as the "opposition between ideology and economic infrastructure," or, more generally, as the divorce of theory from praxis. The dialectic of bourgeois class consciousness, we read, "is grounded in the irreconcilable opposition between the (capitalist) individual—that is, the individual construed after the fashion of the individual capitalist—and the 'natural'-inexorable process of development, a process not amenable to conscious-reflective penetration; thus theory and praxis are placed in irremediable antithesis."[8]

The conflicts beleaguering bourgeois existence form the essential backdrop for Marxism and its intellectual precursor, Hegelian philosophy. As Lukács points out, German idealist thought as a whole was marked by an urge to overcome the dichotomy between individual freedom and objectivist determinism, and to render reality reflectively transparent by unearthing its human genesis. The common goal of idealist thinkers from Kant to Hegel, he writes, was to discover that *subject* or human agent who "can be construed as the productive source of the totality of objective contents"—differently phrased, to advance to "a level of objectivity and of the genesis of objects where the dualism of subject and object (and also the bifurcation of thought and existence) is transcended, that is, where subject and object coincide and become identical." Without denying the plausibility of dualistic constructions for limited purposes, an effort was made to grasp every event ultimately "as the product of this identical subject-object and every duality as a special case derived from this primal unity." In the idealist context, the endeavor reached its most mature expression in Hegelian dialectics. Moving beyond the moralist or aesthetic concerns of his predecessors, Hegel paved the way to the effective resolution of past dilemmas by turning his attention to history and to man's dialectical role in historical development; with this turn, "the genetic problem—the issue of the production of the producer of knowledge, of the removal of the irrational (and inaccessible) 'thing-in-itself,' and of the revival of the 'buried man'—is transformed concretely into a question of *dialectical method.*" From a historical-dialectical perspective, man was finally able to emerge as constitutive social agent, thus revealing the underlying nexus of theory and practice and of freedom and necessity. At this point, we read, "the notion of reality as our product loses its otherwise more or less fictitious character"; for, "once we are able to perceive the whole of reality as history (more specifically: as our history, since there is no other), we have in fact raised ourselves to the position from which reality can be seen as our 'activity.' "[9]

While generally in sympathy with its aims, Lukács finds Hegel's approach marred by its speculative bent and its proclivity to mystification. Despite its focus on historical genesis, in his view the approach failed to clarify the decisive question of reflective thought, namely, *"the question regarding the subject of activity or of genesis."* Instead of pinpointing the historical We-subject—the We which is the "subject of history" and "whose action effectively constitutes history"— Hegel located the "identical subject-object" in the "world spirit" manifest in the "spirits of individual peoples," a world spirit whose intentions are implemented behind the backs of human agents, so that "the action becomes something transcendent for the actor himself." According to Lukács, this is precisely the point where idealist philosophy "gets caught in the hopeless labyrinth of conceptual mythology" and where Hegelianism in particular is "inescapably driven" into this maze; for, "having failed to uncover the identical subject-object in the historical context itself, it is forced to move beyond history and to erect the empire of complete rationality in a trans-historical realm, a realm from which history can be seen as a mere stage and its evolution as 'ruse of reason.' " This is also the point where Marxism provides the crucial corrective to idealist obfuscation by shifting the emphasis from mythological spirits to the struggle of concrete historical classes, and especially to the constitutive historical role of the proletariat. The continuation of Hegelian thought, Lukács observes, and of "dialectics as the true method of history is reserved for that class which is capable of discovering in its own existence and life-experience the identical subject-object, the subject of activity or the 'We' of historical genesis: the proletariat."[10]

Viewed against the long-range process of growing self-consciousness, the emergence of the proletariat fulfills the goal of social transparency. With its rise, the study asserts, "conscious knowledge of social reality reaches its completion; and this is due to the fact that the class outlook of the proletariat provides the vantage point from which the total fabric of society becomes visible." In grasping the structure of society, moreover, the proletariat does not merely gain access to an alien subject matter; although distinguished by cognitive insight, its status is not simply that of a "cognitive subject" as defined by traditional (Cartesian and Kantian) epistemology. The proletariat, we read, "is not a detached spectator of the (historical) process, nor is it merely an active and passive ingredient of the social totality; rather, the growth and development of its cognitive insight, on the one hand, and its own growth and development in the course of history, on the other, are just the two sides of the same real process." By virtue of its role as subject-object, the existence and concrete practice of the proletariat are intimately linked with its cognitive awareness of the social structure and of reality as a whole. According to *History and Class Consciousness,* the unity of theory and practice is only "one manifestation of the social-historical situation of the proletariat—of the circumstance that from its vantage point knowledge of totality and self-knowledge coincide since it is simultaneously the subject and object of its own cognition." In other words: "The self-knowledge of the proletariat converges with the objective comprehension of the nature of society."[11]

In accentuating the role of proletarian class consciousness and its dual accomplishment, the study does not simply rely on contingent psychological dispositions or an empirical *state of mind.* While relatively far removed from the concerns of the phenomenological movement, Lukács shares the aversion of (transcendental) phenomenology to psychologism and to the confusion of rationality with empirical mental processes. Appealing to Engels' statement that contingent human motivations cannot be directly identified with the forces behind historical evolution, the chapter on "Class Consciousness" comments that "the essence of scientific Marxism consists in the realization that the real motor forces of history are independent of man's (psychological) awareness of them." The chief defect of psychologism, according to the study, resides in its inability to segregate *correct* and *false* modes of consciousness, which also prevents it from clarifying the actual function of false awareness in historical dynamics. To overcome these drawbacks, critical Marxism (together with phenomenology) must differentiate between essence and appearance and between genuine and contingent-empirical types of consciousness and cognitive insight; in line with its attachment to dialectical method and *total* social analysis, a crucial Marxist tool for effecting this differentiation can be found in the category of "objective (or essential) possibility." "By relating consciousness to the whole fabric of society," the chapter asserts, "it becomes possible to infer those thoughts and feelings which men in a given life situation *would have* if they were *completely able* to assess this situation and the interests arising from it both with reference to immediate actions and with reference to the social structure congruent with these interests; in other words: it becomes possible to infer the thoughts and feelings appropriate to their objective situation." As used in the study, the term *class consciousness* refers basically to this imputed and objectively possible mode of awareness rather than to a contingent attitude. "Class consciousness denotes in fact the rationally appropriate reaction or outlook which is thus *imputed* to a particular typical position in the process of production; such consciousness is, therefore, neither the sum nor the average of the thoughts and feelings of the individual members composing a class."[12]

To penetrate to the essential or objectively possible form of consciousness is always an arduous undertaking; even in the case of the proletariat, the empirical thoughts and feelings of workers are not immediately synonymous with rational awareness. Just as, under phenomenological auspices, access to essential insight is possible only through bracketing or by wrenching reason away from objectivist beliefs, proletarian rationality requires a strenuous process of awakening and activation; due to the convergence of knowledge and self-knowledge, this process also marks the path of the proletariat's maturation as a class. Without refinement or activation, Lukács notes, the factual views of workers usually display only a false awareness, even if this falseness conceals a latent aspiration or "intentionality toward correctness or truth." The presence of this latent intentionality, he writes, "signifies by no means that this thrust can manifest itself automatically, without the active collaboration of the proletariat. On the contrary: only through the intensification of consciousness, through conscious activity and conscious self-criticism can the mere aspiration toward truth be stripped of its false guises and be transformed into a genuinely correct, historically significant and socially revolutionary form of knowledge." For the typical industrial worker, the requisite activation involves a reversal of his immediate outlook. Enmeshed in the capitalist system of production, the worker initially reflects the thorough objectivism which characterizes that system; in the words of the study, he "appears first of all as the pure and merely passive *object* of social events." The dawn of self-awareness does not abruptly terminate this reified condition, but yields insight into the worker's function as *commodity* in the production process: "To the extent that he is still practically incapable of raising himself above his role as object, his consciousness is in effect the *self-consciousness of a commodity;* differently phrased: it is the self-knowledge or self-revelation of the capitalist system with its reliance on the production and exchange of commodities." Yet, the addition of self-knowledge to the economic structure signals the beginning of a qualitative transformation; by virtue of the nexus of theory and practice, the proletariat as self-conscious commodity turns into an agency of radical innovation: "The self-awareness of the worker as commodity is already as knowledge a practical act; that is to say, this awareness accomplishes an objective, structural change in the object of knowledge." The outlook of the proletariat simultaneously marks the zenith of bourgeois reification and also *"subjectively* the point where this system can be raised to consciousness and be transcended in practice."[13]

Before proceeding to the Frankfurt school, I would like to indicate some quandaries besetting Lukács' study and also some places where his analysis seems to be pushed, by its own momentum, beyond the confines of subject-object identity or a Hegelian We-subject. As it appears to me, little effort is required to show that his preoccupation with reflection and self-knowledge is not politically innocuous; in line with Bacon's equation of knowledge and power, the progressive historical unfolding of consciousness and rationality coincides with the consolidation of man's dominion over all non-human elements. "The 'realm of freedom,' the end of the 'pre-history of mankind,' " we read, "signifies precisely that reification and the hitherto objectified relations between men begin to yield their power to *man*." The growth of class consciousness is politically crucial since it ultimately legitimates the proletariat's exercise of power. As the study observes, "for a class to be ripe for dominion means that its interests and consciousness enable it to organize the whole of society in accordance with these interests; and the finally decisive issue in every class struggle is the question which class can marshal this capacity and this consciousness at a given moment." In this context class consciousness is clearly not the same as a purely contemplative posture; rather, as Lukács admits, it is closely linked with the "role of violence in history," for a variety of reasons: "First, the preconditions enabling particular class interests to prevail can frequently only be established by means of the most ruthless use of force." More importantly, "it is precisely in violent circumstances, in situations where classes are locked in a life-and-death struggle, that questions of class consciousness emerge as the ultimately determining factors." These considerations are poignantly illustrated in the proletariat's struggle against capitalism; in this circumstance, the class consciousness of the proletariat is not just vaguely compatible, but directly coterminous with domination. "Thus it becomes intelligible," the study notes, "why for the proletariat and *only* for the proletariat the correct insight into the *nature of society* constitutes a power-factor of the first magnitude and perhaps the lastly decisive weapon."[14]

Although useful for explaining the role of modern technology, the equation of knowledge and power has limited plausibility on Marxist premises. According to traditional Marxist teachings—teachings which are not contested by Lukács—the history of class struggles is not a perpetual or self-contained process but intrinsically points beyond itself, in the direction of a classless society, that is, a society in which class domination and thereby domination as such comes to an end. Seen against this background, the vocation of the proletariat is to abolish power, not to exercise it; its task is not merely to inaugurate a new form of dominion but a stage of powerlessness or non-domination. To accomplish this, however, entails the dismantling of the prevailing class structure and the proletariat's self-elimination as a class. As Lukács eloquently observes: *"The proletariat only completes its mission by annihilating and transcending itself, by ushering in the classless society as the outcome of its class struggle.* The struggle for this society—in which the dictatorship of the proletariat is a mere phase—is not only a battle waged against the external enemy, the bourgeoisie, but simultaneously a struggle of the proletariat *against itself*."[15] Assuming the correctness of these statements, the study's emphasis on consciousness—and Lukács consistently identifies *true* knowledge or conscious-ness with (proletarian) class consciousness—seems incongruous. If the proletariat is destined to transcend itself as a class, this destiny also embraces the elimination or transcendence of class consciousness; in this case, however, the maturation of proletarian self-knowledge can-not constitute the culmination of social-historical development. In por-traying the mission of the proletariat, *History and Class Consciousness* is led, by the logic of its own arguments, beyond the boundaries of a perspective focused on class consciousness or We-subjectivity (perhaps in the direction of a Heideggerian "end of metaphysics")—although its author did not pursue these implications.

The mentioned incongruence is reinforced by Lukács' professed anti-utopianism. In terms of his analysis, Marxist goals cannot simply be viewed as utopias or speculative fictions, since utopian and empiri-cist approaches are merely the two sides of bourgeois reification. "Rei-fied consciousness must remain trapped simultaneously and inescapably in the two extremes of crude empiricism and abstract utopianism." The projected classless society, together with the self-transcendence of the proletariat and its class consciousness, cannot merely be a utopian vi-sion, but must somehow be anticipated in the proletariat's concrete life-experience. In other words, the slowly maturing outlook of the proletariat must itself contain features which, deviating from tradi-tional epistemological models, facilitate a transgression of conscious-ness. Some passages in the study suggest such a deviant conception— again without elaborating its connotations. From a utopian vantage point, Lukács writes, "consciousness approaches society so-to-speak from another world and leads it from the false path it has followed back to the right one." In the case of the working class, by contrast, "consciousness does not reside outside the real process of history." The proletariat, he adds, "does not have 'ideals to realize.' Translated into practice, its consciousness can only implement those decisions which have been ripened and prepared by the dialectic of history; it can never practically bypass the course of history and impose on it mere desires or ideas."[16] However, if proletarian awareness does not "reside out-side," and is unable in practice to bypass, social-historical development, it is difficult to see how it can plausibly be portrayed as the productive source of this development. Instead of emphasizing its constitutive subject-object role, would it not perhaps be preferable to construe class consciousness in a quasi-ontological vein, as participant in an ongoing historical *disclosure of Being* (or, with Derrida, as an inscribed origin in the play of difference)?

Critical Theory and Non-identity:
Horkheimer and Adorno

Lukács' *History and Class Consciousness* exerted a powerful influence on all non-orthodox versions of Marxist thought in our century; its impact probably was strongest on the founders of the Frankfurt school, especially on Max Horkheimer and Theodor Adorno. Attracted to the working class movement, largely on social-political grounds, but intellectually repelled by the crude determinism propounded by official Marxist doctrine, Horkheimer and Adorno discovered in Lukács' study a way of reconciling their political and philosophical convictions. The echo of Lukács' arguments can be detected in the founders' early attempts to sketch the contours of critical theory (modeled after Marx's critique of political economy); it is particularly noticeable in Horkheimer's programmatic pre-war essay on "Traditional and Critical Theory," which functioned largely as a statement of the school's perspective and was endorsed in this sense by other members. As presented in the essay, *traditional theory* was basically a synonym for the spectator mentality and individualistic epistemology arising from the serial organization of bourgeois society; by contrast, the term *critical theory* sought to capture the striving for self-knowledge and reflective self-determination characterizing anti- or post-capitalist trends, a striving in which cognitive insight is predicated on the constitutive role and productive autonomy of the knowing subject.

In agreement with Lukács' discussion of bourgeois mentality, Horkheimer's account located the source of traditional theory in the Cartesian subject-object bifurcation and detected its aim in the detached observation of empirical processes, independently of the issue of social genesis. "Theory in the traditional sense as it was inaugurated by Descartes and is accepted today everywhere by the specialized sciences," we read, "organizes experience in the light of questions posed by the reproduction of life within the prevailing social structure." From its vantage point, "the social genesis of problems, as well as the concrete situations in which science is applied and the purposes it is made to serve, are all treated as extraneous to science itself." The objective of Horkheimer's essay was not to deprecate the expansion of technological knowledge accomplished under the auspices of the traditional model of cognition; these pursuits were unobjectionable as long as they were animated by the "concrete awareness of their own limitations." Once identified with reason and erected into a universal paradigm of thought, however, traditional theory disclosed its repressive qualities as a manifestation of bourgeois reification. "The technological advances of the bourgeois era," the essay stated, "are inseparably linked with the functioning of the scientific enterprise; under its guidance, facts are incorporated into scientific knowledge relevant to given circumstances while available knowledge is simultaneously applied to facts. Without question, this enterprise is an (important) element in the continuous transformation and development of existing society." To the extent, however, that the "conception of theory" operative in these contexts is "absolutized" or treated "as though it were grounded in the essence of cognition or some other non-historical premises," it quickly "turns into a reified, ideological category."[17]

According to Horkheimer, the ideological character of traditional theory derived chiefly from the concealment of its social basis. Contrary to its claim of neutrality, bourgeois science reflected the rigid division of labor and serial fragmentation of social relations prevalent under capitalism. "The traditional notion of theory," he observed, "is abstracted or distilled from the scientific enterprise as it functions in the context of the division of labor at a given stage; it corresponds to the activity of the scientist as it takes place alongside all the other particular activities performed in society, but without any immediately transparent connection with or between them." In terms of the essay, the proliferation of specialized activities was an outgrowth of the capitalist attachment to individual economic initiative—an attachment which Horkheimer, together with Lukács, regarded as mainspring of the "antinomies of bourgeois thought," especially of the antithesis between freedom and necessity or between individual praxis and social determinism: "Instead of deriving from the nature of their subject matter, the seeming self-sufficiency of activities and work processes actually parallels the seeming autonomy of individual agents in the capitalist economy; while feigning to enact individual decisions, the latter—even in their most complex calculations—are simple cogs in the nontransparent social mechanism." Although extolled as the pillar of economic production, the individual under capitalism was basically a pawn implementing the structural dictates of society (elevated to the status of a "second nature"): "The whole perceptible world as it exists for a member of bourgeois society and is interpreted by the traditional world-view correlated with that society appears to the perceiver as a collection of facts which is simply there and must be accepted as such. The analytical thought of each individual belongs itself to those social reactions which promote social adaptation in a manner most congruent with prevailing needs."[18]

In contrast to the antinomies and dilemmas beleaguering bourgeois thought, critical theory was meant to uncover the unifying linkages behind traditional epistemology by turning to the domain of social genesis or concrete-historical human praxis. In Horkheimer's view, important guideposts for this endeavor could be found in the teachings of German idealist philosophy from Kant to Hegel. "In relating substantive content, that is, the seemingly irreducible facts observed by the specialized scientist, to human production," he stated, "the critical theory of society is basically in accord with German idealism." Although relatively close to Cartesianism, Kantian thought paved the road to the idea of a *supra-individual activity;* while still paying tribute to traditional antinomies, Kant clearly "understood that behind the discrepancy between fact and theory experienced by the scientist in his professional pursuits there lies a deeper unity, namely, the 'general subjectivity' on which individual cognition depends." A further advance toward this unity was contained in Hegelianism, which wrestled with the "unresolved problematic of the relation between activity and passivity, a priori premises and sense data, philosophy and psychology." "Hegel," we read, "pinpointed and developed these contradictions, but finally reconciled them in a higher intellectual sphere; the notion of the 'general subject'—advanced but not concretely described by Kant—was transcended in Hegel's postulate of the 'absolute spirit' as the essence of reality." In the end, however, Horkheimer (like Lukács) saw idealism as marred by its speculative tendencies, a defect which was successfully corrected only by Marxism: From the idealist vantage point, "the activity underlying a given object appeared as purely spiritual—as outgrowth of a supra-empirical 'consciousness as such,' of an 'absolute ego,' or 'spirit'—with the result that the struggle against the opaque, unconscious, and irrational aspect (of reality) was treated in principle as an inner-human process or a matter of mental attitude. In the materialist conception, by contrast, the basic activity is social work or production whose class character puts its mark on all human reactions, including theory."[19]

Seen against this background, critical theory was a continuation of Marxist thought, under the changed circumstances of late or monopolistic capitalism. The critical mode of social thought, the essay asserted, "deals with men as producers of their historical life-form in its totality. The factual conditions which are the targets of science are treated not simply as data to be verified or to be predicted according to the laws of probability. For, contingent facts depend not on nature alone but also on man's control over it; objects, the manner of perception, the questions asked, and the meaning of the answers—all bear witness to human activity and the degree of man's power." Through the stress on human production, the *laws of probability* and similar quasi-natural regularities were not abolished, but were subordinated to human intentionality and the task of self-reflection: "The locus of human self-knowledge in our time is not quantitative natural science hypostatized as eternal 'Logos,' but rather the critical theoretical analysis of prevailing society, an analysis animated by the interest in the establishment of rational life-forms." Being concerned with social rationality, critical theory was necessarily future-oriented (without on this count being synonymous with utopianism); in contrast to bourgeois science, its preoccupation was not an instrument of social adaptation or conducive to the maintenance of existing conditions. Although "emerging from the social structure," we read, the critical outlook "is neither in its conscious intent nor its objective significance designed to promote the better functioning of any part of that structure; on the contrary, it regards the categories of 'better, useful, effective, productive, and valuable' as they are understood in the existing system as intrinsically suspect and by no means as extra-scientific or theoretically irrelevant presuppositions." While the bourgeois individual was as a rule destined "to accept the basic conditions of his existence as given and to adjust to them," critical analysis "is wholly distrustful of the yardsticks which society as presently constituted provides for its members."[20]

Its focus on genetic questions enabled critical theory to overcome the antithesis of individual freedom and social necessity, or at least to point to its resolution. In Horkheimer's words: "The bifurcation of individual and society in accordance with which the individual accepts as natural the limits set to his activity is relativized in critical theory; in fact, the latter considers the structural framework arising from the blind conjunction of individual activities—that is, the existing division of labor with its class distinctions—as a situation which, originating in human action, is also amenable to purposive decisions and rational planning." In bridging the gulf between individual and collectivity, critical thought also opened the way to the removal of the traditional subject-object dichotomy; in line with *History and Class Consciousness* the essay depicted the (progressive) opponents of capitalism as harbingers of a potential subject-object, or as agents able to identify with the goals of society as a whole: "The antinomial character of the existing social fabric develops among the carriers of critical thought into a conscious contradiction; in recognizing the present economic system and the entire culture generated by it as the product of human work and as the organizational form which mankind in the present age has adopted or was able to adopt, these carriers identify themselves with this total fabric and perceive it as a function of will and reason—that is, as their own world." Like the general concern with rationality, the reconciliation of subject and object could not be instantaneously implemented, but required radical social change which would transform society into a transparent mirror of self-knowledge. Critical thinking is "motivated today by the endeavor," we read, to move beyond traditional tensions and to "transcend the antithesis between the individual's intentionality, spontaneity and rationality, on the one hand, and the interrelated work processes structuring society, on the other. Critical thought harbors a concept of man which is in conflict with itself until this identity is established."[21]

As in the case of Lukács' study, the accentuation of self-knowledge and human agency carried political overtones, due to their role in the class struggle and in man's struggle to control the forces of nature (including those of society as "second nature"). Under the auspices of traditional theory, man was seen as basically impotent and governed by "necessity" (external compulsion): "The inability to grasp the unity of theory and practice and the restriction of the concept of necessity to an imposed destiny are grounded epistemologically in the Cartesian dualism of thought and being." From a strictly contemplative perspective "men view themselves as mere onlookers or victims of an overpowering process which can perhaps be predicted but not controlled." Critical theory prepared the ground for a reformulation of necessity in terms of human mastery. "The idea of a theory which becomes a genuine force, residing in the self-awareness of the agents of a great historical transformation," Horkheimer noted, "transcends the mentality which characterizes the (Cartesian) dualism." From the vantage point of these agents the central historical task consisted in the replacement of blind (external) by meaningful (human) necessity, a task which first demanded an "effort of emancipation both from the constraints of nature and from those social life-forms (with their legal, political and cultural dimensions) which have turned into a straitjacket." This effort, in turn, was part of an ambitious endeavor, namely, "the striving for a state of affairs in which human will entails necessary results and in which substantive necessity becomes the necessity of rationally mastered events. The application and even intelligibility of these and similar tenets of critical thought are tied to the activity, initiative, and willpower of the knowing subject."[22]

Although following in large measure in Lukács' footsteps, Horkheimer's essay did not replicate the former's arguments. One difference concerned the role of proletarian class consciousness. Horkheimer did not bypass the proletariat, but seemed much less confident than his mentor regarding its mission as subject-object or its qualification as constitutive We-subject of historical transformation. "Even the situation of the proletariat is in the present society no guarantee of correct insight. Although it experiences society's opacity as the continuation and intensification of the wretchedness and injustice of its own condition, this awareness is prevented from directly asserting itself by the differentiation of social structure imposed from above and by the conflict between individual and class interests which is overcome only in exceptional moments." While these comments appear compatible with Lukács' anti-psychologism and his distinction between empirical and potential (or "objectively possible") class consciousness, their context suggested more than a temporary psychological handicap. "There is no social class," a later passage affirmed bluntly, "by whose insight or consensus (critical) theory could be guided; under prevailing circumstances the consciousness of every stratum can be ideologically restricted or corrupted, no matter how strongly its social position may predestine it to truth."[23] Reservations of this kind, one should note, did not impair the focus on self-knowledge and self-production; though it kept the notion of We-subjectivity, the essay was open-ended regarding its concrete embodiment, preferring to speak vaguely of the subjects or carriers of critical thought. In addition to the proletariat, Horkheimer's account portrayed as potential carriers society as a whole, marginal social groups, concretely interrelated individuals, and even humankind at large. The struggle against repression was once depicted as the "striving for a condition which really witnesses the emergence of a comprehensive subject, namely, self-conscious humanity."[24]

Horkheimer's reservations can be interpreted as an outgrowth of the difference in social-historical context which separated his essay from *History and Class Consciousness*. In this respect, his attitude reflected the self-critical character of critical theory and its ambition (repeatedly stressed in the essay) to avoid doctrinaire rigidity by hewing closely to concrete social-historical developments.[25] On another level, Horkheimer's account can be read as expression of a wavering attachment to, and perhaps a beginning disaffection with, the notion of class consciousness itself and related key ingredients of traditional Marxist thought. Viewed in this light, the essay may be seen as the first step in an extended process of reassessment, a process which gained momentum over several decades and eventually affected a broad range of beliefs, including the concepts of subject-object identity, human self-production, and a constitutive We-subjectivity. This is not the place to trace the stages of this complex intellectual journey, which in large measure was undertaken by both Horkheimer and Adorno and which externally was highlighted by such experiences as emigration, the Second World War, and the emerging East-West conflict. I would now like to review some arguments contained in Adorno's *Negative Dialectics* (of 1966), a study which in many ways forms the culmination of the mentioned theoretical changes; attacking several core tenets of traditional (Hegelian and Marxist) dialectics, the arguments in my view question both serial aggregation and group solidarity as exclusive paradigms of modern intersubjectivity.

Negative Dialectics is a complex, multilayered opus weaving together a broad array of concerns; however, if one were to single out the central motif it is an opposition to the notion of a constitutive subjectivity. The theme is eloquently and emphatically announced in the preface to the study: "Ever since the author trusted his own intellectual impulses, he has considered it his task to dispel the deceit of a constitutive subjectivity by relying on its own competences." According to Adorno, the entire course of Western philosophy, especially in the modern phase, consists in the progressive accentuation of consciousness or subjectivity, together with the steady refinement of the meaning of these terms: "In its preponderant thrust, the development of epistemological reflection was pervaded by the aim to reduce more and more aspects of reality to categories of the thinking subject." The deceit of this movement is evident in the ascription of *being* to consciousness even by the most transcendental epistemological systems: "Every assertion that subjectivity 'is' or 'exists' in some fashion includes already the acceptance of an objective element—an element which subjectivity pretends to found or constitute by virtue of its absolute or pure status." More generally, the distinctive qualities of subjectivity—on account of which traditional philosophy segregated it from being—are basically borrowed from or "modeled after being"; contrary to epistemological allegations, its nature presupposes real experience or "facticity" as a "condition of its possibility." In Adorno's words: "The more autonomously the subject ascends above the ontic realm, the more it turns surreptitiously into an object, in ironic cancellation of its constitutive role."[26]

The study's opposition to subjective foundation extends to the concept of a general subjectivity (or a "subjectivity-writ-large") as articulated in Hegelian philosophy and, more broadly, in modern dialectical thought. Despite his departures from Cartesian or Kantian teachings, Hegel's dialectics in Adorno's view remained a "philosophy of consciousness" and his encyclopedic system an array of concepts superimposed on, but carefully sealed off from, reality. "Hegel's system," he writes, "is not truly dynamic (or open to real change); rather, the entire fabric is implicitly pre-thought or conceptually pre-arranged in every detail." Within this system, every phenomenon appears as the "exemplification of its concept"; despite the "program of objectification," reflection tends to "come to rest within itself and its own tautologies." According to *Negative Dialectics,* the cognitive-conceptual character of Hegelianism—its confinement in the categories of consciousness—is illustrated in its emphasis on totality and on dialectical contradiction. While totality involved a leveling of all "divergent, dissonant, or negative" aspects of reality into an orderly, homogeneous fabric, dialectical contradiction pitted against each other purely logical oppositions which were readily amenable to conceptual reconciliation: "Contradiction is (real) non-identity under the auspices of (logical) identity; the primacy of dialectical antithesis measures difference with the yardstick of cognitive unity or homogeneity." The same tendency was manifest in the treatment of the subject-object correlation. By construing both terms as intellectual categories Hegel "dissolved them in thought" and ensured their possible identification on the level of spirit: "Conceived as an essential structure the dialectic of subject and object was transformed by him into a function of subjectivity."[27]

In Adorno's judgment, one of the most detrimental corollaries of foundational subjectivity (in either its singular or its general sense) is its embroilment in power struggles, particularly in man's struggle for mastery over his environment. Despite the seeming innocence of reflection, rationality and domination have long been reciprocally contaminated: "In its depth 'spirit' suspects that its stable predominance is not purely spiritual but has its *ultima ratio* in the physical force which is at its disposal." The link between rationality and power is tighter than ever in our time due to the unparalleled expansion of technological devices and the resulting *subjugation of nature* in past decades. The longstanding involvement of reason in human domination, Adorno insists, disproves the alleged purity of subjectivity and consciousness, revealing them as (perhaps unwitting) ingredients of objectivist processes. "Contrary to idealist doctrines propounded through the centuries," he writes, "the subject is not so much the source of objects (*obiectum subiectum*) as rather the reverse (*subiectum obiectum*). The primacy of subjectivity continues in spiritual guise the Darwinian struggle for survival: the subjugation of nature to human purposes is itself a merely natural or naturalistic occurrence; accordingly, the superiority of subjugating rationality and its rational dictates emerges as sham." In participating in the struggle for power, reason falls prey to the natural forces it seeks to control, an outcome which gives new meaning to Hegel's master-slave relationship. The sham character of intellectual superiority, we read, is "underscored by the epistemological-metaphysical subject which proclaims itself as lord in Bacon's sense and finally as idealistic creator of all things. In exercising its rule the subject becomes part of the subjugated world, thus succumbing like the Hegelian master."[28]

To counteract the defects of traditional rationality, *Negative Dialectics* suggests a type of reflection which, without abandoning the integrity of thought, opens itself to the domain of non-thought, relinquishing the ambition of control. Instead of seeking to absorb reality or to identify it with its conceptual tools, this kind of thought would be characterized by an attitude of *letting-be* or a respect for *non-identity*. "In encountering its limits," the study notes, "thought begins to transcend itself. Dialectics would be the genuine and consistent awareness of non-identity." In comparison with the legacy of dialectical philosophy, especially its Hegelian version, the suggested outlook has a strongly non-idealist orientation; denying the supremacy of ideas—but not in a purely conceptual or antithetical manner—its main concern is with the intertwining of thought and non-thought: "The endeavor to change the thrust of conceptualization, turning it toward non-identity, is the emblem of negative dialectics. Insight into the constitutive character of the non-conceptual within the conceptual sphere would terminate the constraint of identity which conceptual thought otherwise engenders." From the perspective of non-idealist or negative dialectics, Adorno adds, the "demythologization of concepts" is the proper "antidote of philosophy." The aim of non-possessive or non-domineering thought, in his view, is "literally to submerge itself in heterogeneity, without reducing it to prefabricated categories." Its ambition is "to nestle as close to otherness as (early) phenomenology and Georg Simmel's program had vainly attempted: its motto is unconditional dispossession or surrender. Philosophical substance can be grasped only where it is not dictated by philosophy."[29]

The attitude of negative dialectics toward non-identity applies also to intersubjectivity or to the subject's relation to the Other. "Idealism, particularly Fichte's system," the study observes, "adheres blindly to the ideology according to which the non-ego or the Other (*l'autrui*) and generally everything resembling nature is inferior—an ideology adapted to the voracity of homogeneous thought, its desire to devour otherness in the interest of self-preservation." Non-idealist dialectics is bent on eroding or reversing this presumption: "In experiencing itself as dynamic movement no longer identical with itself, conceptual thought points in the direction of 'otherness' (to use Hegel's terminology) without trying to absorb it." The reversal extends to the notions of reification and alienation, as articulated by traditional dialectical thought. In a passage primarily addressed to Lukács' early work Adorno states: "Thought easily and comfortably imagines to find the touchstone of wisdom in the dissolution of reification or of the commodity character (of social relations). However, the latter is only a manifestation of false objectivity; to focus narrowly on reification as a form of consciousness tends to dress critical theory in idealistic garb, thus rendering it palatable to the ruling ideology as well as to unconscious mass beliefs." According to *Negative Dialectics,* reified (or "thingified") awareness is at best a subsidiary phenomenon and its elevation to a central theoretical category is misleading: "Measured against the possibility of total catastrophe reification is an epiphenomenon; the same is true of alienation or estrangement which denotes a correlated subjective attitude. Both are an outgrowth of fear; but consciousness, 'reified' in existing society, cannot ultimately be recovered as constitutive source. Whoever treats objectivity or 'thing'-quality as radically evil and aims to dissolve reality as a whole in pure praxis or self-production, tends to be animated by hostility to the Other or stranger (a term not by accident contained in 'estrangement')—that is, by hostility to that domain of non-identity which would provide freedom not only for 'consciousness' but for a reconciled humanity."[30]

As employed by Adorno, the term *reconciliation* has close affinity to the *good life* which traditionally has been used to designate the proper human condition or the proper goal of the *polis.* Stripped of idealist or narrowly moralistic connotations, the *good life* in the context of his study intimates not so much the rule of the virtuous or of a homogeneous goodness but rather a situation permeated by the willingness to let others be, or to respect and cherish them in their distinct being and goodness. "The reconciled condition," we read, "would not annex strangeness in an exercise of philosophical imperialism; rather, its delight would consist in recognizing distance and difference even in proximate surroundings, a recognition at odds both with reciprocal isolation and assimilation. The persistent attack on reification prevents or obstructs such a conception, thereby condemning the philosophy of history animating the attack." Recognition of difference, however, especially when joined with non-isolation, presupposes that intersubjectivity is more than a relation of self-contained individuals; in order to *act* in the world or to *interact* with others, the subject must already be infiltrated by the world and by otherness, to the point where both sides are linked in mutual reversibility: "Only insofar as it is also a non-ego can the ego relate to the non-ego or *alter ego* and can it perform an action, including an act of thought. By means of a double reflection thought terminates its supremacy over non-thought, since it is itself shot through from the beginning with otherness."[31]

MODES OF SOCIALITY. A TYPOLOGY

The preceding discussion of the treatment of intersubjectivity by spokesmen of phenomenology and critical Marxism has numerous implications for social and political theory, not all of which can be unraveled in this context. Probably the most important lesson to be derived concerns the relationship between individual and society: contrary to modern political thought with its reliance on an atomistic state of nature which functioned as the explanatory premise of social-political institutions, phenomenology (in its preponderant tendency) and critical Marxism (in at least one of its versions) emphasize the precognitive basis of subjectivity and thus, in a sense, the precedence of sociality over individual autonomy.[1] This emphasis can be seen as the main link between the reviewed writings which have been published since the Second World War. The anti-atomistic implication is manifest in the ontological versions of phenomenology, as articulated by Derrida and Merleau-Ponty, and in Adorno's negative dialectics; however, it can also be detected in Sartrean existentialism. As has been indicated, Sartre's *Being and Nothingness* was strongly antagonistic to traditional cognitive perspectives and, in trying to provide a corrective, construed intersubjectivity as an existential encounter revolving around the dialectic of the look; despite his rejection of Hegelian totalitarianism and despite the continued reference to the subject- and object-poles of ego and *alter ego,* encounter was claimed to imply a process of reciprocal existential transformation, and not just an external juxtaposition of individuals.

To be sure, the accent of these pages has been more on contrast than on affinity. The chief distinction emerging from the comparison is between a relatively individualistic phenomenology and subjectivist idealism, on the one hand, and, on the other, a posture decentering subjectivity to the point of revealing its primary inherence in the world and in Being. Leaving aside Husserl's complex life-work and occasional passages in Merleau-Ponty's early writings, the first perspective is best represented by Sartrean philosophy (even after his turn to dialectical materialism) and by Lukács' quasi-Hegelian dialectics. Although opposing cognitive categories in favor of experiental concreteness, *Being and Nothingness* (as mentioned) tended to define *existence* in terms of subjective intentionality and egological designs; despite the attention given to material and environmental constraints, the *Critique of Dialectical Reason* portrayed intersubjective relations as the clash of individual projects—or else as the merger of individuals into a group subjectivity or joint project designed to overcome the inertia of nature as well as the passivity inherent in collective ensembles. The notion of group subjectivity or of a self-producing We-subject was also a central concern of Lukács' *History and Class Consciousness,* where it served as a primary device for differentiating proletarian class consciousness from the serial aggregation of bourgeois society.

The opposing outlook—first sketched in *Being and Time* and subsequently developed in *Negative Dialectics, The Visible and the Invisible,* and in Derrida's comments on Levinas—does not deny the diversity and possible antagonism between individuals; however, refusing to treat subjectivity as a fixed reference point, and even as a complete negativity, it carries otherness into the heart of selfhood while tracing both ego and *alter* to a prereflective and non-intentional *difference.* As one should note, the distinction does not coincide with an acceptance or rejection of individualism. In Sartre's and Levinas' case, it is true, the separation and multiplicity of individuals is treated on the whole as a metaphysical premise or primordial fact; in a similar vein, the natural attitude described by Husserl and Schutz was said to disclose everyday situations as centered around a (mundane) ego. In the light of available anthropological evidence, this linkage of egology with human *nature* appears precarious. This conclusion does not warrant the opposite thesis, sometimes upheld by defenders of sociality, that everyday life is devoid of subjective-individual traces; especially in modern Western society, little effort is required to show that ego-references have been so strongly sedimented in ordinary experience as to function as taken-for-granted parameters. It seems to me that it would be pointless to deny the importance and effectiveness of individualism in given historical contexts—although one may very well question its ability, as a philosophical doctrine, to account for itself.

Once historical and geographical variability is taken into consideration, the most intriguing challenge implicit in the preceding pages may reside in the possibility of a typology of human interaction or, more precisely, of modes of social and political co-being. The need to find a viable typological scheme has been a longstanding motivation of both sociological and political theory, but the task can hardly be said to have been accomplished. In political thought, the predominant scheme has been the Aristotelian typology of regimes predicated on the number and moral qualifications of the rulers; however, given the almost universal sway of popular regimes in our time and the relative obsolescence of monarchies and aristocracies, the typology retains only a limited applicability. The rise of modern sociology gave a new impetus to typological endeavors precisely at a time when traditional forms of rulership became blurred. Among the founders of sociological theory, Max Weber in particular devised a novel approach for analyzing social and political life by focusing on key forms of social action. As one may recall, his typology comprised chiefly four action modes: namely, *traditional* action determined by *ingrained habituation; affectual* behavior guided by emotions or *feeling states; instrumentally rational* activity involving the employment of effective means for the attainment of ends; and *value-rational* action pursuing a goal *for its own sake.* These action variants were closely related to a new typology of governmental forms differentiating between *traditional, legal* and *charismatic* modes of political authority. Despite the rich insights contained in his arguments, Weber's contribution appears circumscribed by the individualism pervading his outlook—a commitment revealed in his definition of *action* in terms of the *subjective meaning* attached to it by the agent and also in his assertion that only individuals "can be treated as agents in a course of subjectively understandable action."[2]

Modern sociological theory has not remained tied to individualist premises (in both a substantive and methodological sense); however, departures from these premises have frequently been animated by an anti-individualistic and even collectivistic bias—a bias which, like its antipode, pays homage to traditional epistemological dichotomies. In the domain of social formations, Weber's contemporary, Ferdinand Toennies, before the turn of the century articulated his celebrated distinction between *Gemeinschaft* and *Gesellschaft,* or between communalism and association (or associational society). According to Toennies, *Gemeinschaft* was nurtured by natural-instinctual inclinations or organic life-structures, while *Gesellschaft* was the outgrowth of deliberate choice; in the first type the social aggregate preceded any individual initiative, whereas in the second it derived from conscious human de-sign. The two types of aggregates, one should add, were not statically juxtaposed but were assumed to reflect a genetic pattern of develop-ment, in the sense that *Gesellschaft* emerged out of the disintegration of organic communal bonds, especially under the impact of the division of labor and the rise of a competitive market economy.[3] Among the two formations, Toennies clearly preferred the communal pattern—al-though he did not anticipate or endorse some of the abuses to which the notion of *Gemeinschaft* later gave rise, especially in the hands of ideologues advocating the deliberate construction of natural-organic solidarity (a proposal which ignores the boundaries of his typology). Whatever the personal feelings of its author may have been, the *Gemeinschaft-Gesellschaft* dualism could not exhaust the possible modes of interaction; above all, the scheme was unable to account for the formation of non-organic communities deriving from the merger of subjective intentions and deliberate initiatives. Given the waning of organic-traditional bonds and the alienating effects of competitive mar-ket relations, it was precisely this type of interaction which attracted the attention of philosophers and social-political theorists in the early part of this century—as illustrated, for example, in Lukács' study and (less clearly) in Max Scheler's focus on interpersonal communion, predicated on intimate reciprocal empathy.[4]

Relying on suggestions contained in the previous discussion, I would like at this point to propose, in a tentative fashion, a four-fold typology of social interaction concentrating on these key modes of so-ciality or intersubjectivity: *communalism; association* (or associational society); *movement;* and *community.* The typology reformulates and expands Toennies' dualistic scheme; it also takes recourse to Weberian categories, but in such a manner that the focus is on modes of co-being and not on individual action and subjective meaning. My comments on the first type, communalism, can be particularly brief, since it figures least prominently in the reviewed writings. Only *History and Class Consciousness* explicitly makes room for this type, in its references to pre-modern social life-forms. As used in the present context, *commu-nalism* to a large extent corresponds to the notion of *Gemeinschaft* with its emphasis on organic and quasi-natural factors (such as kinship, heredity, and ascribed status) as key determinants of social organiza-tion. Placed in an evolutionary framework, social life at this level is relatively homogeneous and non-specialized, exhibiting little differen-tiation between economic, cultural, and political dimensions of exis-tence. In terms of Weber's classification scheme, communal interaction can be described as traditional, or governed by habituation, custom, or ritual; but one can also detect strands of "affectual" or "affective" behavior—provided "affective" is used in more of a poetic-imaginative sense than a psychological-emotional one. Given its non-intentional, presubjective and prereflective sources, communalism seems close to Heidegger's (and Merleau-Ponty's) notion of anonymous co-being or interaction in the mode of the They; however, as has rightly been pointed out, this notion does not fit a particular social structure but is historically variable—with the result that anonymity implies conformity with prevailing standards in different historical and social settings.[5]

In line with Toennies' *Gesellschaft, association* designates a social aggregate formed through purposive volition which involves a loose juxtaposition of its participants; in view of the stress on volition and a sphere of presocial autonomy, the type assumes a relatively strong sense of individualism and the ability of members to differentiate between ego and Other, as well as between cognitive subjectivity and the world. Sartre's notion of collectives and especially of serial collectivity matches in large measure the associational mode; particularly intriguing is his emphasis on alterity or a general role-structure as common denominator and his assertion that, in the series, "everyone is identical with the Other insofar as the others make him an Other acting on the others." Sartre's and Lukács' descriptions of serial life clearly mark an advance over customary sociological treatments of association; the concepts of *passive synthesis* and *second nature* highlight the material and non-purposive matrix underlying individualistic designs—the way that, as Sartre notes, the "discrete multiplicity of active individuals" in collectives is produced against the backdrop of "a material, inorganic object in the practico-inert field."[6] However, one probably has to go a step further: instead of forming a mute background, non-intentional materiality (as manifest in economic class structures) needs to be seen as the reverse side of individual initiative and thus as inextricably linked with it. In comparison with communalism, association displays considerable heterogeneity and also a steady specialization of social subsectors (such as economics and politics). Viewed in the light of Weber's action categories, the type appears as the main arena for implementing instrumental-rational stratagems and calculations; the social aggregate itself tends to be measured in terms of the utility derived from it by participants. Political authority is guided predominantly by procedural canons, although at the beginning (during the establishment of market relations) a more absolutist regime may prevail. Using Heideggerian vocabulary one might say that interhuman relations in this context are permeated by deficient modes of care, or else by a pronounced degree of managerial solicitude, involving social and political manipulation.

The third type, movement, is distinguished from communalism by its reliance on deliberate intentionality, and from association by its stress on internal unity. Sartre's treatment of the group, especially the fused group, and Lukács' discussion of proletarian class consciousness are pertinent to this type of interaction; Sartre's account even comes close to the terminology chosen here—as when he portrays the group as *moving totality* or writes that "the group is defined by its undertaking and by the constant movement of integration which tends to turn it into pure praxis while trying to eliminate all forms of inertia from it." As in the case of individualistic enterprise, the group or movement carries its own otherness as a correlate, an aspect to which Sartre obliquely alludes in his statement that, in the course of the culture-dialectic, group members "create their own anti-physis by unification so as to construct human power (that is, free relations among men)." It seems to me, however, this allusion needs to be much more strongly accentuated and developed. Group unification means the consolidation of human dominion over nature and the material world, and also unification against non-members; although internally characterized by mutually recognized freedom and genuine devotion, movements typically treat both nature and the rest of mankind as either nonexistent or as deserving to be extinguished. Sartre himself acknowledges the sectarian and potentially violent character of groups when he depicts them as a form of "the Apocalypse" in which complete unity is supposed to be "always *here*." Among Weber's action categories the most relevant types are affective (in the sense of emotional) and value-rational action. Political authority in movements tends to be charismatic, with the leader (or leaders) embodying either unique personality traits or intensely cherished social goals.[7]

The final type mentioned above, community, is least developed in modern sociological and political theory; the tentative outlines of this type derive almost entirely from the contributions of ontological phenomenology and quasi-ontological (or negative-dialectical) versions of critical theory. In contrast to association, community does not imply a simple juxtaposition of supposedly independent agents; at the same time, its relative deemphasis of subjective volition separates it from the sphere of movements or fused groups. As opposed to the homogeneity deliberately fostered in the movement, the communitarian mode cultivates diversity—but without encouraging willful segregation or the repressive preponderance of one of the social subsectors. Not surprisingly (in view of his individualism and philosophical scepticism) Weber did not make allowance for this type among his action categories. Following Heidegger's teachings, as further fleshed out by Merleau-Ponty, Derrida, and Adorno, the pervasive outlook or behavioral mode might be described as anticipative-emancipatory practice or as an attitude dedicated to letting others be—a distinctive and peculiar mode since it is lodged at the intersection of activity and passivity. As a corollary of this outlook, community may be the only form of social aggregation which reflects upon, and makes room for, otherness or the reverse side of subjectivity (and inter-subjectivity) and thus for the play of difference—the difference between ego and Other and between man and nature.

As the terms *anticipative-emancipatory care* and *ontological anticipation* indicate, the type envisaged here does not coincide with an empirically given or presently existing (or historically recorded) aggregate; nor, due to its concern with Being, can it be equated with a regulative principle or abstract utopia. On the level of political theory, anticipation points toward the *end of politics* in a dual sense: namely, the dismantling of political domination and the goal of politics, traditionally formulated as the good life. At least in its qualitative aspect, community evokes the criteria of a well-ordered polis provided by Aristotle: "The best way of life, both for individuals and for polities taken as a whole, is the life of goodness duly equipped with such a store of requisites (that is, material and bodily goods) as to render possible participation in the works of goodness."[8]

CHAPTER THREE

Man and Nature: Prospects of a "Humanistic Naturalism"

THE PHRASE *human nature* is simultaneously baffling and revealing. Despite its commonsense ring and widespread usage, the phrase captures a perplexing enigma. The puzzle arises from more than the proliferation of definitions assigned to the phrase—although this is surely a complicating factor.[1] The trouble emerges because the phrase seems to join terms endowed with distinct and even conflicting connotations. In modern Western thought, in any case, man's *humanity* tends to be seen not only as differentiated from but as antithetical to his *naturalness*. As delineated by Descartes, the mind or spirit of the *ego cogitans* is separated from, and opposed to, the world of extended matter (organic and inorganic nature). In Kant's teachings, man's consciousness and moral autonomy enjoyed a transcendental status completely underivable from worldly experience, while Hegel presented nature simply as antithetical otherness or estrangement of spirit. More recent philosophers, especially in the existentialist camp, have endeavored to treat man's awareness as a complete transparency, as a negative foil against which the positive fullness of the world is silhouetted. The motivation behind this view is easy to detect. The term *nature*—in one of its prominent senses—denotes a self-contained universe of objects governed by inexorable causal laws. Given this definition, how can man be integrated in this universe without being stripped of responsibility and the capacity for valid cognition? In the words of Karl Jaspers: "If I am nothing but nature, nothing but the product of knowable causality, it is not only incomprehensible that I know this nature and use my knowledge to intervene in it; it is absurd that I justify myself."[2]

Viewed against this background, *human nature* appears deeply paradoxical. Its component elements seem unable to coalesce; attempts to produce fusion through reliance on one of the terms entail mutilation and added quandaries. If the core of man is located in a circumscribed *nature* whose dictates he is expected to implement, the dimension of freedom and transcendence is liable to vanish. The situation is not remedied, however, by a simple reversal of emphasis accentuating human freedom. For, given the mutual exclusiveness of terms, how can man's essence—defined as complete malleability and negativity—be meaningfully related to the natural world (which nevertheless remains his habitat)? More importantly, the status of humanity in this case seems elusive if not unintelligible. How can an absence of nature sensibly be construed as human essence, and how can it provide guideposts for cognition and human action? Dilemmas of this kind are not of a merely theoretical import. Behind the sketched quandaries the contours of a concrete drama emerge: the age-old question of man's relationship to and struggle with nature. In the modern era, this relationship has the earmarks of radical enmity and tragedy. The definition of man as a rational agent separate from nature has accompanied man's longstanding quest to control the forces of his environment; aided by the steady advances of science and technology this quest has finally resulted in man's virtually unlimited dominion over nature.

Despite its inherent complexities, the phrase *human nature* should probably not be abandoned too quickly. Its customary usage seems to reveal a deep-seated sense, embedded in language, that man and nature are inextricably linked—no matter how difficult this link may be to comprehend. In our time, the wisdom of ordinary language has been reinforced by a growing awareness of the destructive consequences of unchecked human supremacy. In its famous report on the *Limits to Growth,* the "Club of Rome"—composed of leading scientists of the Western world—depicted in grim colors the perils arising for the human biosphere from rampant environmental spoliation and the progressive depletion of natural resources.[3] Triggered by reports of this type as well as everyday experiences of pollution, concern with environmental issues in industrial nations has spawned a broad ecological movement dedicated to the protection of nature's bounty, or at least to the maintenance of a more judicious balance between supplies and human wants. The conception of human lordship—found to be pernicious for master and servant alike—is beginning to give way to the vision of a more custodial relationship, perhaps an ultimate reconciliation, between man and nature. The same developments place a premium on a careful reconsideration of the meaning of human nature and its theoretical and practical implications.

The idea of a reconciliation with nature is not alien to the tradition of Western thought—notwithstanding the predominant reach toward domination. Relying on speculative constructions or emotional appeals, however, proponents of the notion on the whole tended to stop short of challenging the primacy of human initiative. In the domain of social and political theory, Karl Marx in the last century advanced strong arguments in favor of the reintegration of man and nature, arguments which moved far beyond rationalist or romantic pleas. Adopting a practical stance and stressing the role of human labor and industry, the *Economic and Philosophical Manuscripts* portrayed historical development as a process in which socialization of production would entail the progressive *humanization of nature* as well as the *naturalization of man;* the reappropriation of man's social essence was to usher in a fusion of nature and human endeavors, in the form of a naturalist humanism or a humanist naturalism.[4] In his later writings, including the *Capital,* Marx conceived the same process as a large-scale *metabolism*—a term which highlighted the dialectical character of man's interaction with nature: the aspect that, as producer, man is himself a natural agent and that, in transforming external materials, he simultaneously transforms his own nature (manifest in the forces and relations of production).[5] Despite their suggestive connotations and significant advances beyond earlier formulas, Marx's arguments remained indebted to the legacy of domination through his primary accent on man as producing creature or *homo faber*—an anthropological (and anthropocentric) conception functioning as a pillar of modern industry. To a large extent, socialist thought after Marx continued to cling to the *homo faber* outlook, even compounding its limitations by disregarding the practical-dialectical aspects of Marx's arguments.

The reassessment of the man-nature nexus has received powerful new support in our century, originating from such perspectives as philosophical anthropology, phenomenology, and self-critical versions of neo-Marxism. One of the founders of the first perspective, Helmuth Plessner, endeavored to link human freedom, conceived as *eccentric openness,* with such biological traits as upright posture and instinctual non-specialization.[6] Crucial new vistas in the exploration of human nature were opened up by existential and ontological phenomenology, most notably in Heidegger's writings. More radically than other thinkers of his time, Heidegger challenged the premises of modern Western thought, especially the Cartesian juxtaposition or opposition of human subjectivity and extended matter. His challenge, one should note, was directed both at traditional, psychologically tainted versions of subjectivity and at more recent formulations stressing the deficiency and empty transparency of consciousness and the resulting indefiniteness of man. Heidegger particularly criticized the evasiveness of the recent formulations: their unwillingness to explore the ontic or ontological status of the postulated deficiency and also the issue of how emptiness could be related to presence.[7] Instead of relying on either an abstract or a psychologically concrete subject, *Being and Time* delineated man's condition through the phrase being-in-the-world; in this conception, human existence was centrally marked neither by theoretical reason nor by instrumental adaptiveness (after the model of *homo faber*) but rather by the capacity for care, especially the care for Being or the sense of its own being—a sense which could not possibly disclose itself if it were not latently anchored in existence.

The vistas heralded in Heidegger's writings have not been fully explored in contemporary thought; in some respects his guideposts are exceedingly difficult to unravel. Doubts surround the status of nature in Heidegger's philosophy—although directional hints are certainly present. Provided *Being* is conceived as prereflective fabric underlying thought rather than as a speculative projection of the human mind, its linkage with nature does not seem too remote; also, if—pursuant to the ontological difference—the sense of Being is an oblique implication of ontic beings (rather than their negation), human care would seem to be necessarily mediated through the natural components of existence.[8] I shall not attempt a clarification of Heidegger's own views on human nature and the man-nature relationship; instead, I would like to examine the contributions to the theme made by French phenomenology and post-phenomenology—that is, by thinkers who, in varying degrees, have been influenced by Heideggerian initiatives, although none of them can be described as his disciple. In a first section, I shall delineate pertinent arguments articulated by Paul Ricoeur, a philosopher whose outlook is chiefly indebted to Husserl and transcendental versions of existentialism (as found especially in the writings of Karl Jaspers), and only in small measure to Heidegger's teachings; as it seems to me and as I shall try to show, his arguments are instructive both for pinpointing the philosophical basis of the contrast between man and nature and for indicating, in a tentative fashion, initial steps for remedying the dilemma. In two subsequent sections, the focus will be on Maurice Merleau-Ponty and Jacques Derrida and their endeavors to bring ontological or quasi-ontological considerations to bear on the issue. In conclusion, an effort will be made to sketch some lessons for social and political theory which might be drawn from the reviewed perspectives.

Nature and Human Freedom: Ricoeur

From its inception, phenomenology's posture toward nature has been uneasy. As articulated by Edmund Husserl, phenomenological inquiry

was a continuation and purification of the traditional philosophy of reflection with its accent on consciousness and subjectivity. Despite a
limited legitimacy accorded to the natural (or prereflective) attitude,
the task of philosophy in Husserl's view was to transcend this outlook
in the direction of rigorous intentional analysis; the target of such
analysis was not so much *nature* itself as rather the *noema*, that is, the
intended object as perceived by consciousness. With slight changes,
Husserl maintained this perspective throughout his life. In one of his
last works, *The Crisis of European Sciences,* he outlined some of
the practical implications of pure or transcendental phenomenology.
According to the study, the core and genuine *telos* of man resided in
his consciousness and capacity for rational reflection; the turn to philosophical inquiry heralded the emergence of *humanism* in the proper
sense of the term, as opposed to more primitive and unreflective modes
of human life. As Husserl added, man's telos was never an assured
possession, but had always to be pursued against strong countervailing
trends. Most prominent among these trends was the lure of *objectivism*
or *naturalism*—terms signifying the submergence of thought in external processes. Under the aegis of positivism, this danger had reached
crisis proportions threatening Western culture and its sciences; only
through a "rebirth of Europe out of the spirit of philosophy" was it
possible to overcome "naturalism once and for all."[9]

In the French phenomenological movement, attempts to face the
challenges of nature—the quandaries it raises for consciousness—
emerged hesitantly, and only after an initial vogue of transcendental
and existentialist humanism during and in the aftermath of the Second
World War. Paul Ricoeur's life-work illustrates the changing emphases
of the movement. Although strongly attached to the legacy of transcendental reflection and noumenal autonomy, Ricoeur in the course
of his life wrestled with growing intensity with the problems at the
boundaries of consciousness and freedom; this struggle deepened his
insight into the intimate linkage of man and nature—although his
writings frequently remain satisfied with antinomial formulations.
Focusing on human practice rather than on purely cognitive issues, his
Philosophie de la volonté—a work of several volumes whose publication started in 1950—explored both the eidetic structure of will and
action and their concrete-existential parameters deriving from man's
being-in-the-world. Addressing itself to central philosophical premises,
the first volume portrayed the dialectical nexus or reciprocity between
the *voluntary* and the *involuntary* or between freedom and nature—but
in such a manner that nature (manifest chiefly in organic life and the
domain of the unconscious) supplied material substance, to be molded

by human freedom as agency of purpose and meaning.[10] Subsequent writings further probed the implications of this nexus, by shifting attention to Freudian psychoanalysis, linguistics, and symbolic interpretation. In his study of Freud, Ricoeur compared and contrasted two major types of interpretive inquiry: one directed to the recovery of latent intentional meaning, and another devoted to the deciphering of non-intentional psychic processes obstructing meaning. A similar kind of relationship was still at issue in his comments on the respective merits of hermeneutics and structural analysis, formulated at the beginning of this decade.[11]

Given his impressive productivity and the broad range of his concerns, a brief presentation of Ricoeur's views is difficult and hazardous; rather than attempting a synopsis of his writings I shall concentrate on one essay in which the topic under consideration is succinctly developed. Entitled "Nature and Freedom" (and published in 1962), the essay carefully exposed the paradox inherent in *human nature* by disassembling its heterogeneous elements; such disassembly, however, was meant as a step on the road toward reintegration. "In an initial movement of thought, a regressive and reductive analysis," Ricoeur wrote, "freedom is set in opposition to the whole idea of nature, to both nature in general and to human nature. But," he added, "this triumph by mere opposition is a Pyrrhic victory, for such freedom is merely possible; to become real it must reaffirm nature both in man and outside him. There is no nature *of* man, we say in the first movement of thought. But there is a nature *in* man, we shall have to say in accordance with a second movement, which replies to the first with a progressive synthesis of experience." Thus, the basic task of the paper was to outline the paths of the two opposing movements and to indicate how their dialectical relationship was intelligible: "How can nature appear in turn as both the *'other'* of freedom *and* as its primordial *mediation?*"

According to Ricoeur, the regressive path could be further subdivided into three successive steps, each indicating a progressive intensification of the man-nature conflict. The first step—entailing the initial emergence of the *humanity of man*—erects a prereflective opposition which can be "summed up in the threefold conquest of the institution, the tool, and language." While institutionalization opens the breach between civilization and amorphous natural chaos, the discovery of tools divides the world into artifacts and living beings, just as language produces a dichotomy between signs and mute appearances. In contrast to the human capacities for speech, tool-making, and civil order, nature on this level appears as "violence in man, spontaneity in living organisms, and mute, brute existence in mere objects." Ricoeur conceded that the conflict at this point remains only partial, since it is still possible to regard the mentioned human capacities as the innate telos or goal of nature. It is precisely this notion of a natural teleology which, in modern times, was "shattered by reflection," more specifically by the advance of natural science and the "mathematization of the real" transforming nature into a causal mechanism. This change is the second step in the regressive phase of analysis, highlighted by the confrontation between modern technology and natural resources and also by the antithesis between *is* and *ought* (or between natural and moral causation). Even in this case a linkage persists, rooted in the *homology* between the *law of nature* and the *moral law* of conscience. The third move, involving a further deepening of self-reflection, ruptures this umbilical cord and produces the *"exile of the Cogito"* from *nature* in every sense of that term. "In perceiving the 'I think' as a consciousness which 'is able to accompany all my representations,' I place this 'I' outside the sphere of objectivity," Ricoeur observed. The last step of the reductive analysis is thus a "zero point of nature": "Having withdrawn from things, the *Cogito* now withdraws from that which in itself is a thing. Having absented itself from *nature,* it now absents itself from *its own* nature and, lacking a nature, surrenders to the throes of self-determination."[12]

With this retreat from nature, man's humanity seems completely triumphant; however, what has been gained, in Ricoeur's view, is merely "the most negative, the most unreal, the most impotent of freedoms." A philosophy of total negation, he noted, is bound to remain simply "the opposite of a philosophy," manifesting "the adolescence of freedom." In order to gain a more adequate view of the human condition it is necessary to proceed from reduction to the progressive path of analysis—which again comprises three distinct steps, corresponding in reverse order to the moments of regression. The first step involves a basic change of perspective, from theory or cognition to practice, or from thinking to acting. According to Ricoeur, the misconception of freedom as total negation is due to a cognitive outlook which places consciousness as transparency in opposition to the inert compactness of external things. To overcome this contrast, recourse has to be taken to the conception of existence as practice (rather than as absence or positive presence)—a conception which finds support in a long philosophical tradition of the act of existing, including Spinoza's notion of effort (*conatus*) and Leibniz's theory of appetition. "It is because this meaning of being was forgotten," Ricoeur stated, "that we thought that the emergence of freedom out of nothingness had to be opposed to the essential being, the already completed being, the dead being, of things." This constraint vanishes once it is seen that being is *act* before it is *essence,* and is effort before it is consciousness or idea: "This recovery of what I shall call the active meaning of being is the most fundamental condition for a recovery of nature within freedom."

The second step, as crucial as the first, revolves around the articulation of a proper philosophy of action delineating the concrete emergence of freedom. Two aspects have to be stressed in such an articulation, ones which are commonly ignored in prevalent theories of action, especially those patterned after Kantian noumenal autonomy. The first and central aspect is the linkage of practice and desire, or inclination. Viewed from a non-cognitive vantage point, action has to be seen neither as an absolute project proceeding from consciousness, nor as a biological or psychological impulse, nor finally as the subordination of impulse to rational dictates. Deviating from formulations in some of his earlier writings, Ricoeur insisted that "the becoming-real of freedom does not consist in giving a matter to a form or in subsuming the particular under a rule." Rather, what needs to be taken into account is that "reflective choice always follows from some non-reflective movement, some inchoate act, tendency or inclination which deserves the name of spontaneous will or natural freedom." Given the linkage between effort and desire (highlighted in the Platonic *Eros*), human practice denotes more than a series of isolated decisions; it represents a course of existence or a "way of life": action is a process of habituation and character formation. The second major aspect derives from the deficiency of existence: the circumstance that desire is always a quest for something, but "something which it does not possess, which it lacks." From this perspective, practice is not simply an empirical occurrence; nor is it a gap in existence caused by the intervention of total negativity. The relationship between effort and fulfillment is neither linear nor antithetical but oblique (in the manner of a concrete negation): without being deducible the missing element is anticipated by desire. In Ricoeur's words: "Effort, in its most basic structure, is the affirmation of being in the lack of being."[13]

In its last step, progressive analysis rejoins the level of civilization from which the entire inquiry started. Centered on the realization of freedom, the step penetrates to the "central dialectic of action": namely, the "dialectic of the action and the work," the juncture at which freedom imprints its mark on the world in "those lasting objects" which

"deserve to be known as 'works' " or "*pragmata.*" Permeated by concrete effort, these pragmata are indeed the outgrowth of human activity—without being expressions of willful invention. Construed as
work, human practice is not synonymous with instrumental labor or
production—which is a derivative mode of action predicated on subjective design. Embedded in a non- or precognitive context, Ricoeur
argued, human work is pervaded by the "discipline of the finite" and
manifests "the *naturalizing* of freedom which this discipline of the
work implies. We shall have to say, then," he added, "that freedom is
potency only by means of a fundamental objectification in works." The
focus on work, in Ricoeur's view, finally establishes the "prevalence of
the point of view of mediation over that of opposition" and thus provides at least a tentative answer to the initial query how nature, though
distinct from freedom and reflection, can function as their mediation.
Moving along its regressive and progressive paths, the entire argument
reveals reflection's openness to, and entanglement in, non-thought; the
"successive mediations of freedom" displayed in the course of the analysis can be seen as "a kind of indefinite approximation to the forgotten
nature."[14]

Perceptual Faith: Merleau-Ponty

Ricoeur's discussion of the man-nature dilemma was subtle and penetrating; yet, despite the stress on mediations, the relationship between
regression and synthesis remained precarious and to some degree antithetical. More importantly, the counterpoint of steps seemed to operate
largely within the confines of a purely intellectual dialectic. Comparatively speaking, Merleau-Ponty's outlook was from the beginning less
schematic and more attentive to the concrete nuances of experience.
His concern with human embodiment—prominent in all his writings—
implied a stand against reductionist empiricism and against a self-
confident intellectualism. Nevertheless, at least during their formative
stages, the attitudes of these two phenomenologists were not far apart.
Like Ricoeur, Merleau-Ponty was deeply indebted to Husserl's teachings, and more generally to the legacy of transcendental idealism.
Despite his efforts to overcome traditional dichotomies and to avoid
one-sided empiricist or rationalist positions, his early publications contained traces of this legacy, although they were mingled with novel,
anti-idealist arguments. Thus, as formulated in studies written during
the Second World War, the notion of embodiment heralded not so
much (or not unequivocally) the abandonment of the philosophy of

reflection as the replacement of an abstract *cogito* by a concretely situated subjectivity. "The person who, in sensory exploration, gives a past to the present and directs it towards a future," we read in *Phenomenology of Perception,* "is not myself as an autonomous subject, but myself insofar as I have a body and am able to 'look.' " In a later passage the same study affirms: "If, when reflecting on the essence of subjectivity, I find it bound up with that of the body and that of the world, this is because my existence as subjectivity is merely one with my existence as a body and with the existence of the world, and because the subject that I am, when taken concretely, is inseparable from this body and this world."[15]

The conception of human existence as embodied subjectivity continued to permeate Merleau-Ponty's writings after the war. Although concretely situated in the world, existential experience was endowed with some of the noumenal and negative qualities traditionally associated with consciousness. Commenting on the relations between man and his natural surroundings, an essay dealing with Sartrean existentialism noted: "We cannot help but envy that plenitude of nature—crops growing and seasons succeeding one another in accordance with their perpetual law. In the face of this 'order,' man is the creature who never achieves completion; he is a rift, as it were, in the peaceful fabric of the world." Similarly, an essay devoted to a discussion of Hegel's thought observed that "man, as opposed to the pebble which is what it is, is defined as a place of unrest (*Unruhe*), a constant effort to get back to himself, and consequently by his refusal to limit himself to one or another of his determinations." Accentuating the contrast between subject and object or man and nature, Merleau-Ponty insisted in the same context that "if the only components of the world were things or beings, there would not be even a semblance of what we call man—that is, a being which is not, which denies things, an existence without an essence." Imbued with consciousness, man was portrayed as the carrier of negation, as the source of transcendental negativity in the midst of the world; his substantive (or ontological) deficiency differentiated him from both inorganic and organic nature. Consciousness, we read, "implies the ability to step back from any given thing and to deny it. An animal can quietly find contentment in life and seek salvation in reproduction; man's only access to the universal is the fact that he exists instead of merely living."[16]

As indicated, Merleau-Ponty's position during his early period was far from univocal; the cited comments were interspersed with arguments which transgressed the bounds of consciousness. With regard to the topic under discussion, a passage in *Phenomenology of Perception* stated: "I am thrown into a nature, and that nature appears not only as external world, in objects devoid of history, but is also discernible at the center of subjectivity."[17] His subsequent intellectual development reflected a growing impatience not only with subject-centered reflection but with anthropocentrism in general; as a corollary of these changes the man-nature relationship became the target of intensive reinterpretation. Concern with this issue was clearly evident both in Merleau-Ponty's later writings and in the lectures he delivered at the Collège de France. One of his lecture courses—started a decade after the essay on Hegel and extending over several years—was devoted to a reconsideration of the "Concept of Nature." "The neglect which has fallen upon the philosophy of nature," Merleau-Ponty observed in the synoptic résumé of this course, "is closely linked with a certain conception of spirit, history, and man: namely, the conception which makes them appear as pure negativity." By returning to the "philosophy of nature," he conceded, an impression might be created that the problems surrounding man and history were going to be suppressed; actually, however, the return was meant to encourage a solution of these problems on a "not *immaterialist*" basis: "Naturalism apart, an ontology which leaves nature in silence shuts itself in the incorporeal and for this very reason gives a fantastic image of man, spirit and history. If we have stressed the problem of nature, it is from the double conviction that it cannot by itself solve the ontological problem but that neither is it a subordinate or secondary element in any such solution."[18]

Turning his attention to the history of modern thought, Merleau-Ponty found among leading philosophers either a neglect of nature or else a tendency to treat it as a self-contained universe juxtaposed to mind or spirit and devoid of the mind's negative or creative faculties. This tendency was particularly manifest in the Cartesian view of nature as extended matter. This view, Merleau-Ponty wrote, "obliges every being, under pain of being nothing, to exist completely without hiatus, and with no hidden possibilities. There is to be nothing occult or enveloped in nature any more." Reduced to a material mechanism, nature in Descartes' treatment appeared as *"natura naturata,"* that is, as "a pure product, composed of absolutely external parts, completely existent and clearly combined," while "everything internal" or innovative was "handed over to God's side, the pure *naturans.*"[19] In a more subtle manner, the juxtaposition of thought and extended matter was maintained in Kantian philosophy. In the *Critique of Pure Reason,*

Merleau-Ponty commented, nature was defined "as 'the sum of sense objects' coordinated under the *Naturbegriffe* of human reason. We can only speak of a nature that is nature for us; in this regard nature remains the object which Descartes had in mind, it is a universe conceived by us." Although acknowledging, in the *Critique of Judgment,* the possibility of a non-mechanical and purposive conception of nature, Kant in the end regarded natural teleology as a type of anthropomorphism or as an outgrowth of human subjectivity. In the words of the résumé: "It is in the 'concept of freedom' only and consequently in consciousness and man that the conformity of the elements to a purpose takes on a real sense, so that the teleology of nature is a reflection of 'noumenal man.' The truth of teleology is the consciousness of freedom."[20]

According to Merleau-Ponty, serious efforts to revise the Cartesian and Kantian legacy were first undertaken by Schelling and Marx, but Marx never succeeded in overcoming the *naturans-naturata* dichotomy. In both his early manuscripts and subsequent works influenced by Feuerbach, Marx tried to articulate a concrete dialectic of man and world; however, largely due to the unclarified status of *nature*—a term which meanders through his opus "like a visitation"—the attempt proved abortive. Nature, we read, was "described on the one hand as a state of equilibrium existing in its own right—the stable being which will again close in upon human history at its end—and on the other hand as that which human history negates and transforms. Instead of being mastered or transcended, these two conceptions are simply juxtaposed, and finally forced to mix in the absolute of 'objective activity.' "[21] Unlike the unresolved antithesis in Marx's thought, Schelling's philosophy managed to make some tentative steps in the direction of nature construed neither as external matter nor as a foil of conscious creativity. As delineated in his writings, the notion of a primary nature (*erste Natur*) emerged as "an ambiguous principle, or, as he puts it, a 'barbarous' principle which can be transcended, but will never be as though it had never existed." Schelling's access to this domain was not through reason or reflection, but rather through *intellectual intuition* or intuitive experience—which was "not an occult faculty, but perception as it is before it has been reduced to ideas; it is perception dormant within itself, in which all things are me because I am not yet the reflecting subject." Since it was not the counterpart of consciousness, primary nature could never give rise to "a second science or a gnosis which would objectivate and absurdly convert into a second causality the realities of existing nature as we glimpse them in the 'ek-stasis' of intellectual intuition."[22]

In our century, Merleau-Ponty found promising initiatives in Bergson's life-philosophy, in post-subjectivist phenomenology, and also in post-Newtonian conceptions of science. Despite some affinities with positivist empiricism, Bergson refused to treat nature simply as a "fascinating object" of rational inquiry; rather, he viewed it (at least intermittently) "as a horizon from which we are already far away, a primordial lost undividedness, a unity which the contradictions of the developed universe negate and express in their own way." In Merleau-Ponty's view, Husserl's later writings—especially those focusing on the life-world—intimated a conception of nature which was no longer synonymous with a universe "posited before a purely theoretical subject" or observer. "Beneath Cartesian nature, which theoretical activity sooner or later constructs," he wrote (perhaps bending Husserl's thought too strongly in an ontological direction), "there emerges an anterior stratum, which is never suppressed, and which demands justification once the development of knowledge reveals the gaps in Cartesian science." The anterior stratum uncovered at this point was that of another nature dwelling "at the root and in the depths of Cartesian nature," namely, the arena of an *originary presence,* of "the earth as the seat of pre-objective spatiality and temporality." Comments of this kind seem to capture correctly some of Heidegger's philosophical intentions, especially the basis of his *existence*—a term which another lecture résumé tells us might be taken to denote *non-being,* but not in the sense of complete negativity: "It is beyond such correlatives—object and nihilating nothingness—that philosophy takes its start, namely, in a 'there exists,' in an 'opening' toward 'something,' toward 'that which is not nothing.' "[23]

Paralleling the endeavors of philosophers, developments in contemporary scientific thought also began to challenge the Cartesian conception of nature and its recent offshoot, the positivist thesis of the compactness or empirical solidity of reality. According to Merleau-Ponty, scientific theory in our time was moving away from the Newtonian concept of mechanics and from the deterministic ontology formulated by Laplace. "At the very moment," he wrote, "where twentieth-century physics has increased our power over nature to an unbelievable degree, it raises paradoxically the question of the meaning of its own truth in liberating itself from subjection to mechanical models and from figurative models in general." In attacking traditional notions of space and time, post-Euclidean geometry and relativity physics acknowledged the observer's role in cognition and thus granted "full ontological significance to certain descriptions of perceived space and time—to polymorphous space and time of which common sense and science retain only a few traces." A new view of nature emerged from this attack, one in which elements are no longer "constrained to a unique and fixed location, to an absolute density of being" in the empiricist sense: "In place of Laplace's dogmatic objectivity, we glimpse an objectivity pledged upon the inherence of all thinking subjects in the same core of being which remains amorphous." The sketched changes affected both inorganic physics and the domain of organic life; the latter domain, in particular, was "incomprehensible both to the philosophy of the object (mechanism *and* vitalism) and to the philosophy of the idea" and could be clarified only "through a philosophy of 'something,' or, as one says nowadays, a philosophy of structure." In the end, the lecture résumé noted, "the ontology of life, as well as that of 'physical nature,' can only escape its troubles by resorting, apart from all artificialism, to brute being as revealed to us in our perceptual contact with the world."[24]

As Merleau-Ponty made clear, the new recognition of nature adumbrated in recent philosophy (and corroborated by science) did not signal a lapse into naturalism—for the simple reason that *naturalism* in its traditional meaning presupposes the cognitive role of subjectivity and thus cannot possibly yield access to the arena of prereflective or brute being. "There is a truth in naturalism," we read; "but that truth is not naturalism itself. For to acknowledge naturalism and the envelopment of consciousness in the universe of 'mere things' (*blosse Sachen*) as an occurrence, is precisely to posit the theoretical world to which they belong as primary, which is an extreme form of idealism. It is in fact to refuse to decipher the intentional references which run from the universe of 'mere things,' or extended objects, to 'pretheoretical objects,' to the life of consciousness before science." As soon as theoretical reason was dislodged from its pivotal place, nature no longer appeared as an external assembly of things nor human nature as a pure subjectivity or negativity. "Nature," Merleau-Ponty asserted, "is not simply the object, the accessory of consciousness in its tête-à-tête with knowledge. It is an object from which we have arisen, in which our beginnings have been posited little by little until the very moment of tying themselves to an existence which they continue to sustain and aliment." Viewed from this perspective, man's status in the world was no longer that of an alien spectator, and the "originary relation between man and being" could not be equated with "that of the for-itself to the in-itself"; rather, nature (in Lucien Herr's words) had to be acknowledged as being " 'there from the first day.' It presents itself always as already there before us, and yet as new before our gaze."[25]

Man's being-in-the-world, conceived as involvement in prereflective nature, was inevitably a bodily involvement; the focus of the lectures thus gave new weight to Merleau-Ponty's longstanding preoccupation with embodiment. However, the meaning of the term had by now undergone significant modifications. Embodiment no longer denoted (or not principally) a concretely situated intentional consciousness, but referred to the embeddedness of experience in a bodily world largely impervious to intentional designs. After a long struggle to grasp the core of things, Merleau-Ponty noted, Western philosophy—and phenomenology in particular—had encountered "nature as an oriented and blind productivity"; through the "very exercise of reflective rigor" thought discovered "a natural stratum in which the spirit is virtually buried in the concordant functioning of bodies within brute being." In light of this discovery (or rediscovery) it was necessary to "think of the human body (and not 'consciousness') as that which perceives nature which it also inhabits"; given the corporeal character of experience, perceived things were not simply objects for thought but "caught in this bodily experience like in a cocoon" and "virtually incorporated in my flesh." The relation between man and nature, against this background, was neither one-dimensional (in the sense of naturalism) nor antithetical (as assumed by the philosophy of reflection), for it was neither plausible to assume that "a body-instrument had received from elsewhere a thought-pilot" nor that "an object called the body had mysteriously produced consciousness out of itself." Rather the relation was one of mutual inherence (*"Ineinander"*), of a *double nature* where positive being and transcendence (or negation) were locked together: "The body proper intimates a philosophy of the flesh as the visibility of the invisible."[26]

The notion of a philosophy, or rather ontology, of the flesh, alluded to in the lectures, was elaborated in greater detail in Merleau-Ponty's last major manuscript whose completion was prevented by his premature death in 1961: *The Visible and the Invisible*. In this work, man's primary or prereflective contact with the world and nature was articulated in terms of a *perceptual faith,* that is, an initial acceptance which "knows itself to be beyond proofs, not necessary, interwoven with incredulity, at each moment menaced by non-faith" and which reflects our original *"openness upon being."* Nurtured by this acceptance, man's relation with nature was neither a subject-object confrontation nor a simple convergence, but was an intimate intertwining or chiasm—according to which man cannot have access to the visible world "unless he *is of it,"* unless, "as one of the visibles," he is "capable, by a singular reversal, of seeing them." In line with the lecture résumé, the manuscript placed a crucial accent on the role of embodiment—a term which again signified not merely an enclosure of subjectivity, but the medium of man's insertion into the universe. Man's body, Merleau-Ponty observed, is able to perceive visible things only because, "being of their family, itself visible and tangible, it uses its own being as a means to participate in theirs," because ultimately it "belongs to the order of the things as the world is universal flesh." As used in this phrase, the last expression was not a synonym for ontic reality, but served to highlight a complex linkage, the interpenetration of positive being and transcendence, visibility and invisibility—where transcendence (construed as invisible) functioned not simply as "the contradictory of the visible" or as an "absolute invisible" but rather as "the secret counterpart of the visible," as "the invisible *of* this world" which "inhabits" and "sustains it," as "the Being of this being." Man's inherence in this universal nexus, Merleau-Ponty suggested, could plausibly be described as praxis—provided praxis denoted not so much an intentional design as participation in work viewed as interchange with nature. The last sentence of the "Working Notes" attached to the study offered a new definition of chiasm: "Worked-over-matter-men."[27]

Nature and "Supplement": Derrida

Once the notions of a double nature and of an intricate intertwining of man and nature are taken seriously, a good deal of the traditional terminology of the social or human sciences—including the dichotomies between nature and nurture and between the state of nature and the social state—is thrown into disarray or at least needs careful reconsideration. Significant steps in such reconsideration have been undertaken by Jacques Derrida, in writings which pay tribute both to Heideggerian ontology and to contemporary structuralism (in its non-formalist and non-positivist versions). According to Derrida, nurture or culture has to be seen not as a purely man-made artifact, but rather as a corollary or supplement of nature—provided that nature, instead of being treated as a self-contained and compact universe, is viewed as one dimension in the "play of (ontic-ontological) difference" whose component elements reciprocally supplement each other. Apart from upsetting terminological distinctions, this perspective has the effect of jeopardizing prevalent epistemological beliefs, especially the idea that natural science (positivistically construed) functions as a model for all types of inquiry, or as a foil against which cultural disciplines are silhouetted.

In stressing the supplementary and non-foundational character of nature and its investigation, this outlook also casts doubt on emotional embellishments of nature, as illustrated, for example, in Rousseau's image of the *bon sauvage* or more generally in romantic pleas for a return to nature, conceived as recovery of an unspoiled origin.

In large measure, Derrida's views on the man-nature issue are presented in a commentary on the works of Claude Lévi-Strauss, the pioneer of present-day structuralist anthropology and ethnology. On a theoretical plane, Derrida notes, Lévi-Strauss' opus is based on the philosophical obsolescence of the nature-culture dichotomy—where the defining criterion of nature is placed in its universal, non-volitional, or spontaneous characteristics, in contrast to the artificiality and variability of culture. Key evidence for this obsolescence is found in the immemorial prohibition of incest, a prohibition which Lévi-Strauss repeatedly depicts as a scandal for traditional thought because of its status as both a cultural norm and a universal (thus quasi-natural) principle. We read in his first book, *The Elementary Structures of Kinship,* that if we presuppose "that everything universal in man pertains to the natural order and is characterized by spontaneity, while everything subject to norms belongs to culture and is both relative and particular," then we are "confronted with a fact or rather a group of facts which, in light of the previous definitions, are not far removed from a scandal: we refer to that complex set of beliefs, customs, conditions and institutions described succinctly as the prohibition of incest which, unambiguously and inseparably linked, displays the two traits in which we recognize the conflicting features of two mutually exclusive orders." The prohibition, Lévi-Strauss elaborates, "constitutes a rule, but a rule which, alone among all the social rules, possesses at the same time a universal quality."[28]

Following the intimations of this obsolescence Lévi-Strauss—in at least portions of his writings—explores novel theoretical terrain, in which the status of the prohibition appears no longer as a scandalous anomaly. "There is obviously no scandal," Derrida comments, "except *within* a system of concepts which accredits the bifurcation between nature and culture. By founding his work on the anthropological fact of incest prohibition, Lévi-Strauss places himself at a point at which this distinction—hitherto always taken for granted—finds itself erased or questioned."[29] The theoretical domain whose contours emerge at this point is that of a moving and open-ended structure which, in lieu of conceptual dichotomies, makes room for precognitive complementarity. In its traditional sense, Derrida observes, the term *structure* denoted a set of compact elements amenable to cognitive empirical analysis and endowed with a fixed nucleus. "The function of this center," he writes, "was not only to orient, balance, and organize the structure" but above all "to make sure that the organizational principle of the structure would limit and contain what one might call the *play* of the structure." Once traditional epistemology and its positivist-empiricist offshoot are set aside, a structural arrangement comes into view which—devoid of an (ontic) center—is lodged at the intersection of absence and presence, an intersection or *difference* which antedates and sustains cognitive-conceptual categories. Under the impact of both anthropological findings and the ontological critique of epistemology (or metaphysics), we read, contemporary thought was at long last "constrained to acknowledge that there is no center, that the center cannot be grasped as an (ontic) presence or be pinpointed in its natural location, for the simple reason that it is not a fixed locality or place but rather a function, a sort of non-place where an infinite number of sign-substitutions comes into play. This was the moment when language invaded the universal problematic—the moment when, due to the absence of a center or origin, everything turned into discourse."[30]

According to Derrida, however, Lévi-Strauss' departure from positivism and its epistemological parentage is only halfhearted and, above all, not fully reflected on a philosophical plane; to a large extent his writings combine a naive-intuitive dismissal of the truth-claims of the nature-culture dichotomy with a willingness to utilize the distinction for methodological purposes. This willingness—sometimes described by Lévi-Strauss as *bricolage* or a noncommittal experimentation with available "means at hand"—is in fact evident as an orienting principle in all of his concrete investigations. As he states, for example, in *The Elementary Structures of Kinship,* the "distinction between nature and society ('nature' and 'culture' would seem preferable to us today), while devoid of an acceptable historical significance, does contain a certain logic which fully justifies its use by modern sociology as a methodological tool." This outlook is reaffirmed in his later study entitled *The Savage Mind,* where we read that "the opposition between nature and culture to which I attached much importance at one time now seems to be of primarily methodological importance." As Derrida notes: "Lévi-Strauss believes that in this manner he can separate *method* from *truth,* the methodological instruments from the objective significations intimated by them. One could almost say that this is his primary affirmation."[31]

While appreciating *bricolage* or methodological flexibility, Derrida finds disconcerting Lévi-Strauss' segregation of *truth* and *method* and his reluctance to ponder the philosophical implications of the status of incest prohibition. Due to the failure to explore such questions, the castigated epistemological categories are not so much overcome as converted into opaque paradoxes; the presumed "step beyond" traditional dualisms is in danger of creating theoretical confusion—or of simply truncating the dichotomies in favor of one constituent alternative. "For lack of an explicit formulation of the problem," Derrida observes, "one is condemned to transform the alleged surpassing of (traditional) philosophy into an unnoticed mistake within the same philosophical realm"; in this manner, supposedly "trans-philosophical concepts" risk being "transmuted into philosophical naivetés." In a passage which has more general application, beyond structuralist anthropology, he adds: "What I want to emphasize is simply that to 'go beyond' philosophy cannot signify to turn one's back to philosophy (which usually amounts to philosophizing badly), but rather to continue reading philosophers *in a certain way*. The peril I am speaking of is always shouldered by Lévi-Strauss; it is the very price of his endeavor."[32]

Lévi-Strauss' work is beleaguered by more than general philosophical quandaries; in Derrida's view, it frequently displays a truncation of dichotomies, and particularly shows a submergence of structuralist analysis in empiricism and even in epistemological naturalism. This tendency of truncation can be detected throughout Lévi-Strauss' publications; it surfaces especially in *The Savage Mind,* where we are told: "It would not be enough, however, to absorb particular human groupings into a general category of mankind. This first enterprise opens the way for others" which basically "are incumbent on the exact natural sciences: the reintegration of culture in nature and finally of life within the whole of its psycho-chemical conditions." As Derrida critically comments, the invocation of natural science, although innocuous in itself, amounts to a theoretical abdication in light of structuralism's broader ambitions (manifest in the treatment of incest prohibition). Positivist-empiricist epistemology, he notes, can be defined as the genus which encompasses as different species all the various philosophical mistakes arising from the neglect of philosophy; it forms "the matrix of all the errors threatening a discourse which—like that of Lévi-Strauss—intends to remain scientific." The danger is particularly endemic in the latter's writings, due to structuralism's aversion to subjectivity and the legacy of the *ego cogitans*. However, Derrida suggests that to substitute objectivism for egology, even in a purely experimental way, is an inadequate manner of dealing with epistemological dilemmas: "If we were to probe thoroughly the problem of empiricism and *'bricolage,'* we would probably end up very quickly with a number of absolutely contradictory propositions concerning the status of discourse in structural ethnology."[33]

Apart from, or rather hovering behind, his intermittent inclination to a naturalist epistemology, Derrida detects in Lévi-Strauss a deep emotional attachment to nature, seen as an unspoiled haven or refuge—an attachment linking his outlook with Rousseauism or at least with Rousseau's early writings. The linkage, of course, is not merely an exegetic speculation. Lévi-Strauss himself has been explicit in voicing his indebtedness to the philosopher of Geneva. According to his study on *Totemism,* "Rousseau did not merely foresee anthropology, but founded it"; in the same study, the second *Discourse* ("On the Origin and Foundations of Inequality") is portrayed as "the first treatise of general anthropology in French literature" where "in almost modern terms Rousseau poses the central problem of anthropology: the passage from nature to culture."[34] Derrida exaggerates only slightly when he perceives in Lévi-Strauss' posture "a declared and militant Rousseauism" and when he asserts, as a point of general knowledge, that "Lévi-Strauss not only feels himself to be in *agreement* with Jean-Jacques, to be his heir at heart and in what might be called theoretical affect," but "also often presents himself as Rousseau's modern disciple," reading the latter "as the *founder,* not only the prophet, of modern anthropology." The relevance of Rousseauism for anthropology is highlighted in another context where Derrida writes that, despite Lévi-Strauss' masterful talent to reveal "better than any other" in his structural analyses the complex "play of repetition and the repetition of play," one nonetheless "discovers in his work a sort of ethic of (ontic) presence, a nostalgia for origins, for an archaic and natural innocence, for the presence and self-presence accomplished in speech. This ethic, nostalgia, and even remorse are frequently presented by him as the motivation of the ethnological enterprise with its attentiveness to archaic societies (which are exemplary societies in his eyes)."[35]

In Derrida's view, however, Rousseauism is not an unproblematic ancestry. Following in the footsteps of Heidegger's "destruction of Western metaphysics," he sees Rousseau's work as a particularly instructive manifestation of traditional Western epistemology, whose unifying characteristic he identifies as *logocentrism* or the attempt to render everything present and intelligible to *logos* or human reason. "If the history of metaphysics is the history of the determination of

being as presence, if its adventure merges with that of logocentrism,"
he writes, then "Rousseau's work seems to me to occupy, between Plato's *Phaedrus* and Hegel's *Encyclopaedia,* a singular position." Actually, Derrida divides the history of Western epistemology into two
major periods, the boundary marked by the advent of Cartesianism or
by the focus on certitude associated with the "Cartesian *cogito."* Before that advent, he notes, the "identity of presence" was "constituted
under the 'objective' form of the ideality of the *eidos* or the substan-
tiality of *ousia;* thereafter, this objectivity takes the form of *representation,* of the *idea* as the modification of a self-present substance, conscious and certain of itself at the moment of its relationship to itself."
In terms of the central thrust of metaphysics, the second phase em-
bodies an epistemological refinement since, through its reliance on the
cogito, "the mastery of presence acquires a sort of infinite assurance,"
with *consciousness* indicating the locus of "pure auto-affection"—an
experience which, according to Derrida, finds fulfillment chiefly in
speech rather than in writing, with its dependency on external signi-
fiers. From this perspective, the philosopher of Geneva occupies an
important place in the history of modern thought, due both to his explicit stress on speech and to his more emotive reinterpretation of the
cogito: "Within this period of metaphysics between Descartes and
Hegel, Rousseau is undoubtedly the only one or the first to make a
theme or a system of the reduction of writing profoundly implied by
the entire age. He repeats the inaugural movement of the *Phaedrus*
and of *De interpretatione* but starts from a new model of presence:
the subject's self-presence within *conscience* or *feeling."*[36]

Seen in this broader philosophical context, Lévi-Strauss' attachment to Rousseauism implies his entanglement in logocentric epistemology, with its traditional conceptual dichotomies—a legacy which
he seeks to leave behind in his discussion of the nature-culture issue
and especially in his comments on incest prohibition. From Rousseau's
standpoint, as articulated in the *Discourses* and other well-known writings, *nature* definitely occupies a privileged status in comparison with
the social or cultural condition. Instead of being linked in supplementarity or complementarity (reflecting the ontological "play of difference"), nature and culture in his perspective are both related and separated within a hierarchical order or a system of linear filiation. In one
of his works, Derrida remarks, Rousseau actually designates the domain of culture and human volition as a supplement—but as a "dan-
gerous supplement" which, although perhaps unavoidable, entails the
depravation of natural inclinations and which, far from being a direct

consequence of nature (or of a natural deficiency), befalls nature like an external accident. As Derrida elaborates, Rousseau's outlook is not averse to the notion of supplementation; in fact, his writings sometimes resort to a cumulative supplementarity or a chain of supplements, through which the defects of culture are to be remedied. However, these correctives typically serve as direction signals pointing toward unsupplemented originality and natural immediacy: "Through this sequence of supplements a necessity is announced: that of an infinite chain, ineluctably multiplying the supplementary mediations that produce the sense of the very thing they defer: the mirage of the thing itself, of immediate presence, of originary perception."[37]

The privileged status accorded to nature also overshadows Rousseau's account of the origin of society, which links two separate conditions through the intervention of contractual stipulations. According to Derrida, the closest that Rousseau came to a non-dualistic and non-linear conception was in his "Essay on the Origin of Languages." Instead of emphasizing a contractual connection, the "Essay" focuses on "original festivals" as the "true cradle of nations"; it is in the same essay that incest prohibition plays a key role—for, as Rousseau declares almost in the same breath, "the first men would have had to marry their sisters" but "the law prohibiting the practice is no less sacred for its human institution" or conventional character. "Before the festival," Derrida paraphrases, "there was no incest because there was no prohibition of incest and no society; after the festival there is no more incest because it is forbidden." Thus, "society, language, history, articulation, in a word supplementarity, are born at the same time as the prohibition of incest; the latter is the hinge between nature and culture."[38] However, once the notion of a *hinge* is explored more fully, the terms *before* and *after* and, more generally, the separation of an antecedent state of nature and a subsequent social state, become dubious. People living in a state of non-prohibition could not have committed incest since the practice is defined only by the prohibition. Consequently, society is locked from the beginning with nature in a supplemental embrace; rather than indicating a prior event, its origin operates only in an oblique manner. In Derrida's words: "The festival *itself* would be incest *itself* if some such thing—in itself—could take place; if, by taking place, incest were not to presuppose and confirm the prohibition: before the prohibition, it is not incest; forbidden, it cannot become incest except through the recognition of the prohibition. We are always short of or beyond the limit of the festival, of the origin of society." As he adds: "The *birth of society* is there-

fore not a passage; it is a point, a pure, fictive, unstable and ungrasp-
able limit."[39]

Implications for Political Theory

By way of conclusion I would like to indicate some of the implications
of the preceding arguments for social and political theory. One obvious
corollary is the impact of the arguments on a time-honored formula
which has played an important role in the history of social thought:
the Aristotelian (and Thomistic) conception of man as by nature a
"political (or social) animal." As commonly invoked and without further elaboration, the conception expresses a riddle; in the absence of
Merleau-Ponty's notion of intertwining or Derrida's comments on supplementarity, the formula encourages either an empiricist naturalism or
a cultural essentialism. Closely related to the Aristotelian adage are
other core ingredients customarily used in the philosophical treatment
of politics, such as the categories of *natural law* and *natural right* and
their distinction from positive or socially variable types of privileges
and obligations. The point here is not that these categories and distinctions are obsolete and do not retain a commonsense plausibility, but
that their theoretical status will remain obscure as long as they are tied
to traditional epistemological dichotomies whose cogency has been
questioned by contemporary philosophy, especially by the ontological
critique of the history of Western metaphysics.

Of equally broad philosophical significance are the consequences
of the reviewed writings for the theory of social and political *action*.
In this domain, recent investigations have oscillated between two radically opposed perspectives. On the one hand, *behaviorism* (and positivism in general) has fostered empirical analyses of causally determined
and predictable modes of human behavior—analyses which not only
truncate the range of human experience but also leave unexplained the
epistemological status of the social scientist or observer. On the other
hand, following to some extent Max Weber's lead, defenders of egological versions of phenomenology and existentialism have preferred to
concentrate on subjective intentionality, defining action as a voluntary
design or project. Both alternatives are at odds with the man-nature
nexus delineated above. Derrida's notion of play (or of the "play of
difference") intimates a view of human activity as involvement in an
ongoing practice which is not reducible to factual-ontic processes or to
the outgrowth of purposive freedom conceived as negativity. In a similar manner, Merleau-Ponty's discussion of intertwining and of the cor-

relation of visibility and invisibility is linked with a conception of praxis, placing the emphasis not on willful designs but on cooperation in work, construed as interchange with nature. Probably the most detailed and concrete suggestions for the formulation of a new philosophy of action are contained in Ricoeur's essay. His stress on the active meaning of being and on the connection between action and desire pinpoints (as he says) the "most fundamental condition for a recovery of nature within freedom" as well as some prerequisites for a theory of society and politics which seeks to avoid the pitfalls of naturalism and idealism. His focus also opens access to the investigation of social and political institutions seen as concrete enactments or *pragmata* and, more generally, to the study of social life-forms viewed as manifestations of human work and of "the *naturalizing* of freedom which this discipline of the work implies."[40]

Perhaps the most obvious implications can be found in the areas of political domination and political ideology. Given their central emphasis on the reintegration (and ultimate reconciliation) of man and nature, the discussed writings supply a strong antidote to forms of organized and willful domination in general and to a variant particularly relevant in our age—the force of technocracy, as the systematic domination of man over nature (and, as a corollary, of technocrats over society). Opposition to technocratic rule, which does not mean a simple condemnation of technology, is intimated in Merleau-Ponty's critique of positivist science and in his refusal to treat nature merely as "the object, the accessory of consciousness in its tête-à-tête with knowledge." Similarly, in his essay on "Nature and Freedom," Ricoeur observes that regressive analysis, with its focus on human initiative, yields a radicalization of the man-nature conflict, largely due to the fact that "the world of inertia and mechanics appears as something pure in relation to the activities of (human) domination, exploitation and possession. In industry, the struggle with nature prevails over man's belonging to and participating in nature." In another context, referring to the connotations of technical reason or "instrumental intelligence," he comments that "any reduction of reason to such understanding conspires in the end with violence. For the only thing indeed which then becomes thinkable is the organized struggle against nature."[41]

The critique of ideology is intimately associated with the critical questioning of modes of domination. More precisely, the critique applies to an "ideological politics" which construes politics as an arena for the implementation of theoretical platforms or blueprints. If Merleau-Ponty's political writings contain a basic orientation, it consists chiefly in the rejection of this idea, a rejection whose intensity deepened over the years. His first major political treatise, entitled *Humanism and Terror* (published in 1947) voiced strong objections to rigid ideologies and doctrinaire regimes both in the West and in the East. Regarding Western societies, he discovered a consolidation of capitalist structures coupled with an ossification of liberal ideas in abstraction from concrete human experience. "An aggressive liberalism exists," he wrote, "which is a dogma and already an ideology of war" and which "can be recognized by its love of the empyrean of principles, its failure ever to mention the geographical and historical circumstances to which it owes its birth and its abstract judgments of political systems without regard for the specific conditions under which they develop." Turning to the other side of the Iron Curtain, the study found that "the Marxist transition from formal liberty to actual liberty has not occurred and in the immediate future has no such chance"; instead of promoting this transition, official Marxism has chosen to maintain and aggravate "the dictatorial apparatus while renouncing the revolutionary liberty of the proletariat in the Soviets and its Party and abandoning the humane control of the state." In the face of doctrinaire and repressive trends on all sides, and especially in the face of a communism which is "increasingly strained" and showing "its dark side," Merleau-Ponty considered it "imperative to maintain the habit of discussion, criticism, research, and the apparatus of social and political culture. We must preserve liberty," he added, "while waiting for a fresh historical impulse which may allow us to engage it in a popular movement without ambiguity."[42]

As indicated, Merleau-Ponty's aversion to ideological politics intensified with time. His study of the *Adventures of the Dialectic* (which appeared less than a decade later) traced the pitfalls of official Marxism to a misconception of dialectics as a self-enclosed logical system, according to which thesis and antithesis automatically produce synthesis by a double negation. "The illusion," he observed, "consisted in placing history's entire meaning in one historical fact—the birth and growth of the proletariat—and in assuming that history would accomplish its own goal: differently put, that by acquiring power the proletariat, as negation of the negation, would abolish itself." Such an assumption, in Merleau-Ponty's view, was bound to give rise to political dogmatism and total domination: "If all negativity and the whole meaning of history are identified with one historical formation—the proletarian class—one is inevitably constrained to grant absolute power to its ruling representatives since everything else would be obstruction." The study defended a self-critical dialectic "in which each element opens onto the others" and which is "incomplete as long as it does not pass into other perspectives and into the perspectives of others." Translated into political terms, this outlook vindicated a "new" (left-leaning) liberalism or liberal socialism—a posture which "grants access to its universe even to forces which contest it and finds legitimacy only in understanding these forces."[43] Similar views, though formulated in more subtle philosophical language, can be found in *The Visible and the Invisible*. Stressing the intertwining of "philosophy or the transcendental and the empirical," Merleau-Ponty observed that there could be "no absolutely pure philosophical word" or doctrine; as a corollary, there could also be "no purely philosophical politics, for example, no philosophical rigorism, when it is a question of a Manifesto." The same manuscript also spoke of a *hyperdialectic,* that is, a dialectic which "criticizes and surpasses itself as a separate statement," which is "conscious of the fact that every *thesis* is an idealization, that Being is not made up of idealizations or of things said, as the old logic believed, but of bound wholes" where "the inertia of the content never permits the defining of one term as positive, another term as negative, and still less a third term as absolute suppression of the negative by itself."[44]

Among the thinkers discussed here, Ricoeur has probably been most attentive to concrete institutional arrangements. Surveying political developments on a global scale, his *Political and Social Essays* (containing articles written during the past few decades) detect a strengthening of governmental and managerial controls in both Western and socialist countries. In lieu of a gradual dismantling of sovereignty, he notes, "we see the State multiplying its functions of organization, direction, planning"; this "reinforcement of the State" is happening "in the very epoch which should see the change from political expression to human community." Everywhere, in his judgment, central administration is extending its grip on "all extremities of the social body," while political parties are becoming " 'machines' whose organizational complexities are matched only by the spirit of abstraction that infuses their slogans, programs, and propaganda." According to Ricoeur, the consolidation of central institutions is inevitably accompanied by a "growth in power and in the threat of tyranny." This danger appears particularly pronounced in socialist countries, since "large-scale socialist plans give to the central power methods of pressure on the individual that no bourgeois state has succeeded in mustering." Molded by Lenin and Stalin, official communism or orthodox Marxism vividly demonstrates this danger. In the interval between Marx and Stalin, we read, Marxism "has progressively *closed itself up:* it is understood increasingly dogmatically and mechanistically," while "political Machiavellism has suffocated it as free thought, and its eschatology has been reduced to a technical aspiration." In Ricoeur's view, the theory of proletarian dictatorship and its institutionalization in a single party are chiefly responsible for the "petrification of Marxism." Under the dictatorship principle, Marxism has turned into ideology and an *apology* for violence: for, "again there is the secret, the lie, the cleverness, and the *non-transparence of action,* once action is placed in the shadowy strategy of the proletarian state." Ideological manipulation is enhanced by the one-party structure: "The idea that there exists a group of men who hold a monopoly on the interpretation of history in its entirety, the notion that this group of men constitutes the sole vantage point on the totality—such views are the source of all the dogmatism that has congealed Marxism."[45]

From Ricoeur's perspective, however, Marxist sclerosis and the dangers of centralization in general are unable to impugn the cogency and urgency of socialism. In view of prevailing "disparities of an economic and social nature," he argues, political systems are obligated "to find economic forms of welfare"; actually, the "growing gap between rich and poor" or between developed and underdeveloped areas militates in favor of a global socialism or a "world-wide economy of needs." In its most fundamental sense, he asserts, socialism is not so much a technique as "the cry of distress, the demand and the hope of the most humbled men. This is why today one cannot separate socialism from solidarity with the most underprivileged fraction of humanity, with the misery of the underdeveloped peoples." As Ricoeur realizes, the goal of social and economic equity can only be pursued with governmental intervention and a measure of public economic planning—and consequently must conjure up the peril of the mentioned abuses. Like Merleau-Ponty, he is thus led to champion a liberal version of socialism which would combine endorsement of interventionist measures with the vigilant protection of freedom. In his words: "We have, in effect, to strengthen the State and, at the same time, to *limit* its power: that is the most extreme practical consequence of our entire analysis. It means that in the period in which we must extend the role of the State in economic and social matters and advance along the path of the *socialist State,* we must also continue the task of *liberal politics,* which has always consisted of two things: to divide power among powers, and to control executive power by popular representation."[46]

It seems to me that the opposition to ideological politics articulated by Ricoeur actually captures only a limited and relatively short-range connotation which arises from reassessment of the man-nature issue. In its broader or long-range thrust, the reassessment questions ideological abuses of state power as well as the structure and organization of the modern *state* itself, conceived as embodiment of human rationality or of rational-legal principles, as opposed to *society,* viewed as arena of natural-human inclinations. From this vantage point, the arguments outlined in this chapter point toward the much-belabored "withering-away of the state"—a notion which remains unintelligible as long as it is presented as the potential outgrowth of human initiative or planning. Clearly, the deemphasis on human mastery implicit in the discussed writings must affect the political state, seen (in the tradition of liberalism) as the idealized and rationalized form of mastery; precisely because of this logical connection, however, the disappearance of the institution cannot be expected to derive from the same motivations and conceptual categories which engendered and legitimated it in the history of Western thought (or metaphysics). Only a critical questioning of this legacy and a decentering of the *cogito*—as illustrated, for example, in Merleau-Ponty's attentiveness to wild or brute being—can bring into view, however distantly, a possible obsolescence of the state and state power. In pursuing the intimations of perceptual faith, Merleau-Ponty's perspective sketches the contour of a brute political experience or a wild politics, not reducible to the entrenched dichotomies of state and society or of public and private spheres. Reflecting on this perspective, one commentator speaks of a precognitive and "pre-political suffrage" underlying organized modes of collective life—a suffrage which, not to be confused with the "fiction of a pre-social state of nature," should be seen as "a genetic state in which violence and justice, truth and contradiction are the very matrix from which the option of a specific historical form of society emerges."[47]

The idea of a wild politics does not signify retreat to a condition of pristine innocence or the (presumed) life-pattern of the *bon sauvage;* above all, it does not vindicate the precipitous abandonment of political reflection and political initiative, together with the risks attached to such initiative. According to Derrida, such an abandonment, instead of coinciding with a return to nature, conjures up the danger of complete, unredeemable violence: "the violence of a primitive and prelogical silence, of an unimaginable night which would not even be the opposite of day; an absolute violence which, not being the antipode of non-violence, would be utter nothingness or pure non-sense." In Derrida's opinion, human thought, discourse, and initiative are from the beginning enmeshed in a play of power and violence, although not in an irremediable manner; as a corollary, the obsolescence of the state or state power is not equivalent to its immediate supersession by anarchy or non-power—which historically functioned merely as the state power's accomplice—but to the emergence of a *minimal power* or a power which obliquely foreshadows non-violence. As he writes, struggle "inhabits the philosophical *logos,* although it is only in and through this *logos* that peace may be declared." Even ontological thought, in his view, does not escape this dilemma; for, "the thought of Being, in its unveiling effort, is never completely alien to a certain violence" which entails dissimulation. Yet violence on this level is not inescapable: "Although the first violence is this concealment, it is also the first defeat of nihilistic violence and the first epiphany of Being." Against this background, peace and the good life are not so much the negation of politics and political discourse as their hidden sense: "Peace occurs only in a *certain silence* which is prepared and protected by the violence of language"—a silence which, we read, can also be described as "a certain transgression of the spoken word, a certain possibility, a certain silent horizon of speech."[48]

Viewed as a horizon, however, peace cannot be merely the effect of political machinations. The good life can neither be engineered nor imposed although it is not antithetical to human effort. When it arrives, it is liable to overtake us during the night, not like a thief but like a wealthy benefactor; at its approach, we are likely to discover that we have been heirs all along—but of riches we did not suspect or did not fathom in this form.

CHAPTER FOUR

Human Development and Social Evolution

Suscitans a terra inopem . . .

THE IMPORTANCE OF SOCIAL DYNAMICS or of social-political change in our age hardly needs corroborating evidence. In the period since the Second World War, the dismantling of colonial empires and the rise of nationalist movements has brought onto the global stage a great number of "newly emerging" countries—countries which, having accomplished the short-range goal of independence, find themselves in the throes of social-political evolution, modernization, or development.[1] The same trends have injected new life into evolutionary theory—more precisely, into efforts to formulate theoretical models capable of explaining and guiding the complex processes of change. Such efforts are not of merely academic significance; both developed and developing countries are liable to justify their policies by reference to some developmental scheme, sometimes with profound consequences for present and future generations. Due to its largely Western origin—an aspect which itself reflects the developmental syndrome—contemporary evolutionary theory is strongly suffused with Western experiences and perspectives, although not (or no longer) in an openly avowed manner. Responsive to charges of cultural imperialism—and also to the influence of positivism—social theorists today prefer to limit their sights to strictly pragmatic concerns. Focusing on the presumably central accomplishments of Western civilization, their models offer as developmental yardsticks technological complexity and steering capacity—that is, variations on the neo-Darwinian themes of natural selection and adaptation. Thus, while its technology is transforming the entire globe, Western science, in professing value-neutrality, obscures the possible meaning of this transformation.

Western thought has not always been this reticent or evasive. At least from the Enlightenment era to the end of the last century, philosophers of different persuasions tended to stress both material and moral advancement and emancipation as goals universally applicable to mankind. In our own age, one of the last great philosophers who explicitly paid tribute to this legacy—while refining some of its formulations—was Edmund Husserl. On the eve of the Second World

War, in the midst of a disoriented Europe, Husserl in stirring language depicted as the purpose or mission of European (or Western) culture not the display of technological prowess but the steady cultivation and strengthening of rational reflection and moral-human autonomy. Reflecting on the *immanent teleology* of European history, his *Crisis of European Sciences* spoke of the "breakthrough and developmental beginning of a new human epoch, seen from the standpoint of universal humanity: the epoch of a mankind which now seeks to live, and is only able to live, by freely determining its existence and its historical life on the basis of rational insight in the pursuit of infinite tasks." The breakthrough referred to the emergence of rational thought or *philosophy*—a term which, in its genuine meaning, involved the effort "to gain a deeper and comprehensive grasp of the world unfettered by myth and the whole tradition," that is, to acquire "a universal knowledge of man and world completely untrammeled by prejudice." The emergence, in Husserl's view, first occurred in classical Greece, but its effects shaped European culture as a whole and they intimate a universal human destiny. Regarding long-range developmental implications, the *Crisis* manuscript pondered the possibility that the goal or *"telos* which was inborn in European culture with the birth of Greek philosophy, namely, to be a life-form which seeks to exist, and is only able to exist, through philosophical reflection, moving endlessly from latent to manifest reason"—that this goal, instead of being "a factual historical delusion, the accidental acquisition of merely one among many other civilizations," actually signifies "the breakthrough of an essential dimension of humanity as such, its *entelechy.*"[2]

The emergence of reflection, in Husserl's presentation, was silhouetted against the backdrop of non-reflection or of an unreflective pragmatism. According to the *Crisis* study, the reflective or *theoretical attitude* was differentiated, both logically and historically, from the *natural primordial attitude* or the "attitude of original natural life" which permeated the "originally natural form of cultures." Natural life experienced in the natural primordial attitude was concretely pragmatic in that it was "characterized as a life naïvely and straightforwardly directed at the world, with the world always in a certain sense being consciously present as a universal horizon, but without being thematized as such." In Husserl's opinion, traditional cultures founded on this attitude were not devoid of general interpretive schemes of a religious-mythical type; however, even such schemes served chiefly pragmatic ends: "The mythical-religious attitude prevails when the world as a totality becomes thematic, but in a practical way," that is, when "the whole world is seen as thoroughly dominated by mythical powers, with the result that man's fate depends directly or indirectly upon the manner in which they hold sway." By contrast, the rise of theoretical reason introduced a disengagement from pragmatic concerns; once infected by this new attitude, "man becomes gripped by the passion for a world-view and world-knowledge which disregards all practical interests." Unlike the particular customs or mythical schemes of traditional cultures, the birth of philosophy engendered a "universal critical attitude toward anything and everything handed down by tradition"; it also gave rise to a new question of truth, one preoccupied not with "tradition-bound, every-day truth, but an identical truth valid for all who are no longer blinded by traditions." Originating in Greece, critical reason of this kind was the hallmark of European (Western) civilization, but it was bound to be contagious. The distinctiveness of Europe, we read, "is recognized in us by all other human groups too"; it is a distinctiveness which, "quite apart from considerations of utility and despite their unbroken commitment to cultural self-preservation, becomes for them a motivation steadily to Europeanize themselves, whereas we (if we understand ourselves properly) would never Indianize ourselves, for example."[3]

In tracing the teleological path of rationality, the *Crisis of European Sciences* drew a parallel between individual human development and social-cultural development or, to use social-scientific vocabulary, between ontogenesis and phylogenesis. Human life, we are told, is "a process of constant becoming and, given the correlation of individual-personal and communal-personal existence, this is true of both, that is, of individual man as well as of unified groupings or cultures." With particular focus on individual maturation, the study noted that life "develops in stages of self-reflection and self-responsibility, starting from isolated occasional acts of this kind and proceeding to the stage of universal self-reflection and self-determination, and finally to the conscious perception and enactment of the idea of autonomy, an idea involving the resolution to shape one's whole personal existence into the synthetic unity of a life of universal self-responsibility and, correlatively, to develop oneself into the true, free, and autonomous 'I' which seeks to realize and fulfill his innate reason—the yearning to be true to himself, to be able to remain identical with himself as a rational 'I.' " As Husserl added, however, individual maturation in this sense was inextricably linked with social-cultural development "due to their inner, direct or indirect correspondence or connection of interests, a connection manifesting itself both in harmony and in conflict," and also to the circumstance that individual reason could "come to ever more perfect self-realization only as communal rationality and vice versa." Regarding communal rationality, the study actually envisaged a global or unlimited community of discourse as developmental *telos:* "What is involved is no longer a juxtaposition of different nations influencing each other only through commerce or power struggles; rather, a new spirit stemming from philosophy and its particular sciences—a spirit of free critique and normatively oriented toward infinite tasks—pervades humanity through and through, creating new and infinite ideals."[4]

In the context of twentieth-century thought, Husserl's account of development is probably unmatched in its philosophical rigor; it is certainly unequaled in its eloquence and the loftiness of its vision, which elevates it far above the range of ephemeral political disputes (including disputes regarding cultural imperialism). On a more concrete level and with greater attention to social-political concerns, a comparable type of account—stressing the progressive maturation of reflection—has been sketched by two philosophers influenced by critical Marxism, Georg Lukács and Jean-Paul Sartre, but their formulations hardly approximate the comprehensive thrust of the *Crisis* study. In his *History and Class Consciousness,* Lukács portrayed human and social development as the progressive emancipation of consciousness against the background of traditional life-forms embedded in opaque natural constraints. While pre-modern (especially feudal) society was still too thoroughly natural to permit reflection or social awareness, modern capitalistic society was said to witness the emergence of rational economic structures—which, however (being raised to the status of a second nature), continued to operate in an unreflective manner or in the face of the "unconsciousness of social agents." Only the standpoint of the working class yielded a fully autonomous and reflective perspective, a perspective in which "self-knowledge and knowledge of the social totality coincide." The entire developmental process, in Lukács' view, could be construed as "a constant struggle aiming at higher levels of truth, that is, higher levels of the (social) *self-knowledge of man.*"[5] In a similar vein, Sartre's *Critique of Dialectical Reason* sought to unravel the "meaning of history and its truth" in terms of an unfolding logic of creative action or logic of freedom. As he wrote, a major aim of the (uncompleted) study was "to establish that there is *one* human history, with *one* truth and *one* intelligibility—not by considering the material content of this history, but by demonstrating that a practical multiplicity, whatever it may be, must unceasingly totalize itself by interiorizing its diversity at all levels."[6]

In the present chapter I would like to focus on a more recent approach to human and social development, whose scope and intellectual outlook, in my view, resembles Husserl's earlier presentation: an approach formulated by the German philosopher and sociologist, Jürgen Habermas. Like Husserl, Habermas' formulation emphasizes reflective maturation and seeks to link individual and social development—although, apart from relying extensively on social-scientific terminology and evidence, his treatment accentuates the communal or communicative aspects of all forms of evolution. After offering a synopsis of his pertinent writings, I shall indicate a number of critical reservations which can be, and have been, advanced against the view of rational growth implicit in Habermas' perspective. By way of conclusion, I will delineate a competing model of development, articulated in the same intellectual context (that of the Frankfurt school): Theodor Adorno's conception of natural history and of a negative dialectic, which, without relinquishing the civilizing gains of reflection, also ponders the reverse side of rationality and consciousness. To introduce this train of thought, and in order to convey a flavor of the counterpoint in which reason and rational development seem to be enmeshed, I want to cite a few somewhat somber sentences written by Walter Benjamin, the literary critic and aesthetician whose work exerted a profound influence on Adorno. "A Klee painting named 'Angelus Novus,' " we read,

> shows an angel looking as though he is about to move away from something he is fixedly contemplating. His eyes are staring, his mouth is open, his wings are spread. This is how one pictures the angel of history. His face is turned toward the past. Where we perceive a chain of events, he sees one single catastrophe which keeps piling wreckage upon wreckage and hurls it in front of his feet. The angel would like to stay, awaken the dead, and make whole what has been smashed. But a storm is blowing from Paradise; it has got caught in his wings with such violence that the angel can no longer close them. This storm irresistibly propels him into the future to which his back is turned, while the pile of debris before him grows skyward. This storm is what we call progress.[7]

Habermas on Human and Social Development

In a sense, Habermas has always been preoccupied with questions of evolution or development. His first major publication, *Strukturwandel der Öffentlichkeit* ("Structural Transformation of the Public Sphere"), examined the progressive distintegration of public-communicative discourse in industrial-bourgeois societies and its replacement by the rule of scientific experts, a rule no longer open to general, practical-moral scrutiny. His second, larger work, *Theory and Practice,* reviewed the same decline against the broader background of Western intellectual history; to a considerable extent, the book reasserted the tenor of Husserl's *Crisis* manuscript—although, instead of focusing on positivism and naturalism as basic antipodes of universal reflection, Habermas located the root of contemporary dilemmas in the unchecked sway of *instrumental* or *technical rationality* (a term whose meaning had previously been elaborated by Frankfurt theorists).[8] While containing significant historical insights, none of his early writings was meant to offer a developmental theory in the proper sense of the term. The first attempt to articulate such a theory (or at least to gather important building blocks) occurred a decade after *Theory and Practice,* in a study whose German title referred to "legitimation problems in late capitalism," which has been translated as *Legitimation Crisis.*[9] The study provides a helpful recapitulation of major models of evolution found in recent social-scientific literature; at the same time, a sustained effort is made to correct the positivist and instrumentalist bias implicit in such models. On the whole, the theoretical perspective delineated in *Legitimation Crisis* correlates two main dimensions of social development: namely, structural or *systemic* parameters—as outlined chiefly in structural-functional and system-theoretical models—and normative-cultural meaning or purpose. A central thesis emerging from this linkage is that, at the present evolutionary stage, normative-cultural questions are destined to play a crucial role, with the result that post-industrial (or late capitalist) society is vulnerable to a "crisis of legitimacy."

In order to gain a better grasp of Habermas' contribution, it may be advisable to sketch some of the social-scientific conceptions explicitly or implicitly invoked in the study. One of the author's main points of reference is structural-functionalism or functionalist systems theory, an outlook whose theoretical premises and contours have been elaborated primarily by Talcott Parsons (and subsequently, in the German context, by Niklas Luhmann). As Parsons stipulated, a *social system* can be defined as a set of interrelated elements separated from its environment by boundaries which maintains itself over time through the fulfillment of basic tasks termed *functional requisites.* Systemic boundaries were said to demarcate the range of tolerance within which a system can oscillate or change without losing its defining character.

Regarding functional requisites, Parsonian theory postulated chiefly four, each operating in its own *subsystem,* namely: *pattern maintenance, adaptation, goal attainment,* and *integration.* While the first referred to the preservation of normative-cultural values and while adaptation was concerned with the exploitation and allocation of economic resources, goal attainment was treated as a synonym for effective, purposive (especially political) decision-making; the last requisite insured internal cohesiveness through such devices as socialization and status assignment. In addition to formulating a model of *social statics,* Parsons pinpointed the basic processes involved in *social dynamics* or evolution. Drawing to some extent on the Comtean doctrine of progressive secularization, as well as on Spencer's and Durkheim's arguments regarding growing social complexity and differentiation, his writings advanced the thesis that, as a general tendency, societies develop from ideal-typical patterns prevalent in traditional life to equally ideal-typical patterns of modernity. Among the processes characteristic of such development were the movement from affectivity to affective neutrality (a movement entailing disenchantment, secularization, and rationalization); the advancement from particularism to universalism (that is, from the local-parochial bonds of kinship to a general or global rule system); the change from the ascriptive assignment of status to individual-personal achievement (or from heteronomy to autonomy); and finally the abandonment of amorphic diffuseness in favor of the increasing differentiation and specialization of functions and structures.[10]

Taking his bearings from both functionalism and the Marxist tradition, Habermas adopts Marx's notion of *social formation* to designate the comprehensive structure of a social system. As he argues, every social formation of this kind is marked by a basic principle of organization which, in functionalist terms, delineates the boundaries of systemic variability. In his words, social organization principles determine "an abstract space (or range) of possible social-systemic changes"; differently put, they "delimit the capacity of a society to learn without losing its identity."[11] Within the confines of a social formation, Habermas distinguishes between two major dimensions or subsystems: namely, between system integration and social integration, or, more loosely, between (holistic) system and (experiential) life-world. The term *social integration,* he writes, is used "with reference to a system of institutions in which speaking and acting subjects are socially interrelated; social systems are seen here as *life-worlds* which are symbolically structured." By contrast, *system integration* refers "to the specific steering performances of a self-regulated *system;* social forma- tions are considered here from the vantage point of their capacity to maintain their boundaries and their continued existence by mastering the complexity of a fluctuating environment." As Habermas acknowl- edges, the two dimensions are directly linked with Parsons' theory of functional requisites. "From the life-world perspective," he notes, "we thematize the normative structures (values and institutions) of a so- ciety; events and conditions are treated as dependent on functions of social integration (in Parson's vocabulary: integration and pattern maintenance)." The system perspective, on the other hand, thematizes "a society's steering mechanisms and the expansion of its scope of op- erational capacity; events and conditions are analyzed here in their de- pendency on functions of system integration (in Parsonian language: adaptation and goal attainment), while values are assumed as given." In subsequent passages, the two dimensions are sometimes subdivided into a triad of spheres, with the socio-cultural subsystem performing the task of integration and pattern maintenance and the economic and political subsystems dealing respectively with adaptation and goal attainment.[12]

Although willing to borrow from the concepts and terminology of functional and Marxist theory, Habermas is not ready to embrace these frameworks uncritically. Regarding functionalism, he deplores the positivist and instrumentalist proclivities of its spokesmen, and es- pecially their disregard of the integrity of normative-practical ques- tions. "While undoubtedly encompassing normative structures in its vocabulary," he complains, "the system-theoretical strategy or approach basically conceptualizes every social system from the vantage point of its steering center." Seen from the functionalist perspective, he adds, "social evolution—which actually occurs in the three dimensions of the (economic) development of productive forces, the augmentation of systemic autonomy (political power), and the transformation of normative structures—is collapsed into the single plane of the expan- sion of power through reduction of environmental complexity." What remains completely inaccessible on these premises is the arena of nor- mative (and cognitive) validity: "Admitting as objects of analysis only empirical events and conditions, systems theory must reduce *ques- tions of validity* to *behavioral problems.*" The basic defect of func- tionalism—which does not nullify its other virtues—consists thus in its reductionist one-dimensionality: the advantages of its strategy turn into "weaknesses of conceptual imperialism once steering aspects be- come the sole focus and once the social-scientific problematic is confined to questions of selective capacity."[13] A similar charge of one-dimensionality—this time with reference to economics—is leveled in a later context against Marx. Concentration on "relations of production," we read, "easily leads to a narrow economic interpretation (of development). Which subsystem of a society can obtain functional supremacy and thereby the guiding role in social evolution depends on the underlying principle of organization."[14]

Turning to the issue of evolution, Habermas first outlines three *constitutive properties* or *universal characteristics* of social life and social development.[15] The first characteristic concerns the general growth of a society's systemic capacity deriving from progressive advances in the two spheres of system integration—more particularly, the field of economic adaptation—and social integration. According to Habermas, advances in the two areas correspond basically to society's growing mastery over its external and internal environment or to a steady *appropriation* of its outer and inner nature. "For the specific form in which the reproduction of socio-cultural life takes place," he writes, "the exchange processes with outer and inner nature are of decisive importance." While outer nature is mastered "through (economic) production processes," inner (human) nature is "appropriated through processes of socialization. With expanding steering capacity a social system extends its boundaries into nature both outside and inside." As Habermas adds, however, growth of mastery evolves on more than an instinctive or unreflective level. With regard to outer nature, the expansion of productive forces involves the fashioning of appropriate tools and thus a progressive refinement of instrumental-technical rationality in the direction of testable and scientifically "valid" knowledge. In his words: "A specific accomplishment of social systems I find in their expansion of control over outer nature through the medium of *propositions amenable to validation"* (or incorporating truth claims). A similar refinement occurs in the socio-cultural domain where values or beliefs are increasingly subject to demands for normative justification. In both domains, moreover, advances are said to follow a teleological (and basically unilinear) pattern. In the field of production, Habermas speaks of the "cumulative character of scientific and technical progress," a progress governed by an "inner logic" or a "hierarchy of non-reversible sequences" and leading, via rationalization, to ever-higher levels of scientific rigor. Like the history of science and technology, *Legitimation Crisis* treats the "transformation of normative structures" as a *directional process*. In a passage which seems at least partly inspired by Parsons' theory of pattern variables, the study lists as broad cultural trends the pervasive secularization of world-views, the movement from heteronomy to autonomy, the replacement of particularism by universalistic (and individualistic) orientations, and generally the *increasing reflexivity* of belief systems.[16]

The second universal characteristic mentioned in the study refers to the relationship between systemic and social integration, or, more simply, between system and life-world. Generally speaking, Habermas notes, "changes in the basic regulative parameters of social systems are a function of the evolutionary state of productive forces and of the degree of system autonomy" or capacity; however, functional dependency may not always be complete, since the variation of parameters is "limited by the developmental logic of world-views which is unaffected by the imperatives of system integration" or of the increase of steering power. Actually, the demands of systemic and social integration may (and do) occasionally operate at cross-purposes; for, "while the unfolding of productive forces always extends the system's scope of operational autonomy, evolutionary advances in the structures of cultural-interpretive understanding do not unfailingly entail selective advantages." From this perspective, "normative structures function in relation to imperatives of power expansion in the form of self-inhibiting constraints" or as internal breaking mechanisms; differently phrased, from the vantage point of steering capacity, "socially integrated individuals constitute a paradoxical inner environment." In Habermas' view, the collision or internal social contradiction appears paradoxical only in the confines of an *overextended* or reductionist type of systems theory. The enigmas disappear, he asserts, "once the central focus is placed not on system and self-steering capacity, but on life-world and intersubjectivity, and once socialization is seen from the outset as a process of individuation." As he adds: "Societies are *also* systems, but their dynamics obeys not only the logic of the expansion of system autonomy (or power); rather, social evolution occurs in the bounds of a logic of the life-world, a logic whose structures are determined by linguistically engendered intersubjectivity and founded on critically reviewable validity claims."[17]

The last constituent property of social life in a sense draws the implications from the preceding characteristics, by spelling out the internal wellspring or teleological principle pervading social development. According to Habermas, this wellspring resides in man's reflective capacity, particularly in the tendency of reflection to mature through learning. "It is my conjecture," he writes, "that the fundamental mechanism or motor of social evolution in general can be found in man's built-in inability not to learn: not learning, but non-learning is in socio-cultural development the phenomenon in need of explanation." Reiterating a point made earlier, *Legitimation Crisis* adds that the process of learning—which attests to the *rationality of man*— occurs in two main dimensions, namely, those of systemic integration involving a growth of instrumental-cognitive (or theoretical) knowledge, and of social integration focused on changes in normative-practical awareness; using a shorthand formula, the study sees evolution in the two domains following "a logic, respectively, of growing theoretical and practical insight." In both areas, moreover, learning is said to evolve from a non- or prereflective stage to a reflective or discursive level where validity claims can be raised and tested. *"Non-reflective learning,"* we read, "takes place in action contexts in which implicitly advanced theoretical and practical validity claims are naively taken for granted and accepted or rejected without discursive consideration. *Reflective learning,* on the other hand, proceeds through discourses in which doubtful validity claims—or claims which have been rendered problematic through institutionalized doubt—are explicitly thematized and either redeemed or dismissed on the basis of arguments." Against this background, the evolutionary level of a society is claimed to depend on its "institutionally permitted learning capacity," more particularly on the degree to which the society's organizational principle makes room, first, for "the differentiation between theoretical and practical questions," and second, for "the transition from non-reflective (or pre-scientific) to reflective learning."[18]

In regard to the historical pattern of evolution, Habermas in the study differentiates between four successive types of social formations: the stages of *primitive, traditional, modern,* and *post-modern* social life, with the modern stage being further subdivided into the two phases of early liberal capitalism and of late or organized capitalism. Since the meaning of the post-modern type is not further elucidated, the four stages actually developed in the study are those of *primitive, traditional, liberal-capitalist,* and *late-capitalist* society.[19] With the exception of the primitive or pre-civilized phase, Habermas emphasizes, all other historically recorded formations have been *class societies,* that is, societies sanctioning the structured domination of some social segments by others. As he indicates, his elaboration of the stages is meant to provide general guideposts, but not "to simulate or replace" a fully grounded theory of social evolution (which, instead of proceeding *inductively,* would allow the formulation of evolutionary models *abstractly* or on a rigorously deductive level). For each evolutionary phase, the treatment in *Legitimation Crisis* seeks to describe the society's guiding or underlying principle of organization, while simultaneously indicating the range of variability established by the principle and also the *type of crisis* which is likely to arise in this context. A further aim is to pinpoint the social subsystem or institutional domain which enjoys *functional supremacy* at a given stage of development.[20]

Habermas' comments on primitive and traditional societies are relatively condensed and readily permit brief summary. He finds the organizational principle of the primitive stage in ascription, that is, in the circumstance that status is determined by the *primary roles* deriving from age and sex. The institutional core of society is said to reside in the kinship system which, in Habermas' words, "represents a total institution at this stage of development" in the sense that family structures "govern the entire fabric of social relations" and "simultaneously secure social and systemic integration" by both providing for survival needs (through reproduction and economic activity) and fulfilling the task of socialization or enculturation. Differently phrased: due to the prevalence of family and kinship, social life at this point shows few or no signs of structural and functional differentiation and is devoid of subsystem autonomy. The overlapping of social and systemic integration also implies the confluence of theoretical and practical aspects, or of cognitive beliefs and norms: "both are embedded in rituals and taboos which require no independent sanctions." In view of the family-centered character of the economy, production is resistant to the accumulation of surplus value through exploitation of labor power or physical force—so that primitive cultures are not yet class societies. Crisis, if it happens, tends to befall such cultures as an external catastrophe; typical sources of change are demographic growth or else inter-ethnic dependency linked with warfare or conquest.[21]

In contrast to the undifferentiated and functionally diffuse condition of primitive life, traditional society witnesses the emergence of political or administrative structures dedicated to the enhancement of production and systemic capacity. According to Habermas, the organizational principle at this stage consists in *class domination in political form,* which fulfills both economic-adaptive and steering functions. "With the rise of a bureaucratic apparatus of authority," he writes, "a control or steering center is differentiated out of the kinship system, with the effect that production and distribution of social wealth are shifted from familial forms of organization to ownership of the means of production." In lieu of the kinship system, the state with its bureaucracy represents in traditional contexts the institutional nucleus or dominant subsystem handling the "central power and steering tasks." In addition to introducing a new organizational principle, the emergence of the state initiates a more general process of structural and functional differentiation and specialization: "subsystems arise at this stage of development which serve predominantly either systemic or social integration." However, in Habermas' view, this process is still strongly circumscribed in several respects. First, subsystem autonomy is only partial, as is illustrated by the close linkage of economic and political structures and by the pervasive support given to both by the established legal order. Moreover, both the systemic and the sociocultural domains are marked by the lack of discursive reflection. Technical-instrumental knowledge is not yet "expanded through reflective learning"; similarly, normative structures rely on traditional world-views and on a state-centered civic ethic which remains particularistic and thus incompatible with universalistic modes of interaction. Crisis in traditional settings tends to proceed from internal social contradictions, especially from the contradiction between the prevailing class structure and traditional norms which officially disavow exploitation: "The problem of how socially produced wealth may be unequally yet legitimately distributed is solved temporarily through the ideological bolstering of contrafactual validity claims."[22]

Habermas' treatment of the liberal-capitalist stage is somewhat more elaborate. The organizational principle of this social formation is seen in the relationship between *wage labor and capital,* a relationship buttressed by the "bourgeois system of private law." The new principle implies a relative separation of political and economic subsystems, a separation which alters but does not abolish the class division of society. "With the rise of a sphere—immune from state intervention—reserved for the commerce between private-autonomous owners of commodities," we read, the domain of " 'civil society' is differentiated out of the political-economic system, a development entailing depoliticization of class relations and anonymity of class domination." What emerges at this point as institutional nucleus or dominant subsystem is the market economy, while the state with its political-administrative structures—reduced by and large to the format of a "night watchman"—functions merely as supplement of the self-regulating market. Together with the separation of political and economic structures comes the growing differentiation of the areas of systemic and social integration and thus of theoretical and practical-normative issues. Embodying the principle of instrumental-rational adaptation, the market is freed from traditional (particularistic) norms and tends to give unchecked reign to the pursuit of private interest or profit;[23] actually, commercial relations acquire normative force themselves by sanctioning the yardstick of *fair exchange*. Simultaneously, social learning begins to gain a reflective dimension—especially in the field of economic production where "once the limits of physical exploitation (of labor) are reached," further capital accumulation necessitates reliance on technical or technological innovation and thus "the linkage of technical-instrumental knowledge with reflective learning processes." With regard to normative-practical issues, the predominance of the market encourages the influence of universal rules which at least potentially permit rational justification. In Habermas' words: "Bourgeois ideologies can assume a universalistic stance and appeal to general (or 'generalizable') interests because the property system has shed its political cast and has been converted into a relation of production which seemingly is able to legitimate itself: the institution of the market can rely on the element of justice inherent in fair exchange" (or the exchange of equivalent goods). Despite the mentioned advances in rationality and subsystem autonomy, liberal-capitalist society cannot be considered a fully mature formation. Normative yardsticks are not completely open to discursive inspection; moreover, curbing the process of differentiation, these yardsticks are essentially tied to structures of economic production which perpetuate class division and class domination (thus negating universalism). Due to the central role of the market, crisis at this stage typically erupts in the economic or, more generally, the systemic context: "The organization principle of society transposes the conflict potential of class opposition into the steering dimension where it manifests itself in the form of economic crisis."[24]

As reflected in its original title, the study devotes the most detailed attention to the stage of late (or organized) capitalism; for present purposes the portrayal has to be strongly abbreviated. According to *Legitimation Crisis,* the organizational principle in this phase still resides in the relationship between wage labor and capital; however, the operation of the principle is radically affected by two new developments: first, the process of economic concentration evident in the rise of large-scale (national and multinational) corporations and oligopolies, and second, the practice of massive state intervention in the market. These developments in large measure revoke the previously achieved differentiation of political and economic subsystems—with important systemic as well as normative-cultural effects. While the strengthening of the state engenders a potential growth of steering capacity, the subordination of the economy leads to the obfuscation of the principle of fair exchange which earlier functioned as source of normative legitimacy; thus, precisely in a time of heightened state power, the exercise of such power occurs in a normative void (which does not mean a decrease of normative expectations). In delineating the three subsystems—economy, politics, and normative rules—as found in late capitalism, Habermas (together with numerous other analysts) stresses the mixed character of the economic system, involving the uneasy juxtaposition of three sectors: private competitive enterprise, private market dominated by oligopolies and monopolies, and public sector characterized by a close amalgamation of government and industry. The political or administrative system in his presentation fulfills "numerous imperatives arising out of the economy," but chiefly in two ways: by "regulating the economic cycle as a whole through global planning" and by "creating and improving conditions for utilizing excess accumulated capital." The normative or legitimation system, finally, is described as particularly vulnerable at this stage, due to the collapse of the basic bourgeois ideology (of fair exchange) and the simultaneous growth in state power. "The state apparatus," we read, "no longer, as in liberal capitalism, merely secures the general conditions of production (seen as requisites for the maintenance of the reproduction process), but is now actively engaged in it; for this reason, it must—like the pre-capitalist state—be legitimated, although it can no longer rely on residues of tradition which have been undermined and eroded in the course of capitalist development."[25]

The discussion of the crisis potential in late-capitalist societies— a discussion occupying center-stage in the reviewed study—largely exceeds the thematic confines of this chapter; I shall limit myself here to the barest outline. Habermas finds in late capitalism four system-specific tendencies of possible crisis, labeled respectively *economic crisis, rationality crisis, legitimation crisis,* and *motivation crisis.* He considers the latter two particularly important and the last one ultimately decisive. The first type arises in the economic subsystem and is, in a sense, a continuation or intensification of earlier capitalist dilemmas. "If economic crisis tendencies persist in advanced capitalism," the study asserts, "this indicates that governmental actions intervening in the production process are subject, no less than private exchanges, to spontaneously operating economic laws and thus to the logic of economic crisis as crystallized in the law of the tendential fall of the profit rate." The potential for rationality and legitimation crises is embedded in the political or administrative subsystem, more particularly in its *output* and *input* dimensions. "Output crises," we are told, "have the form of a rationality crisis in which the administrative system fails to harmonize and implement the steering imperatives deriving from the economy. Input crises, on the other hand, take the shape of a legitimation crisis where the legitimation system is unsuccessful in maintaining the level of mass loyalty required for the governmental implementation of economic steering demands." While a deficit in administrative rationality means that the state apparatus "cannot provide adequate steering output for the economy," a similar defect in legitimation highlights the general impossibility "through administrative means to maintain or produce effective normative structures to the extent required." According to Habermas, the latter point underscores the circumstance that growth in state power or steering capacity is not synonymous with an expanding control over the normative domain, a circumstance which is particularly important under conditions of large-scale state intervention. In his words: "The range of political maneuvering is narrowly limited, for the cultural system is peculiarly resistant to administrative control: *there is no administrative production of meaning.*" Although able, to a certain degree, to satisfy consumer demands for concrete goods and services, the late-capitalist state cannot guarantee normative support through administrative fiat: " 'Meaning' is a scarce resource and is becoming ever scarcer."[26]

The preceding crisis tendencies, including the administrative legitimation deficit, in the last resort depend on the functioning of the sociocultural subsystem, which engenders its own disruptive potential in the form of the motivation crisis. Such a crisis is said to arise "as a result of transformations in the socio-cultural system itself"; differently phrased, "when the socio-cultural system changes in such a way that its output becomes dysfunctional for the state and the system of social labor" (or production). In Habermas' view, the chief motivational requisites which the sociocultural domain is supposed to provide in late capitalism consist in the "syndromes of civic and familial-vocational privatism" (that is, in a consumer outlook both in public and private matters); however, these syndromes are prone to malfunction, due both to overall systemic trends eroding their impact and to the internal "developmental logic of normative structures." To show the disappearance of the mentioned motivation patterns as well as the emerging crisis potential, *Legitimation Crisis* advances four main arguments: first, that the residues of pre-capitalist traditions sustaining the syndromes are "being non-renewably dismantled"; second, that the core ingredients of bourgeois ideology (such as possessivism and achievement orientation) are likewise being "undermined by changes in the social structure"; third, that the "denuded normative structures," that is, the remaining elements of bourgeois culture, do not make room for functional equivalents for the decaying syndromes; and finally, that certain key principles of bourgeois culture—"stripped of their traditionalist padding and devoid of their privatistic core"—are still relevant for motivational purposes. In connection with the last two theses the study sketches an outline of normative evolution designed to corroborate the claim of a developmental logic. Starting from the particularism characterizing tribal or kinship systems, the outline traces normative changes over the mixture of primitive-parochial and public or state-centered moral codes in traditional societies to the emergence of relatively universal, though not fully discursively founded, norms in liberal capitalism (a stage illustrated, with varying accents, by modern natural law, utilitarianism, and Kantian ethics). Finding that these changes steadily deepen and expand reflectiveness, the study projects a growing tension between this tendency and remaining class- or nation-based obligations: "If one follows, along the lines of universalization and internalization, the developmental logic of social norm systems (exceeding the domain of historical evidence), a resolution of the conflict is conceivable only if the dichotomy between in-group and out-group morality is obliterated, the opposition between morally and legally regulated behavior relativized, and the validity of *all* norms tied to the discursive choices and deliberations of participants."[27]

The notion of a developmental logic, tentatively delineated in *Legitimation Crisis*, has subsequently been fleshed out by Habermas in several writings—and first of all with primary attention to ontogenesis or the process of individual-psychological maturation (although the relationship with phylogenesis, or social evolution, always remained in view). Initial steps in this direction can be found in an address delivered about half a year after the publication of the discussed study under the title, "Can Complex Societies Develop a Rational Identity?" Relying in part on Hegelian philosophy and in part on findings of contemporary psychology—especially developmental psychology—the address differentiated between three main phases in the emergence and maturation of personal identity: *natural identity, role identity,* and *ego-identity,* with the final phase further subdivided into the periods of the beginning breakthrough toward inwardness and the later consolidation of universalistic ego-structures. Natural identity was said to characterize early infancy and to be anchored in the "boundary-maintaining human organism," that is, in the infant's ability "to distinguish his (or her) body from the surrounding environment in which physical and social objects are still blurred." The next step involves the task of the pre-adolescent child to find his (her) place in the immediate social life-world, that is, in the family and directly experienced social groups. "Once the child internalizes the symbolic rule-properties of a few basic roles in the family setting and later the behavioral norms of larger groups," we read, the organismic selfhood of infancy is "replaced by a symbolically founded role identity." At this point, character is slowly formed through the stabilizing effect of the behavioral expectations associated with roles; however, selfhood is still closely amalgamated with the particularistic fabric of role patterns and habitual rules. This amalgamation is disrupted during subsequent years when "the adolescent learns the important distinction between norms, on the one hand, and on the other, principles according to which norms can be generated" and which "can serve as yardsticks for criticism and for the justification of established norms." In learning to make this distinction the adolescent also discovers that "only *general* (or universal) norms can qualify as rational, since they alone secure the reciprocity of rights and duties among all concerned." The discovery sets in motion a process of growing autonomy and individuation; selfhood from now on cannot be found in prevailing role patterns, but must be reconstituted "so to speak, behind the lines of all particular roles and norms" in a more general and abstract ego-core. This process reaches its zenith in adulthood: "The adult's ego-identity manifests itself in the ability to form new identities and integrate them with previous ones and thus to fashion himself and his interactions into a unique life-history."[28]

Having outlined the ontogenesis of ego-formation, Habermas in his address—taking his cues this time from anthropological and sociological research—sketched a parallel between individual and group identity, by specifying four main stages of social evolution: *archaic-primitive societies, early civilizations* (corresponding largely to the formative phase of traditional societies), *developed civilizations,* and *modern society.* Archaic communities were described as founded on kinship and governed by mythical world-views. Such world-views were as yet unconcerned with the differentiation between physical and cultural contexts, as shown in their anthropomorphic conception of nature and the naturalistic, frequently magical, treatment of society. In myths, everything was integrated in a homogeneous fashion: "individual men are substances just like stones, plants, animals, and gods"; therefore, "one is tempted to compare human identity in archaic society with the natural identity of the infant." Corresponding roughly to the pre-adolescent phase, early civilizations witnessed the rise of sociopolitical organizations and role structures—centered around empire, monarchy, or city-state—which required behavioral norms. With the establishment of role structures and norms, individuals were induced "to emerge from the universal fabric of cosmic substances and forces and to develop their own identity." However, due to the particularistic character of norms and religious beliefs, group identity (like individual identity) at this point was still closely tailored to the confines of the respective communal existence. The first rupture with particularism occurred in developed civilizations, chiefly as a result of the universalistic claims advanced by the "great world religions"—claims which rendered possible "the formation of an ego-identity divorced from all concrete roles and norms." Nevertheless, as Habermas noted, claims of this kind could not be fully satisfied due to the pervasive contradiction besetting the mentioned civilizations, between the prevailing class division and the potential universalism of moral principles and religious beliefs: "Religious teachings and governmental survival imperatives are structurally incompatible at this stage." In modern society this incompatibility is progressively heightened. Under the impact of Protestantism and rationalism, the influence of "strictly universalistic principles and correspondingly individualistic ego-structures" is steadily reinforced; traditional religious beliefs tend to be reduced to "core tenets of a universalistic ethics."[29]

With regard to ontogenesis, Habermas' views were further elaborated in a conference paper presented half a year later (in summer of 1974) on the theme of "Moral Development and Ego-Identity." The paper pointed to relevant trends in contemporary psychology and social psychology and especially those theoretical initiatives most conducive to the formulation of a consistent ontogenetic sequence. Referring to such approaches as ego-psychology, developmental psychology, and symbolic interactionism, Habermas initially summarized a number of common tenets: first, the view that individual maturation is a complex process comprising such aspects as cognitive, linguistic, and motivational development (where the last aspect "seems intimately connected with the acquisition of an interactive competence"); next, that the growth of ego-identity properly speaking consists in a "competence formed in social interactions" and can be differentiated from the more cognitive or *epistemic* dimensions of selfhood; third, the conception of a developmental logic—as "worked out especially by Piaget"—according to which ontogenesis denotes "an irreversible sequence of discrete and increasingly complex developmental stages, where no stage can be skipped over and each higher stage 'implies' the preceding one in accordance with a developmental pattern amenable to rational reconstruction"; further, the notion that maturation is "as a rule crisis-ridden" and that "the resolution of stage-specific developmental problems is preceded by a phase of destructuration and (in part) regression"; and last, the tenet that the developmental thrust of maturation is marked by growing autonomy, that is, by a growing independence deriving from the ego's "increasing problem-solving capabilities" in dealing with external and internal nature and with the "symbolic structure of a partly internalized culture and society." Although noting that none of the current approaches had "as yet yielded a fully explanatory theory of ontogenesis," Habermas singled out as most promising the contributions of Jean Piaget and Lawrence Kohlberg in the field of developmental psychology. Concentrating on the moral aspect of ego-formation, the basic goal of his own paper was "to demonstrate that Kohlberg's stages of moral consciousness satisfy the formal conditions of a developmental logic" once these stages are "reformulated in the general framework of action theory."[30]

In implementing this endeavor, the paper first traced the evolution of communicative action and interaction over the three age levels of infant, child, and adolescent, linking these levels with Piaget's theory of cognitive development (though bypassing the earliest or sensory-motor phase). While the infant or preschool child—cognitively still at the level of pre-operational thought—was found to be involved in particular actions and concerned only with immediate gratifications and sanctions, the preadolescent child—progressing to the cognitive stage of concrete operations—was said to be able to play social roles and thus to participate in a more complex fabric of rule-governed interactions; together with acquiring the ability for formal-operational reasoning, the adolescent, according to this outline, learns to distinguish between principles and conventional rules and to enter into discursive argumentation, withdrawing for this purpose from immediate action constraints. The preceding scheme was then connected with the developmental maturation of ego-identity, in roughly the same terms. At the stage of infancy characterized by natural identity, the paper observed, we find "natural agents to whom comprehensible intentions are *imputed,* but not yet subjects whom one could *hold accountable* for actions on the basis of generalized behavioral expectations." With the emergence of role identity, children become able to act "as role-dependent reference persons and later as anonymous role bearers"; the rise of ego-identity during adolescence finally entails that actors can "meet as individuals across (so to speak) their objective life contexts." The scheme was further enriched by the specification of three dimensions of behavioral or interactive qualifications, dealing respectively with the cognitive understanding of behavioral expectations and with the perception of motivations and co-agents. Each of the three dimensions was again arranged into three age levels, which led to the discovery that behavioral qualifications can be "placed into a certain hierarchy" along the lines of growing reflectiveness, increasing *abstraction and differentiation,* and progressive *generalization.* This finding was said to "provide initial grounds for the assumption that deeper analysis could identify a developmental-logical pattern in Piaget's sense."

In an effort to buttress this assumption, the paper in its remaining portion focused on the stages of moral consciousness as outlined by Kohlberg, with particular attention to the relationship between these stages and the sketched levels of interactive competence. Defining moral consciousness as the "ability to make use of interactive competence for arriving at a *conscious* settlement of morally relevant action conflicts," Habermas found the crucial criterion for a conscious and consensual settlement in the degree of "reciprocity between acting subjects." Once this is granted, he noted, "the stages of moral consciousness can be derived by applying the reciprocity requirement to the respective action structures" encountered at the different levels of maturation. The correlation of moral stages and action structures netted a complex schematic table which defies summary. Suffice it to say that Kohlberg's three stages of *preconventional, conventional,* and *post-conventional* morality—with each stage internally subdivided into two phases, yielding a six-stage sequence—was connected with Piaget's conception of cognitive development, with the levels of interactive competence and identity maturation, as well as with different degrees of interactive reciprocity. One further point deserves notice. While incorporating into his table Kohlberg's stages up to the highest level of *universal ethical principle orientation,* Habermas found the sequence incomplete due to an insufficient attention to discursive validation. "Only at the level of a universal discursive ethics," he wrote, "can need interpretations themselves—that is, what individuals consider and claim as their 'true' interests—become the object of practical discourse. This level is not differentiated by Kohlberg from his sixth stage, although there is a qualitative difference: the yardstick of normative justification is no longer the monologically applicable *principle* of generalizability but rather the jointly adhered to *procedure* of the discursive redemption of normative validity claims."[31]

Habermas' ontogenetic arguments and specifications were soon followed by renewed attempts to explore their implications in the larger framework of social evolution.[32] To conclude this overview, I would like to draw attention briefly to a paper delivered a year later (in 1975) which became the centerpiece in the book bearing the same title: "Toward a Reconstruction of Historical Materialism." The essay treated historical materialism not simply as *heuristic* guideline for a narrative historiography but as a potential theory of social evolution; its basic goal was to reconstruct the Marxist legacy in such an evolutionary sense, with the intent of bringing the legacy more closely in line with the requirements of a developmental logic. Focusing on several key ingredients of historical materialism, Habermas found Marx's notion of "social (or socially organized) labor"—construed as the "manner in which humans, in contradistinction to animals, reproduce their lives"—insufficiently refined to differentiate the properly human form of social reproduction from the pre-human or hominid phase (where labor already was socially organized). "The specifically human mode of life," he argued, "can be adequately pinpointed only if we combine the concept of social labor with that of the familial principle of social organization," a principle entailing behavioral patterns and role structures which, in comparison with earlier types of labor, "mark a new stage of development." Regarding *history of the species* and its linkage with successive *modes of production,* the essay considered the concept suggestive and theoretically promising, especially if forces and relations of production were viewed respectively as manifestations of cognitive-instrumental and moral-practical learning processes; however, notice was also taken of several drawbacks hampering its function as an evolutionary scheme. First of all, orthodox conceptions of base-superstructure relations tended to identify *base* with mode of production in a narrowly economic sense; actually, however, the base or institutional core of society had to be seen as historically variable and as synonymous with the prevalent or stage-specific *form of social integration.* Second, Marxist treatments of social crisis usually presented changes in production relations as dependent on the expansion of cognitive-instrumental productive forces. While agreeing that "an endogenous learning mechanism provides for the accumulation of a cognitive potential which can be used for solving crisis-producing systemic problems," Habermas countered by insisting that cognitive knowledge "can be applied to develop productive forces only once the evolutionary step to a new institutional framework and a new form of social integration has been accomplished." Last, urging its replacement by *principle of organization,* the paper criticized the term *mode of production* as unwieldy and insufficiently abstract when employed to "capture the universals of social development"—a deficiency evident in the haphazard character of the orthodox-Marxist sequence (leading from primitive-communal over Asiatic, ancient, feudal, and capitalist modes to socialism).[33]

The proposed reconstruction of historical materialism in the essay proceeded again first along ontogenetic and then along phylogenetic lines. Regarding individual maturation, the paper recapitulated the main stages of interactive competence, focusing this time on the relationship between speech and action. While at the level of *symbolically mediated interaction* speaking and acting are still closely interwoven, with the result that communicative symbols and actions are reciprocally defined, the two dimensions were said to part company on the level of *propositionally differentiated speech*—in the sense that individuals learn to exchange the perspective of agents for that of third persons or observers, thus acquiring the capacity to discern general behavioral expectations and rules. On the third level of *argumentative speech,* finally, conventional norms are opened up to discursive scrutiny; thus, "their validity can be contested or confirmed with reference to principles." As on previous occasions, these levels were connected with the sequential acquisition of cognitive and moral competences. Turning to social evolution, Habermas treated the levels of interactive maturation as guideposts for the analysis of social infrastructures, more particularly of successive forms of social integration. In order to capture the dynamics of evolutionary change, he distinguished between normal integrative institutions, or institutions dealing with (more or less) undisturbed conditions, and specialized institutions or belief systems tailored to crisis situations; a further differentiation separated general moral world-views from concrete legal-moral structures actually operative in conflictual cases—a separation predicated on the circumstance that, in comparison with normal rules and general beliefs, conflict settlement frequently occurs on a lower level of moral judgment. Adopting a four-stage sequence, the paper found neolithic (or post-hominid) societies characterized by conventional morality on the level of everyday practices and mythical beliefs, and by preconventional morality in the sphere of legal conflict resolution. Early civilizations were described as conventional on all three levels, while developed civilizations were portrayed as marked by conventional everyday structures, post-conventional world views, and conventional-traditional legal systems. Modern society, finally, was seen as exhibiting post-conventional action patterns, universalistic ethical principles, and modes of conflict resolution guided by "a strict separation of legality and morality."[34]

Some Critical Comments

The preceding pages were meant to convey, in a necessarily condensed fashion, an impression of Habermas' endeavors in the area of individual and social development. What should have emerged despite condensation is the bold sweep, the multifaceted complexity, and the analytical rigor of his undertaking. It seems to me that the comprehensiveness of Habermas' approach is virtually unmatched in contemporary social science and social thought: in exploring ontogenetic and phylogenetic processes and their implications, his writings draw upon, and make contributions to, such disciplines as psychology, sociology, anthropology, and political science—in addition to linking social-scientific literature with the history of ideas and overarching philosophical vistas. The substantive content of his arguments also appears to me preferable to most competing perspectives dealing with the topic: especially to the (overt or covert) biological-organismic overtones of current neo-evolutionism, but also to the doctrinaire determinism of orthodox Marxism, and to the unabashed instrumentalism of functionalist systems theory. The following critical observations cannot, and are not intended to detract from these accomplishments; concerning developmental patterns, my purpose is not so much to question the notion of a directional movement (toward higher levels of reflectiveness) as to draw attention to some unresolved issues and to possible contrapuntal corollaries of such evolution.

Before delineating my own observations, I would like to mention a few recurrent objections which have been leveled against developmental schemes of the kind advanced by Piaget, Kohlberg and Habermas—objections which, for a number of reasons, I do not find compelling.

From the vantage point of behaviorist psychology and also from that of positivist social psychology and sociobiology, questions have been raised regarding the reliability of stage theories which postulate a necessary and consistent sequence of human (particularly moral) attitudes not clearly linked through causal processes.[35] Given their strong reliance on empirical findings, such questions seem more pertinent to Piaget's and Kohlberg's arguments than to those of Habermas—although they are also relevant in his case (a point to which I shall return). What prompts me to bypass these queries is their source; in view of the unresolved internal quandaries besetting behaviorism and contemporary sociobiology, challenges issuing from these quarters probably need not be accorded excessive weight. A similar conclusion, though for more complex motives, may be reached with regard to the charge of cultural bias. This charge does not necessarily deny the availability of supportive empirical evidence; but the evidence is seen as so narrowly restricted to Western middle-class samples as to render theoretical inferences hopelessly tainted with Western "liberal" beliefs. To some extent, within the confines of developmental psychology, this criticism appears amenable to empirical resolution, through appropriate studies conducted in cross-cultural contexts (studies which, from what I can see, have so far been inconclusive). In the case of Habermas' more abstract formulation, the charge cannot so readily be resolved in this manner and is also intrinsically more obscure. To the degree that he equates development with growing universality or *universalism*— where universalism denotes the capacity to engage all particular viewpoints in discourse—the criticism amounts to the claim that this capacity reflects in itself a particularistic preference (which strikes me as whimsical at first blush).[36]

While on the whole immune from parochial predilections, Habermas' outlook in my opinion can be said to accentuate a trait which, though potentially universal, has been particularly cultivated in Western societies: the aspect of ego-identity and of ego-based human competences. As I have tried to indicate, human maturation in his writings appears as a process of growing autonomy and individuation; in terms of identity formation, the process is claimed to lead from an embryonic or dormant stage (where men—or infants—have the status of natural "substances just like stones, plants, animals, and gods") over a phase of gradual awakening to the full emergence of universalistic ego-structures and related competences. At another point we read that, both with regard to ego-formation and the dynamics of world-views, development denotes an "ever-more precise categorical demarcation of the subjectivity of internal nature from the objectivity of external nature, as well as from the normativity of social and the intersubjectivity of linguistic reality."[37] Against this background Habermas' posture can be described as *egological* in the sense of traditional epistemology (where the term signifies the juxtaposition of an internal consciousness and an external world). The reliance on epistemological egology is evident in the emphasis placed on the emergence of the observer's or spectator's perspective, which allows first the analysis of action patterns in the light of conventional rules and later the disengaged scrutiny of both actions and rules on the basis of discursive reflection. In several passages, it is true, Habermas seeks to obviate the peril of a self-enclosed subjectivism. In demarcating itself from nature, society, and language, he writes, "the ego knows itself not only as subjectivity but as an agency which, in the domains of cognition, language, and interaction, has 'always already' transcended the confines of subjectivity: the ego can identify with itself precisely in distinguishing the merely subjective from the non-subjective." However, in elaborating on the meaning of the *non-subjective,* Habermas equates it with *object* or *objective environment* as differentiated into the "two regions" of "external nature and society"—thus reaffirming the basic pattern of egological epistemology.[38]

Habermas' attachment to ego-identity and egology (in the mentioned sense) is clearly not a minor ingredient in his outlook; in fact, the enterprise of critical social theory in his view is inextricably linked with the defense and maintenance of ego-autonomy or with the "idea of an ego identical with itself in an uncoerced fashion." "How else could the mode of total (or totalitarian) socialization be discerned," he queries, "if not through the criterion that it neither produces nor tolerates upright individuals?" Noting comments by earlier Frankfurt theorists, especially Adorno and Marcuse, regarding the "obsolescence of psychoanalysis" and the evanescence of ego-structures in our time, Habermas finds their "melancholy" views incapable of eroding the described linkage: "I mention these comments only to draw attention to the fact that critical social theory holds fast to the concept of the autonomous ego, even when it makes the gloomy prognosis that this ego is losing its foundation."[39] At first glance, the stress on ego-identity and autonomy may seem puzzling in light of the "linguistic turn" effected by Habermas in the context of critical theory, that is, his argument that cognition and interactive experience are linguistically structured and thus are built on intersubjective premises. The puzzle disappears once it is realized that his notion of self-identity has individualistic and universalistic connotations; *ego-identity* captures not only a singular congruence but also the dimension where all egos are simultaneously identical with themselves and with each other. Drawing on Hegelian philosophy, Habermas states that "the ego is absolute universality and simultaneously absolute individuality"; he even cites Hegel to the effect that "the nature of the ego and the nature of the concept" converge—a statement which indicates that the coincidence of universality and individuality is established on a purely logical-conceptual plane, from which all personal idiosyncrasies appear as contingent empirical factors.[40] This circumstance is reinforced by the progressive demarcation of the ego from nature and society, referred to above. Needless to say, the relationship between subjectivity and intersubjectivity against this background appears unproblematical (the latter is simply a "subjectivity writ large").

Apart from its general philosophical and epistemological implications, Habermas' focus on subjectivity and ego-identity entails several quandaries with respect to individual and social development. First, one may wonder how a developmental theory built on cognitive-egological premises can claim access to a precognitive and pre-egological condition, such as the phase of natural identity or of archaic world-views. How, in other words, a theory which portrays evolution as leading from *natural* to *ego-identity* and from non-reflection to reflection can account for itself—given the fact that its vantage point and conceptual arsenal are exclusively borrowed from the *goal* stage of the portrayed development. Another question concerns the connection between individual maturation and social change, or between ontogenesis and phylogenesis. The relationship between these two dimensions has long been a strongly debated issue in psychological, sociological, and philosophical literature. Habermas postulates a number of homologies between the two domains, although he cautions against drawing premature comparisons. On the whole, I find plausible his statement that "since the cognitive development of the individual takes place under social boundary conditions, there is a circular process between societal and individual learning." Generally speaking, a post-individualist perspective would seem to have little trouble in accepting the assumed linkage between "individually acquired learning abilities" and "societal learning processes." What appears troublesome is how this linkage can be reconciled with a developmental theory which stresses growing individual autonomy and a steady delimitation of the ego from environmental—including social—conditions; at least in the more advanced phases of such an evolution, one would conjecture, individual and societal learning (or ontogenesis and phylogenesis) are bound to part company. Habermas is aware of this difficulty—as is manifest in his concern with the possibility of a social or *group identity* in *complex societies*. "There remains the analytical question," he notes, "whether a post-conventional ego-identity can at all be correlated with a group-identity, that is, with the fabric of a concrete society."[41]

The issue of the character of the proposed developmental theory has been mentioned briefly, but its ramifications go beyond internal-cognitive accountability. It seems to me that one of the most ambiguous aspects of Habermas' approach is the philosophical and methodological status of the postulated *developmental logic;* what is involved here is not only the question how a *logic* can claim to comprehend both logical and pre- or non-logical phases of experience, but also how logical propositions regarding development relate to concrete-empirical events as well as to practical human aspirations.[42] On the whole, Habermas segregates the notion of developmental logic—construed as a formal-logical *pattern* amenable to *rational reconstruction* and indicative of a priori (or quasi-a priori) conditions of possibility—from the domain of empirical contingency located on an a posteriori level. Assuming that it can be properly "reconstructed and corroborated," he notes at one point, a developmental pattern discloses *"rules for possible problem-solving,* that is, purely formal limitations and not actual mechanisms which could explain particular processes of problem-solving, not to mention the acquisition of general problem-solving capacities." In a similar vein we read in another context: "If we separate the logic from the dynamics of development—that is, the rationally reconstructible *pattern* of a hierarchy of steadily more comprehensive structures from the *processes* through which the empirical substrates develop—then we need to postulate neither the unilinearity nor the necessity, continuity or irreversibility of history." Developmental patterns, the passage continues, "describe the logical space or range within which more comprehensive structural formations can take shape; but whether new structural formations arise at all and if so, when, depends on *contingent* boundary conditions and on empirically observable learning processes." Although seemingly clear-cut, the separation of logical structures and empirical dynamics conjures up numerous quandaries. First, if the logical patterns are truly non-empirical and formal-transcendental, they necessarily have the timeless or transtemporal (and thus non-developmental) character of a priori principles; in this case, however, the relationship between patterns and contingent-historical events becomes an unresolved and irresoluble antinomy. On the other hand, the claimed separation does not seem fully compatible with the research strategy pursued by Piaget and Kohlberg (nor with Habermas' own repeatedly voiced ambition to arrive at an empirical theory, amenable to testing). In the former case, the logic of ontogenetic development is clearly predicated on empirical findings and is meant to capture a pattern of psychological maturation which is not only abstractly possible but "normal." Likewise, Habermas' reconstruction of phylogenesis yields more than an intellectually intriguing though highly improbable sequence; despite his disclaimers regarding a "logification" of history, his developmental scheme corresponds, and is designed to correspond, to the overall "normal" process of historical evolution (thus establishing a yardstick for what is to "count as" evolution).[43]

Similar difficulties beset the relationship between developmental logic and human practice. Repeatedly Habermas indicates that the continued pursuit of the developmental progression presupposes human endorsement. Projected into the future, he writes, assumptions concerning identity formation cannot properly "claim the status of scientific theories; rather, they resemble practical hypotheses which may be confirmed or rejected depending on whether they decisively shape the self-image and world-view of a population." Even more pointedly, the conclusion of *Legitimation Crisis* links the future relevance of discourse and rational reflection with a basic "partisanship for reason," a partiality implicit in man's rational endowment (and thus not synonymous with blind activism). However, the character of the presumed linkage requires further clarification. Some passages suggest a sharp substantive distinction between theoretical reason or logic, construed in an instrumental-cognitive sense, on the one hand, and practice or communicative interaction, on the other; in fact, the differentiation between systemic and social integration (discussed above) is predicated in large measure on this bifurcation. At the same time, the reviewed writings tend to insist on an *internal logic* which governs practical or interactive experience—for example, in the statement that "the rules of communicative action, to be sure, evolve in reaction to changes in the domain of instrumental and strategic behavior; but in doing so they follow *their own logic.*" Thus, while differing substantively from the growth of "technically useful knowledge," the unfolding of moral-practical awareness nevertheless appears to occupy a logical status, in the sense of following a formal developmental pattern (a pattern bound to prevail both retrospectively and prospectively).[44] Seen in this light, Habermas' approach brings into view the specter of a narrowly schematic history as well as that of a "logification" of human practice. A somewhat different conclusion would be reached if, in line with previous considerations, the stipulated logic is seen not simply as an analytic construct but as a shorthand formula for normal empirical processes; but in this case moral-practical or norm-guided action stands in danger of converging with factual behavior.

The notion of a pattern of practical development entails some further complications which deserve to be mentioned. Particularly if, following Kohlberg's model, the accent is placed on stages of moral consciousness, questions arise concerning the significance of stage-specific norms and corresponding moral obligations. In Habermas' reconstruction of the model, the stages disclose an internal hierarchy of advancement toward higher forms of morality, and not merely a random and morally indifferent sequence. "The highest level of moral consciousness," *Legitimation Crisis* states, "consists in a universal morality deriving from the fundamental norms of rational speech. Compared with competing ethics, this morality makes a claim not only to *empirical* superiority (based on the ontogenetically observable hierarchy of stages of consciousness), but to *systematic* superiority as well (predicated on the discursive redemption of its validity claim)." Similarly, the essay on "Moral Development" speaks of the normative implications of ego-formation: "The concept of ego-identity obviously has more than a descriptive meaning. It delineates a symbolic ego-organization which, on one level, lays claim to being a universal ideal."[45] The claim of morally relevant advancement, however, inevitably stirs up the troublesome issue of the origin of norms. Assuming that the stage model is a strictly formal-logical construct, then the connection between a given stage and its normative implications or ethical standards, as well as the connection between successive normative levels, has the character of analytical deduction or inference; the problem in this case resides mainly in the circularity and tautological quality of analytical inferences (and also in the question of how analytical and quasi-transcendental yardsticks are supposed to affect the domain of actual human behavior). On the other hand, presupposing the empirical status of the stage sequence, the assumed normative connotations conjure up the peril of the naturalistic fallacy. Kohlberg, one may note, is little disturbed by this peril—so little, in fact, that he asserts at one point that "the scientific theory as to why people factually *do* move upward from stage to stage, and why they factually *do* prefer a higher stage to a lower, is broadly the same as a moral theory as to why people *should* prefer a higher stage to a lower." While perhaps adequate in the context of positive psychology, this assertion can hardly lay to rest long-standing metaethical dilemmas surrounding this point.[46]

Quite apart from their moral or normative dimensions, Kohlberg's as well as Piaget's models may be questioned with regard to their ability to grasp the complexity of human cognitive and moral development. Queries along these lines have been articulated recently by psychologists engaged in research on developmental problems. Among others, Klaus Riegel has criticized the linear character of Piaget's, and implicitly of Kohlberg's, scheme; relying on the distinction between *dialectics* (revolving around the intimate nexus of "identity and contradiction") and *traditional logic* (stressing the supremacy of non-contradiction), he has urged a more dialectical reinterpretation of cognitive maturation and also an extension of the developmental model through the addition of the stage of *dialectic operations*. According to Riegel, Piaget's theory is not entirely devoid of a dialectical component, especially if the focus is placed on the earliest phase of sensory-motor intelligence (and in part on pre-operational thought); the component in his view is "most clearly revealed in the accommodation-assimilation paradigm," where accommodation denotes "changes of the subject toward the object" and assimilation refers to "changes of the object to (for the benefit of) the subject." At the higher levels of operational thought, however, the dialectical dimension is said to vanish: "As soon as the child reaches the second major period in Piaget's theory, the period of pre-operational intelligence, and as soon as Piaget shifts from a methodology of observational interpretations to that of experimentation, the dialectic paradigm of accommodation and assimilation is being neglected and interpretations are proposed in terms of traditional logic." Differently phrased, cognitive maturation for Piaget signifies "a progression toward abstract thought, away from and toward a denial of contradictions; thus, development represents an alienation of the subject from the object." In addition to reformulating maturational stages, Riegel proposes a new phase which characterizes adulthood: "In contrast to Piaget, we maintain that at the level of dialectic operations at maturity, the individual does not necessarily equilibrate these (cognitive) conflicts, but is ready to live with contradictions; stronger yet, the individual accepts these contradictions as a basic property of thought and creativity."[47]

That prevalent ontogenetic models are inhospitable to dialectic operations of this kind seems scarcely contestable; the same characterization applies to Habermas' reconstructive endeavors, despite occasional ventures into more multidimensional terrain. On the whole, as has been indicated, Habermas' developmental scheme points toward growing ego-autonomy and a steady expansion of universal reflection. In the concluding passages of the article on "Moral Development," however, this teleology is reformulated. Pondering the motivational aspect of personal maturation (in its relation to cognition), the conclusion speaks of the "interdependence of society and nature which reaches into the heart of identity formation," adding that "the model of an unconstrained ego-identity is richer and more ambitious than a model of autonomy fashioned exclusively from a moralist vantage point." The interdependence, according to Habermas, comes to the fore in the transition from the penultimate to the highest (seventh) stage of moral consciousness, a transition said to involve the movement from a "formalistic ethics of duty" to a "universal ethics of speech" where "need interpretations are no longer assumed as given, but are drawn into the process of discursive deliberation." Once this highest level is reached, he elaborates, man's inner nature—that is, the fabric of needs and strivings—is "no longer merely assessed in the light of a monologically applied principle of generalization and then split into legitimate and illegitimate components or into duties and inclinations"; instead, its promptings are rendered "communicatively fluid and transparent." Differently phrased, "inner nature in its contingent cultural preformation is not simply subjected to the demands of ego-autonomy; rather, through the medium of a dependent ego, it obtains free access to the interpretive arsenal of the cultural tradition." Such access, we are told, requires a series of new "sensitivities, openings, and dependencies—in short, a 'field-dependent' cognitive style which the ego, on its way to autonomy, initially overcame, replacing it with a 'field-independent' style of perception and thought."[48]

However meritorious the preceding comments may be, their status within Habermas' developmental theory appears anomalous—at least to the extent that they are concerned with the role of inner nature and not simply with the relatively minor distinction between a monological and a communicative validation of moral principles. It seems to me that a theory which finds the thrust of individual maturation in the increasing demarcation of the ego from natural and environmental conditions—and which, as spelled out in *Legitimation Crisis,* even locates the motor of phylogenetic evolution in the progressive appropriation of inner and outer nature—cannot (without slight of hand) claim to speak in the name of an uncoerced or unmutilated nature. The same consideration applies if human needs and inclinations are reformulated in terms of interests. In several places Habermas distinguishes among interests in accordance with their degree of "generalizability," and suggests that only generalizable interests are properly speaking open to rational discourse and justification. In *Legitimation Crisis* he states that "insofar as they reflect generalizable interests, norms are predicated on a *rational consensus* (or they would attract such consensus if a practical discourse could take place)"; on the other hand, "to the extent that they buttress or regulate non-generalizable interests, norms are based on force." The generalizability of interests is thus closely connected with, and even equivalent to their rationality or their amenability to discursive consensus. Reason or rational discourse, in other words, serves as yardstick to determine the generalizable character of interests; in this case, however, interests or inclinations cannot in turn be invoked as possible correctives to autonomous rationality (or an *ethics of duty*).[49]

Equally unconvincing are Habermas' attempts to temper the movement toward ego-autonomy through caveats against arbitrary or willful human designs. In discussing contemporary crisis possibilities, *Legitimation Crisis* cautions that "there is no administrative production of meaning." The true question is whether meaning can be produced at all, administratively or otherwise. In tracing homologies between the formation of individual and group identity, Habermas notes that "in both dimensions identity projections apparently grow more and more general and abstract, until finally the projection mechanism is consciously recognized as such and identity formation assumes a reflective character, based on the realization that individuals and societies themselves in a sense produce their identities." He states that, in the course of development, both moral norms and social world-views are increasingly "formalized and detached from substantive (content-laden) interpretations." Against this background, mature identity formation can only have a formal-procedural status. "A collective identity," we read in the essay on trends in "complex societies," "can today be anchored, if at all, only in the formal conditions governing the production and change of identity projections." Instead of accepting any given meaning-content, individuals are said to "participate themselves in the learning and deliberative processes connected with the joint formation of a yet-to-be-designed identity. The rationality of the identity content is thus exclusively determined by the structure of the formation or design procedure." The stress on formal structure obscures the distinction between the highest level of morality and the penultimate stage of "formalistic ethics" and raises the questions of whether procedure can yield any content and whether identity is subject to limitless engineering. "A radically futuristic orientation which penetrates into identity formation," the same essay adds, must find "its limit in the foundations of the new identity. If in the light of contingent future scenarios—that is, in the light of a future construed purely as an arena of planning strategies—*everything* would be 'doable' or controllable, something like an identity could not emerge."[50] Since procedure alone hardly provides obstacles to substantive choice, mature identity is bound to be a precarious if not impossible accomplishment—which throws new light on Habermas' statement that "meaning is a scarce resource and is becoming ever scarcer."

Previously I mentioned initiatives in contemporary psychology designed to grapple with these and related dilemmas. As it seems to me, antidotes to developmental linearity and one-dimensionality can be gathered from (dialectical) psychologists, and also from a number of philosophers, past and present. Among phenomenological philosophers of our time, Maurice Merleau-Ponty provides many helpful guideposts in this area, although he does not offer a full-scale model of development on either the ontogenetic or the phylogenetic level. Regarding ontogenesis, his *Phenomenology of Perception* advances insightful criticisms of Piaget's scheme. In infancy and early childhood, Merleau-Ponty notes (agreeing to this point with the psychologist) that "the child lives in a world which he unhesitatingly believes accessible to all around him; he has no awareness of himself or of others as private subjectivities, nor does he suspect that all of us, himself included, are limited to one certain point of view of the world." This initial non-differentiation and inherence in "one single, self-evident world where everything takes place, even dreams" are supposed to be overcome by the rise of operational thought and by the emergence of cognitive self-awareness: "At about twelve years of age, says Piaget, the child achieves the *cogito* and reaches the truths of rationalism. At this stage, it is held, he discovers himself both as a point of view on the world and also as called upon to transcend that point of view and to construct objectivity at the level of judgment." What is neglected in this scheme, according to Merleau-Ponty, is that stages do not simply replace each other without a trace; above all, the rise of self-reflection cannot supplant the child's inherence or "being-in-the-world" without canceling the possibility of concrete human interaction: "Piaget brings the child to a mature outlook as if the thoughts of the adult were self-sufficient and disposed of all contradictions. But, in reality, it must be the case that the child's outlook is in some way vindicated against the adult's and against Piaget, and that the unsophisticated thinking of our earliest years remains as an indispensable acquisition underlying that of maturity, if there is to be for adults one common intersubjective world."[51]

The notion of personal maturation, against this background, acquires a complex tension-laden character. Instead of treating ontogenesis as a straightforward sequence which leads to growing autonomy and reflectiveness, *Phenomenology of Perception* introduces the notion of a *natural time* or natural history, with which all human designs are interwoven: "My voluntary and rational life realizes that it merges into another power which stands in the way of its completion and gives it a permanently tentative look. Natural time is always there." Viewed against this background, personal development appears simultaneously and inextricably as a movement toward greater rational lucidity and transparency and as a lapse into concrete ignorance. "The succession of the instants of time," Merleau-Ponty states, "is both the ground of, and the impediment to, the rationality of my personal history: the ground because it opens a totally new future to me in which I shall be able to reflect upon the element of opacity in my present; and an impediment or source of danger insofar as I shall never manage to seize the present through which I live with apodictic certainty. Since the lived is thus never entirely comprehensible, what I understand never quite tallies with my living experience; in short, I am never quite at one with myself." The limit of rational understanding, he elaborates, resides in the domain of lived experience in its difference (or otherness) from reflection—a domain which, through infancy, stretches back to prenatal existence where there was "nothing but the raw material and adumbration of a natural self and a natural time," that is, an "anonymous life" which is "merely the extreme form of that temporal dispersal which constantly threatens the historical present." In order to "have some inkling" of the character of that "amorphous existence which preceded my own history and will bring it to a close," the study adds, "I have only to look within me at that time which pursues its own independent course and which my personal life utilizes but does not entirely overlay. Because I am borne into personal existence by a time which I do not constitute, all my perceptions stand out against a background of nature."[52]

The implications of these comments for phylogenetic or social development on a global scale are brought out in some of Merleau-Ponty's later writings, especially in *Signs*. Relying on ethnological investigations and findings from Marcel Mauss to Claude Lévi-Strauss, Merleau-Ponty there insists on the need of "constructing a general system of reference in which the point of view of the native, the point of view of the civilized man, and the mistaken views each has of the other can all find a place—that is, of constituting a more comprehensive experience which becomes in principle accessible to men of a different time and country." Construction of such a comprehensive reference system requires in his view a radical openness, namely, a readiness to perceive "what is ours as alien and what was alien as our own"—a readiness which does not imply a lapse into primitivism: "It is not a matter of going in search of truth or salvation in what falls short of science or philosophical awareness, or of dragging chunks of mythology as such into our (Western) philosophy, but of acquiring—in the presence of these variants of humanity that we are so far from—a sense of the theoretical and practical problems our institutions are faced with, and of rediscovering the existential field that they were born in and that their long success has led us to forget." Approached in this manner, non-Western cultures "lacking our philosophical or economic equipment" are bound to assume an "instructive value": "The Orient's 'childishness' has something to teach us, if it were nothing more than the narrowness of our adult ideas. The relationship between Orient and Occident, like that between child and adult, is not that of ignorance to knowledge or non-philosophy to philosophy; it is much more subtle, making room on the part of the Orient for all anticipations and 'prematurations.' " What Western thought can learn from developing countries, and especially from Oriental cultures, Merleau-Ponty adds, is "to rediscover the relationship to being and initial option which gave it birth, and to estimate the possibilities we have shut ourselves off from in becoming 'Westerners' and perhaps reopen them."[53]

Turning to earlier periods of Western thought, Giambattista Vico's philosophy of history strikes me as a storehouse of fertile insights, although most of them were expressed in the metaphysical idiom of his age. Foreshadowing later stage theories (such as those of Condorcet, Comte, and others), Vico's *New Science* divided mankind's profane-historical development into three main epochs—the successive ages of gods, heroes, and men—which epochs were also said to correspond to three different kinds of human nature, of custom, language, and intelligence. During the first (and partially also the second) stage, human life was governed by unreflective experience or by what Vico called vulgar or poetic wisdom, a wisdom congruent with the "vast imagination" of early men who were "entirely immersed in the senses" and "buried in the body." Following a period ruled mainly by authority and speculative thought, mankind in the end was portrayed as entering the properly "human times" or the age of "fully developed human reason," an age when "the intellect was brought into play in great assemblies" and "universal legal concepts" were "abstracted by the intellect," enabling men to recognize "for laws conscience, reason, and duty." Although he depicted the last stage as manifesting the "true and proper nature of man," Vico did not treat the growth of reason as a linear advance; rather, rationalization also tended toward a general atrophy of sensibility, which in turn engenders egocentric caprice, and finally among all men brings about that "extreme form of delicacy, or better of pride, in which like wild animals they bristle and lash out at the slightest displeasure." Once the latter point was reached due to the raging "barbarism of reflection," the *New Science* assumed a cataclysmic reversal or *ricorso* leading mankind back to an earlier stage—not simply a romantic "return to nature" but a return to the initial "barbarism of sense." One further point should be made about the role of human initiative in history. Although he stressed the *verum-factum* principle, according to which insight is linked with authorship, Vico did not identify man's authorship of events with a purely deliberate design, but saw it as part of a larger unfolding practice termed *providence* (which was not synonymous with blind fate).[54]

My intent here is not to give an overview of philosophical teachings relevant to the issues of individual and social development. In the remainder of this chapter, I would like to focus on the writings of one recent philosopher and sociologist whose reflections appear to me particularly thoughtful and significant: those of Theodor Adorno, one of the founders of the same Frankfurt school to which Habermas in large measure claims allegiance. The juxtaposition of the developmental views of Habermas and Adorno seems instructive precisely because they are articulated within similar frames of reference and thus are not rigidly incompatible. Adorno's outlook, in my view, also bears some resemblance to those of the preceding thinkers. Adorno shared with Merleau-Ponty a preoccupation with natural time or with the experiential crosscurrents affecting temporal sequences; in fact, a life-long theme recurring in many of his writings was the conception of natural history. The affinity with Vico resides chiefly in the notion of historical development as a simultaneous progress and regress. Together with the Neapolitan philosopher (and also with Habermas and Husserl), Adorno acknowledged the "humanizing" or civilizing effects of reason and reflection, as opposed to the blind compulsion of mythological beliefs; at the same time, he discovered in rationalization and progressive ego-autonomy the seeds of a growing imaginative debility and the origin of an intellectual anthropocentrism subjecting both nature and society to manipulative human designs. The relationship between the two trends, in his judgment, had to be construed dialectically—not in the sense of Hegel's dialectical logic, but rather in that of a negative dialectics, anticipating the future only in an unplanned and non-predictive manner.

Adorno and "Natural History"

In a tentative fashion, the notion of natural history was first outlined by Adorno in a paper written in 1932, after his break with idealism and shortly before his forced emigration from Germany. Entitled "The Idea of Natural History," the paper challenged a central pillar of Western philosophical thought: the Cartesian legacy of the autonomous thinking subject and of the mind-body bifurcation, a legacy which in more general terms implies a separation between the domains of human intentionality and future-oriented action, on the one hand, and of natural determinism, on the other. As its opening paragraphs stated, the essay's goal was to overcome the customary antithesis of the two domains—labeled briefly *nature* and *history*—by pushing both components to the point where their affinity and reciprocal impact emerge behind their difference. As used in this context, the term *nature* was meant to refer not simply to the object of natural science (itself a derivative of the Cartesian legacy), but more broadly to a realm of substantive, preordained, and necessary reality, as distinguished from the dynamic and innovative features of historical life. As Adorno recognized, the phenomenological movement, especially in its post-Husserlian phase, had repeatedly wrestled with the antithesis and tried to undercut its philosophical moorings; in his view, however, efforts of this kind tended to be marred by the influence of egological-idealist premises. To make headway in this area, he argued, it was necessary to cut loose from the heritage of subjectivity and to open consciousness more fully to the inroads of its counterpart, non-consciousness or nature. Adorno meant not only to establish a speculative synthesis but to show concretely how history in its very historicity is pervaded by nature just as, reversely, nature in its presumed solidity is a historical occurrence. Wrested from its usage in traditional academic disciplines, the term *natural history* could pinpoint this correlation.[55]

As the essay indicated, the intended meaning of the term was not the author's idiosyncratic invention. Two recent thinkers in particular could claim parentage of the notion: Georg Lukács and Walter Benjamin. In his *Theory of the Novel* (published over a decade earlier), Lukács had employed the term *second nature* to designate those layers of historical experience which had been emptied of human intentionality and meaning—which, to use his words, had been turned into "frozen, alien" structures or into a "golgotha of decomposed internality." During the interbellum period, the notion was further developed by Benjamin, perhaps with less speculative fervor and more rigor. While Lukács' second nature was virtually cut off from (purposive) history and recoverable only through an eschatological upheaval, Benjamin presented historical life as an intrinsically "natural" process, due to its largely non-intentional, inchoate, and fragmentary character. At the same time, nature in his view bore a profoundly historical imprint, owing to the fact that it appears transitory or perishable not only in its particular elements but in its core. The connecting link between nature and history, from his perspective, resided ultimately in the common aspect of finitude and mortality: against the foil of nature, the story of human and social evolution revealed itself as a story of suffering and dispersal, or as a universal calvary "significant only at the points of decay." Under Benjamin's radical scrutiny, Adorno commented, "reality is transformed into a panorama of ruins and fragments, into a golgotha of experience where the key to the nexus of history and nature is buried." As inaugurated by Lukács and Benjamin, he elaborated, natural history was clearly not synonymous with mystical reunion or instantaneous harmony. To grasp its import, it was imperative first of all to take seriously the fragmentation of reality, including the discontinuity between nature and history; instead of indulging in synthetic visions, the task was to proceed from this discontinuity by exploring the historical features of archaic, quasi-natural myths as well as the archaic underpinnings of historical innovation.[56]

As presented in the essay, the study of natural history was at best a sketchy program; its pursuit was interrupted by events in Europe which led to Adorno's emigration (first to England and then to America), while simultaneously reinforcing his distrust in the purposive direction of historical evolution. A first sustained effort to carry out the task outlined in the essay can be found in a study written jointly with Max Horkheimer during the war years and published in 1947, under the title *Dialectic of Enlightenment*. In a sense, the study can be viewed as a capstone of Adorno's (and also of Horkheimer's) intellectual development during the preceding decades. The steady disenchantment with idealism and subjectivism, evident in the discussed essay and in other prewar writings, led in the *Dialectic* to the recognition of a deep-seated crisis in Western life: the recognition that *enlightenment,* with its stress on the emancipation of reason from nature, had progressively transformed the world into an assembly of objects for consciousness, and ultimately into an arsenal of utensils for human manipulation and domination. The growth of instrumental rationality and human steering capacity, however, was not identical with the expansion of actual freedom. Due to the dialectical character of the master-slave relationship, man's mastery over nature, according to the authors, entailed his progressive enslavement by natural constraints, more precisely by the dictates of a naturalistic "scientism" governing not only man's contact with nature but social or intersubjective relations as well. For Adorno and Horkheimer, the remedy for the mentioned crisis resided not simply in an abdication of rational inquiry. Despite its problematic effects, rational reflection in their view was an experiential dilemma which had to be sustained in its ambivalence, until thought itself was able to break the spell of instrumental domination. Located at the heart of this experiential dilemma, *enlightenment* was neither a causal occurrence nor a premeditated project but a sinew and manifestation of natural history.[57]

Viewed in connection with the latter notion, the title of the study bears brief elaboration. As employed throughout the volume, the term *enlightenment* was not restricted to the age of Diderot and Voltaire, but was intended to cover the entire period of Western rationalism and "scientific" inquiry from earliest times (that is, since classical antiquity). Contrary to a widespread belief sponsored by its proponents, enlightenment in the authors' judgment signified not so much a linear progression from ignorance to knowledge as a complex movement involving a counterpoint of advance and regress; this counterpoint could be labeled dialectical, but not in the sense of a dialectical logic. The central question motivating the study was why—given the refinement of rationality and the expansion of material productivity—"mankind, instead of entering into a truly human condition is sinking into a new kind of barbarism." Although the *New Science* was not specifically cited, the query carried distinct echoes of the "barbarism of reflection" which Vico had treated as harbinger of a potential new *ricorso* of civilization. According to Horkheimer and Adorno, our contemporary period was marked by a peculiar mixture of intellectual sophistication and concrete-experiential myopia. The rising standard of living even among the lower classes, the study noted, was accompanied by a "glittering display of intellect." While its true concern was the "negation of reification," intellect was bound to decay "where it congeals into a cultural commodity which is distributed for purposes of consumption. The flood of detailed information and candy-floss entertainment promotes simultaneously human cleverness and stultification." Despite its somber diagnosis, the purpose of the study was not simply to indict knowledge, but to find in reason both the source and a possible antidote for the "self-destruction of enlightenment": "We are wholly convinced—and therein lies our *petitio principii*—that social freedom is inseparable from enlightened thought. Yet, we believe to have recognized just as clearly that this type of thought, no less than the concrete historical forms or social institutions linked with it, contains the seeds of the very reversal which is happening today. Unless willing to ponder this regressive element, enlightenment seals its own fate."[58]

The mainspring of Western rationalism, and also the motive of the present reversal, was found by the authors in its ambition to terminate man's bondage to nature and to primitive superstition. "The

basic program of enlightenment," they observed, "was the disenchantment of the world, the dissolution of myths and the substitution of
knowledge for fancy." From the beginning, however, the effort of
demystification and the attack on prejudice were pervaded by a patri-
archal impulse, the impulse to govern: "Having vanquished superstition, human reason shall rule over a disenchanted nature." In order to
gain ascendancy, reason is bent on simplifying the universe, on subsuming all particular details under abstract categories or systematic-logical
schemes—and ideally under handy mathematical formulas: "In advance, enlightenment recognizes as reality or event only what can be
grasped in unity; its ideal is the system from which everything is deduced. . . . Number became the canon of enlightenment." The central ambition of rational analysis is to discover the internal mechanism
of phenomena—a discovery which, by permitting experimental reconstruction or replication, enhances the range of human control. "Enlightenment," we read, "behaves toward things as a dictator behaves
toward men: he only knows them as objects of manipulation. The man
of science knows things insofar as he can make or produce them, thus
chaining their reality to his own ends. The transformation reveals the
nature of things as always the same: an occasion for domination." In
this manner abstract logic and detached analysis reveal their instrumental, utilitarian thrust: "The universality of categories as developed
by discursive logic—emblem of domination in the conceptual sphere—
is erected on the basis of actual domination. The dissolution of the
heritage of magic and of ancient diffuse notions by conceptual unity
heralds a way of life shaped by freemen accustomed to rule."[59]

According to Horkheimer and Adorno, the escape from nature
promised by rationalism was entirely misleading. In combating superstition, scientific reason tries to extricate itself from blind determinism;
however, by focusing attention on causal mechanisms or permanent
laws of nature, science still pays tribute to cyclical recurrence or the
"eternal return of the present." "The doctrine of the equivalence of
action and reaction," the study stated, "maintains the power of repetition over life long after men had renounced the illusory hope to identify themselves through repetition with the repeated reality and thus to
escape its dominion. The more remote the distance into which magical
illusion recedes, the more relentlessly repetition (restyled as lawful-
ness) chains man to that natural cycle whose reification into a law of
nature was supposed to secure his emancipation." As a result of its
universalism and seeming detachment, enlightenment fell prey to the
very ritual whose spell it tried to break: "The principle of imma-

nence—the explanation of every event as repetition—which enlightenment pits against mythical fancy, is the principle of myth itself." Mythology, in the authors' view, was marked by the nexus of guilt and punishment, fate and retribution—a nexus perpetuated by rationalism: "In myths every event must atone for having happened. The same occurs in enlightenment: every particular phenomenon is annihilated as soon as it is noted." Facts, moreover, are obliterated in their particularity, and are also affirmed and worshipped as elements of a universal scheme: "In its figures mythology reflected the essence of existing reality—cycle, fate, mundane dominion—as a truth devoid of hope. Both the vitality of mythical images and the clarity of scientific formulas testify to the permanence of facticity, proclaiming it as the very meaning which it occludes."[60]

From this perspective, the source of the present reversal became evident: in functioning as an instrument of human domination, reason remained a victim and unwitting vehicle of natural constraints. "In the comprehensive sense of progressive thought," the study argued, "enlightenment has always aimed at liberating men from fear and establishing their mastery; but the fully enlightened world radiates triumphant disaster. . . . Every attempt to terminate natural constraints by rupturing nature only intensifies bondage. Such is the course of European civilization."[61] Reduced to a target of instrumental control, nature retaliates not only through counterforce, but also by truncating human sense experience or sensibility toward nature—a paralysis which affects human understanding as well: "The unification of intellectual functions for the sake of gaining control over the senses—reflection's retreat in the interest of conceptual uniformity—entails the impoverishment of thought and experience alike; both are impaired by their mutual segregation." In depicting the human and social costs of rationalism, Horkheimer and Adorno used language whose grimness evoked Vico's portrayal of civilization during the stage of final decay: "The more complex and refined the social, economic and scientific apparatus to whose service the production system has long accustomed the human body, the more perfunctory the experiences of which it is capable. The elimination of qualitative traits and their conversion into functions spreads from science via rationalized modes of labor to the experiential world of nations—which once again tends to be assimilated to that of dinosaurs. The pathology of the masses today is their inability to hear new sounds with their own ears, to touch the untouched with their own hands—a new kind of stupor far outdistancing defunct mythologies. By means of an encompassing society regulating all relations and emotions, men are reduced again to the level from which social evolution and human emancipation departed: the level of species creatures, identical with each other in the atomistic but dictatorial collectivity."[62]

Although somber in tone, the study did not counsel despair; as presented by Horkheimer and Adorno, the dialectic of enlightenment involved neither unidirectional progress nor unmitigated regression but a confluence of the two: "The curse of relentless progress is relentless regression." According to the authors, human thought was irremediably lodged in the tension between image and sign, concrete perception and concept—unable to find rest in either. Inescapably, thought counteracts the unreflected presence of nature, only to fall prey to the dialectic of domination: "Natural bondage derives from the very subjugation of nature without which mind cannot exist." In exerting its analytical capacity, reason opens up the breach between man and nature, subject and object, which, making room for instrumental mastery, cannot simply be healed by synthetic formulas: "Concepts are tools ideally suited to that aspect of things amenable to control. Thought becomes illusory when seeking to conceal its divisive function, detachment and objectifying impact: all mystical reunion is deception." Only by clinging to its own dialectic—especially to the power of concrete negation—can thought hope to overcome its conceit and to dissolve the spell of self-induced bondage. "Reason's battle against prejudice has always meant not only expansion but also exposure of domination," the authors wrote. "Enlightenment is more than enlightenment—nature which becomes accessible in its alienation." By reflecting on its role, that is, "by acknowledging itself as domination and retreating into nature," they added, mind finds it possible to "abandon the claim to mastery subjecting it to nature. Although compelled to flee from necessity and unable to renounce progress and civilization without forsaking knowledge itself, mankind at least does not longer mistake its ramparts against necessity—the institutions and practices of domination which have always rebounded from nature on society—as synonyms of human emancipation."[63]

As indicated, *Dialectic of Enlightenment* was the fruit of a collaborative endeavor; yet, with regard to both style and substance, it is not difficult to detect in the study the influence of Adorno's subtle bent of mind. The intimate correlation of rational-emancipatory initiative and natural constraints, in particular, reflected one of Adorno's central preoccupations, to which he gave detailed attention in his last major philosophical work, his *Negative Dialectics* of 1966. In that work, the issues surrounding the correlation of reason and nature are discussed in a chapter entitled "World Spirit and Natural History," devoted mainly to a critical assessment of Hegel's philosophy of history. Although he appreciates the complexity of Hegel's thought, Adorno challenges both the idealist stress on human culture and the subsumption of particular events under a predetermined pattern of development. In focusing on national cultures as agents of change, Hegelian philosophy—despite its anti-individualism and anti-subjectivism—is said to have identified historical purpose with the intentions of collective (potentially *universal*) subjects. Apart from the pitfalls of cultural bias, the focus on mind—viewed as collective mind—was bound to pit human intentionality against nature, thus enmeshing historical progress in the dialectic of mastery. The glorification of universal reason as epitomized in the *world spirit*—Adorno notes—was synonymous with a glorification of rational control over amorphous nature and over the contingency of particular events. "The apotheosis of universality," he asserts, "is a concession of failure. By banishing particular details, universality reveals itself as particular domination. In its triumph general reason discloses its intrinsic restrictions: instead of simply signifying unity within diversity, it involves a streamlining of reality, a unity superimposed on something. . . . Unity equals division." Ultimately, the conflict between universality and particularity derives from reason's exclusive thrust toward self-knowledge: "Enthroned above the otherness of the world, triumphant reason necessarily constricts itself. The principle of pure identity is in itself contradictory—since it perpetuates non-identity in suppressed and mutilated form."[64]

Seen from this perspective, Hegel's historical conception manifested a dialectic unintended (or not fully apprehended) by its author: rational emancipation had as its counterpoint man's growing entanglement in natural constraints. According to Adorno, Hegel's vision of universal history is spurious if treated as a blueprint of growing moral perfection, yet its accent on uniformity was not entirely misguided. In his words: "There is no point in denying the unity cementing the discontinuous and dispersed fragments of history—the unity of progressive domination extending from nature to society and finally to man's psyche. No universal history leads from barbarism to humanism; but there is one leading from the slingshot to the megaton bomb, terminating in the total threat of organized mankind against living creatures—at a point of total discontinuity." From the vantage point of the world spirit, Adorno continues, historical progress paradoxically annuls itself; submerged in the dialectic of domination, reason falls prey to the cycle of nature and the "eternal return of the present." In Hegel's conception, *Negative Dialectics* comments, "domination is absolutized and projected onto the essence of reality identified with spirit. History, however, as a scheme of events totally explained, acquires the aura of timeless permanence. In the midst of history, Hegel sides with an unchanging immutability—the identical core of a process presumed rational in its totality." Historical progress and cyclical permanence thus presuppose each other; their confluence testifies to the fact that "wedded to identity, mind converges with the spell of blind nature by denying it."[65]

In lieu of the march of the world spirit, *Negative Dialectics* counsels the perspective of natural history, as articulated initially by Lukács and Benjamin. Under the heading of a *second nature,* denoting the fabric of quasi-natural laws governing social life, the perspective is said to preserve Hegel's insight into the objectivity of historical experience—but with a critical bent: "The thesis that society is subject to natural laws is ideology if treated as an immutable dictate of nature; however, it contains a real kernel to the extent that it points to the hidden motor of unconscious society." Contrary to the naturalism and scientism of Marxist orthodoxy, Marx himself—in Adorno's view—stressed natural constraints only as a challenge for human aspirations: "Human history, involving the progressive mastery of nature, continues the unconscious process of nature: devouring and being devoured. Ironically Marx was a Social Darwinist: what Social Darwinists extolled as proper guidelines for human action, was to him a negative foil suggesting the possibility of transformation." That the naturalist thesis cannot be uncritically accepted, he insists, is corroborated by the "strongest theme in Marxist theory, that of the finitude or changeability of natural laws: at the threshold of the realm of freedom they would cease to apply." The realm of freedom, however, is not a simple rejection of nature or its subjugation to the mastery of reason, a relationship which would perpetuate the enmity between man and nature; nor can access to the realm be gained through synthetic formulas. "Once established," Adorno concludes, "the boundary between nature and culture can be blurred but not erased by reflection. Without reflection, to be sure, the distinction would reduce historical movement to a mere adjunct, while enshrining unchanging permanence as essence. It is up to thought, instead, to see all nature (and its equivalents) as history and all history as nature."[66]

CHAPTER FIVE

Ordinary Language
and Ideal Speech

Memoriam fecit. . . .

CONTEMPORARY ETHICS tends to be overshadowed by the so-called fact-value or is-ought split; according to a competent observer, the issue must be viewed as "the central problem in moral philosophy."[1] Opinions differ as to the historical and intellectual origins of the dilemma. While the distinction between normative goals and factual conditions can probably be traced back to antiquity, their segregation into a dichotomy is commonly attributed to modern Enlightenment thought, and frequently to Humean empiricism. Whatever the precise antecedents may be, the fact-value difference was accentuated in our century by the rise of positivism and logical empiricism, a movement committed to the rigorous identification of knowledge with empirical or logical propositions. According to a dominant brand of the movement—usually labeled non-cognitivism—only empirical and logical-analytical statements were amenable to rational validation, while value statements were derived from subjective fancy. Not all members of the movement, one might add, were satisfied with this bifurcation; in the eyes of some—especially adherents of a naturalistic ethics—values could readily acquire cognitive meaning by being submerged in factual and analytical categories. During its period of hegemony, one might also note, the logical-empiricist paradigm held sway not only over its supporters: in seeking to rescue human choice from empirical determinism, even opponents of positivism normally acknowledged the criteria of cognitive validation stipulated by the paradigm.[2]

In the meantime, intellectual alignments have been loosened in many ways, but the fact-value question has not been removed from its central position—nor is it likely to be displaced by a mere stroke of the pen. One of the most significant philosophical developments during recent decades has been the intensive exploration of various non- or presubjective contexts underlying human cognition and experience; while linguistic philosophers have emphasized the primacy of language over individual speech and thought, some Continental thinkers have tried to delineate the prereflective (perhaps ontological) parameters of the life-world shaping individual experience. In the domain of ethics, the focus on language—especially everyday language—has played a crucial role in eroding the rigid contours of the logical-empiricist paradigm; by demonstrating the distinctiveness and at least partial autonomy of normative discourse, linguistic analysts have questioned the narrow restriction of cognitive meaning to factual or logical statements. Despite these advances, linguistic philosophy cannot be said to have banished traditional ethical quandaries, including the fact-value dilemma. The latter issue is bound to reemerge whenever linguistic practices are treated as empirical premises from which moral imperatives can somehow be derived through a process of entailment. It seems to me that the controversy between linguistic empiricists—or descriptivists—and defenders of prescriptive norms is not purely academic, but revolves ultimately around the ethical relevance of human choice. Since responsibility seems inconceivable without at least a measure of autonomy, the persistence of the fact-value problem is hardly fortuitous.[3]

Contemporary ethics—especially when viewed under linguistic auspices—is beset by numerous additional predicaments, all of which are linked with the is-ought correlation. One of the most troublesome questions concerns the character of the entailment which is claimed to tie norms to linguistic practices or similar premises. In large measure, the difficulty centers on whether entailment can be construed as logical deduction or as empirical inference or as a combination of the two. In the first instance, does derivation not simply coincide with a tautological or definitional exercise? The peril of tautology is enhanced when stipulated premises—instead of denoting purely factual conditions—are treated as moral axioms or at least as statements imbued with normative connotations, for in this case entailment easily succumbs to circularity (unless a further effort is made to validate premises, in an infinite deductive regress). Where the factual status of premises is maintained, concrete, non-tautological inferences may indeed be possible—but at the likely price of subverting the normative quality of derived conclusions and of transforming the is-ought correlation into a sequence of empirical events.[4] In the latter instance, however, is not entailment more akin to prediction than to the justification of norms and moral actions? The hazards of entailment have been clearly delineated in a recent essay by a noted moral philosopher. "If the justifying statements are moral ones," he writes, "then there recurs the question of how they are to be justified, since they too are not self-evident, and the question continues to recur as we mount through more general rules and principles. If, on the other hand, the statements from which the moral 'ought'-judgments are to be derived are non-moral ones"— that is, empirical or factual premises—"then there is the difficulty that the 'ought'-judgments are not derivable from those statements either inductively or deductively, unless we define 'ought' in empirical terms; and such a definition raises many questions of adequacy, including how the 'ought'-judgments can pass the tests of prescriptiveness and categoricalness."[5]

The notion (or rather hunch) which I would like to explore in these pages is whether the validation of norms can perhaps be more adequately grasped in terms of recollection than of logical or empirical entailment. As is well known, the concept of recollection or *anamnesis* was first introduced into Western philosophy and epistemology in the Platonic dialogue *Meno*. Confronted with the sophistic dilemma according to which no new knowledge can ever be acquired—since one either knows or does not know what one is looking for and in either case the search is pointless—Socrates argues that, prior to philosophical reflection or demonstration, man "has seen all things both here and in the other world," thus "has learned everything there is" and "can recall the knowledge of virtue or anything else" which he "once possessed."[6] Unfortunately, Plato does not fully spell out the nature of recollection. The geometrical experiment with Meno's slave which illustrates the process of learning seems to approximate recollection to logical-deductive reasoning. However, the remainder of the dialogue casts doubt on this equation, since virtue is found not to be teachable like geometry. What emerges clearly in *Meno* is the difference between recollection and empirical inference: insisting on the acquired character of moral excellence, Socrates rejects naturalism, saying that "good men cannot be good by nature."[7] The present chapter attempts to disentangle, on a limited scale, the quandaries surrounding recollection and entailment, by focusing on several contemporary formulations of the fact-value dilemma. The Ariadne thread through the discussion is provided by a leading example of linguistic ethics: John Searle's derivation of norms from *institutional facts*. After having outlined Searle's main arguments together with key criticisms, I shall shift attention to two ethical theorists, Gewirth and Frohock, and their efforts to correct Searle's weaknesses through a process of rigorous conceptual entailment. Drawbacks of these efforts, in turn, pave the way to a strategy of transcendental justification—as pursued in Apel's *transcendental pragmatics*. The concluding section returns to the theme of recollection and its possible significance in ethical discourse.

Deriving Ought from Is: Searle

As inaugurated by the later Wittgenstein, the investigation of ordinary language was initially motivated not by ethical concerns but by the need to find an adequate *metalinguistic* framework capable of accounting for empirical or scientific propositions. In due course, however, Wittgenstein's suggestive identification of natural languages with *forms of life* encouraged explorations of the full range of statements and *performative* modes encountered in everyday speech patterns, including the dimension of ethical discourse. At the beginning, ventures into the latter domain were modest: still imbued with the positivist commitment to neutral analysis, linguistic thinkers aimed at providing a faithful descriptive record of prevailing discursive practices, without assessing the normative stringency or validity of such practices. Thus Stephen Toulmin's *Examination of the Place of Reason in Ethics* (published in 1950) sought to portray the distinctive features of practical-moral argument or the "logic of moral reasoning," by differentiating this logic from various types of naturalism and non-cognitivist subjectivism; as he acknowledged, the goal of his study was not to corroborate principles but to offer "a descriptive account of the function of ethical concepts." In a similar vein Kurt Baier, although more ambitious in a normative direction, delineated the character of justifying statements ordinarily employed in discourse animated by a "moral point of view."[8] Few analysts at the time were willing to ponder the categorical or ought-quality of norms; if pressed on the issue, many were content to assert the virtual inseparability of facts and values in everyday language. Against this background, Searle's approach involved a significant departure from the prevailing custom: instead of simply depicting habitual speech patterns, his analysis tried to vindicate genuine moral imperatives through a description of linguistic behavior, and thus to demonstrate conclusively "how to derive ought from is."

Presented first in a philosophical journal, Searle's argument appeared in refined form in his *Speech Acts* (of 1970), on which I intend to focus.[9] As its subtitle indicated, the study was conceived as an "essay in the philosophy of language," that is, as an endeavor not merely to solve particular linguistic problems, but "to give philosophically illuminating descriptions of certain general features of language, such as reference, truth, meaning, and necessity." The basic thesis of the book was that language had to be seen as "rule-governed intentional behavior" whose study could not simply rely on external observation or behavioristic analysis; rather, the meaning of words or "linguistic characterizations" could be properly grasped only through participation or by invoking the performative competence of a native speaker. "Speaking a language," Searle noted, "is engaging in a (highly complex) rule-governed form of behavior. To learn and master a language is (*inter alia*) to learn and to have mastered these rules." Consequently, when offering "linguistic characterizations," a native speaker was not merely "reporting the behavior of a group" from the outside, but displaying aspects of his "mastery of a rule-governed skill." Approached from the speaker's perspective, the study of language coincided with the study of speech acts, for—in terms of linguistic communication—the basic unit or token was not, as commonly assumed, the symbol, word, or sentence, but rather "the production or issuance of the symbol or word or sentence in the performance of the speech act." According to Searle, the focus on linguistic acts highlighted the linkage between language and human activity in general, with the result that language theory emerged as "part of a theory of action." As he emphasized, however, the book's practical or pragmatic accent was not designed to replace concern with semantic meaning and syntactical structure (or, in Saussurian terms, to substitute a study of *parole* for that of *langue*). Although these dimensions of language are frequently treated as inconsistent and although "historically there have been sharp disagreements," especially between defenders of semantic reference and pragmatic usage, *Speech Acts* stressed the complementary character and even fusion of such perspectives: "A study of the meaning of sentences is not in principle distinct from a study of speech acts. Properly construed, they are the same study."[10]

The book concentrated on various ingredients, properties, and presuppositions of speech acts, not all of which are relevant for our present purposes. After having differentiated between several types of communicative tokens—such as utterances and propositional and illocutionary acts (all claimed to be intimately linked in complete speech acts)—Searle turned to one aspect which is clearly central in our context: the notion of rules implicit in the rule-governed character of linguistic behavior. Distinguishing between *regulative* and *constitutive* rules—where the former were said to "regulate antecedently or independently existing forms of behavior" and the latter to "create or define new forms of behavior"—the study presented linguistic competence ultimately as under the sway of constitutive principles: "Speaking a language is a matter of performing speech acts according to systems of constitutive rules." The significance of this conception for ethical discussions emerged in the distinction between *brute* and *institutional*

facts outlined shortly afterwards. Relying on "simple empirical observations recording sense experiences," Searle observed, ordinary empiricism or physicalism commonly presented "a picture of the world as
consisting of brute facts"; but the picture was unable to account for a
number of phenomena which yet were undeniably objective: "A marriage ceremony, a baseball game, a trial, and a legislative action involve
a variety of physical movements, states, and raw feels, but a specification of one of these events only in such terms is not so far a specification of it as a marriage ceremony, baseball game, a trial, or a legislative
action." To grasp the latter specification it was necessary to have recourse to the notion of institutional facts: "They are indeed facts; but
their existence, unlike the existence of brute facts, presupposes the existence of certain human institutions." Such institutions, in turn, presupposed or could be defined as "systems of constitutive rules."[11]

On the basis of these kinds of conceptual clarifications the study
tackled the traditional is-ought dilemma. As an opening gambit, Searle
launched a broadside attack on the naturalistic fallacy doctrine, according to which facts and values are separated by an unbridgeable gulf.
Labeling the doctrine the *naturalistic fallacy fallacy* he expressed his
intent to demonstrate through a number of examples how "evaluative
statements *are derivable* from descriptive statements." Surprisingly, in
view of the earlier stress on the intimate linkage between semantic
meaning and usage, the difference in the "illocutionary force" of descriptive and evaluative statements as used in speech situations was said
to have no bearing on the question of derivation or entailment, provided the semantic reference remained constant. "The fact that the
two utterances have characteristically different illocutionary forces is
not sufficient to show that *the proposition* expressed in the first utterance does not entail *the proposition* expressed in the second. Closely
related to this distinction between the proposition expressed in an utterance and the illocutionary force of the utterance is the distinction
between the meaning of the sentence and the force of its utterance, and
also, I shall argue, the distinction—not identity—between meaning
and use." Actually, the obfuscation of the latter distinction was now
claimed to be the core of a misconception termed *speech act fallacy*
and both fallacies were ascribed ultimately to the pragmatic orientation
of ordinary language philosophy. Seeing that the use of evaluative sentences "was different from the use or illocutionary force of the utterance of certain descriptive sentences," Searle commented, linguistic
philosophers "concluded that the meaning must be such that no set of
descriptive statements could entail an evaluative one. But that conclu-

sion does not follow, for from the fact that the point or illocutionary force of uttering a sentence is 'evaluative' it does not follow that the proposition expressed cannot be entailed by a proposition expressed in the utterance of a sentence the illocutionary force or point of uttering which would be 'descriptive.' "[12]

The chief example chosen in *Speech Acts* to undermine the traditional is-ought dichotomy centered on the institution of promising, specifically on the normative obligation which arises from promising seen as an institutional fact. Since the structure of the argument is relatively well-known, I shall limit myself to a summary. Searle at the outset listed a series of five statements whose meanings were subsequently specified in a number of ways. The statements are as follows: "(1) Jones uttered the words 'I hereby promise to pay you, Smith, five dollars'; (2) Jones promised to pay Smith five dollars; (3) Jones placed himself under (undertook) an obligation to pay Smith five dollars; (4) Jones is under an obligation to pay Smith five dollars; (5) Jones ought to pay Smith five dollars." Regarding the preceding list, Searle claimed that "the relation between any statement and its successor, while not in every case one of entailment, is nonetheless not just an accidental or completely contingent relation; and the additional statements and certain other adjustments necessary to make the relationships one of entailment do not need to involve any evaluative statements, moral principles, or anything of the sort." The required tightening of the argument was effected mainly through three further specifications or adjustments. First of all, the linkage between steps (1) and (2) was clarified through insertion of statement (1a), to the effect that "under certain conditions c anyone who utters the words (sentence) 'I hereby promise to pay you, Smith, five dollars' promises to pay Smith five dollars" (where "conditions c" refer to those conditions which render the utterance a successful performance of the act of promising). Next, to evade the effect of supervening circumstances, the five statements had to be seen as occurring simultaneously (a stipulation particularly important for the next-to-last step). Finally, statement (5) was to be interpreted in this sense: "As regards his obligation to pay Smith five dollars, Jones ought to pay Smith five dollars." Surveying the steps of his argument Searle concluded: "We have thus derived (in as strict a sense of 'derive' as natural language will admit of) an 'ought' from an 'is.' And the extra premises which were needed to make the derivation work were in no case moral or evaluative in nature. They consisted of empirical assumptions, tautologies, and descriptions of word usage." As he added, moreover, the *ought* derived in the argument was "in Kant's sense a 'categorical' not a 'hypothetical' ought."[13]

Following the demonstrations of the fact-value nexus Searle offered some general comments on the "nature of the issues" involved in his derivation and then proceeded to respond to some counterarguments. His general observations displayed a keen awareness of the broader philosophical significance of his approach, especially with regard to traditional distinctions between subject and object or between consciousness and world. Factual or descriptive statements, he wrote, are generally regarded as objective, because facts refer to "objectively ascertainable conditions," while evaluative statements carry subjective connotations. The "underlying reason" for this difference, he continued, was that evaluative statements are commonly assumed to "perform a completely different job from descriptive statements. Their job is not to describe any features of the world but to express the speaker's emotions, to express his attitudes, to praise or condemn, to laud or insult, to commend, to recommend, to advise, to command, and so forth." Ultimately, Searle indicated, the fact-value issue reflects metaphysical assumptions revolving around the world-consciousness dilemma: evaluative statements in the traditional view must be segregated from descriptive assertions, "for if they were objective they could no longer function to evaluate. Put metaphysically, values cannot lie in the world, for if they did they would cease to be values and would just be another part of the world." Seen in this context, *Speech Acts* attempted to correct and obviate the traditional mind-world dichotomy—or at least to undertake steps in this direction within the confines of selected human institutions, in particular the institution of promising. The demonstration contained in the example of promising, the study asserted, "started with a brute fact, that a man uttered certain words, and then invoked the institution in such a way as to generate institutional facts by which we arrived at the conclusion that, as regards his obligation, the man ought to pay another man five dollars. The whole proof rests on an appeal to the constitutive rule that to make a promise is to undertake an obligation, and this rule is a meaning rule of the 'descriptive' word 'promise.' "[14]

Although usually focused on concrete examples, the study occasionally seemed to be animated by a more ambitious philosophical objective: in a number of passages the range of concern was expanded from specific institutions to institutions in general, and from particular experiential contexts to human experience as such. As it appears to me, Searle's argument at these points acquired the status of a quasi-

ontological critique of Western metaphysics—a critique loosely akin
to the efforts of some Continental thinkers to uncover the presubjective
underpinnings of subjectivity and to reintegrate the *ego cogitans* in the
broader matrix of being-in-the-world. Thus, reflecting on the possibility of revising and maybe abolishing the *constitutive rules* of such institutions as promising, baseball, or private property, he observed:
"Standing on the deck of some institutions one can tinker with constitutive rules and even throw some other institutions overboard. But
could one throw all institutions overboard (in order perhaps to avoid
ever having to derive an 'ought' from an 'is')? One could not and still
engage in those forms of behavior we consider characteristically human." In a similar vein, the concluding passages of the book pondered
the notion of a complete disengagement from all human obligations, a
notion implicit in the claim of some critics that they can adopt a "detached anthropological standpoint" toward human affairs in general.
"The price of a really consistent application of the 'detached anthropological standpoint' would be an end to all validity and entailment,"
the study noted, adding: "The retreat from the committed use of words
ultimately must involve a retreat from language itself, for speaking a
language—as has been the main theme of this book—consists of performing speech acts according to rules, and there is no separating those
speech acts from the commitments which form essential parts of
them."[15]

However intriguing, statements to this effect cannot be accorded
great weight in Searle's overall argument. Read in context, these passages appear like brief speculative forays—from which the author
quickly recoiled to the safe ground of analytical common sense (heed-
ing John Austin's injunction to avoid the *ivresse des grands pro-
fondeurs*). This retreat is patently evident in Searle's replies to a first
set of criticisms reviewed in the study—replies which clearly acknowledged the particular, contingent, and hence avoidable character of the
institution of promising. Considering the attitude of a "nihilistic an-
archist" who rejects institutional constraints tied to promising or property, he conceded that "we need to make a distinction between what is
external and what is internal to the institution of promising. It is
internal to the concept of promising that in promising one undertakes
an obligation to do something. But whether the entire institution of
promising is good or evil, and whether the obligations undertaken in
promising are overridden by other outside considerations are questions
which are external to the institution." Thus, stressing the internal linkage between promising and obligation did not entail the view that "in-

stitutions are logically unassailable" or that "one ought to approve or disapprove this or that institution"; rather, what the example demonstrated was simply that "when one enters an institutional activity by invoking the rules of the institution one necessarily commits oneself in such and such ways." A similar point emerged from Searle's next reply to the query whether institutional rules could be designed in such a manner as to obligate unwitting bystanders. "The notion of obligation," he wrote, "is closely tied to the notion of accepting, acknowledging, recognizing, undertaking, etc., obligations in such a way as to render the notion of an obligation essentially a contractual notion."[16]

Despite the preceding references to approval or *acceptance,* Searle in his subsequent replies clung tenaciously to the *internal* nexus between promising and obligation—even in responding to more or less *external* challenges or to criticisms hovering at the border between internal and external criteria. Countering the charge that statement (1a)—which forms the bridge "from the brute to the institutional level"—is not so much a descriptive-factual statement as a "substantial moral principle," he insisted that acceptance of this statement was "quite unlike the decision to accept a certain moral principle. (1a) states a fact about the meaning of a descriptive word, 'promise.'" Consequently, "anyone who uses that word in serious literal speech is committed to its logical consequences involving obligations." The further objection that words like *promise* have perhaps a dual meaning—a literal-descriptive and an evaluative sense—and that these meanings reflect the difference in usage "between a committed participant and a neutral observer" was rejected with equal firmness from an institutional vantage point. "There is no literal meaning of 'promise' in which all it means is uttering certain words," the study stressed, adding: "The objection above tries to offer a sense of promise in which the statement 'He made a promise' would state a brute fact and not an institutional fact, but there is no such sense." In the final objection, the neutral observer perspective was accentuated into the outlook of the detached anthropologist reporting about institutions indirectly or in *oratio obliqua.* In Searle's view, however, this external stance was irrelevant to the meaning of terms or definitions and to "the validity of deductive arguments involving the committed use" of relevant terms: "What my argument requires, like any valid argument, is a serious, literal, non-*oratio obliqua* occurrence of the crucial words it contains."[17]

Although admirable in its concise lucidity and impressive in its scope and occasional boldness, Searle's argument in my judgment is marred by a pervasive unevenness and ambivalence. This ambivalence affects both *Speech Acts* as a whole and the treatment of the is-ought dilemma in its concluding part. As an "essay in the philosophy of language" the study, as indicated, oscillates between a philosophical "pragmatics" and a semi-positivist—or rather a mixed positivist-subjectivist—perspective. Despite the insistence in the opening section that linguistic meaning is accessible only through participation, or from the vantage point of the competent speaker, and not through behavioristic analysis, subsequent discussions of linguistic questions almost invariably segregate *propositional* from *illocutionary* acts, or meaning from usage. As a result of this segregation, usage tends to be reduced to a psychological-sociological adjunct of language—a status familiar from the logical-empiricist paradigm. Searle's positivist leanings are evident in his comments on the "method of investigation" employed in his study which he describes as "empirical and rational rather than *a priori* and speculative" and as one constrained to "pay strict attention to the facts of actual natural languages."[18] Linguistic "facts," of course, are neither self-explanatory nor self-sustaining, given the reliance of empirical statements on the predicative functions of consciousness. In Searle's case, this circumstance manifests itself in the correlation of linguistic empiricism and incipiently idealist assumptions. Repeatedly, speaking a language is described as a form of *intentional* (that is, subjectively motivated) behavior; by the same token, the constitutive rules of language and institutions are presumably constituted by human intentionality.

The noted unevenness in language philosophy carries over into the proposed derivation of normative obligations. In this instance, the imbalance resides chiefly in the contrast between sporadic quasi-ontological ventures and the generally commonsense character of the argument, which is reflected in the portrayal of rule-governed actions as institutional facts. Viewed as bundles of facts (and thus under "ontic" auspices), institutions are bound to appear as contingent environmental settings whose obligatory features are coextensive with empirical membership criteria. As part of the environment, however, such settings can at least in principle be critically evaluated, both by members and non-members. Thus, while spelling out the concrete implications of institutional arrangements, Searle's descriptivism also lends support to anti-descriptive voluntarists for whom values are necessarily tied to spontaneous human choice. The same imbalance pervades the internal structure of the stipulated entailment. To the extent that institutional facts are treated as empirical premises, the derivation may indeed be successful, but only contingently for bona fide members; although able to intuitively grasp the sense of the relevant obligations, outsiders can normally claim exemption from their influence. On the other hand, if rule-governed actions are regarded as evaluative premises—and Searle seems at least occasionally undecided or indifferent on this issue[19]—his argument takes the form of an ought-ought derivation, with the resulting perils of circularity and of an infinite deductive regress.

Many of the mentioned drawbacks have been noted by the critics (too numerous to be listed) of Searle's argument. The combination of linguistic empiricism and idealism, in particular, has been succinctly highlighted by Richard Hare in his comments on the "promising game." Focusing chiefly on statement (Ia) in Searle's derivation, Hare challenged the view that the statement was simply analytical or definitional, in the sense of explicating the meaning of terms in "English usage"; more generally, he attacked the claim that entailment relied exclusively on "empirical assumptions, tautologies, and descriptions of word usage." This claim, he observed, involved a confusion of word meanings with human behavior and thus a (quasi-idealistic) substitution of linguistic conventions for rules guiding action in the world. According to Hare, action was not so much an analytical or definitional exercise as a "synthetic" undertaking in a concrete setting: "To conform to the rules of a game it is necessary to act, not merely to speak, in certain ways. Therefore the rules are not tautologies." In the case of Searle's key example, promising and placing oneself under an obligation could not simply be treated as linguistic elaborations or "remarks about word-usage": "For it is a necessary condition for the adoption of these performative expressions that certain synthetic constitutive (and not merely linguistic) rules be also adopted, thus creating the institutions within which the expressions have meaning." Turning to the empiricist aspect of the derivation, Hare argued that, in talking about institutional facts, Searle came perilously close to committing the naturalistic fallacy (notwithstanding his objections to this concept). To be sure, once institutions were established it was possible to "affirm certain 'institutional facts' " by pointing to the occurrence of certain brute facts. "Thus it looks," he wrote, "as if there could be a straight deduction, in two steps, from brute facts to prescriptive conclusions via institutional facts. But the deduction is a fraud. For the brute fact is a ground for the prescriptive conclusion only if the prescriptive principle which is the constitutive rule of the institution be accepted; and this prescriptive principle is not a tautology."[20]

Conceptual Deduction: Gewirth and Frohock

The criticisms leveled at Searle's approach cannot entirely obscure its virtues. Whatever its intrinsic difficulties may be, the attempt to vindicate norms superseding arbitrary individual preferences must surely be recognized as an important and legitimate philosophical endeavor. The particular slant of Searle's argument—his focus on institutional settings—should also not lightly be dismissed; irrespective of the limitations of contingent institutions, it may be feasible to link norms with broader institutional contexts in an overarching experiential narrative. Since the publication of *Speech Acts,* Searle's general initiative has been continued by a number of philosophers and moral theorists, usually with the aim of tightening the structure of entailment and thus of buttressing the categorical and ineluctable status of norms. In lieu of Searle's descriptive and partially inductive strategy—his effort to derive obligations from factual premises—recent writings frequently rely on rigorous conceptual analysis and logical-deductive inference. I want to discuss briefly two writers who exemplify this trend: the philosopher Alan Gewirth, and the moral-political theorist Fred Frohock. In both instances the shortcomings of descriptivism are corrected through recourse to conceptual deduction; the possible costs or side effects of the proposed remedy need to be assessed.

Gewirth has delineated his ethical position in a number of writings, with only slight variations between successive formulations. For the sake of brevity, I intend to concentrate on two relatively succinct lectures, delivered in 1972 and 1974, entitled respectively "Moral Rationality" and "The 'Is-Ought' Problem Resolved."[21] Gewirth's central departure from the descriptivist account consists in the starting point of his argument: instead of focusing on environmental contexts of moral behavior he places the accent squarely on crucial features of the human actor or moral agent. Proceeding in this manner he is able to give due weight to an aspect stressed by voluntarists but neglected in descriptive derivations: that of human autonomy; simultaneously, however, he seeks to overcome arbitrariness by pinpointing the necessary ingredients of moral choice. In the selected essays, these necessary ingredients—labelled *categorial* or *generic* features of action—are identified as *voluntariness* and *purposiveness*. In contrast to "human movements or behaviors" which result from direct or indirect types of external or internal compulsion, Gewirth writes, "actions in the strict sense have the generic features of being voluntary and purposive."[22] Another major aspect of his approach is his insistence on the rigorously binding or ought-quality of norms and his refusal to soften the fact-value conflict in order to facilitate its resolution. His second lecture stipulates five essential traits of ought-judgments against which fact-value discussions must be tested: these judgments must be *moral* (in the sense of dealing with interpersonal concerns), *prescriptive* or mandatory, *egalitarian* or non-discriminatory, *determinate* (in the sense of specifying definite contents), and *categorical* rather than hypothetical. Against this background, the "real 'Is-Ought' Problem" in Gewirth's view can be formulated in these terms: "How can 'ought'-judgments having these five characteristics be logically derived from, or be justified on the basis of, premisses which state empirical facts?" As he adds, the entailment structure of the question gives rise to a sixth condition: that of *non-circularity*, "especially in the respect that the premisses from which the 'ought'-conclusions are derived must not themselves be moral or prescriptive."[23]

Using these criteria as yardsticks, Gewirth examines previous efforts to resolve the fact-value dilemma—either on a concrete-material level or through formal-logical procedures—and finds them wanting for various reasons. Regarding material or chiefly inductive strategies,[24] he reviews a number of proposed derivations including means-ends calculations; arguments relying on human wants or needs; eudaemonist approaches; and several types of contextual and institutional theories. Means-ends calculations center on rational choice governed by self-interest, that is, on the selection of "the most efficient means to one's desired ends" where the agent is typically "an individual whose end is to maximize his own happiness or well-being."[25] In contrast to the stress on rationality evident in choice models, arguments from wants or needs focus more broadly on empirical living conditions and dispositions, usually adding the conclusion that "all men ought equally to have the means" of satisfying their needs or desires. Eudaemonist approaches regard happiness as the universal goal of human endeavor; translating this goal into ethical terms, they define moral obligation as the duty to do everything required "for the attainment of human well-being or for the avoidance of ill-being." Turning to descriptive frameworks relying on rule-governed contexts or institutions, Gewirth considers both looser and more tightly constructed versions of this outlook. A broadly suggestive version of descriptivism in his view can be found in writings which invoke the context or "institution of morality itself," or which concentrate on settings permeated by a "good reasons morality" or by "the moral point of view." On the other hand, the "most famous examples" of appeals to specific institutional arrangements in recent literature are said to be those "concerned with the institutions of promising and of buying and selling." In this case, "the argument has been that if one participates in these institutions by making a promise or a purchase, then, by virtue of the rules of the respective institutions, one is obligated to keep the promise or to pay for what one buys, and so forth."[26]

Surveying these metaethical endeavors, Gewirth initially offers his overall assessment of their merits and shortcomings. On the negative ledger he finds chiefly "three sharp limitations of these material 'is-ought' derivations." First of all, the derived norms or obligations are without exception "only hypothetical, not categorical." As he points out, the structure of entailment in the above instances invariably takes this form: if stipulated premises or contexts (such as the satisfaction of needs, the pursuit of happiness, or the means-ends nexus) are accepted with their implications, "*then* such and such actions ought to be done." Consequently, the obligatory character of norms is in every case "contingent on persons' variable choices or decisions to accept the context in question, or on some independent justification of the context itself as setting forth valid requirements for action." The second drawback is the lack of prescriptive force: "For to say that 'ought' means what is required by some structured context is not to say that the speaker who uses such an 'ought' necessarily accepts this requirement as binding either on himself or on his hearers." This absence of prescriptiveness, according to Gewirth, is tied to a third defect which he calls the *dilemma of commitment* and which involves the twin perils of circularity and arbitrary freedom. If the agent or speaker chooses to commit himself to the stipulated premises or contexts, he writes, "then the 'ought' he will derive will be circular in that he will simply be resuming in the conclusion a commitment or advocacy which he had already chosen to make in the premise." On the other hand, if the agent refrains from committing himself, "then his derivation will not be circular"; but in this case the derived norm "will not be prescriptive" or binding on himself or his hearers.[27]

Descending from the synoptic plane, Gewirth then subjects individual strategies to detailed analysis. While means-ends calculations are criticized chiefly for yielding non-categorical and indeterminate norms, eudaemonist and needs arguments are attacked because of their circular as well as indefinite and hypothetical character. In the present context, Gewirth's comments on institutional models seem most pertinent. Regarding the institution of morality, or the moral point of view treated as an institutional setting, his assessment basically recapitulates the dilemma of commitment; finding "no significant advance" in this approach over emotivism, he concludes that "the moral point of view itself requires justificatory argument: neither it nor its subordinate rules are self-evident, and both have alternatives which, in terms of a non-question-begging definition of morality, are themselves moral ones." Derivations stressing specific institutions or institutional facts—in Searle's case, the institution of promising—are likewise charged with being unable to satisfy the criteria of ought-judgments. By presupposing different institutional contexts, Gewirth notes, one is able to "infer diametrically opposed 'oughts' "—a consequence incompatible with the requirement of determinacy. This defect, moreover, cannot simply be remedied by adding voluntary endorsement to the premises. If one were to stipulate, for instance, "that only those arrangements are to be considered institutions which are voluntarily accepted or agreed upon by all their participants, then this would not only restrict unduly the concept of an institution, but it would also violate the condition of non-circularity. For now the derivation would not begin from a morally neutral 'is'-statement, since the initial presumption would be that the institution in question fulfills the moral requirement of not being coercively imposed on its participants."[28]

Given the many pitfalls to be overcome—obstacles which successfully thwarted previous attempts—the task of linking *is* and *ought* is clearly an arduous undertaking. Gewirth sees the advantage of his own counterproposal chiefly in two aspects: his chosen starting point and his method of analysis and derivation. As previously indicated, the former concentrates on the categorial or generic features of action (where *action* refers to voluntary and purposive human behavior). According to Gewirth, this frame of reference is "both logically prior to and more invariable and inescapable" than the premises or contexts invoked in earlier derivations. The main defects of these earlier attempts can be labeled *acceptance-variability* and *content-variability*—the first relating to the need of prior commitment, the second to the diversity of possible contexts. The focus on generic features avoids both defects: "There is no acceptance-variability, for it is not open to any person intentionally to evade or reject the context of action." Similarly, content-variability disappears, "for although actions may, of course, be of many different sorts, they all have certain generic features in common," features which "logically generate certain requirements or 'oughts' regardless of the specific differences of kinds of action." Regarding the method and structure of his argument Gewirth describes it as a "dialectically necessary" approach adhering chiefly to the "model of deductive inference." The approach is said to be dialectical in that "it begins from assumptions, statements, or claims made by protagonists—in this case, the agent—and it examines what these logically imply." Furthermore, the method is claimed to be dialectically necessary in that "the assumptions or claims in question are necessarily made by agents" or belong to "the necessary structure of purposive action as viewed by the agent."[29]

The resolution of the is-ought dilemma, as outlined in Gewirth's counterproposal, proceeds in four major steps. From the initial premise that all actions in general—and the specific action of a given agent in particular—are voluntary and purposive, the first step draws immediately an *evaluative* conclusion. Stressing the distinction between action and "a mere physical occurrence" involving "no choices" and "no purposes," Gewirth argues that the agent's relation to his endeavor "is conative and evaluative, for he acts for some purpose which seems to him to be good," envisaging "more or less clearly some preferred outcome" or goal "worth aiming at or pursuing." Consequently, he writes, "since the agent values, at least instrumentally, the purposes or objects for which he acts, it can also be said that he regards these objects as at least instrumentally good according to whatever criteria lead him to try to achieve his purpose." The second step leads from subjective preference to tentative justification by means of *right-claims*. "In virtue of his positive evaluation," Gewirth continues, "the agent regards himself as justified in performing his actions and in having the freedom and basic well-being which generically figure in all his actions, and he implicitly makes a corresponding right-claim." Differently phrased, in considering his action warranted by its goodness, the agent also views himself as entitled to the preconditions for acting; justification at this point "takes the logical form of a claim on the part of the agent that he has a right to perform his actions and to have freedom and basic well-being." The next step involves the universal application of the agent's right-claims to other agents, an extension deriving from the generic basis of these claims. Since the agent's claimed entitlement to freedom and basic well-being is predicated on his status as "a prospective agent who has purposes he wants to fulfill," he is said to be "logically committed to a generalization of this right-claim to all prospective agents and hence to all persons" who similarly want to fulfill their purposes. The fourth and final step moves from the generalized claim to a corresponding normative or ought-judgment. Since the agent had to admit the universal right to freedom and well-being, he must also recognize the obligation "to refrain from interfering with the freedom and basic well-being of all prospective purposive agents." Labeling the maxim underlying this duty the *principle of generic consistency* (PGC), Gewirth summarizes the yardstick emerging from his derivation in these terms: "Apply to your recipient the same generic features of action that you apply to yourself."[30]

In terms of logical rigor and tightness of construction, the preceding entailment model clearly has many advantages over competing conceptions; the effort, above all, to buttress freedom while evading arbitrariness must be counted among its most salient assets. It seems to me, however, that these and related merits cannot blot out some intrinsic weaknesses. Like Searle's approach, Gewirth's argument is characterized by an oscillation between contingent empiricism and subjective-cognitive idealism—although these two alternatives have different connotations and are differently weighted in his case. While in Searle's derivation the chief accent rests on empirical-contextual factors, Gewirth's outlook is slanted toward cognitive-conceptual abstraction. The empiricist ingredient in Gewirth's perspective is evident primarily—though not exclusively—in his basic premise. Despite the stress on generic features of action and their differentiation from "mere physical" occurrences, Gewirth in his second lecture insists on treating the agent's particular action as a factual event. "That purposive actions occur or that some person performs an action," he writes, "is an empirical fact which can be stated in descriptive, empirical propositions regardless of whether the statements are made by the agent himself or by other persons." Actually, his entailment model is concerned less with outside observation than with the actor's self-description. Thus, since the focus is on "actions as they are viewed and referred to by the agent himself," the initial "empirical premise" of the model is simply "the agent's statement that he performs an action." Empiricist connotations are also present in the moral obligations derived from the argument. Apart from prohibiting the infliction of "serious gratuitous harm on other persons," the principle of generic consistency in Gewirth's view also imposes the "positive duty to perform such actions as rescuing drowning persons or feeding starving persons, especially when this can be done at relatively little cost to oneself." The same principle is said to entail as indirect consequences "sociopolitical moral 'ought'-judgments requiring actions in support of civil liberties and in opposition to great inequalities of wealth and power."[31]

The above assertions are hardly fortuitous—given the author's intent to link norms and facts. Yet, in the context of Gewirth's overall account, the statements appear as alien and perplexing components. At a closer look, the factual status of the initial premise seems at best tenuous; on the other hand, its factuality, if rigorously maintained, jeopardizes the entailment model. As will be recalled, the defining characteristics of human actions are found in their voluntariness and purposiveness, that is, in their rootedness in free will and purposive intentionality. Actions in this sense are carefully distinguished from types of behavior which arise from compulsion or are due to external or internal causation; in Kantian terms, the latter types belong to the domain of nature or of synthetic phenomenal experience—a domain amenable to empirical-scientific inquiry. To present actions in the initial premise as empirical events amounts thus to their reintegration in the world of causal explanation, from which they are claimed to be segregated by a rigid barrier. Reliance on the agent's self-description cannot remedy this predicament, for self-description merely transforms actions into psychological states of mind—and empirical psychology is ignorant of free will and teleological purpose. The fragility of the factual premise permeates Gewirth's entire argument to its prescriptive conclusions. Taken by themselves or as internal qualities of agents, free will and purposiveness are not necessarily or obviously impaired by external misfortunes or material deprivations, including "great inequalities of wealth and power"; on the contrary, in the view of some, such qualities are tested and enhanced by hardship. As Gewirth recognizes at one point, the moral duty implicit in the principle of generic consistency may on occasion collide with physical or material well-being; thus, when lying in order to prevent a murder, an agent is formally inconsistent (in violation of the principle)—although his act may be justified by reasons "more basic than those that would be fulfilled by telling the truth or being propositionally consistent in this situation."[32]

Actually, Gewirth's general model seems incongruent with the notion of an empirical premise for a number of reasons. Apart from the confluence of action and behavior, a main reason is epistemological and methodological: since facts depend on a predicating consciousness, a factual starting point would be subject to deliberate choice—a result at odds with the dialectically necessary character of the model; similarly, such a starting point would encourage inductive generalization—which conflicts with Gewirth's repeated stress on the primarily deductive character of his argument and on the analytic status of the principle of generic consistency and of "the moral rules and judgments which follow from it."[33] Construed as an analytical-deductive endeavor, of course, his proposal conjures up a host of quandaries endemic to such endeavors. No one has formulated these quandaries more concisely and compellingly than Gewirth himself. In every case of deductive reasoning, he notes in his first lecture, a major problem concerns the correlation between the justifying maxim—such as the principle of generic consistency—and the events in need of justification. Since a principle is "logically prior" in the sense that "everything else in the field depends for its justification more or less directly on the principle," the notion of "justifying a principle seems contradictory for it requires showing the dependence of what is independent, the logical posteriority of what is logically prior." Furthermore, he adds, the attempt to validate a principle deductively appears to involve "either an inevitable circularity or a certain superfluity": "For the only things left to justify the principle are the very *justificanda* or consequents which it is the function of the principle itself to justify." In the field of ethics, deductive validation encounters the additional problem that the justifying principle can be either moral or non-moral. If it is a moral maxim, then validation takes the form of an ought-ought derivation, which "obviously begs the question," for "a moral justification of a moral principle already assumes, in its criterion of justification, the very principle which is to be justified." On the other hand, if the superior axiom is non-moral, then the question arises how a moral *ought* or norm "can be justified by premises which are theological, or biological, or psychological, or sociological, and the like, which do not themselves contain any 'ought.' The familiar problems of naturalism and heteronomy arise here."[34]

It is highly doubtful, in my judgment, that Gewirth's model is able to evade the difficulties of deductive inference. Although he tackles a number of objections, his replies are hardly more persuasive than Searle's rejoinders. His comments on the issue of circularity seem particularly elusive. Pointing to the "necessary deductive" structure of his arguments, Gewirth acknowledges "that the moral principle is in some sense implicitly present in the premises." However, "vicious circularity" is claimed to be avoided by virtue of the merely *implicit* character of the entailment (although the distinction between explicit and implicit entailment and its relevance to the point at issue are far from evident): "The conclusion arrived at is genuinely informative, in that it has not been recognized that implied in the concept of being an agent is the further concept of making right-claims on the ground of having purposes and envisaging goods, that this ground logically requires an extension of the rights in question to the recipients of the agent's action." Gewirth's reply regarding the specific quandaries besetting deduction in the field of ethics is mainly twofold. Although he has just admitted a linkage (albeit implicit) between premises and conclusions, he first sidesteps the charge of an ought-ought derivation by stressing his initial focus on the generic features of action. Since these features, he writes, "are logically prior to specifically moral considerations, because the moral is subsumed under the rational and the practical, the difficulties of deriving a moral principle from some superior principle are to this extent resolved." Since this response, however, conjures up the problem of how norms can emerge from non-moral premises, Gewirth immediately tightens the entailment structure again by insisting that "right-claims, with their correlative obligations or 'oughts,' are logically implied in all purposive action." If this point is granted, he adds, then "the sequence from action to morality is not merely from an 'is' to an 'ought' but rather from a context which implicitly contains an 'ought' to another context in which this 'ought' is made explicit."[35]

Circularity is not the only pitfall of deductive entailment; employing Gewirth's own criteria, the yardsticks of determinacy and categoricalness also deserve attention. Despite his strong claims in these areas, I am not convinced that his model successfully overcomes the content-variability—and also the acceptance-variability—noted in Searle's approach. Given the derivation of norms from the generic features of action, *any* action which displays free will and purposiveness is by definition morally justified—a conclusion which clearly leaves the content of action (within the confines of its generic features) infinitely variable. Referring to the generalization maxim, Gewirth claims that his application of the principle "restricts the agent's action-description to necessary contents, that is, to the categorial features of action, voluntariness and purposiveness." However, it is doubtful that the term *contents* is appropriate at this point, since the mentioned features chiefly describe qualities of the human agent. Equally questionable, at least in the ethical domain, is the claim that analytic-deductive statements "signify objective properties" and that "some analytic truths arise because men can conceptually understand extra-linguistic properties and make linguistic classifications based on that understanding." Responding to the criticism that analytic propositions are devoid of "substantive content," Gewirth asserts blandly that "we must distinguish between explicitly and implicitly analytical statements and between logical and psychological vacuity" and that "analytic moral judgments may give practical guidance if they are only implicitly analytic." The moral significance of analyticity is also at the heart of the query whether it is sensible to assign to an agent right-claims which are part of the definition of agency and which entitle him "to do what he cannot avoid doing." Gewirth's reply points to future transactions, arguing that a *prospective* agent's participation in transactions is not something that he "cannot avoid." Yet, it is clear that "insofar as he is an agent" the prospective agent's right-claims are likewise "analytic" or true by definition.[36] On the other hand, if it is left to the individual to decide whether or not to perform as an agent in future transactions, then agency depends on prior endorsement—which conjures up the specter of acceptance-variability.

While formulating a similarly analytical framework, Fred Frohock is relatively candid about its drawbacks. My necessarily brief reference is to his study entitled *Normative Political Theory* (published in 1974). Together with Gewirth and prescriptivist thinkers, Frohock in this study stresses the importance of autonomy and free choice in ethics, countering to this extent the ambitions of descriptivism—and cognitivism in general—to derive norms from environmental settings or factual propositions. "One provision of the denial of value cognitivism normally considered desirable," he writes, "is moral freedom. If value statements have truth value, then moral judgments are true or false. This means not only that some moral claims are then ruled out because they are false, but also that one is then not free to choose any moral principle." By contrast, "the *absence* of a necessary connection between facts and values" in his view makes room for "legitimate moral dissent." The comments are not, however, meant as a defense of moral relativism. Like Gewirth, Frohock wants to preserve freedom while simultaneously curbing arbitrariness—an arbitrariness implicit both in non-cognitivist doctrines and also, in more subtle form, in descriptivist accounts, where the element of prior choice tends to be glossed over. Although cautiously pursued, the goal of *Normative Political Theory* is to overcome the fact-value dichotomy, under whose influence investigations of justice or the good life have frequently been reduced to matters of private preference. The arguments of the study, we are told, are "concerned to demonstrate the limitations of positivism and the alternatives to it"; endeavoring "to revive the traditional emphasis on the good polity" with "analytic tools," they aim to explore not merely "how one dimension of a society, the law, can be moral but how the larger society itself can be moral."[37]

As a preparatory step to formulating his own perspective, Frohock examines several entailment models proposed by spokesmen of ethical descriptivism (some of which are labeled *new naturalism*). A loosely conceived model, allowing at best a "warranted inference," is found in the *good-reasons* approach, advanced chiefly by Toulmin, where ordinary language serves as quasi-institutional setting for moral evaluation and where the justification of norms derives from the rules of conventional discourse. Frohock's critical objections are akin to those articulated by Gewirth and also by Hare. The chief defect of the approach, he asserts, is that "the reliance on a system of rules, with a purpose, does not in itself avoid the necessity of endorsing a primary *ought*," but "merely moves the *ought* from the premises to the rules of inference." As he adds, a second deficiency resides in the notion that conventional rules can limit ethical inquiry, a notion in conflict with the unbounded quality of ethics which entails that "any ethical principle or any goal advanced for ethics may be evaluated ethically" and thus is "challengeable from the outside." More detailed attention is devoted in the study to Searle's institutional derivation of *ought* from *is*. While acknowledging the importance of the "distinction between physicalist (or 'brute') and institutional facts"—mainly because of its implication "that the phenomena of the natural world are not wholly continuous with social phenomena"—Frohock in the end considers Searle's argument unsuccessful, primarily due to its dependence on prior endorsement (in Gewirth's terms: its inability to remedy acceptance-variability). "To be bound by the institution of promising," he observes, "is to choose or decide to be bound. *This* choice or decision is the primary endorsement which provides for the deduction, and since it is freely entered into it can be denied without a logical contradiction." The study also refers to the possibility of a mental reservation in the act of promising (a possibility previously stressed by Hare). If this possibility is granted, we read, then it is logically possible to move from the first to the second step in Searle's derivation "with a suppressed premise on endorsement," a premise which alone "provides for the nontautological proposition that one ought to keep one's promises."[38]

As indicated, Frohock's own outlook, like Gewirth's, takes essentially the form of conceptual analysis or analytical deduction; however, while the latter concentrates on the concept and generic features of action, Frohock focuses on the concept of morality itself. Four chief characteristics are said to be directly implied in, or derivable from, this concept. Morality or moral discourse, he argues, involves first of all a *prescriptive* (rather than merely persuasive) element, in that norms are meant to serve as "a guide or directive for action"; second, the concept invokes *evaluative principles* or criteria on which prescription can be based; third, morality is *external in form* in the sense that its precepts are "open-textured" and permit unrestricted evaluative inquiry; and last, its scope is *universal* since prescriptions usually make no reference to particulars. The sketched characteristics of the concept of morality are subsequently applied to the political domain where they serve as cornerstones of an ideal or *moral polity*. According to Frohock, such a polity is marked by a number of distinctive traits, among which the following seem particularly important: given the prescriptive and *principled* nature of morality, a primary feature of *moral politics* must be "public consistency and similarity on the criteria of the principles used to direct or guide action in policy." The same qualities of morality entail that *public policy* must be seen "as the prescriptive system for society generally," with the result that "moral policy will override all contrary actions in the area in which it is implemented." Due to morality's *openness* and reliance on principles, moral policy cannot simply be a command or demand but "must always provide for some criteria" which are "valid or worthy" not merely because they are dictated or wanted "but because they are moral." The universality of norms, finally, implies that a moral polity likewise will be universal in scope: "If moral universals are to be taken as applying to all men as such, and not to men in their particular roles or characteristics, then the policy propositions and structural arrangements comprising a moral polity are right for all men."[39]

The advantage of conceptual analysis, in Frohock's view, resides in its relative aloofness from partisanship, or the narrow advocacy of particular codes. Yet, as he frankly concedes, this merit is offset by several drawbacks—especially those associated with content-variability and, to a lesser degree, with acceptance-variability. What conceptual analysis yields, he writes, is "a *formal* definition of morality" which can be accommodated to diverse substantive contents: "The immediate disadvantage of this is that nothing then can rule out the fanatic" for "the prescription 'Everyone ought to kill one another' is as congenial with this system of morality as the prescription 'Everyone ought to love one another.'" In short, he adds, the cost "of formality is the moral rationality of fanaticism, though at the bargain price of setting out certain necessary requirements which all moralities must fulfill in order to be moralities." Related to this defect is another which Frohock does not directly ascribe to his conceptual framework but which he freely castigates in the discussion of competing approaches: his conceptual outline may provide a definition of theoretical-analytical *rationality* rather than of *morality* or moral discourse.[40] The problem of acceptance-variability arises from the study's disclaimer regarding the definitive status of the proposed outline. "It is obvious," we read "that the strategy adopted here has not been to rule out the alternative ways to define morality" suggested by other perspectives but rather "to build a case for the justification of the particular conceptualization of morality developed here. If the justification is unconvincing, then the supporters of alternative definitions will go away unnourished intellectually."[41]

Given Frohock's intent to overcome arbitrariness and to pinpoint necessary requirements of morality, the mentioned variabilities are bound to be grounds for discomfort. Repeatedly, *Normative Political Theory* suggests corrective measures—without pursuing the matter beyond the level of brief (occasionally cryptic) hints. "There *is* a case which can be made against the requirement of a primary *ought*," Frohock asserts in discussing good-reasons morality. "It relies on ethics as a system of rules, but it elevates the system of rules to a state of natural necessity impossible to accommodate in Toulmin's instrumental philosophy." In contrast to Toulmin's reliance on conventional rules, "only a naturalistic case for requirements in experience, and language" is said to "permit the derivation of an *ought* without an endorsement." Similarly, the critical assessment of Searle's descriptivist approach concludes with the comment: "If some institutions are necessary conditions for the possibility of human life, not chosen but required for experience to take place at all, then *oughts* do follow deductively from the description of such institutions." In its final paragraphs, the study offers slightly more explicit direction signals, alluding especially to the *a priori conditions of possibility* of ethics. "One can investigate claims, once commonly accepted in rationalist philosophy," we read, "that conditions can be identified which are necessary for certain kinds of experiences to occur, in the sense in which Kant asked this question of experience generally. In the context of normative political interests, the question is: What conditions are necessary for political or moral experience to occur, in the sense that if they are absent such experiences are impossible?" Noting that this question can be posed "either in the philosophy of language, or in phenomenology," Frohock observes: "It is clear that if necessity can be demonstrated of experience, then the derivation of *ought* from *is* becomes more reasonable."[42]

Transcendental Pragmatics: Apel

As it happens, the notion of reviving the Kantian quest for a priori conditions is not confined to a marginal gloss in *Normative Political*

Theory; in fact, the endeavor to uncover transcendental premises, or conditions of possibility, is a pervasive preoccupation in contemporary ethics, especially among Continental thinkers.[43] I would like to glance briefly at arguments advanced by Karl-Otto Apel, a philosopher influenced in equal measure by phenomenology and by linguistic analysis; the particular focus here will be on his essay entitled "Theory of Speech Acts and Transcendental Pragmatics of Language with Reference to Ethical Norms" (published in 1976). As employed by Apel, the phrase *transcendental pragmatics of language* has several important connotations. Instead of pointing broadly to the pragmatist tradition, the middle term derives its significance chiefly from concerns indigenous to contemporary semiotics (the theory of signs): from the distinction—inaugurated by Peirce and Morris—between referential meaning (semantics), logical-analytical structure (syntax) and performative usage by competent speakers (pragmatics). Given Searle's stress on semantic context and Gewirth's primary reliance on conceptual-analytical deduction, Apel's perspective may be said to round out the options provided by the three dimensions of language. One should note, however, that performative usage in his case is not the same as empirical-linguistic behavior governed either by psychological learning mechanisms or by conventional rules; rather, his inquiries are directed toward the non-contingent parameters of pragmatic performance, that is, toward the a priori premises underlying human communication. While faithful to the basic trend of Kantian thought, his outlook reformulates this legacy by shifting attention from the role of consciousness to the constitutive functions of language. "Construed as a transcendental pragmatics of language or communication," Apel writes, "transcendental philosophy today must radicalize Kant's approach by reflecting on the *a priori 'conditions of possibility' of discursive argumentation.*"[44]

In the cited essay, the contours of transcendental pragmatics and its normative implications emerge largely in the course of a review of Searle's descriptivism—a review which combines partial approval with critical dissent. What Apel considers attractive in Searle's position is the treatment of language as rule-governed intentional behavior and the underlying premise that linguistic meaning is tied to pragmatic usage or the performance of speech acts. If properly developed, he sees as equally valuable the distinction between regulative and constitutive principles and the presentation of linguistic performance as governed by systems of constitutive rules. The central defect of *Speech Acts,* on the other hand, is found in the halfhearted elaboration of these views and in the persistent tendency to misconstrue pragmatic performance in an empiricist or purely conventional sense—a misconstrual which vitiates the proposed derivation of norms. "As I think I can show," the essay states, "Searle's thesis regarding the possibility of deriving normative or evaluative statements from descriptive propositions is unable to undermine the 'naturalistic fallacy' doctrine, for the simple reason that his arguments leveled against this doctrine are either untenable or irrelevant." At the same time, Apel acknowledges that "the analysis of the preconditions and consequences of speech acts (as it has been launched by Searle and partially already by Austin) is indeed relevant for the justification or derivation of ethical norms—provided such analysis is not or not purely conceived as a descriptive portrayal of 'institutional facts,' but rather as a reflective enterprise aiming to uncover the *universal rules* of communication which are merely 'contingently implemented' in existing linguistic institutions."[45]

A major inconsistency of Searle's argument, from Apel's perspective, resides in the ambivalent treatment of the respective roles of meaning and usage. Despite the initial assertion of a close correlation, Searle's normative derivations—as previously indicated—focus on propositional content while disregarding pragmatic performance. In articulating the so-called speech-act fallacy, Apel notes, Searle advances the "strange claim that the *propositional meaning* of statements can be entirely segregated from the *illocutionary force of their utterance;* differently put: that the *truth conditions* of a stated proposition can be specified without reference to the statement's *point* or *illocutionary function.*" As he adds, this attempted segregation is not merely a trivial imbalance, but goes against the grain of the theory of speech acts which—in comparison with purely syntactical or semantic doctrines—derives its significance precisely from the postulated or *"ideal-typical reciprocity or functional interdependence* of linguistic sentences and speech acts construed as forms of communicative behavior," a relationship which entails a similar reciprocity between "linguistic *propositions* and the *illocutionary force of utterances.*" To be sure, propositional content and pragmatic usage are not always congruent and may even collide in actual speech situations; according to Apel, the theoretical remedy in such instances cannot reside in the suppression of the performative dimension: "It seems more plausible and also more in conformity with Searle's basic approach to follow the lead of the later Wittgenstein and to trace apparent divergences between propositions and the illocutionary force of corresponding utterances to a difference between the syntactic-semantical *surface structure* and the semantic-pragmatical *depth-structure* of sentences."[46]

Turning to Searle's arguments on the implications of promising,

Apel questions the feasibility of deriving normative conclusions from an empirically construed institutional fact. To illustrate the shortcomings of this strategy, he examines two main attitudes which one might adopt toward promising as a factual institution: those of the judge and of the cultural anthropologist. In the case of the judge, the factual ascertainment that a promise has been made is indeed conclusive evidence of a binding obligation, but only because this ascertainment is itself tied to a normative endorsement; in other words, the "normative consequence follows *not solely* from the ascertained *fact* of the promise, but from this fact combined with the legally sanctioned normative premise which the judge accepts as a matter of course." The second case is somewhat more difficult to disentangle: while not sharing the judge's professional commitment, one can justifiably claim that the anthropologist cannot properly describe the "promising institution" without simultaneously understanding the normative implication that promises should normally be kept. As the essay concedes, "the neutral anthropologist who *understands* the meaning of the promising institution and ascertains the fact of a promise made *under the auspices of this institution,* knows also that—in terms of the institution—the promisor is obligated (*ceteris paribus*) to keep his promise and to undertake or omit a certain action." According to Apel, however, interpretive understanding, although methodologically indispensable in anthropology and all the social sciences, is not identical with moral approval. "There is a definite difference," he writes, "between the *hermeneutical* inference of an obligation in the context of an ascertained institutional fact and the morally binding derivation of an 'ought' on the basis of an *accepted normative premise.*" By disregarding "this difference between a *normatively-categorical* and a merely *hermeneutical* derivation of normative statements," he adds, "Searle's meta-critique of the 'naturalistic fallacy' doctrine misses its aim."[47]

Apel's rejection of Searle's particular derivation strategy does not imply a dismissal of speech act theory as such, nor of the ethical relevance of the promising institution. As the essay indicates, Searle's focus on this issue may reflect the correct hunch that "it may be impossible for us to treat the 'promising institution' (with its obligatory quality) as simply an empirically reportable 'institutional fact' among other contingent facts," since this institution seems to function as "a basis or better: a *condition of the possibility* of all justifiable conventions or institutions among men." In the concluding passages of *Speech Acts,* this intuition is articulated when Searle voices the apprehension that "the retreat from the committed use of words ultimately must involve a retreat from language itself." Read in context, this statement, in Apel's view, alludes to the "necessary conditions of argumentation" and thus points to "the *legitimacy and even necessity of a transcendental-philosophical interpretation of speech act theory.*" For why, he asks, should the retreat from language be cause for alarm, if not for the fact that such a retreat "would cancel not simply an empirically describable 'institutional fact,' but rather the *condition of possibility* of all factual descriptions and of all logical deductions, and in this manner would eliminate discursive argumentation itself whose constraints cannot argumentatively be shirked." Speech act theory can thus indeed claim to have normative implications, but only when formulated in transcendental terms: "Once the *rules of speech acts*—and among them especially those of promising—are no longer viewed as conventional or empirically describable 'institutional facts,' but (via transcendental reflection) as *normative conditions of the possibility of argumentation itself,* then one does not have to derive norms from facts in order to highlight the significance of language and of speech act theory; rather, one is then able to show that *certain norms must always already have been endorsed by us and are thus available a priori as transcendental-pragmatic premises of any normative derivation.*"[48]

Seen from the perspective of transcendental pragmatics, ethical norms are not the outgrowth of private decisions or subjective whim, nor can they be detected as part of empirical environmental settings—mainly because such settings, including the context of ordinary speech, invariably fall short of, and even run counter to, normative standards. In Apel's words: "To the extent that they are based on *rules of communication,* interpersonal moral obligations have to be uncovered or unearthed by means of a critical analysis of the perversion and alienation of communication as it is manifest in conventional adaptations of its rules in existing institutions." To be successful in this endeavor, critical analysis must have recourse not to contingent speech patterns, but to the standards of ideal communication, standards which—though not fully implemented in reality—are both implicitly presupposed and "counterfactually anticipated" in ongoing communicative practices as conditions of their possibility and intelligibility. The promising institution can be said to form part of these ideal premises, since without promise-keeping human interaction and discursive justification would ultimately be impossible. Expressed as a substantive maxim, the basic yardstick of transcendental pragmatics can be formulated as the universal demand to respect and obey the transcendental rules of communication as the norms of a "counterfactually anticipated and (in the long run) to be implemented" community of ideal or unlimited speech; differently put, as the "inescapable obligation of all participants in argumentation to honor the principle of the 'discursive justification' of all normative claims in accordance with the *intersubjective universalizability* of particular interests." As Apel adds, this yardstick can be viewed as a reconstruction of Kant's categorical imperative—provided its foundation is no longer sought in an intelligible ego but in the dimension of intersubjective communication.[49]

Ethics and Recollection

As it seems to me, Apel's perspective of transcendental pragmatics is for many reasons superior to the metaethical postures previously sketched. By focusing on transcendental reflection and the transcendental premises of discourse, his approach avoids the pitfalls of inductive derivation which beset Searle's descriptivism; the same focus also erects some safeguards against the perils of circularity and variability noted in the conceptual-analytical schemes advanced by Gewirth and Frohock. In a more general vein, the stress on performance or the pragmatics of communication serves as antidote to the potential absorption of ethical standards by the rules of empirical verification or deductive inference. Notwithstanding these advantages, I find Apel's argument not entirely persuasive. Despite his differentiation between reflection and deduction, transcendental pragmatics seems to share some of the drawbacks of analytical schemes and of traditional rationalist philosophy in general. While revising Kant's non-linguistic concept of cognition, the reliance on transcendental parameters conjures up the Kantian bifurcation between a priori categories and a posteriori experience and also the dualism between form and content; in the ethical domain these dichotomies revive the familiar question of how categorical imperatives can affect contingent reality, or more specifically, how standards of ideal speech are capable of molding and perfecting ("in the long run") existing patterns of discourse. Speaking more broadly, Apel's pragmatics, like Kant's practical philosophy, appears to overaccentuate cognitive-intentional design at the expense of experiential practice: advances in rational knowledge or awareness of transcendental rules tend to be equated with the progressive implementation of an ideal speech community construed as "kingdom of ends." What this emphasis neglects is the possibility that growing rationality may be accompanied by a decline of moral sensitivity, a possibility which underscores the point that ethics is not purely a matter of thought but also of action.

Apart from its practical consequences, rationalism—transcendental or otherwise—also has implications for the process of cognition or the search for knowledge (including the search for normative standards). As initially indicated, the dilemma of cognition resides in the difficulty of rendering intelligible the search for a goal which can neither be fully known nor unknown in advance. Applying this dilemma to preceding discussions, descriptivism or empirical induction can be seen to stress an initial ignorance, but fails to show how moral standards can be learned through the study of environmental contexts; by contrast, rationalism in its different forms insists on a nucleus of at least implicit prior knowledge, at the price of rendering experience irrelevant. For these and similar reasons I consider it preferable, following Plato's suggestion in the *Meno,* to approximate cognition more closely to the process of *recollection.* In contrast, however, to interpretations which equate the Platonic notion with a priori principles of reflection or with a return to an unspoiled rationality I am inclined to the reverse view: one which sees recollection as a probing of opacity or as an effort to decipher the signals of a precognitive or prereflective practice—a practice which is not synonymous with individual or collective designs and which seems less akin to reason than to imagination (or to the poetic wisdom discussed by Vico). Since such practice bypasses subjective predication and the consciousness-object bifurcation, its lessons are not amenable to procedures of inductive inference or conceptual deduction, but only, if at all, to a process of decoding, a translation which requires all the more diligence as it proceeds not only from fragments but from gaps and partial insinuations.[50] I would next like to draw attention to some recent or contemporary thinkers whose writings, in my view, contain hints of a recollective ethics.

In the context of critical theory as formulated by the Frankfurt school, hints of this kind can be found especially in Adorno's meditations on "Freedom"—subtitled "Toward a Metacritique of Practical Reason"—contained in his *Negative Dialectics.* The chapter seeks to probe and unsettle the traditional dichotomies of *is* and *ought,* form and content, free will and natural necessity—dichotomies which, deriving largely from Kantian teachings, have been codified in our time in the injunction against the naturalistic fallacy. As Adorno attempts to show, these dualisms, at least in their Kantian formulation, are not so much the expression of fixed and ineluctable contrasts as indications of unresolved puzzles. Thus, the expectation that norms would eventually direct empirical behavior was an important ingredient of Kantian thought, but unwarranted by its premises, especially by the *noumenal* quality of the categorical imperative. "While rigorously proclaiming the gulf between 'is' and 'ought' in his practical philosophy," Adorno observes, "Kant was forced to accept mediations; but in this manner his notion of freedom becomes paradoxical since the latter is injected into the causality of the phenomenal world, in contravention of its Kantian definition." The same quandary is also manifest in the correlation between form and content in the moral domain: while claimed to be an agency in the world, free will in Kant's account is identified with the axioms of pure reason and thus reduced to a formal "condition of possibility" of action, divorced from substantive change. In Adorno's view, these quandaries have their ultimate source in the paradoxical character of Kant's concept of freedom. Distilled into an absolute noumenal autonomy, freedom coincides with reason's ascendancy over internal and external nature; human emancipation in this light inaugurates a new form of domination and bondage. Kant's practical philosophy, *Negative Dialectics* states, erects "formal rational logic into the highest moral tribunal," insuring "its primacy over the diffuseness of nature and over the multiformity of the non-identical world" (or the world non-identical with reason); in line with its overall tendency, "it can grasp freedom only as repression."[51]

The entanglement of rational autonomy and domination, Adorno suggests, can be counteracted only through the recovery of a precognitive or preconscious freedom, not yet marred by aggression against nature. "The emerging consciousness of freedom," he writes, "still harbors the memory of an archaic impulse not yet guided by a fixed ego or subjectivity," and he adds: "Without anamnesis or recollection of this unrepressed and pre-subjective impulse—an impulse later banished (by reason) into the domain of natural constraints—the idea of freedom could not be conceived, although this idea subsequently contributes to subjectivity's consolidation." A recollective effort of this kind, according to Adorno, brings into view a conception of practice which does not coincide with noumenal designs, but is equally irreducible to contingent whim. "True praxis," the chapter notes, cannot be divorced from, or be placed in antithesis to, "theoretical consciousness," yet "praxis requires also another element transgressing consciousness: a bodily or sensual element which is only indirectly related to, and qualitatively distinct from, reason." Seen from this perspective, ethics cannot be compressed into abstract rational yardsticks—yardsticks which are inevitably enmeshed in rationality's domineering ambitions; what counts more than imperatives is the impulse of compassion, the "sense of solidarity" with "bodily suffering," and the immediate revulsion against violence. In Adorno's words, men will react spontaneously only to the extent that they "recognize evil without being satisfied with its pure cognition." The stress of immediacy, one should note, does not imply a submergence of noumenal aspirations in a descriptive ethics content with mirroring existing life patterns. Such aspirations, we read, "would be betrayed" were they "incorporated, however cautiously, in a description of reality"; nevertheless, their significance can be salvaged only if, instead of "hovering above reality" like clouds, they are seen as "part and outgrowth of reality's evolving nexus of guilt."[52]

To a considerable extent, Adorno's arguments are echoed in Merleau-Ponty's *Phenomenology of Perception,* particularly in its concluding chapter devoted to a discussion of "Freedom." Like Adorno, Merleau-Ponty in this chapter criticizes the traditional segregation of a priori dictates and a posteriori contingency. "The rationalist's dilemma," he writes, according to which "an act is either free or it is not and an event either originates in me or is imposed on me from outside, does not apply to our relations with the world and with our past." The assumption of a noumenal freedom or choice seems particularly implausible, "not only because there is no time anterior to time, but because choice presupposes a prior involvement and because the idea of an initial choice is contradictory." In Merleau-Ponty's view, moral action is neither derivable from empirical contexts nor equivalent to a pure condition of possibility, but rather involves "our manner of being in the world." Even if this manner of being were seen as the outgrowth of conscious design, he observes, the latter would presuppose "an earlier acquisition which choice merely modifies, thereby founding a new tradition—which leads us to ask whether the complete diremption in terms of which freedom is initially defined is not simply the negative aspect of our universal adherence to a world, and whether our indifference to each determinate thing does not express our involvement in all." Drawing in part on lessons from *Gestalt* analysis, the chapter adds: "If freedom is to have *room* in which to move, if it is to be describable as freedom, there must be something to hold it away from its objectives, it must have a *field,* which means that there must be for it concrete possibilities, or realities which tend to cling to being."[53]

Together with Adorno, Merleau-Ponty perceives moral judgment as harking back at least obliquely to an impulse not defined in antithesis to nature. Probing beneath cognitive designs or subjective projects, he detects the stirrings of a *natural self* obscurely sensitive to moral issues (although the term *self* may be misleading in this context). "Underlying myself as a thinking subject who is able to take its place at will on Sirius or on the earth's surface," we read, "there is as it were a natural self which does not budge from its terrestrial situation and which

constantly adumbrates categorical valuations. What is more, my projects as a thinking being are clearly modelled on the latter." Emphasizing the aspect of moral sensitivity or imagination, Merleau-Ponty speaks
even of "the presence within us of spontaneous evaluation," as differentiated from reflective yardsticks or rational imperatives. Without such
evaluations, he observes, we would be bereft of orientation and unable
to maintain our manner of being-in-the-world: "We would not have a
world, that is, a collection of things which emerge from a background
of formlessness by presenting themselves to our body as 'to be touched,'
'to be taken,' 'to be climbed over.' We should never be aware of adjust-
ing ourselves to things and reaching them where they are, beyond us,
but would be conscious only of tailoring our thoughts to the immanent
objects of our intentions; thus we would not be in the world, ourselves
implicated in its practice and, so to speak, intermingled with things,
but would merely enjoy the spectacle of a universe."[54]

As is well known, the phrase *being-in-the-world* as used in *Phenomenology of Perception* first made its appearance in Heidegger's
writings. As he indicates in the *Letter on Humanism,* the phrase does
not express a mundane confinement, mainly because the term *world*
does not refer to a contingent environment but rather to the "clearing
of Being" or the open arena in which Being can manifest itself. Reflective attentiveness to this opening or approach of Being is designated as
Andenken—a term which may be translated as recollective or commemorative thinking—in contradistinction to both logical-rationalist
analysis and empirical induction. In the same *Letter,* Heidegger also
raises the question of ethics, but immediately places this question in the
context of commemorative thought. In its initial Greek usage, he observes, the term *ethos* denoted neither a derivation nor a positing of
values, but rather man's manner of *dwelling* or being-in-the-world.
Seen against this background, he adds, a thinking which reflects on this
dwelling and its relation to Being can be said to be "the original ethics"—although this expression may be confusing, for, if modern terminology is applied, commemorative thought can be equated neither
with a theoretical ontology nor with a descriptive or rationalist ethics.
To illustrate the meaning of the Greek term, Heidegger refers to a
fragment ascribed to Heraclitus: *ethos anthropo daimon.* In a somewhat free translation, he renders the statement as follows: "The manner of man's dwelling is an opening for the approach of a God" (or
of Being).[55] Perhaps, in our context, we might translate the fragment
still more freely in this sense: Man's being-in-the-world involves an
intimation or solicitation of goodness.

Appendix

ABEUNT STUDIA IN MORES:

BERLIN ON VICO AND HERDER

The transformations occurring in contemporary philosophy and social thought are casting new light on a number of modern thinkers previously overshadowed by Cartesianism and the philosophy of subjectivity. Foremost among them is Giambattista Vico, who was an early opponent of Descartes' perspective, without championing either scholasticism or a narrow brand of empiricism. A similar resurgence is experienced by some figures of the pre-Romantic and Romantic era—such as Hamann, Schelling, and Herder—who remained outside the Kantian and Hegelian frameworks. Isaiah Berlin's study on *Vico and Herder* thus appears at a propitious time. As is evident from numerous recent conferences and publications dealing with Vico, there is widespread interest in the Neapolitan's multifaceted opus. To a slightly lesser extent, the same might be said about the German thinker. In an age when historiography is increasingly assimilated to statistical analysis and when socioeconomic models of development threaten to rob newly emerging countries of the chance to view the world on their own terms, Herder's stress on the uniqueness of historical contexts is bound to strike a responsive chord.

Sir Isaiah brings to his study broad erudition and a solid grounding in historical and cultural *Geisteswissenschaften*. Actually, his close attachment to the latter illuminates both the book's strength and its major limitation. On the one hand, historical sensitivity in Ranke's and Dilthey's sense clearly is of invaluable aid in unraveling the complex panorama of seventeenth- and eighteenth-century thought. On the other hand, the legacy of historicism and *Geisteswissenschaften* may obstruct

Isaiah Berlin: *Vico and Herder: Two Studies in the History of Ideas* (New York: Viking Press, 1976).

access to earlier conceptions of history. The chapter on Vico carries as an epigraph this statement by Ballanche: *Singulière destinée de cet homme! Lui, qui fut si intuitif, il sort du tombeau lorsqu'il n'a plus à enseigner.* Written in 1830, the statement expresses the self-confidence of the epoch to have absorbed and brought to full fruition Vico's embryonic ideas. Apart from flying in the face of the canon of historical differentiation, however, Vico's treatment as a mere "forerunner" or predecessor shortchanges the task of theoretical exegesis: despite numerous affinities and linkages, Vico (as well as Herder) may have something to "teach" which historicism was unable to grasp.

One of the study's most important and original contributions to Vico scholarship is in the domain of "sources" or intellectual parentage. Focusing on Vico's "two dominant doctrines"—the conviction "that the *verum/factum* formula could be applied to human history conceived in its widest sense," and "arising out of it, the very conception of culture as a category of historical thought" (p. 117)—Sir Isaiah inquires into their origins. He finds unconvincing the arguments advanced by leading Italian interpreters (including Fausto Nicolini and Nicola Badaloni) who ascribed a central influence to Vico's immediate milieu, especially to the background of philosophical and scientific ideas in Naples. Countering attempts to detect sources more broadly "in the fields of philosophy, theology and scientific theory," the author turns to the history of philology and especially to "early modern jurisprudence" which, he notes, lay "closer to Vico's dominant interests" and where thus "the long-sought-for clue may at last be found" (pp. 123, 125). The *Mos Gallicus* in particular, with its intimate blending of classical-linguistic and legal learning, in his view provided inspiration for the historically grounded exegesis of texts and also for the conception of historically differentiated cultures. "There is a similarity of approach, both basic and in detail," he writes, "between the historical jurists, especially Hotman and Baudouin, and Vico." Although it does not amount to conclusive proof, this similarity has at least presumptive value: "We cannot say, in the present state of knowledge, that there is positive evidence that Vico derived some of his central notions from the historical jurists: only that it is exceedingly unlikely that he did not do so; for this is the world that he knew best" (pp. 131, 133). The thesis has much plausibility, provided historical jurisprudence is not segregated too neatly from theological and philosophical exegesis; its novelty also should not be exaggerated: Dilthey much earlier had traced modern hermeneutics to its philological, juridical, and theological roots.

Regarding the tenor of Vico's teachings, the study unfortunately is much less satisfying and persuasive. This is in part attributable to the manner of presentation which is excessively rambling, repetitive, and discursive. Perhaps an excess of empathy has induced the author to imitate too closely the baroque style of the *Scienza Nuova* (and also Herder's romantic effusiveness). Repeatedly, the presentation exhibits signs of forgetfulness in the sense that statements at different points of the study unintentionally seem to collide with each other. Thus, according to one passage (p. 111), Vico "supposes that we can, by a species of imaginative insight, turn every *an sich* (to use Hegelian language)— an entity observed from outside by the agent . . . —into a *für sich*, an element in, assimilated to, his purposive, 'spiritual' activity." Somewhat later one is told (p. 122) that Vico's vision "does not move from nature to mind, nor from the contingent to the logically necessary (as that of Leibniz does), nor (as in late Idealism) from the *an sich* of things to the *für sich* of persons." A similar conflict or at least tension seems to exist between the stress on Vico's rootedness in philology, as opposed to "philosophical or theological or scientific ideas," and the assertion that he was after all "a philosopher and a jurist" who "thought in terms of general ideas buttressed by occasional examples" (pp. 83, 140).

More important are shortcomings of substantive exegesis. The study does not contribute significantly to a clarification of the *verum-factum* principle, which Sir Isaiah rightly treats as Vico's pivotal contribution to the history of ideas. No doubt, the discussion of the theme contains numerous insightful observations which deserve careful attention. Particularly striking is the epistemological comment (p. 121) that Vico "did not draw a line at the point at which Descartes drew it—between mind and matter, or between *a priori* knowledge of the real world and *a posteriori* perception of the world of senses"; although he drew a line, he "drew it elsewhere: between activity and passivity, between, on the one hand, *mens* in human affairs, incarnated in human beings, guided, indeed determined, by God and Providence, but themselves creative agents, who have constructed the civil or political-historical world; and, on the other, *mens* in nature, which God, whose instrument it is, can understand, but which to men, who have not made it, is opaque and inscrutable." Unhappily, the author does not explore the implications of this comment. Above all, he does not examine what *mental* activity and creativity might mean on non-Cartesian premises; nor does he indicate how an understanding of such activity—of the *factum* in history—can aspire to true knowledge in the sense of *verum*.

On the whole, his elaborations on the thrust of Vico's key principle seem readily compatible with Cartesian and even neo-Kantian maxims. The epistemological "break," he notes at one point (p. 122), is "between what men's minds 'make,' and what they do not make but find or act upon: the former is, or can be, transparent to mind: the latter resists it." In a simplified formula (p. 12), the dividing line is said to run "between 'outer' and 'inner' knowledge, what later came to be distinguished as *Naturwissenschaft* and *Geisteswissenschaft*."

Assessments of this kind serve to buttress Vico's role of precursor—a role repeatedly stressed in the study. After recapitulating central ingredients of Vico's teachings, the author affirms that "this is the whole doctrine of historicism in embryo" (p. 38). Elsewhere Dilthey's life-philosophy seems to be the implicit goal (p. 67): "In history we are the actors; in the natural sciences mere spectators. This is the doctrine, above others, on which Vico's claim to immortality must rest. For upon it rests the crucial distinction between *Geisteswissenschaft* and *Naturwissenschaft*." Affinity with historicism entails a proclivity toward relativism and subjectivism. According to Sir Isaiah, Vico's argument "points to an easily neglected truth: that all classification, selection, interpretation is subjective"; to some extent, he can even be viewed as "ancestor of those romantic voluntarists, idealists, pragmatists and existentialists who stress the role played in men's experience by their transforming acts" (pp. 109, 141). To be sure, he "does, at times, remind himself that Christian values are timeless and absolute; but for the most part he forgets this, and speaks as if necessarily *autres temps, autres moeurs*" (p. 41). Seen in this light, Vico's overall conception emerges as profoundly paradoxical: his relativistic bent seems wholly incongruent with his stress on providence and his vision of an "ideal eternal history." Sir Isaiah sometimes tries to mollify the conflict through deemphasis, as when he dismisses the notion of *corsi e recorsi*—an aspect of "ideal history"—as "the least interesting, plausible, and original of his views" (p. 64). More commonly he simply records the conflict (pp. 82, 114): "The tension between Vico's theism and his humanistic historicism, between his conception of the cunning of Providence, and his constant emphasis on the creative and self-transforming labours of men, is not resolved in the *New Science*. . . . As for the nature of the relation between God's creation and men's self-creation: between what is given or determined by powers beyond human control or understanding, and what men can mould—this our author, either from excess of prudence, or because of sheer failure to think it through, does not tell us."

Perhaps some hints might have been gleaned from the previously mentioned comparison with Cartesianism. As Sir Isaiah correctly observes, Vico in his early, semi-Cartesian phase tended to identify truth with a priori axioms, with "clear and distinct ideas" directly evident to the human mind. Can one not plausibly assume that his deepening quarrel with Descartes affected his conception both of mind (or *thinking substance*) and of truth? An indication of this change can be found in a passage in *De Antiquissima* (quoted by Sir Isaiah, p. 20) according to which the Cartesian yardstick of a priori intelligible ideas "not only cannot be the criterion of other truths, but it cannot be the criterion of the mind itself; for while mind apprehends itself, it does not make itself, and because it does not make itself, it is ignorant of the former mode by which it apprehends itself." Vico's notions of mental activity and of the nexus between *factum* and *verum* probably need to be viewed against this background; history in this case can no longer be reduced to the categories either of *res cogitans* or of an empirical *res extensa*. Sir Isaiah resurrects this bifurcation when he claims (p. 66) that the pattern of "ideal eternal history" is knowable as "an *a priori* truth" and that "in Leibniz's language it is a *vérité,* not *de fait* but *de la raison."* (This claim does not prevent him from asserting a little later, p. 73, that—contrary to Leibniz and other rationalists—Vico worked on the "opposite" premise "that only empirical knowledge, at times abstruse and peculiar, of what actually occurred, and exceptional imaginative power brought to bear upon it, reveals the working of the 'eternal' pattern that shapes the characteristics of human beings.") At a minimum, the concept of *activity* would seem to deserve more careful delineation than it receives in the study, where one reads (p. 107, n. 1) that Vico did not differentiate "between 'doing' and 'making'; nor, for his purposes, was this necessary."

The discussion of Herder in the second part of the book betrays the same broad learning and familiarity with sources as the first part. What is missing chiefly is a comparison between the roles of the two thinkers in the history of ideas. As the author makes clear, there is little evidence of direct influence: Herder apparently did not read Vico's *Scienza Nuova* "until at least twenty years after his own theory of history had been formed" (p. 147). Yet a study devoted to *Vico and Herder* clearly should have room for an examination of intellectual affinities, convergences, and dissimilarities; presumably Herder's stress on intuition and feeling (one of his writings contained the phrase "I feel! I am!") was not simply a replica of Vico's notion of *poetic wisdom.* Only one passage (pp. 119–20) alludes briefly to a possible distinction. Commenting on neo-Platonic and Leibnizian speculations concerning a continuity between nature and human activity, Sir Isaiah observes: "So far from deriving his ideas from these monistic forerunners of Schelling, Ravaisson, Bergson, Teilhard de Chardin and all other modern adherents of various kinds of *Naturphilosophie,* Vico opposed them." On the other hand, he notes that "philosophers of nature before him, Paracelsus, perhaps, and Campanella, and after them Herder, Schelling, the Romantics, did believe, as against both Descartes and Kant, in precisely such continuity, and it forms the heart of their doctrines." Although pregnant with implications, the comparison is not further pursued; nothing follows from it for the two parts of the study, so that Herder emerges basically as another precursor.

In presenting the latter's views, the author concentrates on "three cardinal ideas," mainly because they "have had great influence for two centuries" and went "against the main stream of thought of his time" (pp. 146–47): namely, populism, expressionism, and pluralism. The first term is chosen chiefly to convey Herder's attachment to "kinship, social solidarity, *Volkstum,* nationhood" (p. 158) and his defense of natural as against artificial life-forms. His view of nationhood, one is reminded, was worlds apart from support for the nation-state with its centralizing and dehumanizing effects; also, his opposition to French *lumières* was not simply an outgrowth of aristocratic or feudal preferences (p. 165): "He is the profoundest critic of the Enlightenment, as formidable as Burke, or de Maistre, but free from their reactionary prejudices and hatred of equality and fraternity." The second category is intended primarily to capture Herder's role as father of the *Sturm und Drang* with its commitment to the full expression of all human faculties and to the intimate fusion of art (conceived as creativity) and life. The main emphasis of the study is on the third category, termed *pluralism:* "the belief not merely in the multiplicity, but in the incommensurability, of the values of different cultures and societies" and the corresponding rejection of "the classical notions of an ideal man and of an ideal society" (p. 153). Sir Isaiah treats this aspect as "the most revolutionary of the implications of Herder's position" and he endorses as essentially "valid" Meinecke's thesis "that the heart of Herder's doctrines is a systematic relativism" (pp. 206, 209, n. 1). In his view, the "cloven hoof of relativism, or rather pluralism" can be found even in Herder's "most orthodox discussions of universal ideals," including his enunciation of the "general ideal of *Humanität*" toward which mankind was said to be climbing: "If Herder's notion of the equal validity of incommensurable cultures is accepted, the concepts of an ideal state or of an ideal man become incoherent" (pp. 208–11).

Although richly suggestive, the three mentioned categories are not obviously congruent or compatible; the study makes little effort to articulate their relationship. As in the case of Vico, there is an acknowledgment of internal contradictions. "There is a tension," one reads (pp. 213–14), "between Herder's naturalism and his teleology, his Christianity and his enthusiastic acceptance of the findings of the natural sciences"; still more significant is "the contrast between, on the one hand, his notion of the continuity of overflowing nature, the *Natura naturans*," and "on the other hand, the crucial role attributed to the unaccountable leaps of genius, miraculous events, sheer chance." In the end, such tensions are unable to impede the study's relativistic exegesis. This assessment, however, carries a price: instead of merely rendering Herder's thought interestingly paradoxical, it is prone to vitiate his main argument. For, given the complete incommensurability of historical and cultural contexts, how should Herder or any other student of history be able to decipher their meaning and to "feel himself into everything"? More importantly, for what purpose should such an effort be undertaken, once the past is transformed into a *musée imaginaire* or an aesthetic display of idiosyncrasies? What seems to be chiefly lacking in the study is an appreciation of Gadamer's concept of *Wirkungsgeschichte*—the notion that historical understanding carries over into conduct (which cannot be entirely non-directional). Despite the stress on the linkage between "thought and action, language and activity" (p. 171), the study tends to restrict empathy to a whimsical pastime. It may be well to recall Gadamer's views at this point. Countering Meinecke's verdict he comments: "We have to ask ourselves whether the 'undissolved residue of transcendence' which the epoch of triumphant historicism detected in Herder's writings may not be essential for the synopsis of nature and history which sustains his entire outlook" ("Nachwort," in *Auch eine Philosophie der Geschichte zur Bildung der Menschheit*, Suhrkamp, 1967, p. 151).

TALE OF TWO CITIES:

RICOEUR'S POLITICAL AND SOCIAL ESSAYS

The opinion is often voiced that phenomenology is completely unrelated to, and irrelevant for, social and political theory. To the extent that the writings of Sartre and Merleau-Ponty are not sufficient counterevidence, Ricoeur's *Political and Social Essays* should lay this view definitely to rest. In these essays, which were first published in French between 1956 and 1973, Ricoeur emerges as a subtle and penetrating thinker deeply concerned about contemporary social and political problems. The essays, one should note, are by no means private "after-hours" ruminations but are intimately connected with Ricoeur's lifework as a professional philosopher. This linkage accounts in large part for the fascination of the essays. Broadly speaking, Ricoeur's philosophical position appears to be located somewhere between Husserl and Heidegger—or else between Jaspers and Lévi-Strauss; and it can plausibly be argued, I believe, that some of the most crucial issues for social and political thought today arise precisely in this field of coordinates.

As is evident in all of his publications, Ricoeur's thinking prefers to move in broad arenas and resists premature synthesis; typically, his endeavor is to delineate the boundaries of a theme in antithetical fashion before embarking on the task of coordination or reconciliation. The procedure is amply illustrated in this volume. Repeatedly the collection speaks of "balanced tensions" or mediated conflicts and "oppositions" (pp. 39, 72). A striking example of the procedure occurs in the discourse on *freedom* where, steering a course between categorical principles and dialectics, the author appeals simultaneously to Kant and to Hegel: the former for securing "the conditions of possibility of

Paul Ricoeur, *Political and Social Essays,* collected and edited by David Steward and Joseph Bien (Athens, Ohio: Ohio University Press, 1974).

freedom" and the latter for establishing "the conditions for its actualization" (p. 65). The reader may recall in this context other "balanced tensions" which characterize Ricoeur's philosophical opus. Although profoundly indebted to transcendental phenomenology (a debt manifest in his study on Husserl and in his translation into French of the first volume of *Ideas*) and to the entire legacy of the philosophy of consciousness, Ricoeur early in his intellectual career shifted his focus from cognition to questions of human will and action and, in doing so, built a bridge to existentialism. His *Philosophie de la volonté* in particular juxtaposed the analysis of transcendental freedom and autonomy to the experiences of guilt, finitude, and fallibility endemic to man's status as a being-in-the-world. Somewhat later, when the problem of language and the interpretation of symbols moved to the center of his thought, he contrasted and correlated two major types of hermeneutics (in *Freud and Philosophy*): one directed to the recovery and recollection of latent intentional meaning, and another concerned with the decoding and removal of systematic distortions of meaning. Almost simultaneously, responding to the challenge issuing from contemporary linguistics and anthropology, Ricoeur endeavored to establish a *modus vivendi* between hermeneutics and structuralism (especially in *The Conflict of Interpretations*).

In the present collection, tensions and their mediations are discussed on the level of ideas and methodologies, but are also seen to be operative in all facets of practical life. Building on the earlier study on human will, the opening essay explores the correlation or dialectic of *nature* and *freedom* and presents two complementary interpretations of human history: in terms of an "ascending genesis of *libido*" and a "descending genesis of freedom" (p. 43). A subsequent essay probes further the conflict between freedom and social-cultural institutions, in the context of a critique of Skinner's behaviorism. In a modified form, the same conflict emerges in an essay on "Violence and Language" which examines the tension between organized power and normative meaning in diverse settings, including politics, poetry, and philosophy. Politics in particular is said to be lodged at the crossroads of two conflicting imperatives: an *ethic of conviction* stressing internal perfection and autonomy and an *ethic of responsibility* concerned with concrete options and outcomes in a given situation. Among political institutions, the volume pays special attention to the modern state and its "adventures," stressing the Janus-faced character of its role and impact: while meant to function as a pacemaker of enlightenment, rationalization, and large-scale planning in the public interest, it also has served as a tool of tyranny and oppression. In Ricoeur's words: "The State is, among us, the unresolved contradiction of rationality and power" (p. 208).

A similar ambiguity is said to be at work in the entire modern process of secularization and urbanization: although they engender anonymity, rootlessness, and bureaucratic domination, these trends are also perceived as possible harbingers of human autonomy and social renewal. According to Ricoeur, incidentally, social and political renewal today cannot be restricted to the reform of established institutions (typically anchored in the state) but must foster the growth of global structures embracing mankind as a whole—although such structures should not simply replace or dismantle inherited frameworks. The dialectic of freedom and institutions at this point gives rise to another dialectic of innovation and social change: while important as a corrective to the arrogance of nation-states, *planetary consciousness* (p. 135) can also entail global uniformity and anonymity—an insight which renders desirable the maintenance of the tension between *mondialization* and local or national particularism. The same dialectic pervades the discussion of the respective merits of hermeneutics or historical understanding and the critique of ideology (as exemplified in the works of Gadamer and Habermas). Ricoeur at this point counsels a balance between *participation* in tradition and critical *distantiation* or emancipation. The concluding essay identifies as chief task of the political educator the mediation between past and future, between the temporalities of *creation* and *memory*. The preservation of culture, we are told (p. 292), is possible "only to the extent that we entirely assume our past, its values and its symbols, and are capable of reinterpreting it totally."

Although significant in their domains, the sketched tensions are overshadowed by a more deep-seated antagonism: the drama of the interplay between the Augustinian "two cities." As a Christian thinker, Ricoeur views politics not simply as the clash of competing ideologies, but as the meeting ground of secular arrangements and eschatological hopes. His conception of the relation between the two cities, one should note, is by no means a replica of the medieval juxtaposition of temporal and spiritual powers. Ricoeur is firmly opposed to a direct political role of the Church or to any institutionalized Christian politics: "The new type of witnessing which will appear must be completely dissociated from any institutional aspect" (p. 149). Far from vouchsafing political abstinence, the rejection of clericalism is meant to allow the Christian to become an "efficacious" participant in the "earthly city."

Christians are reminded of the Biblical injunction to be the "salt of the earth"—an injunction which is bypassed by a retreat to a holy mountain or an exclusive preoccupation with personal salvation. According to Ricoeur, there is perhaps tension but not a stark opposition between personal piety and "commitment in the world" (p. 124). With regard to the modern state—a structure "simultaneously instituted and fallen" (p. 203)—Christians are exhorted to assist both in strengthening its rational operation and in curbing its proclivity to abuse of power. The leavening role of Christians, however, extends beyond the state to all aspects of modern life. The process of secularization in this context emerges less as a threat to organized religion than as an opportunity for Christian involvement in the world. The essay "Urbanization and Secularization" speaks of a theology of the *secular city* and of social change, indicating how the modern "disenchantment of nature" and "desacralization of politics" (p. 185) can encourage an endeavor to sanctify and redeem the profane. Ultimately, believers viewed as "God's avant-garde" are assigned three services or ministries in the midst of the world (p. 193): the services of *proclamation* (*kerygma*), of *healing by reconciliation* (*diakonia*), and of *eschatological communion* (*koinonia*). Performance of these services keeps the "salt" of faith intact. "The non-parish will save the parish. We shall have to learn to see the face of the Church wherever the ministries of announcement, of diakonia, and of concrete community confront the city as a whole, such as the modern world has made it: that is, the secular city" (p. 197).

The goal of communion, in Ricoeur's view, requires not only spiritual pleas but also efforts to establish social preconditions for community life. Regarding economic wealth he writes that "the cards will have to be reshuffled" and that "it is one of the basic tasks of the Christian Church to show the 'haves' that they must give to the 'have-nots' on a world-wide scale" (p. 117). Statements to this effect are not incidental. In terms of political outlook, the entire volume is an argument in favor of Christian socialism or of a socialism tempered by religiously motivated liberal principles. Concerning economic and social policy, Ricoeur even is a friendly critic or critical friend of Marxism—provided the latter is seen as a "humanist realism" rather than as a "crude materialist" doctrine. The essay "Socialism Today" defines socialism as a comprehensive movement operative in the domains of economics, politics, and culture. On the economic level socialism denotes "the transition from a market economy to a planned economy that is responsive to human needs" and that is characterized by "collective or public" ownership of the means of production (p. 230); on the political and social level, the movement advocates "the participation of the greatest number of individuals in economic decisions," that is, the establishment of "industrial democracy" or a "democracy of labor" (pp. 234, 237), while culturally it implies a struggle against alienation and for "solidarity with the most underprivileged fraction of humanity" (p. 241). As Ricoeur recognizes, however, large-scale planning and public ownership may also entail new forms of exploitation and manipulation. From this danger arises the need for a "revindication of true liberalism, that is, the revindication of an area recognized and guaranteed by the State for critical and creative activity of the man of culture" (p. 83). Precisely at a time when socialist planning is required for the removal of social injustice, liberal safeguards have to be jealously maintained: "In the period in which we must extend the role of the State in economic and social matters and advance along the path of the *socialist State,* we must also continue the task of *liberal politics,* which has always consisted of two things: to divide power among powers, to control executive power by popular representation" (p. 213).

Written two decades ago, these lines still have a timely ring. Ricoeur's pleas for a liberal socialism or socialist liberalism are bound to strike responsive chords in a generation (in France and elsewhere) numbed by bloc politics and weary both of capitalist exploitation and Stalinist tyranny. On a more strictly theoretical level, the volume contains numerous observations which are prone to captivate readers familiar with contemporary philosophical trends. Given the prominence of language philosophy today, Ricoeur's comments on the topic—especially on the twin pitfalls of cultural relativism and universalism—deserve careful attention. The "partial possibility of translating certifies that humanity, in its depth, is one," he writes (p. 282), adding: "Whereas on the technical level men can become identical with one another, on the deeper level of historical creation, diverse civilizations can only communicate with each other according to the model of the translation of one language into another." In the discussion of hermeneutics and critical theory, the reader is likely to be struck by the comparison of Habermas' notion of *interest* both with the Heideggerian category of *care* and the Marxist concept of *praxis* (p. 261). In the same intellectual context, one may wish to ponder the relationship between Habermas' three types of interests and the three dimensions of civilization—"industries, institutions, and values" (p. 272)—delineated by Ricoeur in his comments on political education. His views on "disengaged" thought and literature, incidentally, bring back to memory the earlier Frankfurt school, in particular Adorno's defense of artistic freedom against propagandistic manipulation (p. 84).

Despite its considerable merits, the volume occasionally tends to leave the reader perplexed. The predilection for tensions and antinomies sometimes impales arguments on the proverbial horns of dilemmas, while mediations acquire overtones of weak compromise. Although not obliged to offer solutions, the author might at times have probed more thoroughly the challenges opened up by philosophical quandaries. Thus, concerning the dialectic of nature and freedom, it is probably not sufficient to be told that a clue for tackling the antinomy can be found in the Leibnizian notion of *appetition* and the Spinozistic concept of *effort* (*conatus*)—especially if one learns shortly afterwards that one must reject "the wholly positive ontology of Spinoza" (pp. 32, 34). Cryptic is also the description of the dialectic (in terms borrowed from Nabert) as "the *appropriation* by the ego of a certainty of existing which constitutes the ego, but of which it is in many ways dispossessed" (p. 33). More generally, the role of the ego or of man in relation to nature, culture, or the universe is never fully clarified in the volume. The essay "Humanism" acknowledges that "man determines and chooses himself," while insisting simultaneously on a "philosophy of limits" which treats man as "only human" (pp. 75, 87). The latter qualification does not prevent Ricoeur from arguing at another point that "God, in creating man, creates his creators" and that "through the passion for the limit beyond all vanity, man unfolds the *magisterium* which was entrusted to him at the beginning" (pp. 131, 133). The ambivalence of man's status carries over into ethics and especially into the question of the origin of values. The essay on hermeneutics affirms that "ethical life is a perpetual transaction between the project of freedom and its ethical situation outlined by the given world of institutions" (p. 269)—leaving the origin of the ethical situation in doubt. Another passage states more ambitiously, but no less elusively, that man "invents concrete values, but within a realm of value which determines his will on primordial grounds" (p. 129). Political theorists and students of philosophy must be grateful to Ricoeur for having broached issues whose further elucidation demands their best efforts.

The writings of the Frankfurt school are fast acquiring *droit de cité* outside the school's original habitat; in North America, critical theory— a shorthand label for the school's perspective—enjoys wide attention among intellectuals and academic practitioners in a broad spectrum of disciplines. The volume *On Critical Theory,* edited by John O'Neill, illustrates this pervasive reception. With one exception, all the contributors to the volume are either natives or long-term residents in North America; even the exception has spent several years in Canada and the United States. It is hardly correct to say, as one contributor does (p. 142), that "critical theory is dead in Germany while thriving in America." After all, Jürgen Habermas, whom the volume treats as the school's major contemporary representative, still works primarily in the German setting; so do many of his students as well as students of Horkheimer and Adorno. The remarkable transatlantic influence of the theory can probably be ascribed to the largely uniform character of *post-industrial society* or (better) *organized capitalism* with its tendencies toward technocracy and cultural one-dimensionality—tendencies which, however, are particularly pronounced in North America. Though still exaggerating, the same contributor seems closer to the mark when he writes (p. 135) that "in spite of its language and constant references to European culture, critical theory came into being in the late 1930s and early 1940s specifically as a theory of American society. Although it still spoke German and had no initial impact in the United States, critical theory had irrevocably moved beyond its European origins."

Its transatlantic migration, to be sure, has not left critical theory unaffected. Several of the essays are couched in the distinct idiom of North American "counterculture" or "youth culture." According to

John O'Neill, ed., *On Critical Theory* (New York: Seabury Press, 1976).

one writer (pp. 12–13), in being "transplanted from Germany to North America," critical theory had tended to import "a crabbed style of philosophical analysis, replete with a scholastic structure of authority." Instead of concentrating on its "philosophical inheritance," he argues, its insights can only be renewed by "writing the theory in a direct and unmediated way." Whatever its other merits may be, a renewal of this kind is bound to complicate the book's central topic and its differentiation from parallel movements and symbiotic accretions. To some extent, of course, haziness of contours is endemic to the outlook of Frankfurt theorists, regardless of geographical transplantation: intended by its spokesmen chiefly as a scrutiny of established doctrines or a critique of ideology, critical theory cannot readily be treated as a systematic doctrine or set of positive propositions. The demarcation problem is aggravated by pronounced contrasts of personal style and accent as well as by generational differences between members of the school. In his contribution, Christian Lenhardt speaks of "a process of diversification, if not dissolution," which marked the Frankfurt school during the last decade—a process ascribed chiefly to the fact that Habermas "went off on a philosophical journey of his own which has had few points of contact with that of his mentors" (p. 34). While Lenhardt may be overstating his case, the undeniable diversity of formulations would seem to make it imperative to explore carefully the affinities as well as the discontinuities in the writings of Frankfurt theorists. Unfortunately the volume does not provide such an exploration, except in its last section, the essay by Albrecht Wellmer whose title ("Communications and Emancipation: Reflections on the Linguistic Turn in Critical Theory") does not fully convey the range of the author's concerns.

Background: Marx, Weber, and Lukács

On Critical Theory shares the hazard of most edited collections: the unevenness and only partial complementarity of contributions. Instead of following the sequence of essays (which does not seem to disclose an immediately perceptible pattern), I shall arrange my discussion by and large along chronological lines. The reader who desires an overview of the background and development of critical theory is strongly advised to begin with Wellmer's perceptive and well-informed account. Tracing the antecedent motivations of the Frankfurt school back to Marx's own work, Wellmer notes that—despite his distinction between *forces* and *relations* of production and despite his stress on "real, sensuous activity" in the Feuerbach Theses—Marx tended to shortchange the meaning of *praxis* by identifying it narrowly with labor or instrumental-material productivity. "In his *anthropological* and meta-theoretical considerations," he writes (p. 233), "Marx tries to incorporate the symbolic function into the productive one in order to save the anthropological *primacy* of the category of 'material production.' Man, *primarily*, is conceived as a tool-making animal." Marx's implicit tendency emerged in Engels' writings as an overt doctrine, with the result that the "transition of socialism from utopia toward science" is taken literally and "dialectical materialism degenerates into a naturalist metaphysics" (p. 235). The dangers of scientism and instrumentalism became obvious with the rise of managerial elites and corporate industry—trends which Max Weber tried to grasp theoretically under the labels of *rationalization* and *bureaucratization*. Weber's analysis was incorporated by Georg Lukács into his theory of the progressive *reification* of consciousness under capitalism—although Lukács still expected an imminent dismantling of reification through class struggle and failed to take into account the corporate-technological transformation of capitalist society. In Wellmer's opinion, the latter transformation provided the immediate incentive for critical theory as articulated by the founders of the Frankfurt school: "What they held in common was the view that with the emergence of organized capitalism a closed universe of 'instrumental reason' or 'one-dimensional rationality' was being created" and that any further emancipation, instead of resulting from unfolding economic contradictions, "would have to be achieved *against* the internal logic of the development of capitalism" (p. 244).

References to Weber and Lukács occur repeatedly in the volume, but their relevance to critical theory is not always as judiciously assessed. In his essay, "Science, Critique, and Criticism: The 'Open Society' Revisited," H. T. Wilson expresses the belief that "it is Weber who constitutes a basic point of departure and problematic for *both* Popperians and critical theorists" (p. 205). The belief seems plausible in Popper's case, given his segregation between scientific objectivity and the subjective choice of values and philosophical premises, a distinction reducing social inquiry to the investigation of effective means. "Popper," he notes (pp. 211–12), "is left with a very Weberian bifurcation between science and politics, with the social sciences treated as 'technological' problem-solvers and therefore part of practice rather than science." From this vantage point, "the social sciences become handmaidens in the effort to formulate 'responsible' social and political aims," which implies "that theories in these disciplines function exclusively as instruments whose value lies not in their search after truth but rather in the degree to which their assessments are correct and their utilization achieves the desired practical results." The founders of the Frankfurt school—Wilson concurs with Wellmer on this point—adopted Weber's concept of *rationalization,* but insisted on the political character of this allegedly "formal" concept: its entanglement in structures of domination. For some critical theorists, movement toward socialism therefore implied changes both on the level of economic-political institutions and on the level of scientific rationality. In Habermas' writings, however, Wilson detects a return to Weber's original bifurcation. Habermas' epistemology, he asserts (p. 218), displays a "fragmentation" which is "derived directly from the distinction in Weber between rationalization and the disenchantment of the world. For rationalization Habermas substitutes *work,* or 'systems of rational-purposive action'; for the disenchantment of the world he substitutes *interaction,* or 'symbolically-mediated interaction.' The first is governed by technical rules, the second by consensual norms." Phrased in this manner, the allegation appears lopsided. While a linkage with Weber (and Popper) may persist in the domain of "empirical-analytical science," Habermas' notion of *interaction,* and especially his stress on the discursive justification of *consensual norms,* can hardly be reconciled with Weber's decisionism or with an instrumentalist view of social inquiry.

The essay by Paul Piccone entitled "Beyond Identity Theory" contains additional observations concerning Lukács and the repercussions of his work. Together with Korsch and Gramsci, Lukács is presented as a spokesman of "Hegelian Marxism," a perspective which arose chiefly as a reaction to the positivism of the Second International. According to Piccone (p. 132), Lukács' originality resided "not in introducing the theme of alienation" but rather "in analyzing it in terms of the division of labor and the resulting objectified conceptual forms" prevalent under capitalism: "The framing of alienation within the logic of capitalist production, and the re-interpretation of Marxism through the Hegelian dialectic of whole and part, produced a theory which could locate the proletariat as the historical agency of change and its political aim as the re-integration of that hopelessly fragmented cultural whole typified by commodity fetishism." The perceptiveness displayed in this statement and in the portrayal of Korsch's and Gramsci's arguments, however, is not a uniform trait of the essay. Thus, the assertion (p. 132) that "Lukács', Korsch's, and Gramsci's contributions were not the result of their immediate political efforts, but of the reflection on that work and its failure" seems doubtful at least in application to *History and Class Consciousness,* whose élan still reflected revolutionary (if not millenary) expectations. More important are Piccone's comments on subsequent developments. The introduction of the assembly line and of "scientific" management in his view ushered in the decline of the first wave of Hegelian Marxism, a decline made irreversible by the Great Depression and Fascism. Given the trends of the time, he observes (p. 135), "it is not surprising that the new generation of Hegelian Marxists in the 1930s took as its point of departure the objective impossibility of collective subjectivity, and sought to preserve whatever free space had been created for the bourgeois individuality that the system increasingly seemed to rule out. In carrying out this theoretical retreat, the new Hegelian Marxists in the 1930s called themselves 'critical theorists' and concentrated their analysis on culture and on the psychological dimension." What is questionable in this statement is not so much the deemphasis of *collective subjectivity* (read: the proletariat), but rather the identification of the Frankfurt program with Hegelian Marxism and the presumed focus on *bourgeois individuality.* Actually, the assumption of successive generations of Hegelian Marxists seems to me to obscure some of the most distinctive features of critical theory.

Some of these features emerge in a short but superbly written essay by Ioan Davies, entitled "Time, Aesthetics, and Critical Theory." The essay concentrates on the relationship between Lukács and Walter Benjamin, and thus on an important juncture in the transition between Hegelian Marxism and early critical theory. In large part, the discussion revolves around a central theme in aesthetic (as well as social) theory: the nexus of form and content. "Benjamin's thesis on form and content," we read (p. 64), "differs substantially from that of Lukács where, notwithstanding the different media discussed by the two authors, the major distinction made is that the great work of art must express a totality of experience and conflict." In general terms, Lukács' aesthetics was geared toward a substantive totality "which in turn dictates certain forms." By contrast, Benjamin's writings, especially his notes on Haussmann's architecture in Paris, stressed the complexity of the relationship and "the danger of not taking form seriously enough." Behind the two approaches were more fundamental differences of philosophical premises. Lukács' outlook reflected a view of history as an outgrowth of human intentionality and as evolving synthesis of meaning. "With Lukács," Davies observes (p. 65), "the reading of history in relation to art and social change requires searching for those totalizing forms which reflect the wholeness of experience." Benjamin's *Illuminations,* on the other hand, contains the statement that "there is no document of civilization which is not at the same time a document of barbarism"—a statement which points not only to the discontinuity of history, but to vast stretches of non-meaning and non-intentionality. From Benjamin's perspective, the task of the historian was to construct historical *tableaux* by interrupting the gestures and designs of participants. In Davies' words (pp. 67–68): "We interpret the gestures of the actors in mid-nineteenth-century France not simply to examine the relationships between people, but between people and *things.* And for this purpose history itself is a thing." As he adds: "If Marxism is a dialectical materialism, Benjamin is the materialist *par excellence.* The bourgeois politicians and merchants turned matter into a spiritual wave of progress. The historical materialist confronts matter as matter, and progress as the débris of matter." Regarding social change, Lukács derived movement from immanent contradictions, while Benjamin based his hope on "moments salvaged out of the débris," moments which were "shot through with chips of Messianic time." (The volume contains another essay dealing with aesthetics, titled "Aesthetic Experience and Self-Reflection as Emancipatory Processes," from which, however, I am only able to gather that modern aesthetics pursues an emancipatory thrust which is somehow related to self-reflection.)

Adorno and Marcuse

In view of Davies' paper, one might expect a similarly sensitive discussion of Adorno's work who, after all, was more strongly influenced by Benjamin than other members of the Frankfurt school. The expectation, however, is disappointed; in fact, among critical theorists Adorno receives by far the most hostile and vituperative treatment in the volume. A measure of empathy or appreciation—though canceled toward the end—can be found in Lenhardt's contribution on "The Wanderings of Enlightenment." The essay deals with Horkheimer's and Adorno's *Dialectic of Enlightenment,* and especially with the excursus on the *Odyssey* contained in that study. "Far from being straightforward emancipatory," Lenhardt writes (pp. 36–37), enlightenment in Horkheimer's and Adorno's view "has had a dialectical character," since it signifies "at once emancipation from myth and the destruction of areas of freedom already won." In its departure from unilinearity, he adds, *Dialectic of Enlightenment* issued a radical challenge to the "idea of historical totality," a challenge which signaled "the Copernican turn critical theory has effected in dialectical thought, Hegelian and Marxist alike." As presented in the study, primitive or prehistorical man "acts in a setting characterized by the omnipresence of nature," a situation in which he has "no ego, no consciousness of himself, no identity apart from nature" (p. 39). Lenhardt's comments on the study's conception of archaic nature are striking and worth quoting at greater length (pp. 48–49): "If the historical mission of enlightenment is a man's progressive deliverance from fear, this means that nature, the seat of mythical threats, is not an indifferent otherness which has progressively become 'for us' through toil and the thetic-constitutive powers of the subject. Instead, archaic nature was determinate, saturated with spirit, and man existed 'for it.'" By contrast, "the neutralized, clawless concept of nature in Hegel and Marx was no more than a product of modern secularization and demythologization, not nature as natural man saw it." The excursus on the *Odyssey* depicts the agonies, triumphs, and penalties involved in the emergence of individual consciousness and rationality from the collective forces of myth; enlightenment in this context denotes "the formation of a subject or human self which survives the onslaught of ever-present mythical dangers," a process typified by Odysseus, "the individual *in statu nascendi*" (p. 43). The chief costs of the process were progressive self-enclosure and insensitivity toward others: "Since Odysseus, frigidity is the inevitable shadow of individuation: To be able to see one's companions devoured by the monster without experiencing guilt, and perhaps even physical pain, was the condition of subjectivization" (p. 56).

Turning from description to assessment, Lenhardt offers a few comments or "lines of possible reflection" which he himself describes as impressionistic (p. 48) but whose common tenor is hardly favorable. One major comment concerns the "theme of fear" as developed in *Dialectic of Enlightenment*. Claiming to detect a "dephobization" of modern life, Lenhardt argues that the study "wrongly implies that fear and panic are the psychic accompaniments of everyday life in an age of computerized welfare" (pp. 49, 51). Quite apart from the question whether the implication is as stated, one may wonder whether Lenhardt's concern with fear does not unduly shift the study's focus from a philosophical-historical to a psychological terrain. Moreover, neurotic *anxiety*—which he readily admits to have been on the rise during recent centuries—may well be a modulation of fear and can hardly be segregated neatly from the "real psychic terror" (p. 52) of earlier ages. More important are Lenhardt's comments on the overall outlook displayed in the study—and in Adorno's work as a whole—which he finds marked by the bleakest pessimism. Adorno's posture in his view can be summarized in the statement: "Everything we do is wrong no matter how generously or radically it is conceived." Time and again in Adorno's writings, he adds, "the Gnostic idea of a *civitas terrena* where all cows are black and all things indistinguishably evil gained the upper hand over the discriminating perception and critique of determinate socio-political landscapes" (pp. 53, 55). One key phrase in these writings which Lenhardt finds particularly offensive is the notion of a "universal context (or nexus) of guilt" (*universaler Schuldzusammenhang*). "How can there be guilt," he observes (p. 53), "when there is no conceivable course of right conduct, no moral code for the autonomy-seeking subject? This is the point where Adorno unwittingly assumes the posture of a kind of world spirit, one who behaves, to be sure, more like a vengeant fury than a benefactor of mankind or an embodiment of its highest aspirations." In my judgment, these comments are entirely misconceived. Contrary to Lenhardt's allegation, Adorno was not simply an amoralist or anti-moralist for whom there was no moral code and no distinction between right and wrong conduct; his views on ethics were developed not only in the aphorisms of *Minima Moralia* but also in the Kant chapter in *Negative Dialectics* (a work, incidentally, which is not pervaded by hopelessness, although hope is not anchored in subjective intentions). The notion of a universal nexus of guilt, however, does not properly belong to the level of private ethics, but rather to the level of *Sittlichkeit* (stripped of idealist overtones); instead of focusing on the autonomy-seeking subject, the phrase points to the circumstance that our actions are implicated in broader social and historical structures whose change cannot simply derive from, but does not render obsolete, individual good will.

Lenhardt's arguments are subdued compared with the animosity evident in other parts of the volume. In his essay "On Happiness and the Damaged Life," Ben Agger contrasts "Adorno's nearly unmitigated pessimism" with Marcuse's "guarded and sophisticated optimism" and with O'Neill's perspective of "wild sociology." While Adorno, he writes (pp. 12–13), "employed a negative language and favored negative culture," Marcuse and O'Neill "have responded to the libidinal rebellion of American youth as a potentially revolutionary phenomenon." What grieves Agger most is Adorno's "ban on images" or refusal to portray the promised land: "For too long, Marxism has been under the sway of a taboo prohibiting the depiction of the image of socialism"; the central thesis of the paper is "that this taboo must be lifted and Adorno's dismal reluctance to sing about socialism opposed" (pp. 13–14). As presented in the paper, critical theory and socialism in general have strongly musical or aesthetic connotations. "Adorno," we read (p. 13), "saw negative theory captured in the mind-boggling rows of twelve-tone music where Marcuse and O'Neill hear the crash and flight of rock music as a new promise of freedom, providing a vision of the preverbal harmony of socialist life: the *carnal* grounds of socialism." Advances toward socialism in Agger's view require chiefly aesthetic and symbolic efforts since, he asserts (p. 15), "modes of expression like music and theory *themselves* constitute a new body politic and socialist relations." The gulf between the discussed writers on this score is radical: "The way of O'Neill and Marcuse is a direct attempt to create a socialist body politic through the medium of musical and theoretic harmony. Adorno's way is a form of abstract negation through dissonance." The term *theory,* as used in this context, is not meant to convey cerebral endeavors—whose attractions would be pale in comparison with the "non-linear spacetime of rock and drugs"; rather, we are told, "theory sings, paints, writes, makes love" (pp. 19, 32). Genuine critical theory follows the same pattern in that it "sings the world" and in this sense coincides with praxis (pp. 18, 24).

As Agger indicates, the contrast between critical theorists is anchored primarily in their different assessment of subjectivity and its social function. Long before the rise of structuralism, Adorno in some of his writings discerned the malaise if not demise of this centerpiece of modern life. In Agger's words: "Adorno supposed that the subject was an effete residual of bourgeois philosophy which perished in the Nazi death camps." On the other hand, the "theory of liberation" offered by Marcuse and O'Neill "treats the subject as a relatively undamaged agent of revolutionary praxis" (pp. 24, 26). Both Marcuse's "new sensibility" and O'Neill's "wild sociology" draw support from libidinal components of Freudian psychoanalysis. "Whereas Adorno read Freud as the prescient prophet of the completely eradicated subject," the two thinkers employ "the allegedly 'gloomy' Freud to postulate a buried libidinal substratum capable of healthy creativity and socialist relations." From Marcuse's and O'Neill's perspective, "the kernel of positive opposition lies in the 'libidinal rationality' beginning to emerge from the embodied subject"; they thus are able "to restore the experience of the embodied subject to Marxism" (p. 26). In contrast to the tradition of philosophical *subjectivity* from Descartes to Husserl, the subject uncovered in this manner is claimed to be concrete and tangible and directly linked with nature through the medium of natural instincts. According to Agger, Marcuse's and O'Neill's Freudianism allows them to "harness the natural subject as the new agent of body politics." Supported by psychoanalysis—he states in a later context (p. 31)—the two writers are capable of formulating a "theory of the objective character of subjectivity," thus bringing into view the "objectivity of subjectivity" or the "objective subject."

Marcuse's work is cited in other portions of the volume, commonly in a favorable light. In his own contribution entitled "Critique and Remembrance," O'Neill refers to Marcuse's elaborations on the "concept of essence" and their implications for the "essence of man." While "premodern conceptions of being" revolved around the "tension between essence and existence," he writes (p. 5), modern philosophy has tended to reduce essence to a "problem of logic and epistemology," a reduction particularly evident in the focus on transcendental consciousness "from Descartes and Kant to Husserl." This trend has been halted only in "critical materialism" where "the tension between essence and appearance becomes a historical theory of the development of man through specific forms of social and economic organization"; the "critical Hegelian-Marxist concept of essence" thus denotes chiefly a "historical relationship between men." According to O'Neill (pp. 6–7), critical materialism operates basically on two levels: "at one level concepts deal with the relations between reified phenomena, and at another level they deal with the real or essential relations between reified phenomena whose subjective constitution has been revealed as an historically specific praxis." Marcuse's writings in his view have recaptured this central insight; departing from both abstract idealism and crude materialism they embed "the concept of the essence of being and the subjective praxis of modern knowledge in the Hegelian unity of reason and freedom demanded by the critical concept of the essence of man." Another essay by Ken O'Brien, "Death and Revolution," deals with one of Marcuse's competitors in the domain of Freudian exegesis, Erich Fromm; but the argument is basically that Fromm's "contributions to the corpus of the Frankfurt School's critical theory should be reappraised in a more positive light" and that especially in his earlier writings "the analysis is more Marcusean—in the tradition of sections of *Eros and Civilization*" (pp. 104, 123).

As portrayed in the volume, Freudian or Marcusean Marxism invites a number of comments. None of the authors displays an awareness of, or concern with, more recent reinterpretations of Freud from both hermeneutical and structuralist perspectives; Jacques Lacan's writings in particular cast doubt on the creative-affirmative character of instinctual drives—a vision extolled with special fervor in Agger's paper. The latter's account is questionable also in other respects. The notion of libidinal rationality in his formulation strikes me as an exuberant synthesis which neglects the complex mediations of reason and experience; a theory which "sings" and coincides with praxis is liable to shortchange the integrity of both thought and action. At least equally dubious and detrimental is the concept of an embodied subject or objective subject—terms whose relevance, to be sure, is not restricted to Marcuse's work but extends to a good deal of existentialist literature. Far from offering a *via media* or a road leading beyond idealism and materialism, the phrase in my view combines only the disadvantages of the two perspectives without sharing their virtues: while abandoning the rigorous cognitive standards associated with the tradition of transcendental subjectivity, the concept simultaneously is unable to capture materialism's non-intentional or structural connotations. Agger's claim to find in the embodied subject a bridge reconciling man and nature seems to me entirely unfounded. Reduced to a synonym for the "bodily and libidinal health of the subject" (p. 27), nature functions at best as a concrete adjunct of human endeavors.

From a slightly different vantage point the critique of Adorno is also taken up by Piccone. In the latter's contribution, Adorno appears as a wayward or renegade Hegelian Marxist who ultimately—contrary to Lenhardt's charge of amoralism—lapsed into a stern Kantianism. Arguing that Marxist *metatheory,* in contradistinction to its historical applications, "can only exist as *faith,"* Piccone asserts (pp. 137–38) that "what eventually happens to Adorno is that he loses faith. He no longer believes in the possibility of universal history and must reject the Hegelian teleology to fall back on an abstract Kantian moralism which can neither explain itself nor realize its ethical ideals." Entrenched in his "privileged position" of categorical imperatives or the "logic of essence," Adorno proceeded not only to "throw critical thunderbolts at the reified phenomena of the administered society," but also to "nail all other theories down as frozen images, and hence as accomplices of that same administered society" (p. 141). As antidote to Adorno's austere negativity, Piccone invokes not Marcuse's "new sensibility" but rather Husserl's phenomenology—for which, he stresses (p. 138), "critical theory never developed an appreciation." As he surmises (p. 139), this lack of appreciation was due mainly to the (mistaken) "interpretation of Husserl's own work as a preparatory step to Heidegger's ontology," an ontology which completely "ruled out *collective* salvation as well as the very possibility of qualitatively changing the human predicament." Most Husserl students, it seems to me, will be surprised to learn (as their teacher would have been) that "Husserl provided the only genuinely *materialist* theory of knowledge adequate to the new phase of capitalist development" (p. 140). The contemporary reader may also be intrigued by the claim (p. 142) that in the present stage of monopoly capitalism "not only are official organs of repression dismantled *from above,* but some free space is artificially created to allow for the growth of the needed critical dimension."

Antagonists: Popper, Luhmann

The remainder of the volume is devoted chiefly to the review of a number of disputes between members of the Frankfurt school and spokesmen of competing intellectual positions, such as Popper's *critical rationalism,* systems theory, and hermeneutics. As they are apt to highlight distinctive aspects of critical theory, these disputes clearly deserve attention. The opposing camps, one should note, do not always espouse strictly antithetical views but tend to share common premises—a circumstance complicating the respective arguments and their assessment. A relatively straightforward antagonism prevails between Popperians and critical theorists, a conflict examined in Wilson's paper. As Wilson notes, one of the climactic points of the dispute was the confrontation between Popper and Adorno (and their respective followers) at the meeting of the German Sociological Association in 1961. The heart of the controversy was—then and subsequently—the proper role of reason and rational reflection. While Popperians have tended to restrict reason to scientific inquiry (chiefly in the natural sciences), critical theorists are bent on extending reflection's range to the broad domain of social and historical experience. Popper's posture, Wilson comments (p. 208), "begins by abstracting the individual out of a social structure with which he is reflexively involved *as a member* in order to reconstitute him as an observer with a problem. The idea that society itself (in contradistinction to nature) has a problem to which reflexivity is a response borders on heresy for Popper, hostaged as he is to the man-nature, mind-body, subject-object, value-fact, and ends-means dichotomies." Whereas, in Popper's view, the Frankfurt school was guilty of espousing historicism, holism, and the "myth of total reason," critical theorists have attacked the former's scientism and practical decisionism. As previously indicated, Wilson discovers in Habermas' writings a partial convergence with Popper's outlook or at least an attempt to articulate "a revised version of Popper's open society thesis" (p. 225)—an argument which I consider excessive for the mentioned reasons. Despite its opacity, the following statement (p. 227) referring to Habermas may be more to the point: "The loss of that tension between concept and object given in critical theory as a negative dialectics would then signify the triumph of Hegel, but the unreflexive Hegel who endorsed civil society rather than the author of the modern teaching whose method Marx sought to recover and whose vision he sought to redirect."

The controversy between critical theory and systems analysis is of more recent origin and derives chiefly from successive exchanges between Habermas and Niklas Luhmann during the last decade. Friedrich Sixel's essay, entitled "The Problem of Sense: Habermas v. Luhmann," offers a well-informed and well-written synopsis of the debate (although the German term *Sinn* would probably have been better rendered as *meaning,* rather than *sense*). In contrast to the older conflict, the lines of demarcation in this case are less clearly drawn, not only because of a partial overlap of initial premises but also because of a reciprocal *rapprochement* on some points. In Sixel's words (p. 185), "the Habermas-Luhmann debate is far from the kind of trench warfare that the Adorno-Popper controversy certainly was. While in the sixties the two discussants tried mainly to demarcate their positions against each other, Habermas and Luhmann make every effort to listen to and learn from what the other has to say." As a result of this learning process, "the adoption of a systems-theoretical language increasingly influences Habermas's way of arguing in the debate while in turn Habermas's attack on Luhmann's notion of complexity forces the latter to reformulate the meaning of that concept as the argument goes on." Sixel identifies as one of the initial affinities the common reliance on cognitive categories rooted in consciousness (p. 186): "Luhmann, like Habermas, departs from the firm result of transcendentalism that the object depends on the cognitive faculties—Kant speaks of categories—of the subject." While Habermas seeks to overcome the monological structure of Kantian consciousness through a turn to language, Luhmann finds the remedy in a "combination of Edmund Husserl's phenomenology and modern systems theory." Relying on Husserl's notion of "transcendence immanent to consciousness" but focusing on a strictly mundane-sociological level of awareness, Luhmann detects a parallel between Husserl's noetic-noematic framework and the relation between the internal structure of social *meaning systems* and their complex environment. In order to remain viable, he argues (p. 187), such systems need to reduce the environment's complexity and they do this by adopting a strategy of selecting information which is manageable "in terms of the systems' internal structures." His claim is thus that, akin to phenomenological inquiry, meaning systems "have in the reduction of external complexity a transcendental relation to their environment." Systemic change, according to Luhmann, is typically "initiated by information that the system cannot incorporate" and effected by internal structural rearrangements. *Meaning* in his usage does not denote individual or subjective designs but rather a socially sanctioned practice of information selection and management.

Habermas objects to Luhmann's perspective chiefly on two counts: its idealism and its merger of thought and practice reminiscent of the "sociology of knowledge." Regarding the first point, he deplores his antagonist's ignorance of dialectical materialism and of the cognitive function of material production. Paraphrasing Habermas, Sixel comments (p. 195): "Man being a citizen in the world of matter and of mind depends for the construction of his reality on both material production and the senseful (read: meaningful) organization thereof." Concerning the second point, Habermas criticizes Luhmann's reduction of social meaning to a strategy of information management governed by the standard of systemic efficiency and viability; since, in contemporary society, compliance with this standard is typically determined by experts, systems theory truncates normative discussion. Instead of offering a theory of praxis or theory of society conducive to universal discourse, Habermas charges (p. 197), Luhmann's approach promotes "the *administrative* management of problems in society" by providing "the conceptual basis for a sociology that is functionalized as a *social technology*." In opposing functionalism Habermas also challenges the individual's subordination to social practices, thus recovering the autonomy of human choice and action. In Sixel's words (pp. 197–98), "Habermas hangs on to the concept of the reasonable subject as the key concept of sociology," while his "theory of cognition returns to the human subject in his totality and historical concreteness." What is not entirely clear is the meaning of these statements, and especially why the stress on the rational subject involves "certainly not an idealist concept of man." Despite the earlier reference to material production and its significance for cognition, it is not directly evident how the worlds "of matter and of mind" are related and how the stress on the subject "as the only condition of order" (p. 199) is reconcilable either with systemic concerns or with dialectical materialism. The assertion that "man's grounding in nature provides him with a secure rail for not venturing off into strange horizons of possible sense alien to that of praxis" offers hardly sufficient guidance in this area. The following statement also remains puzzling (p. 198): "It is Habermas's suggestion that establishing sense and the constitution of the self take place 'uno actu,' in one act. The individual constitutes itself as an Ego *not after* having distinguished itself from Alter, but *in* the act of making that distinction; or, while one identifies oneself with others, one retains one's discreteness."

Critical Theory and Hermeneutics

Easily the most tangled—and most intriguing—controversy discussed in the volume concerns the status of philosophical hermeneutics. Dieter Misgeld's essay, entitled "Critical Theory and Hermeneutics: The Debate Between Habermas and Gadamer," makes an important contribution to a clarification of relevant issues; several of the other papers also touch repeatedly on aspects of the dispute. Quite apart from its difficult subject matter, the complexity of the debate derives from the lack of bipolarity, from the intricate mixture of conflict and consensus between the two contestants. While systems theory may be related to the notion of technical interest, hermeneutics has direct affinity with Habermas' category of communicative interaction—a category central to his argument since it serves as threshold for both *discourse* and reflective *emancipation*. As Misgeld correctly states (p. 166): "Habermas, it seems, noticed that hermeneutical reflection on historical understanding had faithfully described the origin of understanding in the practice of communication and had, therefore, made communal reflection thematic." Misgeld proceeds to list at least six considerations "in terms of which Gadamer's hermeneutics could become relevant to Habermas' redesign of a foundation for critical theory," including: their common critique of instrumental reason and of the "objectifying methods of the sciences"; their distinction between *praxis* and *techné;* their shared focus on dialogue and interpretive understanding; and their attempt in some fashion to link theory and practice (pp. 168–70). Other similarities should emerge in the course of the following discussion. In its opening pages, the essay also introduces the reader to the central point of dissension. "Critical theory," we are told (p. 171), "is not hermeneutics: it aims at a critique of society and of our history. It is oriented toward emancipation from our historical past, in so far as this history can be seen as a history of the exercise of domination and repression."

Before entering into the thick of the dispute, Misgeld offers a perceptive account of the basic ingredients of Gadamer's hermeneutical project, as outlined mainly in *Truth and Method*. Gadamer, he observes (pp. 172–73), takes Dilthey's notion of the *Geisteswissenschaften* with its stress on interpretive method as his point of departure, but proceeds beyond Dilthey in an ontological direction by incorporating Heidegger's existential analytic: "Hermeneutics cannot merely be a 'doctrine of method,' not even for the *Geisteswissenschaften*. If there are experiences of truth transcending the sphere of control of scientific method, interpretation is to be seen as an element of all 'prescientific' experience." The ontological posture of hermeneutics implies that "the movement of understanding is encompassing and universal," instead of simply denoting "procedures peculiar and restricted to the humanities." Hermeneutics, from Gadamer's perspective, is thus a reflection of our inescapable involvement in a world which precedes and nurtures our judgment and with which experience and thought have to come to terms. The primary medium in which we are involved prior to conscious analysis is language (p. 174): "We can never account for language by reference to principles of a reasoning activity which is initially conceived as outside or beyond language. We participate in language, Gadamer says, by 'belonging' to it." Language grants access to other prereflective domains, especially to the matrix of history as an ongoing accretion of experience: "History, as mediated by language, gains supremacy over our individual consciousness, expectations, and practical intentions. Hence we speak of the *tradition-context of language,* as that to which we belong." Given the crucial role of prereflective frames of reference, judgment can never entirely clear out the underbrush of prejudgments, nor reason completely vanquish the "authority" of historical legacies (p. 180): "Gadamer's rehabilitation of authority and prejudgment should be taken as an illustration for the dependency of our schemata of interpretation on the tradition-context of language. Preunderstandings of historical texts, brought to a reflective presence in hermeneutical insight, can never be put aside once and for all." The same argument applies also to social inquiry: "A communicative access to the data of social science implies, according to Gadamer, the recognition of the dependency of theorizing on the modes of understanding embedded in social practice, where they are always at work."

In stressing the importance of prereflective understanding and ongoing social practices, Gadamer takes a stand against manipulative social engineering and against the longstanding effort of rationalist enlightenment to denigrate history and tradition. This effort, in his view, can be traced ultimately to Descartes' radical doubt and his ambition to buttress the self-sufficiency of reason independently of historical antecedents. An important theme in *Truth and Method,* Misgeld notes (pp. 166, 178), is the "critique of the Cartesian model of self-certainty and its effects on the epistemology of historical understanding and comprehension." With Descartes, "the method of universal doubt takes the place of a historical understanding which initiates into the normative tradition of a culture"; once his "model of self-reflection" is joined with scientific method, "the contrariety of reason and authority results." Cutting thought loose from its prereflective moorings, rationalist enlightenment ultimately aims to subject both nature and society to external (or third-person) analysis and technical control. "Technology, scientific method, and even the rationalism of the tradition of critique in philosophy from Kant to Hegel, Marx, Husserl, and the Frankfurt school have something in common," Misgeld comments (pp. 175–76). "They either aim at presuppositionless objective knowledge and ignore the historical embeddedness of those modes of knowing which convey self-understanding, or they aim at knowledge having the practical effect of making societal and historical actors totally rational. Both lend themselves to a fateful combination of technological and political utopianism." Once the "standards of rationality" are erected outside or beyond historically structured interaction situations, the "tradition-context of language" appears only as "a source of continuous misunderstandings."

Viewed against the background of the modern self-glorification of reason, Gadamer's work undoubtedly provides a valuable antidote. The merits of his perspective come readily into view when juxtaposed to a *critical theory* construed as a synonym for reflective self-sufficiency—a construction offered in Jeremy Shapiro's essay, "The Slime of History: Embeddedness in Nature and Critical Theory." According to Shapiro, human freedom hinges on the rupturing of all non-reflective bonds or contexts deriving from historical or natural sources; although necessarily mediated by these contexts, *emancipation* signifies man's continuous transcendence of the "slime of history" and the "embeddedness in nature" (a free translation of the German *Naturwüchsigkeit*). Appealing to the philosophy of self-reflection, he asserts that "the transcendental subject that constitutes time is itself the result of an empirical genesis, one that contaminates the transcendental subject with the traces of a real past, an unfinished past of unfreedom and suffering that seems to seep continually into the present and drag the transcendental subject down into the mire of repetition that constitutes its prison" (p. 147). In Shapiro's view, Marx was the first to outline a concrete dialectic of human freedom in terms of the transcendence of "embeddedness in nature," the latter seen as "the domination of the past over the present"; in communism or the "state of post-embedded-ness," the individual is expected to be "entirely self-created, ceaselessly going beyond its own limits by means of its creativity, and continuously participating in the movement of its own becoming" (p. 149). As he adds, however, Marx's account of transcendence was incomplete because he focused narrowly on economic factors, ignoring the constraining role of "the family and the nation"; the significance of the Frankfurt school is found in the circumstance that it "turned its attention to social phenomena previously considered by Marxism as part of the 'superstructure' or as ideology: personality, family, and authority structures and the realm of aesthetics and mass culture" (pp. 153, 155). By emphasizing broad-scale emancipation, critical theory is said to round out the Marxist vision and to bring to fruition the effort "to penetrate to deeper and deeper layers of the roots of embeddedness in nature in order to make possible free action and the installation of rationality." The instrumental or managerial overtones of this installation are evident in Shapiro's account: the specific function of the emancipatory dialectic is defined as "the control and direction of the evolutionary process itself" (p. 157).

The conception of critique as the termination of natural and historical conditions appears both untenable and obnoxious: stripped of its prereflective beginnings reason turns either into idle curiosity or an instrument of domination. On the level of praxis, emancipation construed in this manner vitiates the formation of character; for where should human responsibility and care be *practiced* if not in concrete communities? Misgeld (speaking on behalf of Gadamer) has no difficulty in deflating this view. The notion of emancipation, he writes (p. 171), "implies reference to a shared form of life in which we have come to an understanding with one another which need no longer be revoked." O'Neill's introductory essay contains a full-fledged attack on a futuristic Marxism forgetful of the past or relegating it simply to the "slime of history." "What is required of critical theory," he writes (p. 2), "is not at all that it separate itself from its own legacy"; rather what is needed is to "take a responsible stand towards the apocalyptic separation of the past from the future." The function of *remembrance,* in his view, is chiefly to preserve Marxism from the vagaries of rationalism and the "logic of domination" (p. 3): "I believe that by stressing the fundamental notion of our historical memory of guilt and unredeemed suffering we recover the deepest grounds of the ethical materialism that motivates critical theory." Pointing to the prereflective matrix of experience, O'Neill speaks of the "necessary recognition of the claims of that anonymous labor in the history of man's senses and intellect which have left us a world with any vision of human solidarity"; remembrance, he adds (pp. 4–5), "is the womb of freedom and justice and must be cultivated long before men are able to name their slavery within the discourse of rational freedom and consensus."

Compared with a rootless rationalism, Gadamer's outlook clearly proves itself superior to his detractors. However, the question remains whether his argument makes sufficient room or provides criteria for critique, that is, for the differentiation between prejudgments and corrigible prejudices, or between legitimate authority and repression. Unfortunately, Misgeld's essay does not explore this question; his valid argument that judgment always arises in a "tradition-context" does not indicate how this context can generate the basis for critique. O'Neill's advice to critical theory to concentrate on the development of descriptive accounts of action-contexts (or tradition-contexts) also does not seem helpful on this score. Critical theorists, he writes (p. 10), "must commit themselves to the ordinary work of a social science that will deliver competent ethnographies of the practical exigencies of daily living in the modern world," before climbing "once more the ascending heights of theory." As it seems to me, Gadamer himself has been reluctant to spell out criteria for the mentioned differentiation. Wary of the manipulative dangers of a transhistorical tribunal of reason, he has tended to stress the patient exegesis of varying cultural situations. Yet, one may ask, does the elaboration of critical standards necessarily presuppose a transhistorical or extramundane vantage point? Does history, in its successive epochs, not itself testify to the continuing human effort not only to develop descriptive accounts but to differentiate in a normative sense between regimes and life-forms? Differently phrased: do ordinary life-contexts—the "practical exigencies of daily living"— not themselves contain clues for such a differentiation?

Perhaps, in order to clarify somewhat the meaning of tradition-contexts (or life-contexts), it is desirable to take a closer look at the main thrust of the hermeneutical project. Reference has already been made to Gadamer's rejection of the model of self-reflection deriving from Descartes. As Misgeld correctly observes, this rejection is part of a more comprehensive attack on the modern concern with subjectivity. "Gadamer," he states (p. 166), "pursues a critique of the epistemological subject's role in historical understanding which shows how the subject, even if he is armed with the methods of science, is not able to extricate himself from the very traditions which he attempts to study."

Disenchantment with subjectivity entails that hermeneutics does not focus exclusively on subjective intentions or conscious human designs; rather, "subjective meaning-intentions, which we can explicitly ascertain as our own and objectify, only describe a limited range of those meanings, in which we *participate*" (p. 174). The ontological quality of hermeneutics derives in large measure from its deemphasis of intentionality. In Gadamer's view, the effort to come to terms with the world requires a basic human openness: a willingness to expose oneself to unfamiliar and unsettling life-forms and experiences. The main concern of hermeneutics, *Truth and Method* affirms, is "not what we do or what we ought to do, but what happens to us, over and above our wanting and doing" (p. 173). Concentrating on the subject's vulnerability in historical encounters, Misgeld comments (p. 170): "We may learn to risk our preunderstandings and prejudgments in acquiring an openness for new experience in which we experience ourselves as transformed and changed."

Given the injunction against self-enclosure one might assume hermeneutics to be particularly sympathetic to efforts to overcome individual or social prejudices or misjudgments and to modify habitual action patterns. Rigorously pursued, should the transcendence of subjectivity not pave the way to the domain of non-understanding and non-intentionality and even to the Kantian limit-concept of the thing-in-itself—a dimension providing a (restricted) warrant for "objective," non-hermeneutical analysis? Similarly, would willingness to risk oneself not also imply a readiness to expose propositions and action standards to intersubjective and cross-cultural scrutiny and validation? Yet, hermeneutics on the whole has tended to shy away from such ventures. Akin in this respect to existentialism (and to some of Marcuse's arguments), its ontological or anti-Cartesian turn has meant primarily the abandonment of cognitive subjectivity and a focus on evolving life-contexts as experienced by concrete-historical or embodied subjects. The role of subjective experience can readily be detected in *Truth and Method;* thus, opposing the scientific treatment of history, Gadamer comments (pp. 179–80): "We always stand within tradition—and this is no objectifying process, i.e., we do not conceive of what tradition says as something other, something alien. It is always part of us." It seems to me that hermeneutics in its ambivalence toward subjectivity reveals its intellectual origins or sources of inspiration. Misgeld correctly pinpoints this legacy when he writes (p. 169) that hermeneutics is "heir to the late Husserl's and the early Heidegger's phenomenology." As is well known, Husserl in his later years was chiefly preoccupied with the concrete life-world forming the matrix of subjective experience and reflection. On the other hand, presented as a hermeneutical phenomenology, Heidegger's *Being and Time* still showed traces of subjective-intentional inquiry—although, in my view, the study's central focus on the question of Being radically altered the direction and significance of this inquiry. (The same focus, I would add, ultimately also militates against a purely descriptive hermeneutics: in distinguishing between authentic and inauthentic modes of existence *Being and Time* does not merely juxtapose different historical life-contexts or subjective experiences, but erects a qualitative contrast between forms of life predicated on attentiveness to the question of Being.)

The unresolved status of subjectivity colors the hermeneutical treatment of life-contexts or "tradition-contexts"; betraying the continued influence of the Cartesian subject-object bifurcation, these contexts appear either as subjective-intentional experiences or else as environments conditioning such experiences. Misgeld's essay amply testifies to this ambivalence. In several passages tradition is described as an *authority* circumscribing human intentions. Responsiveness to tradition, he writes, "may imply a recognition not only of what one cannot change, but even more an insight into what one ought not to attempt to change" (p. 173). Referring to basic *orders* of human life he notes somewhat later (p. 177) that "the more fundamental the orders referred to are, the less it seems they can be intended, and the more they assert themselves on their own accord, with a power of persuasion which cannot be broken by reflection." At the same time, the essay stresses the experiential basis of history and tradition. Each varying life-context, we read (p. 174), "be it a 'form of life,' an institution, a social role, or a tradition," we can "know about somehow," but we cannot give an "objective account" of it "of a kind that would not require or even *a limine* forbid the use of personal pronouns." Given its character as "our" context, tradition cannot be approached from an external (or third-person) perspective or from a vantage point transgressing interpretive understanding. In Misgeld's words (p. 175): "We cannot objectify or transcend the tradition-context of language toward, e.g., the material conditions of factual history, as if we could look at language as a tradition-context from outside it."

Habermas' critique capitalizes on the noted ambivalence of the hermeneutical project. In challenging its universality claim, he attacks hermeneutics basically on two levels: as a descriptive account (and conservative defense) of factually given traditions, and simultaneously as an idealist treatment of history preoccupied solely with its intentional and intelligible dimension. While Misgeld seems mainly concerned with the first charge—objecting particularly to the "mobilization of political invective" (p. 167)—Wellmer elaborates at some length on the second point. "According to Habermas," he writes (p. 254), "the idealism of the hermeneutic position consists in the fact that it itself is the expression of an inadmissible *idealization,* namely, the idealization that the linguistic organization of social relations and of the motivational base of social interaction has attained a state of 'perfection.' " As he adds, the idealist view of linguistic organization implies chiefly the assumption of a complete "consistency and comprehensibility" of communication patterns in historical life-contexts. Such an assumption renders difficult if not impossible the distinction between meaning and non-meaning, and between genuine understanding and distorted or false types of consciousness. "The linguistic organization of social reality," Wellmer observes (pp. 256–57), "is by no means incompatible with an opposition between this reality and its ideological self-presentations. It is precisely because of the internal relationship which every society has to the idea of truth that social science can question the self-interpretation of groups and individuals and exhibit the delusion as well as the 'rational' function of false consciousness: ideology as rationalization (in the Freudian sense)." The attack on idealization, one should note, does not signify a rejection of hermeneutics itself, but only of its universality claim. "Hermeneutic analysis," he continues, "is necessary because any historical reality is intrinsically meaningful, and the objectifying methods of causal and functional analysis are necessary because the meaning of history still crystallizes behind the back of individuals who make it. Historical materialism, correctly understood, is only the elaboration of this truth."

While it captures the limits of an intentional hermeneutics, the preceding statement also points to a further convergence of the two protagonists of the debate. Construed as the interpretation of subjective meaning, hermeneutics ineluctably seems to call for the "objectifying methods of causal and functional analysis" as its supplement and corrective. In Habermas' writings, hermeneutical inquiry and communicative understanding almost invariably refer to a context of subjective (or intersubjective) meaning and purpose; as an antidote to this intentional focus recourse is typically taken to empirical-analytical science as typified by such approaches as systems theory or structural analysis (including the structural aspects of psychoanalysis). As can readily be seen, what surfaces behind this distinction—and even behind the precarious linkage of science and hermeneutics in "critical social inquiry"—is the Cartesian bifurcation of thought and matter, a bifurcation which also was seen to be operative in Gadamer's argument and which ultimately is rooted in the premise of subjectivity. Actually, the legacy asserts itself more forcefully in Habermas' work than in the confines of philosophical hermeneutics. Whereas Gadamer's ontological leanings entail at least a tentative transgression of intentionality, Habermas' outlook—as portrayed especially in more recent writings—reflects a growing fondness for a quasi-Cartesian or quasi-Kantian (though linguistically revised) rationalism. This trend is noticeable, I think, in his "reconstructionist" efforts, in particular in the reconstruction of dialectical materialism as a theory of social evolution patterned after psychological theories of cognitive and moral development with their emphasis on the growth of rational-analytical capacities. The same trend can also be detected in his "discursive theory of truth," a conception which tends to divorce rational discourse entirely from the context of practical experience, despite the concession that some requisites of *ideal speech* (especially truthfulness) cannot be ascertained apart from the domain of practice.

Habermas' rationalist proclivity has been noted by friends and critics alike. Pointing to the genetic reconstruction of individual or social development, Wellmer finds troublesome the adoption of a strictly external or metatheoretical perspective. "As far as the genetic explanations *also* have the meaning of a rational reconstruction of the implicit knowledge of the adult," he writes (pp. 260–61), "they themselves assume epistemological meaning: they become fragments of an empirical phenomenology of mind. If this is true, however, the theoretical explanation and the genetic reconstruction of the implicit knowledge of the adult can no longer be considered as being in the relationship of metatheory and theory with each other." Misgeld expresses a similar preoccupation, couching it in terms of the relationship between theory and practice (pp. 182–83): "Habermas' problems arise because he aims at an all-inclusive theory of the contemporary age. Yet he also wants to retain a linkage with praxis, which he himself understands as not capable of being fully guided by a theory." As he concludes: "Reflection transcending tradition will either have to learn to appraise itself as involved in the formation of tradition or forego the possibility of becoming practical." In O'Neill's paper (pp. 8–9), concern with the "formation of tradition" or an "empirical phenomenology of mind" is translated into the idiom of "pedagogic practice," particularly of a "pedagogy of the oppressed." Apprehensive that "communicative competence" may remain "the one-sided talent of party theorists and organizers" and insisting that socialism "works only with men and not upon men," O'Neill stresses the need for reciprocal learning between theorists and workers, a reciprocity governed by mutual care. "The pragmatics of communicative competence," he writes (correctly and eloquently in my view), "belong to a larger critical theory of socialist education which is broader than either the cognitive theory of proletarian consciousness or a linguistic approach to the critique of ideology. Socialist education cannot succeed except where men *love* the world and the society of men."

NOTES

INTRODUCTION

1. José Ortega y Gasset, *What is Philosophy?* (New York: W. W. Norton, 1960), pp. 149–50. Ortega himself did not indulge in this illusion, but preferred to move in the opposite direction. "On the contrary," he added, referring to subjectivity, "we must set ourselves within it, understand it and completely dominate it. Otherwise we could not even try to overcome it." (I am indebted to Marvin Zetterbaum for alerting me to this passage.)

2. Élie Halévy, *The Growth of Philosophic Radicalism,* trans. Mary Morris (first published 1901–04; new ed., Boston: Beacon Press, 1955), p. 504. A similar thrust is evident in Lindsay's observation that "all modern political theory, except the theory of Bolshevism and of Fascism, is . . . individualistic in that it seeks to find room for and encourage the individual moral judgement and is based on toleration and the maintenance of a system of rights. Most of the differences between modern individualism, strictly so-called, and socialism are differences within these common assumptions." See A. D. Lindsay, "Individualism," in *Encyclopedia of the Social Sciences,* vol. 7 (New York: Macmillan, 1935), p. 677.

3. Steven Lukes, *Individualism* (New York: Harper and Row, 1973), pp. 73, 125, 138–39, 145–46, 148. Regarding epistemological individualism he writes (p. 107): "Descartes' thought began from this position, from the individual's certainty of his own existence—*cogito ergo sum*—from which he derived knowledge of the external world and the past via the transcendental route of assuming God's veracity; Malebranche took a similar course. . . . Kant saw the categories as innate in the (abstract) *individual.* But the paradigm epistemological individualist is perhaps the empiricist, who holds that (individual) experience is the source of knowledge, that all knowledge arises within the circle of the individual mind and the sensations it receives."

4. In this sense I find little difficulty in endorsing (at least in good part) Lukes' statement (ibid., p. 153) referring to the chief gains of "abstract" individualism, formal equality and formal freedom: "These are crucial and indispensable gains but, if we are to take equality and liberty seriously, they must be transcended. And that can only be achieved on the basis of a view of un-abstracted individuals in their concrete, social speci-

ficity who, in virtue of being *persons,* all require to be treated and to live in a social order which treats them as possessing dignity, as capable of exercising and increasing their autonomy, of engaging in valued activities within a private space, and of developing their several potentialities."

5. See Martin Heidegger, "Überwindung der Metaphysik," in *Vorträge und Aufsätze,* Part I, 3rd ed. (Pfullingen: Neske, 1967), pp. 64, 70. The terms *difference and reciprocal envelopment* are an admittedly awkward rendering of the complex Heideggerian notion of *Zwiefalt.*

6. See Jacques Derrida, *Writing and Difference,* trans. Alan Bass (Chicago: University of Chicago Press, 1978), p. 284. "What I want to emphasize," he adds (p. 288), "is simply that to go 'beyond' philosophy cannot mean to turn one's back to it (which usually leads to bad philosophy), but rather to continue reading philosophers *in a certain way."* For Adorno's argument compare his *Negative Dialektik* (Frankfurt-Main: Suhrkamp, 1966), p. 19.

7. Given the comprehensiveness and complexity of Heidegger's writings (and the limits of my understanding) I can only offer some glimpses of his thought. With regard to the meaning of individualism and post-individualism his previously cited essay, for example, contains many helpful guideposts which would deserve further scrutiny. Thus, examining the relationship between metaphysics and human nature he writes: "Metaphysics belongs to the nature of man. But what is nature itself, and what is metaphysics? Who, within the purview of this natural metaphysics, is man? Is he simply an I that, by appealing to a Thou, is further solidified in his ego-character, manifest in the I-thou relationship. . . . This (ego-character) is present even where the single I does not protrude but rather recedes to make room for 'society' or other (intersubjective) aggregates; even and especially in this case, the strict dominion of 'egotism' in the metaphysical sense holds sway (which has nothing to do with a naïvely construed 'solipsism'). Philosophy in the age of fully developed metaphysics is anthropology." See "Überwindung der Metaphysik," pp. 66, 78.

8. *Writing and Difference,* p. 145. Derrida's comments were written in response to the Heidegger critique formulated by Emmanuel Levinas; it seems to me, however, that his rejoinder to Levinas is applicable in large measure also to Adorno's arguments. With regard to the epistemological issue compare my "Genesis and Validation of Social Knowledge: Lessons from Merleau-Ponty," in Joseph Bien, ed., *Phenomenology and Social Science* (The Hague: Nijhoff, 1978), pp. 74–106, also "Marxism and Truth," *Telos,* No. 29 (Fall, 1976), pp. 130–59; concerning the relationship between Adorno and Heidegger see "Phenomenology and Critical Theory: Adorno," *Cultural Hermeneutics,* vol. 3 (1976), pp. 367–405.

CHAPTER ONE

1. In the words of Élie Halévy: "Individualism is the common characteristic of Roman law and Christian morality. It is individualism which creates the

likeness between the philosophies, in other respects so different, of Rousseau, Kant, and Bentham." See *The Growth of Philosophic Radicalism,* trans. Mary Morris (Boston: Beacon Press, 1955), p. 504. For a survey of the semantic history of individualism in major Western countries compare Steven Lukes, *Individualism* (New York: Harper and Row, 1973), pp. 1–42.

2. Max Horkheimer, *Zur Kritik der instrumentellen Vernunft* (Frankfurt-Main: Fischer Verlag, 1967), p. 94. "The history of human efforts to subjugate nature," he added (p. 104), "is also the story of man's subjugation by man. The development of the ego reflects this dual history." Concerning Bacon's notion of science compare especially William Leiss, *The Domination of Nature* (Boston: Beacon Press, 1974), pp. 45–71.

3. See C. B. Macpherson, *The Political Thought of Possessive Individualism: Hobbes to Locke* (Oxford: Clarendon Press, 1962), pp. 1, 3, 272–73; for a fuller statement of the assumptions implicit in *possessive individualism* see pp. 263–64. As one should note, the general-human aspirations of early liberalism did not cancel its possessivism nor the (latent) linkage between possessivism and domination.

4. Robert Nozick, *Anarchy, State, and Utopia* (New York: Basic Books, 1974), p. 160.

5. Ibid., pp. 51–53. For the defense of survival needs see Ayn Rand, *The Virtue of Selfishness* (New York: New American Library, 1964), and for Nozick's critique of this position see *Anarchy, State, and Utopia,* p. 179, note.

6. Nozick, *Anarchy, State, and Utopia,* pp. 33–34.

7. Separateness of existence and interests may lead plausibly to a Hobbesian "war of all against all," unless complete mutual isolation is assumed. In this condition there is no *mutually* binding prohibition against aggression, although everyone can be expected to defend himself against attack.

8. Ibid., pp. 48–50.

9. Ibid., p. 51.

10. Compare Karl-Otto Apel, "Das Apriori der Kommunikationsgemeinschaft und die Grundlagen der Ethik," in Apel, *Transformation der Philosophie* (Frankfurt-Main: Suhrkamp, 1973), vol. 2, pp. 359–435. For a discussion of some aspects of Apel's ethical (or metaethical) position see the section on transcendental pragmatics in chapter 5; also my "Toward a Critical Reconstruction of Ethics and Politics," *Journal of Politics,* vol. 36 (1974), pp. 926–57.

11. As he writes at one point: "So the fact that we partially are 'social products' in that we benefit from current patterns and forms created by the multitudinous actions of a long string of long-forgotten people, forms which include institutions, ways of doing things, and language (whose social nature may involve our current use depending upon Wittgensteinian matching of the speech of others), does not create in us a general floating debt which the current society can collect and use as it will." See Nozick, *Anarchy, State, and Utopia,* p. 95.

12. Actually, two stages of this process are differentiated. The emergence of the *ultraminimal state* in which a protective agency acquires monopoly over the use of force is said to be completely automatic. A complication arises with the transition to the *minimal state* in which the dominant protective agency grants protection to all individuals living in a given territory. As Nozick realizes, the actual behavior of the agency at this point may diverge from its morally required behavior; in his view, however, the difficulty does not affect the non-intentional character of the entire process: "We should note that even in the event that no nonmoral incentives or causes are found to be sufficient for the transition from an ultraminimal to a minimal state, and the explanation continues to lean heavily upon people's moral motivations, it does not specify people's objective as that of establishing a state. Instead, persons view themselves as providing particular other persons with compensation for particular prohibitions they have imposed upon them. The explanation remains an invisible-hand one." Ibid., p. 119.

13. "Why must differences between persons be justified?" he queries, adding: "We have found no cogent argument to (help) establish that differences in holdings arising from differences in natural assets should be eliminated or minimized." Ibid., pp. 50, 223, 226.

14. "As it stands," he writes, "there is no reflection of entitlement considerations in any form in the situation of those in the original position; these considerations do not enter even to be overridden or outweighed or otherwise put aside." For a moment Nozick even seems aware that this circumstance casts the shadow of bias over his approach: "Since to specially tailor principles is to tailor them *unfairly* for one's own advantage, and since the question of the fairness of the entitlement principle is precisely the issue, it is difficult to decide which begs the question: my criticism of the strength of the veil of ignorance, or the defence against this criticism which I imagine in this note." See ibid., pp. 203, note, and 204. Compare also John Rawls, *A Theory of Justice* (Cambridge, Mass.: Harvard University Press, 1971), pp. 12–15.

15. Jean-Paul Sartre, "Existentialism is a Humanism" (1946), trans. Philip Mairet, in Walter Kaufmann, *Existentialism from Dostoevsky to Sartre* (Cleveland: Meridian Books, 1956), pp. 287, 289–91. As Sartre adds (p. 291), the notion that "man primarily exists" signifies "that man is, before all else, something which propels itself towards a future and is aware that it is doing so. Man is, indeed, a project which possesses a subjective life, instead of being a king of moss, or a fungus or a cauliflower. Before the projection of the self nothing exists, not even in the heaven of intelligence: man will only attain existence when he is what he purposes to be."

16. Ibid., p. 302.

17. Ibid., pp. 291–92.

18. Ibid., pp. 288, 303. In Sartre's words (p. 303), the *limitations* of the hu-

cause we meet with them everywhere and they are everywhere recognizable; and subjective because they are *lived* and are nothing if man does not live them—if, that is to say, he does not freely determine himself and his existence in relation to them." In another context, Sartre defines the relationship between man and world in terms of the antithesis between for-itself and in-itself, an antithesis incapable of being reconciled in the (Hegelian) synthesis of the in-and-for-itself; see Jean-Paul Sartre, *Being and Nothingness, An Essay on Phenomenological Ontology,* trans. Hazel E. Barnes (New York: Philosophical Library, 1956), esp. pp. 617–25.

19. "Existentialism is a Humanism," p. 303. Regarding the topic of intersubjectivity compare Sartre, *Being and Nothingness,* pp. 221–430 (being-for-others), and the section on French phenomenology in chapter 2.

20. "Existentialism is a Humanism," pp. 291, 310. The self-possessive quality of the *cogito* emerges also from Sartre's comments on the *two senses* of subjectivism (p. 291): "Subjectivism means, on the one hand, the freedom of the individual subject and, on the other, that man cannot pass beyond human subjectivity. It is the latter which is the deeper meaning of existentialism." For a later reformulation of the significance of existentialism (a reformulation still focusing on intentional human *projects*) see the chapter on "Marxism and Existentialism" in Jean-Paul Sartre, *Search for a Method,* trans. Hazel E. Barnes (New York: Knopf, 1963), pp. 3–34.

21. See Eric Voegelin, *Order and History,* vol. 4: *The Ecumenic Age* (Baton Rouge: Louisiana State University Press, 1974), pp. 260–63, 269. For a sustained critique of the role of subjectivity in Husserl's thought compare also the essays "On the Theory of Consciousness," in Voegelin, *Anamnesis,* trans. and ed. Gerhart Niemeyer (Notre Dame: University of Notre Dame Press, 1978), pp. 14–35, and "Brief an Alfred Schütz über Edmund Husserl," in *Anamnesis: Zur Theorie der Geschichte und Politik* (Munich: Piper, 1966), pp. 21–36. Despite the critique of subjectivity, one should note, Voegelin maintains the central position of philosophical anthropology and especially the primacy of man over society and history within the *realm of man;* see "About the Function of Noesis," in *Anamnesis,* pp. 208–9.

22. See Niklas Luhmann, "Systemtheoretische Argumentationen: Eine Entgegnung auf Jürgen Habermas," in Habermas and Luhmann, *Theorie der Gesellschaft oder Sozialtechnologie—Was leistet die Systemforschung?* (Frankfurt: Suhrkamp, 1971), pp. 317, 322–23, 327. Systemic processes and decisions, incidentally, do not necessarily imply or entail human responsibility. "The universality of systems theory," we read (p. 325), "can be maintained only if one concedes the existence of social systems which—though composed of interactions—are not the locus of responsibility for their behavior."

23. Louis Althusser, *Lenin and Philosophy, and Other Essays,* trans. Ben Brewster (New York: Monthly Review Press, 1971), pp. 218–19. Compare also his comments in another context (p. 195, note) that "Marx

based his theory on the rejection of the myth of the *'homo oeconomicus,'* Freud based his theory on the rejection of the myth of *'homo psycho-logicus.'* "

24. Ibid., pp. 167, 170–71, 173, 176.
25. Ibid., pp. 120–23. Compare also his statement in Louis Althusser and Étienne Balibar, *Reading Capital,* trans. Ben Brewster (London: Unwin Bros., 1977), p. 25: "It is literally no longer the eye (the mind's eye) of a subject which *sees* what exists in the field defined by a theoretical problematic: it is this field itself which *sees itself* in the objects or problems it defines."
26. Michel Foucault, *The Order of Things: An Archaeology of the Human Sciences* (first French ed., 1966; New York: Vintage Books, 1973), pp. 374–75, 378, 381.
27. Ibid., pp. 379, 382–83.
28. Ibid., p. 385. Compare also his comments in another context: "To awaken us from the confused sleep of (Hegelian) dialectics and of (philosophical) anthropology, we required the Nietzschean figures of tragedy, of Dionysus, of the death of God, of the philosopher's hammer, of the Overman approaching with the steps of a dove, of the Return. . . . The breakdown of philosophical subjectivity and its dispersion in a language that dispossesses it while multiplying it within the space created by its absence is probably one of the fundamental structures of contemporary thought." See Michel Foucault, *Language, Counter-Memory, Practice: Selected Essays and Interviews,* trans. Donald F. Bouchard and Sherry Simon (Oxford: Basil Blackwell, 1977), pp. 38, 42.
29. Jacques Derrida, "Les fins de l'homme" (1968), in his *Marges de la Philosophie* (Paris: Editions de Minuit, 1972), p. 144. (An English version of the essay under the title "The Ends of Man" appeared in *Philosophy and Phenomenological Research,* vol. 30 [1969], pp. 31–57.)
30. *Marges de la Philosophie,* pp. 136–37. To some extent, Derrida found traces of metaphysical humanism not only in French existentialism but also in the work of Hegel, Husserl, and Heidegger.
31. Ibid., pp. 162–63.
32. Derrida fully recognizes this danger when he writes that the stress on discontinuity may conceal the attempt "to take refuge more naively and more directly in human internality which one claims to have left behind." Ibid., p. 162. The above comments on anti-humanism, incidentally, are aimed chiefly at its more doctrinaire versions; to some extent its differentiation from non-possessivism may be more strategic than substantive in character. Compare in this respect also Derrida's statements in another context: "Our discourse irreducibly belongs to the system of metaphysical oppositions. The break with this attachment can be announced only through a *certain* organization, a certain *strategic* arrangement which, within the field of metaphysical opposition, uses the strengths of that field to turn its own stratagems against it." See his *Writing and Difference,* trans. Alan Bass (Chicago: University of Chicago Press, 1978), p. 20.

33. See Martin Heidegger, *Sein und Zeit,* 11th ed. (Tübingen: Niemeyer, 1967), paragraphs 41 and 64, pp. 191–200, 316–23.

34. Martin Heidegger, *Über den Humanismus* (Frankfurt: Klostermann, 1949), p. 35. The term *existence,* Heidegger observed, (p. 17), "does not denote the implementation of an essence, nor does it designate the cause or constitutive origin of essence. Construed as theoretical constitution, the term 'project' used in *Being and Time* is treated as the accomplishment of a subjectivity"—and thus submerged in metaphysical categories. Pointing to the tenet of traditional metaphysics according to which essence precedes existence, he added: "Sartre reverses this tenet; but the reversal of a metaphysical proposition remains a metaphysical proposition."

35. Ibid., pp. 35–36. Noting the tendency to retreat into subjective privacy as a refuge from the anonymity and reification of public life, the *Letter* states at another point (p. 8): "So-called 'private existence' does not yet coincide with genuine, that is, autonomous human life; it merely insists obstinately on the negation of the public domain. Thus, privacy remains a dependent offshoot, sustaining itself through the mere retreat from society; involuntarily it testifies to its subjection to public opinion. The latter, in turn, involves the stabilization and sanctioning of overt, ontic reality to the point of the complete reification of everything—a process engendered by metaphysics or the rule of subjectivity."

36. Ibid., pp. 29, 31, 37–38.

37. Compare Martin Heidegger, "Das Ding," in *Vorträge und Aufsätze,* Part II, 3rd ed. (Pfullingen: Neske, 1967), pp. 152–78. Against this background one has to treat warily Ricoeur's claim that Heidegger substitutes a "hermeneutics of the 'I am'" for the traditional principle of the *cogito;* at least to the extent that the phrase "I am" suggests a solid or self-contained *I* or *ego,* the claim is misleading. See Paul Ricoeur, "The Critique of Subjectivity and Cogito in the Philosophy of Heidegger," in Manfred S. Frings, ed., *Heidegger and the Quest for Truth* (Chicago: Quadrangle Books, 1968), pp. 62–75.

38. As the study added, it was important to recognize "consciousness itself as a project of the world, meant for a world which it neither embraces nor possesses, but towards which it is perpetually directed—and the world as this pre-objective individual whose impervious unity decrees what knowledge shall take as its goal." See Maurice Merleau-Ponty, *Phenomenology of Perception,* trans. Colin Smith (New York: Humanities Press, 1962), pp. xi, xvii–xviii; also "The Battle over Existentialism" (1945), in Merleau-Ponty, *Sense and Non-Sense,* trans. Hubert L. and Patricia A. Dreyfus (Evanston: Northwestern University Press, 1964), pp. 72, 79–80.

39. Maurice Merleau-Ponty, *The Visible and the Invisible,* trans. Alfonso Lingis (Evanston: Northwestern University Press, 1968), pp. 23, 35, 130–31.

40. Ibid., pp. 131, 143, 159. The "Working Notes" attached to the study (p. 201) speak of "the *self* of perception as 'nobody,' in the sense of Ulysses, as the anonymous one buried in the world, and that has not yet traced

its path. Perception as imperception, evidence in non-possession: it is precisely because one knows too well what one is dealing with that one has no need to posit it as an ob-ject."

41. Ibid., pp. 134–35, 159–60.

42. Theodor W. Adorno, *Negative Dialektik* (Frankfurt: Suhrkamp Verlag, 1966), pp. 131, 141, 179, 185, 189–90, 382. With specific application to individualism Adorno adds (p. 272): "Subjectivity is falsehood since—for the sake of absolute mastery—it conceals the objective preconditions of its rule; individuality could emerge only from the rejection of this falsehood, from an effort—born out of the strength of self-identity—to discard the armor of subjectivity." Concerning the role of the subject in Adorno's earlier writings see Susan Buck-Morss, *The Origin of Negative Dialectics* (New York: Free Press, 1977), pp. 82–95. For additional literature on the issues raised in the present chapter see Michael Landmann, *Das Ende des Individuums: Anthropologische Skizzen* (Stuttgart: Klett Verlag, 1971); Jürgen Habermas, "The End of the Individual?" in his *Legitimation Crisis,* trans. Thomas A. McCarthy (Boston: Beacon Press, 1975), pp. 117–30; Paul Ricoeur, "The Question of the Subject: The Challenge of Semiology," in his *The Conflict of Interpretations: Essays in Hermeneutics,* ed. Don Ihde (Evanston, Ill.: Northwestern University Press, 1974), pp. 236–66; Anthony Giddens, "Structuralism and the Theory of the Subject," in his *Central Problems in Social Theory: Action, Structure and Contradiction in Social Analysis* (Berkeley: University of California Press, 1979), pp. 9–48; and Reiner Schürmann, "Anti-Humanism: Reflections on the Turn Towards the Post-Modern Epoch," *Man and World,* vol. 12 (1979), pp. 160–77.

CHAPTER TWO

Introductory paragraphs

1. Compare in this context Ortega's comments: "I shall never forget the surprise mingled with shame and shock which I felt when, many years ago, conscious of my ignorance on this subject I hurried, full of illusion, all the sails of hope spread wide, to books on sociology . . . and found something incredible—namely, that books on sociology have nothing clear to say about what the social is, about what society is." See José Ortega y Gasset, *Man and People* (New York: Norton, 1957), p. 13.

2. In this respect Ortega writes correctly: "One of the greatest misfortunes of our time is the acute incongruity between the importance that all these questions have at present and the crudeness and confusion of the concepts of them which these words represent." Ibid., p. 12.

Husserl and Heidegger

1. Jacques Derrida, *Writing and Difference*, trans. Alan Bass (Chicago: University of Chicago Press, 1978), p. 31. As he adds: "The archaeology to which Husserl and Heidegger lead us by different paths entails, for both, a subordination or transgression or in any case a *reduction of metaphysics*— even though, for each, this gesture has (at least apparently) an entirely different meaning." (Translation slightly altered.)

2. Edmund Husserl, *Formal and Transcendental Logic*, trans. Dorion Cairns (first German ed., 1929; The Hague: Nijhoff, 1969), paragraph 95, p. 237 (translation slightly altered).

3. Edmund Husserl, *The Crisis of European Sciences and Transcendental Phenomenology: An Introduction to Phenomenological Philosophy*, trans. David Carr (Evanston, Ill.: Northwestern University Press, 1970), pp. 184, 186 (translation slightly altered).

4. Apart from his major works (mentioned subsequently), Husserl's intensive preoccupation with the theme is reflected in the voluminous working papers and fragments written between 1905 and 1935 which have been published posthumously: Edmund Husserl, *Zur Phänomenologie der Intersubjektivität: Texte aus dem Nachlass*, 3 vols., ed. Iso Kern (Husserliana Volumes XIII–XV; The Hague: Nijhoff, 1973).

5. Edmund Husserl, *Ideas: General Introduction to Pure Phenomenology*, trans. W. R. Boyce Gibson (London: George Allen and Unwin, 1931), paragraphs 28, 29, 53, 135. Husserl's conception of empathy was deeply indebted to the leading study of the time devoted to this topic: Theodor Lipps' *Zur Einfühlung* (Leipzig: Engelmann, 1913).

6. Edmund Husserl, *Ideen zu einer reinen Phänomenologie und phänomenologischen Philosophie*, vol. 2: *Phänomenologische Untersuchungen zur Konstitution*, ed. Marty Biemel (Husserliana Volume IV; The Hague: Nijhoff, 1952), paragraphs 12, 19–21, 34, 43–47, 49–51 (especially pp. 190–200). For an instructive review of the study compare Alfred Schutz, "Edmund Husserl's Ideas, Volume II," in Schutz, *Collected Papers*, vol. 3, ed. Ilse Schutz (The Hague: Nijhoff, 1966), pp. 15–39.

7. See Edmund Husserl, *Erste Philosophie* (1923–24); Second Part: *Theorie der phänomenologischen Reduktion*, ed. Rudolf Boehm (Husserliana Volume VIII; The Hague: Nijhoff, 1959), p. 59; also his *Formal and Transcendental Logic*, paragraphs 95 and 96, pp. 237–44.

8. Edmund Husserl, *Cartesian Meditations: An Introduction to Phenomenology*, trans. Dorion Cairns (The Hague: Nijhoff, 1973), esp. paragraphs 44, 49–56. For a brief summary of the Fifth Meditation compare Marvin Farber, *The Foundation of Phenomenology* (Cambridge: University Press, 1943), pp. 528–36; also Alfred Schutz, "Phenomenology and the Social Sciences," pp. 124–26, and "Sartre's Theory of the Alter Ego," pp. 195–96, both in his *Collected Papers*, vol. 1, ed. Maurice Natanson (The Hague: Nijhoff, 1967).

9. Husserl, *The Crisis of European Sciences,* pp. 172, 255, 258, 340 (translation slightly changed); also *Die Krisis der europäischen Wissenschaften und die Transzendentale Phänomenologie,* ed. Walter Biemel (Husserliana Volume VI; The Hague: Nijhoff, 1976), p. 416.

10. Husserl, *The Crisis of European Sciences,* pp. 103, 108, 111, 142–44. At another point (p. 292) Husserl observes: "Natural man (let us consider him as man in the pre-philosophical period) is directed toward the world in all his concerns and activities. The field of his life and his work is the surrounding world spread out spatiotemporally around him, of which he counts himself a part." These statements suggest that the relationship between life-world and reflection involves a teleology leading from unreflective to reflective subjectivity, from imperfect to perfect insight (with the life-world functioning merely as a preamble to knowledge). Several other passages corroborate this view. "Objective science," one reads ((pp. 110–11), "presupposes the being of this world, but it sets itself the task of transposing knowledge which is imperfect and prescientific in respect of scope and constancy into perfect knowledge. . . . To realize this in a systematic progress, in stages of perfection, through a method which makes possible a constant advance: this is the task."

11. Ortega was not the first to translate Husserl's chiefly cognitive outlook into a more concrete, experiential vocabulary. Some three decades earlier, Max Scheler—Husserl's contemporary and an early pioneer of phenomenological sociology—had endeavored to cast egology in the mold of a philosophical anthropology culminating in the *person* or human *personality* conceived as center of transcendental acts. In a free adaptation of Husserlian teachings his anthropology distinguished between two main levels of experience: a mundane or *vitalistic* level governed by human instinct and an essentially transcendental or *spiritual* level inhabited by personality. Compare especially his *Wesen und Formen der Sympathie* (Bonn: Verlag F. Cohen, 1923), and *Die Wissensformen und die Gesellschaft* (Leipzig: Neue Geist-Verlag, 1926).

12. José Ortega y Gasset, *Man and People* (New York: Norton, 1957), pp. 38–39, 46, 51, 73, 89–92, 95. Compare also his statements (pp. 118, 120): "When, among minerals, plants, and animals, a being appears to me consisting in a certain corporeal form that I call human—even though only that corporeal form is *present* to me, something that is invisible in itself and, more generally still, imperceptible becomes *com-present* to me in it, namely, a human life, something, then, that is similar to what I am, since I am nothing but a 'human life'. . . . This world of the Other is unattainable to me, inaccessible, if we are to speak strictly. . . . Here is the immense paradox: that, with the being of others, there appear in my world worlds alien to me as such, worlds that present themselves to me as unpresentable, that are accessible to me as inaccessible, that become patent as essentially latent."

13. *Ibid.,* pp. 122–25. In human interaction the contrast is obvious particularly

when the body of the Other is that of a female, since—as Ortega notes (pp. 127–28)—"the transposition of my ego, which is irremediably masculine, into a woman's body could only produce an extreme case of a virago."

14. Ibid., p. 127.

15. Ibid., pp. 106, 109. According to Ortega, human interaction on this level is predicated not so much on appresentation, but rather on an exchange of signals and expressive gestures. Regarding the sense of these signals he assumes (with Scheler) the possibility of immediate understanding (p. 126): "The expression that is sorrow or irritation or melancholy, I did not discover in myself but *primarily* in the Other and it at once signified inwardness to me—grief, annoyance, melancholy."

16. Ibid., pp. 97 99, 140, 144, 174–75, 221. Countering communitarian visions Ortega adds (p. 174): "This idea of the *collective soul,* of a *social consciousness,* is arbitrary mysticism."

17. Alfred Schutz, "Das Problem der transzendentalen Intersubjektivität bei Husserl," *Philosophische Rundschau,* vol. 5 (1957), pp. 81–107, translated under the title "The Problem of Transcendental Intersubjectivity in Husserl," in *Collected Papers,* vol. 3, pp. 51–84.

18. Schutz, *Collected Papers,* vol. 3, pp. 59, 63, 65, 69, 73. Similar criticisms were contained in Schutz's earlier review of *Ideas,* "Edmund Husserl's Ideas, Volume II" (1953), ibid., esp. pp. 36–39. Compare in particular the comment (p. 38): "The communicative environment, basic for all constitution of the intersubjective world, originates, according to Husserl, in relationships of mutual understanding and mutual consent, which in turn are founded upon communication. But communication presupposes already a social interrelationship upon which it is founded. . . . And the vehicles of such communication—significant gestures, signs, symbols, language— have necessarily to belong to the common environment in order to make communication possible and, therefore, cannot constitute it."

19. Schutz, "The Problem of Transcendental Intersubjectivity in Husserl," pp. 76–77, 79, 82. Compare also Schutz's comment in another context: "Sartre's statement that Husserl has not succeeded in explaining the problem of intersubjectivity in terms of a relationship between transcendental subjectivities seems to be correct. . . . Husserl, so it seems, has shown in a masterful way how within the mundane sphere man and fellow-man are compossible and coexistent, how within this sphere the other becomes manifest, how within it concordant behavior, communication, etc., occur. Yet he has not shown the possibility of a coexisting transcendental Alter Ego constituted within and by the activities of the transcendental ego." See "Sartre's Theory of the Alter Ego," *Collected Papers,* vol. 1, p. 197. The view that Husserl's argument entails basically a "reduplication of the ego" is also voiced by Eugen Fink in comments attached to Schutz's paper. As Fink adds, some of Husserl's late manuscripts point to "the curious idea of a primal ego, of a primal subjectivity which is prior to the distinction between the primordial subjectivity and the transcendental subjec-

tivity of other monads." See "The Problem . . . ," pp. 84, 86. The latter idea is in fact adumbrated in some of Husserl's working papers, especially in the "Nocturnal Dialog" (*Nachtgespräch*), written in June of 1933; see Husserl, *Zur Phänomenologie der Intersubjektivität*, vol. 3, pp. 580–88.

20. As he writes: "It is only if the we-community manifests itself in the life of the transcendental ego as transcendental, that transcendental phenomeno-logical idealism can be saved from appearing solipsistic. . . . But how can the appearance of solipsism come about? Obviously only by artificially suspending the hidden intentionality of the founding mundane intersubjec-tivity and eliminating, by means of the reduction, the essential content of the world accepted by me as a world for everyone." See Schutz, "The Problem . . . ," p. 83.

21. For a critique of Schutz's assessment of transcendental phenomenology compare Peter J. Carrington, "Schutz on Transcendental Intersubjectivity in Husserl," *Human Studies,* vol. 2 (1979), pp. 95–110.

22. Schutz, "Some Structures of the Life-World," *Collected Papers,* vol. 3, p. 122. "What belongs to the former, the ontological component of the situation," he adds, "is experienced by the individual as imposed upon, and occurring to him, as a condition imposed from without upon all possible free manifestations of spontaneity. The biographical state determines the spontaneous definition of the situation within the imposed ontological framework. To the experiencing subject's mind, the elements singled out of the pregiven structure of the world always stand in sense-connections, connections of orientation as well as of mastery of thought or action. The causal relations of the objective world are subjectively experienced as means and ends, as hindrances or aids, of the spontaneous activity of thought or action."

23. Ibid., pp. 117–20. Compare Aron Gurwitsch, "The Common-Sense World as Social Reality—A Discourse on Alfred Schutz," *Social Research,* vol. 29 (1962), pp. 50–72, reprinted as the introduction to the *Collected Papers,* vol. 3, pp. xi–xxxi; also Richard M. Zaner, "The Theory of Intersubjectiv-ity: Alfred Schutz," *Social Research,* vol. 28 (1961), pp. 71–94.

24. Michael Theunissen, *Der Andere: Studien zur Sozialontologie der Gegen-wart* (Berlin: Walter de Gruyter, 1965), pp. 87, 141.

25. In Theunissen's view, "joint work is not an incidental supplement to the other types of communicative interaction"; rather it constitutes a *central medium* of human contacts in the life-world. See ibid., p. 115.

26. Ibid., p. 126. Compare in this context also Alexandre Métraux's com-ments: "It is not sufficient merely to postulate a return to the 'world of the natural attitude' without at the same time taking seriously the implied theoretical and methodological consequences of this return. . . . Recogni-tion of the fact that the 'world of the natural attitude'. . . . represents in-deed the correct starting point is not yet equivalent to the required radical elimination of conceptions which are irreconcilable with this 'world'. . . . Although taking as its point of departure quite correctly the 'world of the

natural attitude,' Husserl's accounts continue to be permeated by a dualist conception of the relationship between subject and world which finds no warrant in everyday experience." See his preface to Aron Gurwitsch, *Die mitmenschlichen Begegnungen in der Milieuwelt* (Berlin and New York: Walter de Gruyter, 1977), pp. xviii–xx.

27. Theunissen, *Der Andere,* pp. 140, 150. As an antidote to the egological conception of intersubjectivity, Theunissen advanced the notion of dialogical encounter, patterned after Buber's I-thou relationship. Several years prior to Theunissen's study, a similar critique had been articulated by Emmanuel Levinas in his *Totality and Infinity: An Essay on Exteriority* (first French ed., 1961; Pittsburgh: Duquesne University Press, 1969). Arguing (p. 67) that the Other, in his true or *infinite* otherness, "does not lie at the limit of a cognitive process that begins as constitution of a 'living body,' as according to Husserl's celebrated analysis in the fifth of his *Cartesian Meditations"* and that the "relation with the Other" is "as primordial as the constitution from which it is to be derived," Levinas insisted that "the primordial sphere, which corresponds to what we call the same (or self), turns to the absolutely Other only on call from the Other." (Although treating intersubjectivity as a *face-to-face* encounter, the study departed from Buber's account chiefly by stressing the *asymmetry* of the I-thou relationship, pp. 68–69.) Reviewing Levinas' critique, Derrida finds the argument flawed by its insufficient recognition of the "irreducibly mediated" and transcendent status of the *alter ego* in Husserl's analysis, a status precisely demonstrated in Husserl's recourse to "analogical appresentation." According to Derrida, appresentation signifies the attempt to thematize the Other's essential *absence* or non-presence, with the result that Husserl's theory of intersubjectivity assumes the tension-laden (if not antinomial) features of a phenomenology of *non-phenomenality.* As he writes: "By transforming the Other, notably in the *Cartesian Meditations,* into the ego's phenomenon, constituted by analogical appresentation on the basis of the ego's own or proper sphere, Husserl (according to Levinas) missed the infinite alterity of the Other, reducing him to the self. . . . But it would be easy to show the degree to which Husserl, especially in the *Cartesian Meditations,* takes pains to respect the alterity of the Other in its significance. He is concerned with describing how the Other *as Other,* in his irreducible alterity, is presented to me, or how he is appresented . . . as an originary non-presence. It is the Other as Other who is the ego's phenomenon: but a phenomenon of a certain non-phenomenality which is irreducible for the ego as ego in general (or the eidos ego)." See Derrida, *Writing and Difference,* p. 123 (translation slightly altered; for a fuller discussion of Levinas' position see the section on French phenomenology below). Relying on Derrida's exegesis one might conclude that Husserl's transcendental intersubjectivity signifies a simultaneously present and absent community: present as phenomenon of the ego in general, and absent in its otherness or its aspect of general non-phenomenality.

28. Compare these statements in the *Letter on Humanism:* "Ek-sistence is neither the implementation of an essence, nor does it cause or constitute essence. If the term 'project'—as used in *Being and Time*—is interpreted in a cognitive-constitutive sense, then it is viewed as achievement of a subjectivity, rather than as man's ecstatic relationship to the clearing of Being (which is the only proper 'ontological' construction in the context of the 'existential analysis' of 'being-in-the-world'). . . . In the phrase 'being-in-the-world' the term 'world' does not designate the worldly in contrast to the heavenly domain, nor does it refer to the 'temporal' in contrast to the 'spiritual' realm. 'World' in that phrase does not mean any ontic object nor any ontic domain, but rather the openness of Being. . . . 'World' is the clearing of Being into which man reaches out from his thrown existence." See Martin Heidegger, *Über den Humanismus* (Frankfurt: Klostermann, 1949), pp. 17, 35.

29. Compare in this context especially Friedrich-Wilhelm von Herrmann's *Subjekt und Dasein: Interpretationen zu "Sein und Zeit"* (Frankfurt: Klostermann, 1974).

30. Martin Heidegger, *Being and Time,* trans. John Macquarrie and Edward Robinson (London: SCM Press, 1962), pp. 19, 21, 27 (in the above and following citations the translation is slightly altered for the sake of simplicity and clarity).

31. Ibid., pp. 72, 365–66.

32. Ibid., pp. 45–46, 366–67. According to Heidegger, a further merit of Kant's perspective was his attempt to construe the *I think* in the sense of *I think something.* However, the attempt was not rigorously pursued or implemented; presenting cognition as the mere coexistence of subjectivity (or a priori principles of consciousness) and substantive representations, he failed to explore the repercussions of the phrase on the *cogito:* "Although Kant avoided isolating the 'I' from thought, he did so without grasping the 'I think' in its essential core as 'I think something' and especially without perceiving the ontological 'presupposition' of the 'I think something' as basic determining feature of selfhood." Ibid., pp. 367–68.

33. Ibid., p. 73. Concerning Husserl's notion of consciousness or spirit, compare his comments in the *Crisis:* "The spirit, and indeed only the spirit, exists as an entity (*seiend*) in itself and for itself, is self-sufficient; and in this self-sufficiency, and only in this manner, it can be treated truly rationally, genuinely and from the ground up scientifically. . . . Only when spirit returns from its naive external orientation to itself and remains with itself and purely with itself, can it be sufficient unto itself." See *The Crisis of European Sciences,* p. 297.

34. Heidegger, *Being and Time,* pp. 365–66, 369. In the same context Heidegger cautions against the temptation to treat selfhood as new foundation or a priori premise in lieu of subjectivity: "From the circumstance that ontologically the self can be derived neither from an ego-substance nor from a 'subject' and that, on the contrary, everyday-fugitive I-talk has to be un-

derstood against the background of an authentic potentiality for Being, one should not draw the conclusion that the self is then the permanently given ground of care. Selfhood can existentially only be detected and grasped in self's authentic potentiality for Being, that is, in the authenticity of *Dasein*'s being *as care*."

35. Ibid., pp. 150–52. Heidegger, one should note, does not completely reject the practice of treating the commonsense notion of the ego as a given starting point for inquiry; this treatment, he grants, provides the basis for egological phenomenology in its own limited domain (p. 151): "Perhaps this kind of givenness (or rather 'giving') contained in simple, formal ego-awareness is indeed evident. This insight even affords access to an autonomous phenomenological problematic which has its basic significance within the confines of a 'formal phenomenology of consciousness.'"

36. See Eberhard Grisebach, *Gegenwart, Eine kritische Ethik* (Halle: Niemeyer, 1928), pp. 51, 77, 94, 131. The "question of Being", he added (p. 512, note), was articulated simply "on the basis of a prior, explicit decision in favor of a closed system of thought, in favor of a self-reflective and constitutive selfhood and thus in favor of 'man' as construed by humanism." In contrast to traditional metaphysics and the legacy of subjectivity, Grisebach advocated a radical reversal aiming at the replacement of constitutive human intervention by an attitude of patient *listening* and attentiveness (*Hörigkeit*)—notions which do not seem alien to Heidegger's perspective.

37. Karl Löwith, *Das Individuum in der Rolle des Mitmenschen* (Munich: Drei Masken Verlag, 1928), esp. pp. 79–82. For comments on this study compare Gurwitsch, *Die mitmenschlichen Begegnungen in der Milieuwelt*, pp. 142–43, and Theunissen, *Der Andere*, pp. 413–39.

38. See, for example, Ludwig Binswanger, *Grundformen und Erkenntnis menschlichen Daseins* (Zurich: Max Niehans, 1953); Martin Buber, *Between Man and Man* (London: Routledge and Kegan Paul, 1947), esp. pp. 163–81.

39. Theunissen, *Der Andere*, p. 166. The entire passage in which this statement occurs reads: "Husserl stands in the long and venerable tradition of thinkers for whom truth emerges from visual perception and from the contemplative gaze of theoretical cognition. By contrast, probing beneath the cognitive truth of perception, Heidegger explores the discovery or disclosure of worldly entities through practical involvement. Thus the 'understanding' of fellow-men—implicit in *Dasein*'s openness to Being as such—is not so much a cognitively acquired knowledge, but rather a manifestation of human care or 'solicitude'—a care which may be qualitatively different from 'concern' with things but which shares with the latter the connotation of practical involvement."

40. Ibid., pp. 160–61, 167.

41. Ibid., pp. 171, 174.

42. Ibid., pp. 173, 176, 179, 182–83. To my knowledge the only detailed examination of co-being in the English language is Carol C. Gould's unpub-

lished doctoral dissertation, entitled "Authenticity and Being-with Others: A Critique of Heidegger's Sein und Zeit" (Yale University, 1971). Without mentioning Theunissen, the dissertation basically endorses the latter's interpretation, especially the dichotomy between solitary authenticity and inauthentic being-with-others (under the dominion of "the They"). According to Gould, Heidegger's *Being and Time* is marred by a glaring contradiction or inconsistency: namely, by the presentation of co-being as a structural attribute of *Dasein* and its simultaneous denigration as a deficient or inauthentic mode of experience. "In our interpretation," she writes in the summary of her thesis, "authenticity was revealed as fundamentally 'non-relational'; in achieving totality, *Dasein* is individualized and its relations to others 'fail' it. I argue that this basic position of *Sein und Zeit* is inconsistent with another of Heidegger's claims: that *Dasein* is always Being-with others. This suggests that Heidegger's understanding of *Dasein*'s completeness involves an inconsistency."

43. Heidegger, *Being and Time,* pp. 153–55.

44. Ibid., p. 160. Also, on the *referential* context of ready-to-hand equipment compare pp. 95–122, especially this comment (p. 101): The mode of being of equipment "must not be taken as a matter of mere interpretation—as if ready-to-hand 'aspects' were superimposed on an empirical 'entity' or as if a primarily given substance were simply 'subjectively colored.'" Heidegger's stress on practical involvement, incidentally, does not mean an endorsement of willful or *subjective* behavior. "Practice," he writes (p. 99), "is not 'atheoretical' in the sense of blindness or lack of vision. Its difference from theory does not merely reside in the fact that the emphasis is in one case on observation and in the other on *action,* or that action to obtain guidance or direction applies theoretical insights; rather, practice has its own vision, just as observation arises originally from practical concern."

45. Ibid., pp. 161–62. As he writes at another point (p. 156): "Even when the *Dasein* of others becomes, as it were, a theme of study, they are not encountered as given ego-substances (or person-things); rather we meet them 'at work,' that is, primarily in their being-in-the-world. . . . The Other is encountered in his co-presence in the world."

46. Ibid., pp. 158, 161, 166. "Through such solicitude," Heidegger notes (p. 158), "the Other may become dependent or the victim of domination, even if this domination is tacitly exercised and remains hidden from him."

47. Ibid., pp. 166–68.

48. Ibid., pp. 158–59.

49. Ibid., pp. 303, 307–08.

50. Ibid., pp. 307–08.

51. Ibid., p. 308. As he adds (pp. 308–09): "Free for its innermost possibilities—possibilities which derive from the *end* (that is, death) and thus are understood as finite—*Dasein* dispels the danger that, mired in its own finite self-conception, it might fail to recognize the existential possibilities of others which surpass it or that it might misconstrue these possibilities and

identify them with its own—thus renouncing its own factual existence. As non-relational possibility, death individualizes; but, in light of its unsurpassable character (for each existence), it does so only in order to render *Dasein* as co-being sensitive for the others' potentiality for Being."

52. Ibid., p. 344.

French phenomenology

1. The renewed interest in Hegel was manifest chiefly in Jean Hyppolite, *Genèse et structure de la phénoménologie de l'esprit de Hegel* (Paris: Aubier, 1946), and Alexandre Kojève, *Introduction à la lecture de Hegel* (Paris: Gallimard, 1947).

2. The phrase "phenomenology with an ontological foundation," to characterize Sartre's early position, is used by Klaus Hartmann in his *Sartre's Ontology: A Study of "Being and Nothingness" in the Light of Hegel's Logic* (Evanston, Ill.: Northwestern University Press, 1966), p. 30; but perhaps the reverse formulation is more appropriate.

3. Jean-Paul Sartre, *Being and Nothingness, An Essay on Phenomenological Ontology,* trans. Hazel E. Barnes (first French ed., 1943; New York: Philosophical Library, 1956), pp. 233–35. As Sartre adds (p. 235), his previous attempt to obviate this conclusion by simply eliminating Husserl's notion of the transcendental ego was insufficient, for abandoning this notion "does not help one bit to solve the question of the existence of Others. Even if outside the empirical ego there is *nothing other* than the consciousness of that ego—that is, a transcendental field without a subject—the fact remains that my affirmation of the Other demands and requires the existence beyond the world of a similar transcendental field. Consequently the only way to escape solipsism would be here again to prove that my transcendental consciousness is in its very being affected by the extra-mundane existence of other consciousnesses of the same type." The reference is to Sartre, *The Transcendence of the Ego: An Existentialist Theory of Consciousness,* trans. F. Williams and R. Kirkpatrick (New York: Noonday Press, 1957).

4. Sartre, *Being and Nothingness,* pp. 235–43.

5. Ibid., pp. 244–47. The alleged equivalence of co-being and togetherness is underscored particularly in these passages (pp. 246–47): "The empirical image which may best symbolize Heidegger's intuition is not that of conflict but rather a *crew.* The original relation of the Other and my consciousness is not the *you* and *me;* it is the *we.* Heidegger's being-with is not the clear and distinct position of an individual confronting another individual. . . . It is the mute existence in common of one member of the crew with his fellows, that existence which the rhythm of the oars or the regular movements of the coxswain will render sensible to the rowers and which *will be made manifest* to them by the common goal to be attained."

6. Ibid., pp. 247–49.

7. Ibid., pp. 244, 250–52.

8. Ibid., pp. 253, 255–57.

9. Ibid., pp. 258, 260–63.

10. Ibid., pp. 263, 265–67.

11. Ibid., pp. 268, 270–72. With regard to transcendental reduction Sartre adds (p. 272) that I cannot make the Other's look "fall beneath the stroke of the phenomenological 'epoché.'" The Other cannot be bracketed "since as a look-looking he definitely does not belong to the world. I am ashamed *of* myself *before* the Other, we said. The phenomenological reduction must result in removing from consideration the object of shame in order better to make shame itself stand out in its absolute subjectivity. But the Other is not the *object* of the shame; the object is my act or my situation in the world. They alone can be strictly 'reduced.'"

12. Ibid., pp. 287–89, 292.

13. Ibid., pp. 296–97, 364. Compare also these statements (p. 408): "We can never hold a consistent attitude toward the Other unless he is simultaneously revealed to us as subject and as object, as transcendence-transcending and as transcendence-transcended—which is on principle impossible. Thus ceaselessly tossed from being-a-look to being-looked-at, falling from one to the other in alternate revolutions, we are always no matter what attitude is adopted, in a state of instability in relation to the Other."

14. Ibid., pp. 414–15, 417–21. As Sartre adds (p. 421): "Thus the oppressed class finds its class unity in the knowledge which the oppressing class has of it, and the appearance among the oppressed of class consciousness corresponds to the assumption in shame of an Us-object."

15. Ibid., pp. 424–29. With regard to class struggle Sartre initially ascribes an active possibility to the oppressed class (p. 422): "The assumption of the 'Us' in certain strongly structured cases, as, for example, class consciousness, no longer implies the project of freeing oneself from the 'Us' by an individual recovery of selfness but rather the project of freeing the whole 'Us' from the object-state by transforming it into a We-subject." But the possibility is not further pursued, beyond a reference to "mob psychology" and the emergence of a crowd under "the look of the leader."

16. Hartmann, *Sartre's Ontology,* p. 114 (italics added). Compare also Schutz's comments: "In being looked at I turn into an object for the Other-subject, whose subjectivity escapes me entirely. And objectifying the Other, I again seize the Other merely as an object. How is all this, if true, compatible with the assumption that my experiencing the Other and his experiencing me are interchangeable? . . . *Why from Sartre's position should we, then, assume that the Other acts at all, that he like me, has open possibilities?* Why assume that he has freedom, which to Sartre is the first condition of action? And how can we come to an understanding of what the Other's action means to him, the actor? . . . How explain, in a word, social action and social relationship?" See "Sartre's Theory of the Alter Ego," in Alfred Schutz, *Collected Papers,* vol. 1, *The Problem of Social Reality,* ed. Maurice Natanson (The Hague: Nijhoff, 1967), pp. 200–01.

17. Sartre, *Being and Nothingness,* pp. 230–32, 252, 283–85. In Hartmann's words: "A recognition of myself in the Other is not possible for Sartre. I am myself in negating the Other. As in the case of my negating being-in-itself, my reference to the Other is a negation of exclusion. . . . This antagonism between subject and object, which makes it impossible to have cognitive access to the Other as a subjectivity, or to recognize oneself in the Other, forms one of Sartre's basic convictions." *Sartre's Ontology,* pp. 115–16.

18. Sartre, *Being and Nothingness,* pp. 243, 299–301. "The multiplicity of consciousnesses," Sartre concludes (p. 301), "appears to us as a *synthesis* and not as a *collection,* but it is a synthesis whose totality is inconceivable."

19. Ibid., pp. 263, 286.

20. Jean-Paul Sartre, *Critique of Dialectical Reason,* vol. 1: *Theory of Practical Ensembles,* trans. Alan Sheridan-Smith (first French ed., 1960; London: NLB, 1976), pp. 79–80.

21. Ibid., pp. 64–69. "Since our starting point is individual praxis," Sartre writes (p. 65), "we must carefully follow up every one of those threads of Ariadne which lead from this praxis to the various forms of human ensembles; and in each case we shall have to determine the structure of these ensembles, their real mode of formation out of their elements, and finally their totalizing action upon the elements which formed them. But it will never be sufficient to show the production of ensembles by individuals or by one another, nor, conversely, to show how individuals are produced by the ensembles which they compose. It will be necessary to show the dialectical intelligibility of these transformations in every case."

22. Ibid., pp. 101–05 (translation slightly altered). As Sartre adds (p. 105): "Each center stands in relation to the Other as a point of flight, as an *other* unification. This is a negation of *interiority,* but not a totalizing negation. . . . The plurality of doubly negated centers at the level of practical unification becomes a plurality of dialectical movements, but this plurality of exteriority is interiorized in that it characterizes every dialectical process in interiority."

23. Ibid., pp. 106, 108, 111, 115 (translation slightly altered). Compare also these comments (pp. 108–09): "If I try to locate myself in the social world, I discover around me various ternary and binary formations, the first of which are constantly disintegrating and the second of which arise from an ongoing totalization and may at any moment integrate themselves into a trinity. . . . A binary formation, as the immediate relation of man to man, is the necessary ground of any ternary formation; but conversely, a ternary relation, as the mediation of man among men, is the basis on which reciprocity becomes aware of itself as a reciprocal connection."

24. Ibid., p. 230. In an effort to reconcile ontic determination with his earlier theory of freedom he comments (p. 227, note 68): "For those who have read *Being and Nothingness,* I can describe the foundation of necessity in terms of practice: it is the For-Itself as agent, revealing itself initially as inert or,

at best, as practico-inert in the milieu of the In-Itself. This, one could say, is because the very structure of action as the organization of the unorganized primarily relates the For-Itself to its alienated mode as Being-in-itself. . . . Necessity, for man, is conceiving oneself originally as other than one is or in the dimension of alterity."

25. Ibid., pp. 253–54 (translation slightly altered). The two formations seem to be ideal types in Weber's sense, although Sartre (p. 255) describes them as "extreme, though frequent and *normal* cases"; he insists in any event on the possibility of erecting a "clear separation between the two social realities."

26. Ibid., pp. 255, 260, 263, 267 (translation slightly altered). The serial link between men, Sartre writes (p. 263), "cannot be explained in terms of reciprocity" since seriality "excludes the relation of reciprocity: everyone is the reason for the other-being of the Other in so far as an Other is the reason for his being. In a sense, we are back with material exteriority, which should come as no surprise since the series is determined by inorganic matter. On the other hand, to the extent that the ordering was performed by *some practice* and that this practice included reciprocity within it, it contains a *real interiority:* for it is *in his real being,* and as an integral part of a totality which has totalized itself outside, that each is dependent on the Other in his reality."

27. Ibid., pp. 238–39, 250, 312, 316 (translation slightly altered). In general terms, Sartre adds (p. 317), class "produces itself as a contradictory double unity: for the inert-being-of-seriality, as the basis and material of every ensemble, is really the unity of workers in their being and *through being,* in so far as their destiny owes its rigidity to their dispersal and increases it; whereas an active organization constitutes itself against being and its unity is purely practical. In other words: praxis, as the organizing transcendence of inert being toward the reorganization of the serial field, is the unity of the multiple through perpetual labor."

28. Ibid., pp. 118, 255, 340–41, 357, 367, 372–73 (translation slightly altered).

29. As one should note, the preceding discussion of the *Critique* concentrated only on the main types of aggregates, while bypassing many subtypes and sociological nuances; above all, no attention was given to the disintegration or ossification of group life, a process leading from *fused* over *statutory* to *organized* groups and finally to the emergence of *institutions.*

30. Actually, Sartre in his early study distinguishes between three aspects of embodiment: the body as being-for-itself on the level of facticity; the body as body-for-others; and the body as accepted by me and simultaneously as known by others, or as "this perpetual 'outside' of my most intimate 'inside' "; see *Being and Nothingness,* pp. 303–59, esp. p. 352. For a comparison of Sartre's and Merleau-Ponty's views of embodiment compare Willi Maier, *Das Problem der Leiblichkeit bei Jean-Paul Sartre und Maurice Merleau-Ponty* (Tübingen: Mohr, 1964).

31. Maurice Merleau-Ponty, *Phenomenology of Perception,* trans. Colin Smith

(first French ed., 1945; London: Routledge and Kegan Paul, 1962), pp. xii–xiii. As one will notice, the Preface does not abandon reference to consciousness or to the *cogito,* although their significance is reassessed. "The true *cogito,*" we read in the same context (p. xiii), "does not define the subject's existence in terms of the thought he has of existing, and furthermore does not convert the indubitability of the world into the indubitability of thought about the world, nor finally does it replace the world itself by the world as meaning. On the contrary, it recognizes my thought itself as an inalienable fact, and does away with any kind of idealism in revealing me as 'being-in-the-world.' "

32. Ibid., pp. 347–48 (translation slightly altered).

33. Ibid., p. 349 (translation slightly altered). As he adds (p. 350): "In so far as I constitute the world, I cannot conceive another consciousness, for it too would have to constitute the world and, at least as regards this other view of the world, I should not be the constituting agent. Even if I succeeded in thinking of it as constituting the world, it would be I who would be constituting the consciousness as such, and once more I should be the sole constituting agent."

34. Ibid., p. 351 (translation slightly altered).

35. Ibid., pp. 352, 354.

36. Ibid., pp. 352–54 (translation slightly altered).

37. Ibid., pp. 355–58 (translation slightly altered). As he adds (pp. 356, 358): "The conflict between myself and the Other does not begin only when we try to *think ourselves into* the Other and does not vanish if we reintegrate thought into non-thetic consciousness and unreflective living. . . . Although I am outrun on all sides by my own acts and submerged in generality, the fact remains that I am the one by whom they are experienced, and with my first perception there was launched an insatiable being who appropriates everything that he meets. . . . The generality of the body will never make it clear how the indeclinable *I* can estrange itself in favor of another, since this generality is exactly compensated by the other generality of my inalienable subjectivity."

38. Ibid., pp. 358–59 (translation slightly altered).

39. Ibid., pp. 359–60 (translation slightly altered).

40. Ibid., pp. 360–61. Even the refusal to communicate, he notes (p. 361), is still "a form of communication. Unbounded freedom, the thinking nature, the inalienable core, existence without qualification—which in me and in others mark the bounds of sympathy—do interrupt communication, but do not abolish it. . . . Transcendental subjectivity is a revealed or manifest subjectivity, manifest to itself and to others; and for this reason it is an intersubjectivity." (One may wonder, of course, whether the terms *core of our thinking nature* and *natural difference* do not still betray an "inside-outside" distinction which Merleau-Ponty otherwise rejects.)

41. Ibid., p. 448 (translation slightly altered). Concerning being-for-itself and being-for-others he adds: "If the others who empirically exist are to be for

me other human beings (or egos), I must have a means of recognizing them, and the structures of the For-Others must, therefore, already be dimensions of the For-Itself." Likewise, "I must apprehend myself immediately as centered in a way outside myself, and my individual existence must diffuse round itself, so to speak, an existence in qualitative space. The For-Itselfs—me for myself and the Other for himself—must stand out against a background of For-Others—I for the Other and the Other for me. My life must thus have a significance which I do not constitute; there must strictly speaking be an intersubjectivity." (Translation slightly altered.)

42. Ibid., p. 362 (translation slightly altered).

43. Ibid., pp. 363, 445–46 (translation slightly altered). When I adopt a class position in a revolutionary context, he adds (pp. 446–48), "this taking of a stand is not the outcome, through some mechanical causality, of my status as worker or bourgeois (which is why all classes have their traitors), but neither is it an unwarranted evaluation, instantaneous and unmotivated; it is prepared by some molecular process, maturing in co-existence before bursting forth into words and being related to objective ends. . . . Idealism and objectivism both fail to pin down the emergence of class-consciousness: the former because it deduces actual existence from consciousness, the latter because it derives consciousness from *de facto* existence, and both because they overlook the nexus of motivation."

44. Ibid., pp. 363–64.

45. Ibid., p. 365.

46. Maurice Merleau-Ponty, *The Prose of the World,* ed. Claude Lefort, trans. John O'Neill (Evanston, Ill.: Northwestern University Press, 1973), pp. 134, 137, 140, 142–43, 145 (translation slightly altered). Regarding embodiment, the manuscript added (pp. 138–39) that "there would not be others or other minds for me, if I did not have a body and if they had no body through which they slip into my field, multiplying it from within, and seeming to me prey to the same world, oriented to the same world as I. . . . The solution . . . consists, as far as our silent relation to the Other is concerned, in understanding that our sensibility to the world, our synchronized response to it—that is, our body, the thesis underlying all our experiences—removes from our existence the density of an absolute and unique act, making a transferable signification out of our 'corporeality,' creating a 'common situation' and finally yielding the perception of another like ourselves."

47. Maurice Merleau-Ponty, *The Visible and the Invisible,* ed. Claude Lefort, trans. Alphonso Lingis (Evanston, Ill.: Northwestern University Press, 1968), p. 264. Regarding ontology compare his comments (p. 84) that Being "only shows through at the horizon, at a distance which is not nothing, which is not spread out by me . . . and which finally makes what merits the name of Being be not the horizon of 'pure' being but the system of perspectives that open into it, thus making the integral Being be not before me, but at the intersection of my views and at the intersection of my views with those of the others." Concerning chiasm and its relation to Hei-

deggerian teachings see Rudolf Boehm, "Chiasma: Merleau-Ponty und Heidegger," in *Durchblicke: Martin Heidegger zum 80. Geburtstag* (Frankfurt-Main: Klostermann, 1970), pp. 369–93.

48. Merleau-Ponty, *The Visible and the Invisible,* pp. 22–23, 32, 48 (translation slightly altered). "Here too," he added (pp. 48–49), "the reflective attitude would be inexpugnable if it did not belie in the hypothesis and as reflection what it affirms in the thesis about what is reflected on. . . . My access to a universal mind via reflection, far from finally discovering what I always was, is preceded by the intertwining of my life with other lives, of my body with the visible things, by the intersection of my perceptual field with that of the others, the blending in of my duration with the other durations."

49. Ibid., pp. 79–81 (translation slightly altered).

50. Ibid., pp. 80–82 (translation slightly altered). The reference to the *same* Being should not be misconstrued in the sense of an ontological identity, for elsewhere (e.g., p. 221) Merleau-Ponty pointed to the polymorphous character of Being: "Describe the pre-egology, the 'syncretism,' indivision or transitivism. What is the givenness (the 'there is') at this level? There is the vertical or carnal universe and its polymorphic matrix."

51. Ibid., pp. 82–83, 94. As he added (p. 95): "In other words, what we exclude from the dialectic is the idea of the pure negative; what we seek is a dialectical definition of Being that can be neither the being-for-itself nor the being-in-itself—rapid, fragile, labile definitions which, as Hegel rightly said, lead us back from the one to the other—nor the in-itself-for-itself which is the height of ambivalence." With specific reference to Sartre, the "Working Notes" observed (pp. 236–37): "The problem of negativity is the problem of depth. Sartre speaks of a world that is not vertical, but in-itself, that is, flat, and for a nothingness that is absolute abyss. In the end, for him depth does not exist, because it is bottomless. —For me, the negative means absolutely nothing, and the positive neither (they are synonymous), and that not by appeal to a vague 'compound' of being and nothingness; for the structure is not a 'compound.' I take my starting point where Sartre ends, in the Being taken up by the for-itself. —It is for him the finishing point because he starts with being and negentity and *constructs* their union."

52. Ibid., pp. 139, 264. Similarly, the chiasm was described (p. 264) as "the doubling up of my body into inside and outside—and the doubling up of the things (their inside and their outside)."

53. Ibid., pp. 138, 174. Compare also this comment (p. 172): "The passage to intersubjectivity is contradictory only with regard to an insufficient reduction, Husserl was right to say. But a sufficient reduction leads beyond the presumed transcendental 'immanence'; it leads to the absolute spirit understood as *Weltlichkeit,* to *Geist* as *Ineinander* of spontaneities, itself founded on the aesthesiological *Ineinander* and on the sphere of life as sphere of *Einfühlung* and intercorporeality."

54. Ibid., pp. 160, 263. "By reason of this mediation through reversal, this

chiasm," he added (p. 215), "there is not simply a for-itself for-the-Other antithesis; there is Being as containing all that, first as sensible Being and then as Being without restriction. . . . One cannot account for this . . . 'chiasm' by the cut of the for-itself and the cut of the in-itself. A relation to Being is needed that would form itself *within Being.* —This at bottom is what Sartre was looking for. But since for him there is no *interior* except me, and every *Other* is exteriority, Being for him remains intact after this decompression that occurs in it; it remains pure positivity, object, and the for-itself participates in it only through a sort of folly." Regarding third party intervention compare this passage (p. 263): "Reversibility: the finger of the glove that is turned inside out. —There is no need of a spectator who would be *on each side;* it suffices that from one side I see the wrong side of the glove that is applied to the right side, that I touch the one *through* the other."

55. See Jacques Derrida, *"Ousia* and *Grammé:* A Note to a Footnote in *Being and Time,"* trans. Edward S. Casey, in F. Joseph Smith, ed., *Phenomenology in Perspective* (The Hague: Nijhoff, 1970), pp. 54–93; and his *Positions* (Paris: Editions de Minuit, 1972), pp. 19–20, 37–38. Compare also Hugh J. Silverman, "Self-Decentering: Derrida Incorporated," in *Research in Phenomenology,* vol. 8 (1978), pp. 45–65, especially his comment (p. 54) that Derrida's "deconstruction involves both destruction and construction. It operates at the juncture which Merleau-Ponty described as the chiasm or intertwining between the visible and the invisible, between philosophy and non-philosophy; it fills out the Heideggerian 'in-between' as indicated by the crossing out of Being."

56. "Intersubjectivity," he observes at one point, "is not simply the application of the category of multiplicity to the domain of the mind. It is brought about by Eros, where in the proximity of another the distance is wholly maintained, a distance whose pathos is made up of this proximity and this duality of beings. What is presented as the failure of communication in love in fact constitutes the positive character of the relationship; the absence of the Other is precisely his presence qua Other." See Emmanuel Levinas, *Existence and Existents,* trans. Alphonso Lingis (first French ed., 1947; The Hague: Nijhoff, 1978), p. 95.

57. Ibid. Elsewhere he writes: "The absolutely other is the Other *(autrui)*; he and I do not form a number. . . . The absolutely foreign alone can instruct us; and it is only man who can be absolutely foreign to me—refractory to every typology, to every genus, to every characterology, to every classification—and consequently the term of a 'knowledge' surpassing objectification. The strangeness of the Other, his very freedom. . . . If totality cannot be constituted it is because Infinity does not permit itself to be integrated; it is not the insufficiency of the I that prevents totalization, but the Infinity of the Other." See Emmanuel Levinas, *Totality and Infinity: An Essay on Exteriority,* trans. Alphonso Lingis (first French ed., 1961; Pittsburgh: Duquesne University Press, 1969), pp. 39, 73, 80.

58. For a critique of the inside-outside structure—which is claimed to be still operative in Heideggerian thought—compare Levinas, *Existence and Existents,* pp. 81–82. Regarding exteriority the same study affirms (p. 95): "The exteriority of the Other is not simply an effect of space which keeps separate what conceptually is identical, nor is there some difference in the concepts which would manifest itself through spatial exteriority. It is precisely in as much as it is irreducible to these two notions of exteriority that social exteriority is an original form of exteriority and takes us beyond the categories of unity and multiplicity which are valid for things." The concept is further developed in *Totality and Infinity,* subtitled *An Essay on Exteriority.*

59. See Jacques Derrida, *Writing and Difference,* trans. Alan Bass (first French ed., 1967; Chicago: University of Chicago Press, 1978), pp. 112–13 (translation slightly altered). As he adds (p. 133): "To say that the infinite exteriority of the Other is *non*-spatial, that it is *non*-exteriority and *non*-interiority—thus failing to designate it otherwise than negatively—is this not to acknowledge that the infinite (also designated negatively in its presumed positivity: in-finite) cannot be expressed? Does this not amount to acknowledging that the structure of 'inside-outside'—coeval with language itself—marks the original finitude of language and of all that language seeks to grasp? No philosophical language will ever be able to eradicate the 'naturality' of the spatial praxis in language." For a fuller treatment of the inside-outside structure of language compare Derrida, *Of Grammatology,* trans. Gayatri C. Spivak (first French ed., 1967; Baltimore: Johns Hopkins University Press, 1976), pp. 30–65.

60. Derrida, *Writing and Difference,* pp. 125–27 (translation slightly altered).

61. Ibid., p. 114 (translation slightly altered).

62. Ibid., pp. 114–16 (translation slightly altered). Regarding embodiment he adds (p. 115): "Body: that means *also* exteriority, locality in the fully or literally spatial sense of the term; a zero point, the origin of space, although an origin which has no meaning before the *of* and which is inseparable from genitivity and from the space it engenders and orients— thus, an *inscribed* origin."

63. Ibid., pp. 138, 142, 317, note 66, 318, note 70 (translation slightly altered). In an effort to highlight its non-conceptual, not-purely-ontic, and constantly unfolding character, Derrida sometimes injects difference into the word itself by spelling it *différance.* One must admit, he writes at one point, "a systematic production of differences or the *production* of a system of differences—that is, a 'differance,'" adding that "I have tried to distinguish 'differance' (whose 'a' indicates, among other things, its productive and conflictual character) from the Hegelian difference" or antithesis; *Positions,* pp. 40, 59. Elsewhere we read: "Differance is not simply active (any more than it is a subjective accomplishment); it rather indicates the middle voice, preceding and setting up the opposition between passivity and activity. With its *a,* differance more properly refers to what in classical lan-

guage would be called the origin or production of differences and the differences between differences, the *play* of differences." See Jacques Derrida, *Speech and Phenomena, and Other Essays on Husserl's Theory of Signs,* trans. David B. Allison (Evanston: Northwestern University Press, 1973), p. 130.

64. Derrida, *Writing and Difference,* pp. 141, 143–44. As he adds (p. 141): "Since Being is what it is only through the letting-be of thought and since the latter is thought only by virtue of the presence of Being which it lets be, thought and Being or thought and otherness are the 'same'—which, we should recall, does not signify their identity, oneness, or indifference."

65. Ibid., pp. 137–38, 146. Criticizing both Levinas and Sartre, Derrida (p. 319, note 85) opposes the interpretation of co-being "in the sense of camaraderie, team effort or the like," adding: "The *with* of *being-with* (*Mitsein*) denotes *originally* as little the structure of a team animated by a neutral common task as does the *with* in the phrase 'dialog *with* God.' The Being alluded to in *being-with* does not signify (as Levinas repeatedly suggests) a third term, a common truth and the like."

Critical Marxism

1. In trying to explicate social interaction, adherents of these trends typically rely on symbolic, normative, or linguistic frameworks; however, the origin and philosophical status of these frameworks tend to remain in doubt. With regard to the first perspective compare Herbert Blumer, *Symbolic Interactionism: Perspective and Method* (Englewood Cliffs, N.J.: Prentice-Hall, 1969); concerning ordinary language theory see Peter Winch, *The Idea of a Social Science and Its Relation to Philosophy* (London: Routledge and Kegan Paul, 1958); and on communications analysis see Claus Mueller, *The Politics of Communication* (New York: Oxford University Press, 1973).

2. That Lukács' early thought may appropriately be ranked under the rubric of critical Marxism is corroborated by the assertion, in his major opus during the interbellum period, that genuine Marxism "does not imply the uncritical acceptance of the results of Marx's investigations; nor does it denote the 'belief' in this or that thesis or the exegesis of a 'sacred' text." See Georg Lukács, *History and Class Consciousness: Studies in Marxist Dialectics,* trans. Rodney Livingstone (Cambridge, Mass.: MIT Press, 1971), p. 1 (translation slightly altered). In a later context (p. 81), the same study notes that "the proletariat must not shy away from self-criticism, for its victory can only be based on truth; therefore, self-criticism must be its natural element." (In these and subsequent citations I have slightly altered the translation in the interest of clarity and readability.)

3. Ibid., pp. 111–12, 188.

4. Ibid., pp. 19, 55, 57–58.

5. Ibid., pp. 55–57.

6. Ibid., pp. 19, 58–59.
7. Ibid., pp. 19, 62, 64.
8. Ibid., pp. 62–64. As Lukács adds (p. 62), bourgeois individualism is itself a fragile and contradictory phenomenon; for, "on the one hand, the rise of the bourgeoisie endowed the individual with an unprecedented importance while, on the other, it tends to annihilate every type of individuality by subjecting it to economic preconditions and to the process of reification associated with commodity production." Moreover, even to the extent that it is cultivated, individualism under capitalism tends to be restricted to the minority of capital owners.
9. Ibid., pp. 122–23, 141, 145.
10. Ibid., pp. 145–49. As he notes in another context (pp. 17–18), "Marx's dialectical method arose as consistent continuation of the aims which Hegel himself pursued but never concretely achieved. . . . By recognizing 'the production and reproduction of real life' as the *in the last instance* decisive factor in history,' Marx and Engels gained the vantage point from which they could settle accounts with all (conceptual) mythologies. Hegel's absolute spirit was the last of these grandiose mythological schemes, a scheme which already gave expression (albeit in opaque or unconscious fashion) to historical totality and its dynamics. If in historical materialism reason—that reason 'which has always existed though not always in rational form'—finally reaches its rational form by discovering its real substratum or basis from which human life can really become conscious of itself, then this achievement means the implementation of Hegel's philosophy of history (even though at the cost of the destruction of his system)."
11. Ibid., pp. 19–21, 149. The stress on its subject-object character differentiates Lukács' notion of the proletariat at least in a minor fashion from the Sartrean We-subject; due to the pervasive opposition between for-itself and in-itself, the latter's subject-object quality remains precarious and limited to the (short) periods of *fusion*.
12. Ibid., pp. 47, 51. "This analysis," Lukács adds (p. 51), "establishes right from the start the distance which separates class consciousness from the empirically given and psychologically describable and explicable views which men form about their life situation."
13. Ibid., pp. 72–73, 165, 168–69, 172.
14. Ibid., pp. 52–53, 68–69.
15. Ibid., p. 80.
16. Ibid., pp. 77–78, 177–78. Some of Lukács' epistemological observations, especially those dealing with the relation between thought and being, point in a similar direction. "Only by being treated as a form of reality, as an element in the total process," we read at one point (pp. 203–04), "can thought overcome its own rigidity dialectically and assume the character of becoming. . . . Thought and being are thus not identical in the sense that they 'correspond' to each other, 'reflect' each other, 'run parallel' or 'coincide' with each other (all terms that conceal a rigid duality); rather,

their identity resides in the circumstance that they are components of one and the same concrete-historical and dialectical process." What remains questionable is whether the term *identity* is still appropriate to designate a situation where thought is a mere *component* unable to embrace reality as a whole. For a comparison of Lukács' dialectics and Heideggerian ontology see Lucien Goldmann, *Lukács and Heidegger: Towards a New Philosophy* trans. William Q. Boelhower (London: Routledge and Kegan Paul, 1977).

17. See Max Horkheimer, "Traditional and Critical Theory" (1937) in *Critical Theory: Selected Essays,* trans. Matthew J. O'Connell and others (New York: Herder and Herder, 1972), pp. 194, 199, 244. (For the sake of convenience I treat the postscript, dating from the same year, as part of the essay; in the above and subsequent citations the translation is slightly altered.)

18. Ibid., pp. 197, 199. Stressing the role of (abstract) individualism Horkheimer added (pp. 210-11): "Bourgeois thought is so constituted that, in reflecting on the cognitive subject, it discovers with logical consistency the supposedly autonomous 'ego.' Its approach is essentially abstract and its guiding principle is an individuality which is sealed off from concrete events and which bombastically considers itself the ground of the universe, if not the universe itself. . . . The thinking subject (*ego cogitans*) is not the locus where thought and object coincide and which could function as launching pad for the acquisition of absolute knowledge. Such an illusion—nurtured by idealism since Descartes—is ideology in the strict sense; for the limited initiative of the bourgeois individual here takes on the illusory form of absolute freedom and autonomy. However, in a non-transparent and unconscious society, the ego—whether as thinking or as practical subject—cannot have a secure footing. In the (traditional) conception of man, subject and object are sundered; their identity lies not in the present but the future."

19. Ibid., pp. 203-04, 244-45. Going beyond idealism Horkheimer discovered an important inspiration for critical theory in classical Greek philosophy (p. 246): "Irrespective of the interrelation between critical theory and the specialized sciences . . . the former never aims simply at an increase of information as such, but rather at the emancipation of man from slavery or repressive conditions. In this respect, it resembles Greek philosophy as it was practiced not so much in the Hellenistic period of resignation as in the golden age of Plato and Aristotle. While, following the unsuccessful political projects of these two thinkers, Stoics and Epicureans retreated to the doctrine of individualistic practice, the new dialectical philosophy clings to the realization that free individual development depends on the rational structure of society."

20. Ibid., pp. 198-99, 207, 244. For a critique of utopianism compare this statement (p. 250): "Dialectical theory does not practice criticism based solely on ideas. . . . Its standard of judgment does not lie beyond time, but in the dictate of time itself."

21. Ibid., pp. 207, 210.

22. Ibid., pp. 230–31. Regarding the two types of necessity compare also these comments (p. 229): "A consciously critical attitude belongs to the development of society. The conception of historical events as necessary products of an economic mechanism entails itself the protest (nurtured by the mechanism) against this order of things and the idea of the self-determination of the human species, that is, the idea of a situation in which man's actions are no longer the outgrowth of a mechanism but of his own decisions. The judgement regarding the necessity of past events implies here a struggle for its transformation from a blind into a meaningful necessity."

23. Ibid., pp. 213–14, 242. Even when recognizing its role, Horkheimer's references to the proletariat were at least ambivalent. Commenting on the interest in establishment of a rational society he observed, in a somewhat noncommittal fashion (p. 213): "The notion that this interest is necessarily generated in the proletariat is the doctrine of Marx and Engels." The following statements can perhaps be read as an oblique critique of Lukács himself, or at least of some of his disciples (p. 214): "The intellectual who, in reverent admiration, extolls the creativity of the proletariat and is content to canonize it, overlooks the fact that every evasion of theoretical effort . . . and of a possible temporary conflict with the masses induced by this effort only renders these masses blinder and weaker than they need be. His own thinking belongs as a critical, progressive factor to their development."

24. Ibid., p. 241. For references to other agents compare pp. 200 (society as active subject), 211 (interrelated individuals), 237–38 and 241 (marginal groups). While defending different types of solidarity or We-subjectivity, Horkheimer was careful to distance himself from spurious (fascist) doctrines of a quasi-biological *folk community*. "Behind the clamoring for a 'social spirit' or a 'folk community,'" he wrote (p. 243), "the gulf between individual and society widens every day."

25. "This influence of social development on the structure of (critical) theory," we read at one point (ibid., p. 238), "is part of the theory's own teachings. Thus new contents are not just mechanically added to pre-existing components. As a unified whole which gains its distinctive meaning only through its relation to the contemporary situation, the theory is itself caught up in an evolution—an evolution, however, which does not change the theory's foundations, any more than recent trends alter the nature of its chosen target, namely, contemporary society."

26. See Theodor W. Adorno, *Negative Dialektik* (Frankfurt-Main: Suhrkamp, 1966), pp. 8, 176, 184. As he added (p. 176): "Ontically mediated is not only the pure by the empirical ego . . . but the transcendental principle itself in which philosophy claims to find its origin or privacy vis-à-vis reality."

27. Ibid., pp. 15, 36, 174.

28. Ibid., pp. 73, 177, 179.

29. Ibid., pp. 15, 22. "Almost unconsciously consciousness would have to bury itself in the phenomena it encounters," the study notes at other points (pp. 36, 142). "In this manner dialectics would be qualitatively transformed, since systematic homogeneity would vanish. . . . Thinking does not have to remain imprisoned in its own rules; without relinquishing its role, it can think against itself. If a definition of dialectics were possible, this formulation might usefully be proposed." With regard to the role of cognition compare also this passage (pp. 187–88): "The 'thing itself' is by no means a mere product of thought; rather, it is non-identity piercing through (cognitive) identity. Such non-identity is not an 'idea,' but a hidden reference point. The experiencing subject strives to disappear in its folds; truth would be his dissolution."

30. Ibid., pp. 31, 157, 189. "Absolute dynamics," the study adds (p. 189), "would coincide with the kind of absolute praxis or activity which in domineering fashion finds satisfaction in its own deeds, while abusing the realm of non-identity as a mere stimulus or occasion." Regarding alienation another passage observes (p. 172): "The theory of alienation, treated as ferment of (idealist) dialectics, contaminates the need to come close to the heteronomous and, to this extent, irrational world—in the words of Novalis 'to be everywhere at home'—with the archaic-barbaric belief that the yearning subject is incapable of cherishing strangeness or otherness, and thus with the lust for incorporation and persecution. If strangeness were no longer ostracized, alienation or estrangement could scarcely persist."

31. Ibid., pp. 190, 199.

Modes of Sociality: A Typology

1. For a juxtaposition of individualism and sociality against the background of modern social philosophy compare David M. Rasmussen, "Between Autonomy and Sociality," *Cultural Hermeneutics,* vol. 1 (1973), pp. 3–45. In my view the term "autonomy" is applicable at this juncture only if used as a synonym for self-centeredness or willful segregation.

2. See Max Weber, *Economy and Society,* ed. Guenther Roth and Claus Wittich (New York: Bedminster Press, 1968), vol. 1, pp. 4, 22, 24–26. Compare also Rasmussen's comments: "Weber and Schutz were both willing to define social experience as the mutual interaction of two or more individuals. In my judgment this view is not adequate because, although it acknowledges the necessary recognition of the Other implicit in the social situation, it fails to come to terms with the *actuality* of a situation in which definition of self is based upon and finds its meaning in definition of self by another." "Between Autonomy and Sociality," p. 41. The above comments do not intend to disparage the Aristotelian scheme; with suitable modifications and adaptations, his distinctions (especially between oligarchy, polity, and democracy) seem still relevant to our age.

3. Compare Ferdinand Toennies, *Community and Society,* trans. Charles P.

Loomis (first German ed. 1887; East Lansing, Mich.: Michigan State University Press, 1957). To some extent Toennies' typology resembled distinctions developed during the same period by students of social evolution, especially Sir Henry Maine's dichotomy of *status* and *contract* and Durkheim's differentiation between *mechanical* (traditional) and *organic* social solidarity; see Henry Sumner Maine, *Ancient Law* (first ed. 1861; New York: Henry Holt, 1906), and Émile Durkheim, *The Division of Labor in Society,* trans. George Simpson (first French ed. 1893; New York: Free Press, 1964), esp. chapters 2 and 3.

4. In several of his writings Scheler differentiated between four main types of social coexistence or sociality, namely: *herd* (or *mass*) governed by causal-psychological mechanisms; *vital community* bound together by quasi-organic traditional ties; *society* denoting a juxtaposition of separate individuals; and *person-community* (or *love community*) involving the spiritual union of *persons* considered as sources of transcendental acts. Compare, for example, Max Scheler, *Formalism in Ethics and Non-Formal Ethics of Values: A New Attempt Toward the Foundation of an Ethical Personalism,* trans. Manfred S. Frings and Roger Funk (first German ed. 1916; Evanston, Ill.: Northwestern University Press, 1973), pp. 526–61; and his "Vorbilder und Führer," in *Schriften aus dem Nachlass,* ed. Maria Scheler, vol. 1 (Bern: Francke, 1957), pp. 265–66; see also Ernest Ranly, *Scheler's Phenomenology of Community* (The Hague: Nijhoff, 1966). The typology outlined below bypasses the notion of *herd* or *mob,* mainly because of its ambivalent status: the notion could designate either a societal (or serial) gathering produced through psychological contagion, or else a *fused* group intentionally welded together by charismatic leadership.

5. This point is made by Aron Gurwitsch in his study entitled *Die mitmenschlichen Begegnungen in der Milieuwelt,* ed. A. Métraux (written 1931; Berlin: Walter de Gruyter, 1976), p. 156, note 28. Gurwitsch distinguishes in that study between three main types of social formation: *Gemeinschaft,* characterized by ascriptive *belongingness* (*Zugehörigkeit*); *Gesellschaft,* founded on associative *partnership;* and *Bund,* formed through interpersonal *fusion* (*Verschmelzung*). The term *quasi-natural* was used above to indicate that, when serving as criteria of social organization, the mentioned factors cannot be viewed as completely pre- or non-social.

6. See Jean-Paul Sartre, *Critique of Dialectical Reason,* trans. Alan Sheridan-Smith (first French ed., 1960; London: NLB, 1976), pp. 255, 264. In his discussion of partnership, Gurwitsch focuses chiefly on common role-structure and presocial autonomy; *Die mitmenschlichen Begegnungen in der Milieuwelt,* pp. 154, 167.

7. For Sartre's comments see *Critique of Dialectical Reason,* pp. 118, 255, 341, 357. The importance of charisma in unified or fused groups is stressed by Gurwitsch who writes that "precisely because it is one and the same charismatic power which grips group members and because everyone of them senses this power, it is possible to say that something like a *'fusion'*

occurs between them." He also refers to the "non-worldly" character of charisma, an aspect which conjures up the problem of the "mundanization" and "routinization of charisma" discussed by Weber; *Die mitmenschlichen Begegnungen in der Milieuwelt*, pp. 203, 213–14. Weber's own discussion of charismatic communism and also of sects seems to corroborate the category of movement; see his *Economy and Society*, vol. 1, pp. 153, 456, vol. 3, pp. 1119–20, 1204–10, and his *Gesammelte Aufsätze zur Religionssoziologie* (Tübingen: Kohlhammer, 1922), vol. 1, pp. 152–70, 211. In contemporary political science the notions of movement-regime and mobilization system seem equally pertinent; compare Robert C. Tucker, "Towards a Comparative Politics of Movement-Regimes," *American Political Science Review*, vol. 55(1961), pp. 281–89, and David E. Apter, *The Politics of Modernization* (Chicago: University of Chicago Press, 1965), pp. 357–90.

8. Aristotle, *Politics*, 1323b 37–1324a 1 (Book VII, Chapter 1, par. 13).

CHAPTER THREE

1. For an overview of definitions or conceptions of human nature compare Leslie F. Stevenson, *Seven Theories of Human Nature* (Oxford: Clarendon Press, 1974), and Erich Fromm and Ramon Xirau, eds., *The Nature of Man* (London: Macmillan, 1968). Compare also J. R. Pennock and John W. Chapman, eds., *Human Nature in Politics, Nomos* XVII (New York: New York University Press, 1977).

2. Karl Jaspers, *Philosophy I*, trans. E. B. Ashton (Chicago: University of Chicago Press, 1969), pp. 233–34.

3. D. L. Meadows, *The Limits to Growth* (Washington, D.C.: Potomac Associates, 1972). Compare also M. Mesarovic and E. Pestel, *Mankind at the Turning Point* (London: Dutton, 1974), and David A. Kay and Eugene B. Skolnikoff, eds., *World Eco-Crisis* (Madison: University of Wisconsin Press, 1972). Regarding human and social connotations see Hwa Yol Jung and Petee Jung, "Toward a New Humanism: The Politics of Civility in a 'No-Growth' Society," *Man and World*, vol. 9 (August, 1976), pp. 283–306. For a shortened and revised version see Hwa Yol Jung, *The Crisis of Political Understanding: A Phenomenological Perspective in the Conduct of Political Inquiry* (Pittsburgh: Duquesne University Press, 1979), chapter 3, pp. 41–56.

4. As Marx writes: "Communism as a fully developed naturalism is humanism and as a fully developed humanism is naturalism. It is the *definitive* resolution of the antagonism between man and nature, and between man and man. . . . The *natural* existence of man has here become his *human* existence and nature itself has become human for him. Thus *society* is the accomplished union of man with nature, the veritable resurrection of nature, the realized naturalism of man and the realized humanism of nature."

See T. B. Bottomore, ed., *Karl Marx: Early Writings* (New York: Mc-Graw-Hill Book Co., 1964), pp. 155–57.

5. In the words of Alfred Schmidt: "Nature becomes dialectical by producing men as transforming, consciously acting Subjects confronting nature itself as forces of nature. Man forms the connecting link between the instrument of labour and the object of labour. Nature is the Subject-Object of labour. Its dialectic consists in this: that men change their own nature as they progressively deprive external nature of its strangeness and externality, as they mediate nature through themselves, and as they make nature itself work for their own purposes." See *The Concept of Nature in Marx* (London: NLB, 1971), p. 61. On the notion of metabolism see pp. 76–93.

6. Compare Helmuth Plessner, *Philosophische Anthropologie* (Frankfurt-Main: Fischer, 1970); *Conditio Humana* (Pfullingen: Neske, 1964); also my "Plessner's Philosophical Anthropology: Implications for Role Theory and Politics," *Inquiry,* vol. 17 (1974), pp. 49–77.

7. See Martin Heidegger, *Sein und Zeit,* 11th ed. (Tübingen: Niemeyer, 1967), pp. 47–48 (par. 10).

8. On the notion of nature see especially Martin Heidegger, "Vom Wesen und Begriff der Physis (Aristoteles' Physik B, 1)," in *Wegmarken* (Frankfurt-Main: Klostermann, 1967), pp. 309–71; also Karl Löwith, "The Nature of Man and the World of Nature (for Heidegger's 80th Birthday)," *Southern Journal of Philosophy,* vol. 8 (Winter, 1970), pp. 309–18. In his post-war writings, Heidegger repeatedly depicted man as part of a quadripartite structure (composed of earth and sky, mortals and immortals) in which all elements presuppose each other; compare, for example, "Das Ding," in *Vorträge und Aufsätze,* Part II, 3rd ed. (Pfullingen: Neske, 1967), pp. 37–55.

9. Edmund Husserl, *The Crisis of European Sciences and Transcendental Phenomenology,* trans. David Carr (Evanston, Ill.: Northwestern University Press, 1970), pp. 277, 299 (translation slightly altered). Compare also Maurice Merleau-Ponty, "Husserl et la notion de nature," *Revue de Métaphysique et de Morale,* vol. 70 (July-September, 1965), pp. 257–69; and William Leiss, "Husserl and the Mastery of Nature," *Telos,* no. 5 (1970), pp. 82–97.

10. As the study noted: "This reciprocity of the voluntary and the involuntary leaves no doubt even about the direction in which we must read their relations. Not only does the involuntary have no meaning of its own, but understanding proceeds from the top down, and not from the bottom up. Far from the voluntary being derivable from the involuntary, it is, on the contrary, the understanding of the voluntary which comes first in man. I understand myself in the first place as he who says 'I will.' The involuntary refers to the will as that which gives it its motives and capacities, its foundations, and even its limits." See Paul Ricoeur, *Freedom and Nature: The Voluntary and the Involuntary,* trans. with introduction by Erazim V. Kohák (Evanston, Ill.: Northwestern University Press, 1966), p. 5. Com-

pare also Kohák's comments (p. xv) that "while nature makes freedom actual, freedom makes nature more meaningful, and neither can ultimately be separated from the other. . . . While my freedom is actual only in and through my nature, the voluntary only by reason of the involuntary, that very 'nature,' that involuntary, becomes meaningful only in relation to the Cogito incarnate in and through it."

11. See Paul Ricoeur, *Freud and Philosophy: An Essay on Interpretation,* trans. Denis Savage (New Haven & London: Yale University Press, 1970); *The Conflict of Interpretations: Essays in Hermeneutics,* ed. Don Ihde (Evanston, Ill.: Northwestern University Press, 1974).

12. Paul Ricoeur, "Nature and Freedom," in *Political and Social Essays,* ed. David Stewart and Joseph Bien (Athens: Ohio University Press, 1974), pp. 23–30. Compare also his comments (pp. 29–30); "The idea of nothingness (néant), introduced as a gap between the 'I' and the sum of its motivations, is the symbol of the extreme *denaturing* to which it is undoubtedly necessary to go in order to comprehend the problem posed by the notion of human nature. . . . *Wesen ist gewesen.* The essential is the having been; to know this is to deliver oneself from the prestige of essential nature."

13. Ibid., pp. 30–37. As he added (p. 34): "In this sense we must reject both the wholly positive ontology of Spinoza, who can understand negation only as external destruction . . . , and the wholly negative ontology of Sartre, who in symmetric fashion relegates all positivity in being to the exteriority of the thing."

14. Ibid., pp. 39–40, 44. For a distinction between labor and work, but along somewhat different lines, compare Hannah Arendt, *The Human Condition* (Garden City, N.Y.: Doubleday, 1958), pp. 71–153.

15. Maurice Merleau-Ponty, *Phenomenology of Perception,* trans. Colin Smith (London: Routledge and Kegan Paul, 1962), pp. 240, 408 (translation slightly altered). The above point is noted by Frank Tinland who, referring to Merleau-Ponty's early studies, writes that the "embodiment of the *cogito*—however intriguing it may be—goes hand in hand there with a kind of disembodiment of the body. . . . The descriptions of the body in the first person singular and of the significance of embodiment for human existence have no doubt helped in conferring a new respectability on examinations of the body; however, they have also provided an alibi for the neglect of somatic structures whose analysis from a third-person perspective appears as a merely secondary, derivative construction." See *La différence anthropologique: Essai sur les rapports de la nature et de l'artifice* (Paris: Aubier Montaigne, 1977), pp. 22–23. Commenting on *Phenomenology of Perception* Merleau-Ponty himself observed at a later point that "the problems that remain after this first description" are "due to the fact that in part I retained the philosophy of 'consciousness' "; *The Visible and the Invisible,* ed. Claude Lefort, trans. Alphonso Lingis (Evanston, Ill.: Northwestern University Press, 1968), p. 183.

16. Merleau-Ponty, "The Battle over Existentialism" (1945) and "Hegel's Exis-

tentialism" (1946), in *Sense and Non-Sense*, trans. Hubert L. and Patricia A. Dreyfus (Evanston, Ill.: Northwestern University Press, 1964), pp. 66–67, 73.

17. Merleau-Ponty, *Phenomenology of Perception*, p. 346 (translation slightly altered). Concerning negativity, the same study noted (p. 215): "As for the subject of sensation, he need not be a pure nothingness with no terrestrial weight. That would be necessary only if, like constituting consciousness, he had to be simultaneously omnipresent, coextensive with being, and in process of thinking universal truth. But the spectacle perceived does not partake of pure being. . . . I am not, therefore, in Hegel's phrase, 'a hole in being,' but a hollow, a fold which has been made and which can be unmade."

18. Merleau-Ponty, "The Concept of Nature, I," in *Themes from the Lectures at the Collège de France, 1952–60*, trans. John O'Neill (Evanston, Ill.: Northwestern University Press, 1970), pp. 62–63 (translation slightly altered).

19. Ibid., p. 69. As Merleau-Ponty recognized, however, Descartes' view of nature was not entirely one-dimensional (p. 70): "By maintaining the contingency of the act of creation, Descartes upheld the facticity of nature and thus legitimized another perspective on this existent nature than that of pure reason. To this nature we have access not only through mind, but through the vital relation that we have with a privileged part of nature: namely, our body, through the 'natural inclination' whose lessons cannot coincide with pure reason" (translation slightly altered).

20. Ibid., pp. 71, 73 (translation slightly altered).

21. Ibid., pp. 63–64. In another lecture course Merleau-Ponty noted: "In Marx at the time of the 1844 Manuscripts, alongside a conception of history as man's 'act of birth' and as negativity, which he defends against Feuerbach, we found a naturalist philosophy which localizes the dialectic in the preparatory phase of human 'prehistory' and assumes as its horizon beyond communism as the 'negation of the negation,' the wholly positive life of man as a 'natural' or 'objective' being which is the resolution of the enigma of history. The latter philosophy is definitely predominant in *Capital* (that is why Marx could there define the dialectic as 'the positive intelligence of things as they exist') and much more so among Marxists." See Merleau-Ponty, "Dialectical Philosophy," in *Themes from the Lectures*, pp. 58–59.

22. Merleau-Ponty, "The Concept of Nature, I," ibid., pp. 75–76.

23. Ibid., pp. 78, 82–83; see also "Philosophy as Interrogation," ibid., p. 110. As Merleau-Ponty added (p. 111): "What has been called the 'mystique' of Being—a word expressly rejected by Heidegger—is the effort to integrate truth with our capacity for error, to relate the incontestable presence of the world to its inexhaustible richness and consequent absence which it recuperates, to consider the evidence of Being in the light of an interrogation which is the only mode of expressing this eternal elusion."

24. See Merleau-Ponty, "The Concept of Nature, I," pp. 85–87, "The Concept

of Nature, II," pp. 91, 98, and "Nature and Logos: The Human Body,"
pp. 125–26, all in *Themes from the Lectures.* On the relations between
Merleau-Ponty and structuralism compare James M. Edie, "Was Merleau-
Ponty a Structuralist?," *Semiotica,* vol. 4 (1971), pp. 297–323.

25. Merleau-Ponty, "The Concept of Nature, I," *Themes from the Lectures,*
pp. 64–65, 80. From the vantage point of theoretical reason, man's involvement in prereflective nature was bound to be perplexing; due to long habituation, reflection was wedded to the classical space-time coordinates and
thus "disoriented by this implication of the immemorial in the present."
However, Merleau-Ponty affirmed (pp. 65–66), "if we are not to be re-
signed to saying that a world from which consciousness is cut off is nothing
at all, then in some way we must recognize that primordial being which is
not yet the subject-being nor the object-being and which in every respect
baffles reflection. From this primordial being to us, there is no derivation,
nor any break; it has neither the tight construction of the mechanism nor
the transparency of a whole which precedes its parts."

26. Merleau-Ponty, "The Concept of Nature, I," pp. 81, 83, and "Nature and
Logos: The Human Body," pp. 128–29, both in *Themes from the Lectures.*
From the perspective sketched above the unconscious was neither a product
nor simply the reversal or repression of consciousness, but rather a layer of
archaic or prereflective experience (p. 131): "The repressed unconsciousness would be a secondary formation, contemporary with the formation of
a system of perception—consciousness—and the primordial unconsciousness
would be a permissive being, the initial yes, the undividedness of feeling."
Concerning the notion of a double nature compare also Heidegger's view
of the twofold character of being, in the sense of the *presence of absence;*
see "Vom Wesen und Begriff der Physis," p. 367.

27. Merleau-Ponty, *The Visible and the Invisible,* pp. 28, 88, 135, 137, 151,
201, 215, 275.

28. See Claude Lévi-Strauss, *The Elementary Structures of Kinship,* trans.
James H. Bell, John R. von Sturmer, and Rodney Needham (Boston: Beacon Press, 1969), p. 8 (translation slightly altered).

29. Jacques Derrida, *Writing and Difference,* trans. Alan Bass (Chicago: University of Chicago Press, 1978), p. 283. In a more general vein he adds
(pp. 283–84): "It could perhaps be said that the whole conceptual arsenal
of philosophy—which is systematically linked with the nature-culture dichotomy—is designed to leave unthought or unreflected the very condition
of its own possibility: the origin of the prohibition of incest." (Translation
slightly altered.)

30. Ibid., p. 280. What Derrida finds "most fascinating" in Lévi-Strauss' studies of myth is "the explicit renunciation of any reliance on a *center,* a *subject,* a privileged point of *reference,* an origin or absolute foundation
('*arche*')" (p. 283). Summarizing his distinction between types of structure or modes of structuralism he concludes (p. 292): "There are thus two
interpretations of exegesis, of structure, of sign, and of play. The one seeks

to decipher a truth or an origin immune from play and the order of the sign, and consequently experiences the need of interpretation like an exile. The other, no longer turned toward the origin, affirms play and tries to move beyond man and humanism, given the fact that 'man' is the name of the creature who throughout the history of metaphysics or onto-theology— in other words, throughout his entire history—has dreamed of full presence, a reassuring foundation, an origin and the end of play." (Translation slightly altered.)

31. Ibid., p. 284. Compare also Lévi-Strauss, *The Elementary Structures of Kinship*, p. 3, and *The Savage Mind* (Chicago: University of Chicago Press, 1966), p. 247.

32. Derrida, *Writing and Difference*, p. 288 (translation slightly altered). In a similar vein he writes at another point (p. 284): "The step 'outside (or beyond) philosophy' is much more difficult to conceive than is commonly imagined by those who think they have accomplished it long ago with cavalier ease, and who in general remain prisoners of metaphysics with the entire discourse which they claim to have disengaged from it."

33. Ibid., p. 288 (translation slightly altered). Compare also Lévi-Strauss, *The Savage Mind*, p. 247.

34. Claude Lévi-Strauss, *Totemism*, trans. Rodney Needham (Boston: Beacon Press, 1963), pp. 30, 99.

35. Derrida, *Writing and Difference*, p. 292 (translation slightly altered). Compare also Jacques Derrida, *Of Grammatology*, trans. Gayatri C. Spivak (Baltimore: The Johns Hopkins University Press, 1976), pp. 105–06.

36. Derrida, *Of Grammatology*, pp. 97–98 (translation slightly altered).

37. Ibid., pp. 150–51, 157. Compare also his comment (p. 259): "The passage from the state of nature to the state of language and society, the advent of supplementarity, remains outside the grasp of the simple alternative of genesis and structure, of fact and principle, of historical and philosophical reason. Rousseau explains the supplement in terms of a negativity perfectly exterior to the system it comes to overturn, intervening in it therefore in the manner of an unforeseeable factum, of a null and infinite force, of a natural catastrophe that is neither in nor out of nature and remains non-rational as the origin of reason must (and not simply irrational like an opacity within the system of rationality). The graphic of supplementarity is irreducible to logic, primarily because it comprehends logic as one of its *cases* and may alone delineate its origin."

38. Ibid., pp. 262–65. Due to the description, in *The Social Contract*, of the fundamental social order as a sacred right, Derrida feels justified in establishing a parallel between the "Essay" and Rousseau's more famous treatise (p. 265): "Everything in fact permits us to respect the coherence of Rousseau's theoretical discourse by reinscribing the prohibition of incest in this place. If it is called sacred although instituted, it is because, although instituted, it is universal; it is the universal order of culture. And Rousseau *consecrates* convention only on one condition: that one might universalize

it and consider it, even if it were the artifice of artifices, as a quasi-natural law conforming to nature. That is exactly the case with this prohibition."

39. Ibid., p. 267. Compare also his comment (p. 266): "The displacing of the relationship with the mother, with nature, with being as the fundamental signified—such indeed is the origin of society and languages. But can one speak of origins after that? Is the concept of origin, or of the fundamental signified, anything but a function, indispensable but situated, inscribed, within the system of signification inaugurated by the interdict. . . . The fundamental signified, the meaning of the being represented, even less the thing itself, will never be given us in person, outside the sign or outside the play (of difference); even that which we say, name, describe as the prohibition of incest does not escape play."

40. For an instructive dialog between an (egological) phenomenologist and a (structural-functional) positivist on the meaning of social action compare Richard Grathoff, ed., *The Theory of Social Action: The Correspondence of Alfred Schutz and Talcott Parsons* (Bloomington: Indiana University Press, 1978); for a recent effort to formulate a non-positivist and non-subjectivist theory of action focusing on the role of *habitus* see Pierre Bourdieu, *Outline of a Theory of Practice,* trans. Richard Nice (Cambridge: Cambridge University Press, 1977).

41. Ricoeur, *Political and Social Essays,* pp. 27, 98. For a distinction (partially inspired by Heidegger) between the ontological meaning of technology and its possible political repercussions compare Derrida, *Writing and Difference,* p. 318, note 79.

42. Maurice Merleau-Ponty, *Humanism and Terror: An Essay on the Communist Problem,* trans. John O'Neill (Boston: Beacon Press, 1969), pp. xxi–xxiv. As he continued (pp. xxiii–xxv): "The right to defend the values of liberty and conscience is ours only if we are sure in doing so that we do not serve the interests of imperialism or become associated with its mystifications. . . . There is a way of discussing communism in the name of liberty which consists in mentally suppressing the problems of the u.s.s.r. and which, as the psychoanalysts would say, is a sort of symbolic destruction of the u.s.s.r. In contrast, true liberty takes others as they are, tries to understand even those doctrines which are its negation, and never allows itself to judge before understanding."

43. Maurice Merleau-Ponty, *Adventures of the Dialectic,* trans. Joseph Bien (Evanston, Ill.: Northwestern University Press, 1973), pp. 204–05, 207, 225–26 (translation slightly altered).

44. Merleau-Ponty, *The Visible and the Invisible,* pp. 94, 266. As one should note, the opposition to philosophical rigorism did not imply a denial of philosophy, including political philosophy. In Merleau-Ponty's words (p. 266), philosophy cannot simply surrender itself to non-philosophy. "It rejects from non-philosophy what is positivism in it, militant non-philosophy—which would reduce history to the visible, would deprive it precisely of its depth under the pretext of adhering to it better." As examples of

militant non-philosophy he listed "irrationalism, *Lebensphilosophie,* fascism and communism, which do indeed have philosophical meaning, but hidden from themselves."

45. Ricoeur, *Political and Social Essays,* pp. 139, 207, 217, 225–27. As he adds (p. 227): "It is a question of knowing what the audience is today for non-Stalinist, non-dogmatic Marxists who are not enmeshed in the party ortho-doxy. Only the history of the coming decades will show if open Marxism can yet renew from the inside scholastic Marxism."

46. Ibid., pp. 142, 150–51, 213, 241. Going beyond the traditional separation-of-powers doctrine Ricoeur suggests (p. 214) that division of power today "implies perhaps an invention of new powers," especially in the cultural domain; precisely because of its "concentration of economic power," so-cialism "needs the independence of the judge and that of the university and the press."

47. See John O'Neill, *Perception, Expression, and History: The Social Phe-nomenology of Maurice Merleau-Ponty* (Evanston, Ill.: Northwestern Uni-versity Press, 1970), pp. 72, 78; also his *Making Sense Together: An In-troduction to Wild Sociology* (New York: Harper Torchbooks, 1974). The notion of a *wild politics* can also derive inspiration from some of Herbert Marcuse's writings, especially from his stress on a *new sensibility.* For comments on Marcuse in this light (and also for remarks cautioning against interpreting his thought in the sense of a simple return to nature) compare Herbert G. Reid, "Critical Phenomenology and the Dialectical Foundations of Social Change," *Dialectical Anthropology,* vol. 2 (1977), pp. 107–30.

CHAPTER FOUR

1. The three terms are frequently used interchangeably in the literature, and are so used here. Sometimes, however, a differentiation is made in the sense that *evolution* refers to material-biological underpinnings, while *mod-ernization* denotes sociocultural, and *development* economic and political trends. For the latter distinction compare, e.g., Lucian W. Pye, *Aspects of Political Development* (Boston: Little, Brown, 1966), pp. 3–48 (especially his comment, p. 8, that *modernization* is "the process of profound social change in which tradition-bound villages or tribal societies are compelled to react to the pressures and demands of the modern, industrialized, and urban-centered world. This process might be called Westernization, or sim-ply advancement and progress; it might, however, be more accurately termed the diffusion of a world culture").

2. See Edmund Husserl, *The Crisis of European Sciences and Transcen-dental Phenomenology: An Introduction to Phenomenological Philosophy,* trans. David Carr (Evanston, Ill.: Northwestern University Press, 1970), pp. 8, 15, 274 (translation slightly altered). For Husserl, the mentioned

telos was not an accomplished fact—and could not be fulfilled in the absence of a rededication of Western life to reason. Only through such a renewal, we read (p. 16), could it be "decided whether European culture bears within itself an absolute idea, rather than being merely an empirical-anthropological type like 'China' or 'India'—whether the spectacle of the Europeanization of all other civilizations testifies to the unfolding of an absolute meaning, one which pertains to the sense of the world, rather than to a historical non-sense." Husserl's argument, incidentally, was not meant as a simple defense of Enlightenment philosophy or traditional rationalism: "We are now certain that the rationalism of the eighteenth century, the manner in which it sought to grasp the essential roots of European culture, was naïve. But in giving up this naïve and (if carefully examined) even absurd rationalism, is it necessary to sacrifice the *genuine* sense of rationalism?"

3. Ibid., pp. 275, 281, 283–86, 288 (translation slightly altered). As he added (p. 275): "I mean that we feel (and in spite of all obscurity this feeling is probably legitimate) that our European culture contains an inborn *entelechy* which holds sway throughout all historical transformations, bestowing on them the sense of a development toward an ideal shape of life and existence as an eternal goal. We are not dealing here with one of those well-known types of teleology which characterize the physical realm of organic nature, especially not with something like a biological evolution from a seminal point through stages of maturity to a subsequent phase of aging and dying. For essential reasons, there cannot be anything like a zoology of peoples (or nations)."

4. Ibid., pp. 289, 338. These ideals, he continued (p. 289), "exist for individuals in their nations, and also for the nations themselves. But ultimately they are also infinite ideals for the expanding synthesis of nations in which each nation, precisely by pursuing its own ideal task in an infinite direction, contributes its best to the co-united nations."

5. See Georg Lukács, *History and Class Consciousness: Studies in Marxist Dialectics,* trans. Rodney Livingstone (Cambridge, Mass.: The MIT Press, 1971), pp. 19–20, 52–54, 188 (translation slightly altered). As Lukács soberly added (pp. 23–24): "The path of consciousness in the course of history does not become smoother, but on the contrary more and more difficult and demanding in terms of human responsibility."

6. Jean-Paul Sartre, *Critique of Dialectical Reason,* vol. 1: *Theory of Practical Ensembles,* trans. Alan Sheridan-Smith (London: NLB, 1976), p. 69. As one should note, however, Sartre's view of development was not entirely unilinear. "It must be understood," he observed (p. 222), "that there is a dialectic within the dialectic. That is to say, from the point of view of a realist materialism, the dialectic as totalization produces its own negation as absolute dispersal. . . . Thus it is not a process which is transparent to itself in so far as it is produced in the unity of a project, but an action which escapes from itself and diverts itself according to

laws which we know and clearly understand in so far as they effect an un-
balanced synthesis between interior and exterior."

7. See Walter Benjamin, *Illuminations,* ed. with introduction by Hannah
Arendt (New York: Harcourt, Brace and World, 1968), pp. 259–60.
(The citation is from the "Theses on the Philosophy of History" written
around 1940.)

8. See Jürgen Habermas, *Strukturwandel der Öffentlichkeit: Untersuchungen
zu einer Kategorie der bürgerlichen Gesellschaft* (Neuwied: Luchterhand,
1962); and *Theorie und Praxis: Sozialphilosophische Studien* (Neuwied:
Luchterhand, 1963), trans. John Viertel under the title *Theory and Practice* (Boston: Beacon Press, 1973). Regarding instrumental rationality
compare Max Horkheimer, *Zur Kritik der instrumentellen Vernunft*
(Frankfurt-Main: Fischer, 1967), trans. Matthew J. O'Connell and others
under the title *Critique of Instrumental Reason* (New York: Seabury
Press, 1974); also his *Vernunft und Selbsterhaltung* (first published in
1942; Frankfurt-Main: Fischer, 1970).

9. Jürgen Habermas, *Legitimationsprobleme im Spätkapitalismus* (Frankfurt-
Main: Suhrkamp, 1973), trans. Thomas McCarthy under the title *Legitimation Crisis* (Boston: Beacon Press, 1975).

10. Regarding the general features of structural-functional systems theory see
Talcott Parsons, *The Social System* (New York: Free Press, 1951), *Essays
in Sociological Theory Pure and Applied* (New York: Free Press, 1949),
and *Structure and Process in Modern Societies* (New York: Free Press,
1960); also Niklas Luhmann, "Moderne Systemtheorien als Form gesamt-
gesellschaftlicher Analyse," in Jürgen Habermas and Niklas Luhmann,
*Theorie der Gesellschaft oder Sozialtechnologie—Was leistet die System-
forschung?* (Frankfurt-Main: Suhrkamp, 1971), pp. 7–24. Concerning social development and the theory of pattern variables compare especially
The Social System, pp. 45–67; also Talcott Parsons, "Pattern Variables
Revisited," *American Sociological Review,* vol. 25 (1960), pp. 467–83, and
"Some Considerations on the Theory of Social Change," *Rural Sociology,*
vol. 26 (1961), pp. 219–39.

11. Habermas, *Legitimation Crisis,* p. 7 (translation slightly altered). As he
adds, such principles are "highly abstract rule systems which arise as emer-
gent properties from improbable evolutionary mutations and characterize,
at each stage, a new level of development." A task of historical systems
analysis is precisely to "ascertain the respective range of tolerance within
which the values of a given system may vary without endangering its continued existence. The boundaries of this range of variability coincide with
the boundaries of historical continuity."

12. Ibid., pp. 4–6.

13. Ibid., pp. 5–6 (translation slightly altered). As one may note, Habermas
does not abandon functionalist systems theory, but seeks to correct or supplement its deficiency through a stronger concern with normative-practical
aspects. As he writes (p. 4): "Both paradigms, life-world and system, are

important; the problem resides in their interconnection." To tackle this problem, Habermas turns to *crisis analysis* in an evolutionary context. Crisis analysis, he notes (p. 7), "requires an analytical framework through which the *connection* between normative structures and steering problems can be grasped. I find this framework in a historically oriented analysis of social systems."

14. Ibid., p. 17 (translation slightly altered).

15. To a degree, these *universal characteristics* can be compared with the *evolutionary universals* which Talcott Parsons delineated in his "Evolutionary Universals in Society," *American Sociological Review*, vol. 29 (1964), pp. 339–57.

16. Habermas, *Legitimation Crisis*, pp. 8–12 (translation slightly altered). Habermas at this point incidentally postulates a basic symmetry between ontogenesis and phylogenesis (p. 12): "The identity-stabilizing and socially integrative components of world-views—that is, the moral systems with accompanying interpretations—follow with growing complexity a pattern which has a parallel at the ontogenetic level in the logic of the development of moral consciousness. As long as the continuity of tradition endures, a collectively attained stage of moral consciousness can just as little be forgotten as a collectively acquired empirical knowledge (which does not exclude regression)."

17. Ibid., pp. 8, 12–14 (translation slightly altered).

18. Ibid., pp. 8, 14–15 (translation slightly altered). Habermas in this context (p. 150, note 10) finds some merit in systemic theories concentrating on an evolutionary process of learning, such as those formulated by Karl W. Deutsch in *The Nerves of Government* (New York: Free Press, 1963) and Amitai Etzioni in *The Active Society: A Theory of Societal and Political Processes* (New York: Free Press, 1968), however, he considers their conceptions "too narrow to encompass discursive learning."

19. Habermas, *Legitimation Crisis*, p. 17. Under the rubric of *modern* society, Habermas also lists the variant of a *post-capitalist* phase, a term meant to designate contemporary "state-socialist societies" characterized by a "political-elitist management of the means of production"; however, the study's focus is on *late capitalism* rather than post-capitalism of this type.

20. Ibid., pp. 17–18. As it seems to me, the study's developmental scheme bears affinity in many respects to the functional-evolutionary model outlined (in the context of American political science) by Gabriel A. Almond and G. Bingham Powell in *Comparative Politics: A Developmental Approach* (Boston: Little, Brown, 1966). Leaving aside the post-modern type, Almond and Powell like Habermas distinguish between primitive, traditional, and modern systems (subdividing the latter further into democratic and authoritarian variants, which correspond broadly to liberal capitalism, and late and post-capitalism). Again like Habermas, Almond and Powell focus on two main dimensions—systemic and normative-cultural—of social life, postulating that development involves both growing systemic or *struc-*

tural differentiation and increasing *cultural secularization.* As they write (pp. 215–16): "We propose to divide political systems into three classes, according to the degree of structural differentiation and cultural secularization. These classes are (1) systems with *intermittent political structures* (i.e. primitive systems), in which there is a minimum of structural differentiation and a concomitant diffuse, parochial culture; (2) systems with *differentiated governmental-political structures* (i.e. traditional systems), characterized on the attitudinal side by the spread of what we have called a 'subject' culture; and (3) systems in which *differentiated political infrastructures* (political parties, interest groups, and media of mass communication) have developed along with some form of participant political culture" (i.e. modern systems). Although the authors are unconcerned with questions of reflective or discursive validation, these comments on normative-cultural development deserve attention (p. 60): "It is through the secularization of political culture that these rigid, ascribed, and diffuse customs of social interaction (i.e. of parochial culture) come to be overridden by a set of codified, specifically political, and universalistic rules. By the same token, it is in the secularization process that bargaining and accommodative political action become a common feature of the society, and that the development of special structures such as interest groups and parties becomes meaningful." Regarding cultural development compare also Lucian W. Pye and Sidney Verba, eds., *Political Culture and Political Development* (Princeton: Princeton University Press, 1965); Gabriel Almond and Sidney Verba, *The Civic Culture* (Boston: Little, Brown, 1965); and regarding crisis analysis, Leonard Binder and others, *Crises and Sequences of Political Development* (Princeton: Princeton University Press, 1971), a study which concentrates on the five crises of *identity, legitimacy, participation, penetration,* and *distribution.*

21. Habermas, *Legitimation Crisis,* p. 18. Habermas cites in this context such works as Claude Lévi-Strauss, *The Savage Mind* (Chicago: University of Chicago Press, 1966), and Marshall D. Sahlins, *Stone Age Economics* (Chicago: Aldine-Atherton, 1972).

22. Habermas, *Legitimation Crisis,* pp. 18–20 (translation slightly altered). Habermas does not cite social-scientific literature at this point; some relevant works might be S. N. Eisenstadt, *The Political Systems of Empires: The Rise and Fall of the Historical Bureaucratic Societies* (New York: Free Press, 1963); and Joseph LaPalombara, ed., *Bureaucracy and Political Development* (Princeton, N.J.: Princeton University Press, 1963).

23. Habermas, *Legitimation Crisis,* pp. 20–21 (translation slightly altered). As Habermas writes (p. 21): "Only the relative uncoupling of the economic from the political system allows the development of bourgeois society as a domain which is free from traditional (normative) ties and given over to the strategic-utilitarian action orientations of market participants."

24. Ibid., pp. 22–23. "The opposition of interests, grounded in the relation of wage labor and capital," Habermas adds (pp. 23, 26), "comes to light not

directly in class conflicts but in the interruption of the process of accumulation, that is, *in the form of steering problems.* A general concept of system crisis can be derived from the logic of this economic crisis. . . . Economic growth takes place through periodically recurring crises, due to the fact that the class structure, transplanted into the economic steering system, has transformed *the contradiction of class interests into a contradiction of systemic imperatives."*

25. Ibid., pp. 33–36. The decline of the *fair exchange* principle, in Habermas' view, does not eliminate universal normative expectations, and especially not the demand for universal or general political participation (through suffrage). The conflict between eroded legitimacy and normative expectations is patched over through the device of *formal democracy* through which citizens are reduced to *consumers* of economic products and political decisions (p. 36): "Genuine participation in political decision processes— that is, substantive democracy—would render evident the contradiction between administratively socialized production and the continued private appropriation and use of surplus value. In order to conceal this contradiction from view, the administrative system must be sufficiently independent or immune from legitimating choices and decisions. The arrangement of formal democratic institutions and procedures permits administrative policies to be adopted largely without reference to the specific wishes of citizens; this happens through a legitimation process which elicits generalized preferences—that is, a diffuse mass loyalty—but avoids participation." Regarding the three subsectors of late capitalist economy Habermas relies chiefly on such studies as Michael D. Reagan, *The Managed Economy* (New York: Oxford University Press, 1963); Andrew Shonfield, *Modern Capitalism* (New York: Oxford University Press, 1965); and John K. Galbraith, *The New Industrial State* (Boston: Houghton Mifflin, 1967).

26. Habermas, *Legitimation Crisis,* pp. 45–47, 70, 73 (translation slightly altered). As he adds, however, a crisis can occur on this level only if expanded state intervention coincides with growing normative deficiency or unfulfilled legitimation needs (p. 71): "A crisis argument can be sustained only in connection with the broader point that the expansion of state activity produces the side effect of a disproportionate increase in the need for legitimation. I consider such a disproportionate increase probable, not only because the enlarged volume of administratively regulated issues necessitates the generation of mass loyalty for new functions of state activity, but because the boundaries of the political vis-à-vis the cultural system shift as a result of this expansion."

27. Ibid., pp. 48, 75, 79, 86–87 (translation slightly altered). As Habermas notes (p. 89), the advance of a fully discursive *communicative ethics* over the *"formal"* universalism of liberal-bourgeois (especially Kantian) principles resides not only in its global reach, but also in its ability to render wants and inclinations accessible to reflection: "The limits of formalistic ethics can be seen in the fact that inclinations incompatible with duties

must be excluded from the domain of moral relevance and actually be suppressed. The interpretation of needs prevalent at a given stage of socialization must thereby be accepted as given; they cannot in turn be made the object of discursive choice and deliberation. Only a *communicative ethics* guarantees the generality of admissible norms and the autonomy of agents by relying on the discursive justification of the validity claims connected with norms, that is, by according validity only to *those* norms to which all individuals affected could (freely or without constraint) consent as participants of a discourse if they entered a discursive process of deliberation." The conception of a communicative ethics relying on universal consensus—a consensus reached in an unconstrained discourse (or an *ideal speech situation*)—is spelled out at greater length in the concluding portion of the study, dealing with the "logic of legitimation problems"; ibid., pp. 95–117.

28. See Jürgen Habermas, "Können komplexe Gesellschaften eine vernünftige Identität ausbilden?" in his *Zur Rekonstruktion des Historischen Materialismus* (Frankfurt-Main: Suhrkamp, 1976), pp. 94–95. Compare also the statement (p. 93): "Successful ego-identity denotes the peculiar capability of speaking and acting subjects to remain identical with themselves even in profound transformations of the personality structure occurring in response to the challenges of conflicting situations." (The address was given in January 1974 when Habermas received the Hegel Prize.)

29. Ibid., pp. 97–101. (Portions of the address were translated under the title "On Social Identity," in *Telos*, no. 19 [1974], pp. 91–103).

30. See Jürgen Habermas, "Moralentwicklung und Ich-Identität," in *Zur Rekonstruktion des Historischen Materialismus*, pp. 67–74. With slight alterations I follow the English version in Jürgen Habermas, *Communication and the Evolution of Society*, trans. Thomas McCarthy (Boston: Beacon Press, 1979), pp. 73–78. Compare also the comment (p. 82) that Kohlberg's "empirically based classification of types of moral judgement is meant to satisfy the theoretical claim to represent developmental *stages* of moral consciousness. If we assume the burden of proof for this claim—a claim not fully redeemed by Kohlberg—we commit ourselves to demonstrating that the descriptive sequence of moral types manifests a developmental logic. . . . I would like to reach this goal by linking moral consciousness with general qualifications of role behavior."

31. Ibid., pp. 82–90. Kohlberg's six moral stages are: obedience and punishment orientation; instrumental hedonism; good boy-nice girl orientation; law and order orientation; contractual-legalistic orientation; universal ethical principle orientation.

32. In fall of 1974 Habermas presented an instructively synoptic conference paper on the topic "Comparison of Sociological Theories: With Reference to the Theory of Evolution." The paper distinguished between four main approaches to social evolution: historical materialism; social action theory; behaviorism; and functionalist systems theory. Ontogenetically the paper

relied on "Piaget's concept of a developmental logic" to buttress a maturational sequence of cognitive, linguistic, and interactive competences. Attention to the successive "moral institutionalization of behavioral expectations"
yielded a four-stage phylogenetic sequence: primitive societies; early (archaic) civilizations; developed civilizations; and early modernity. See Jürgen Habermas, "Zum Theorienvergleich in der Soziologie: am Beispiel der
Evolutionstheorie," in *Zur Rekonstruktion des Historischen Materialismus,*
pp. 129–43.

33. Habermas, "Zur Rekonstruktion des Historischen Materialismus," ibid.,
pp. 144–68. With slight alterations I follow the English version in Habermas, *Communication and the Evolution of Society,* pp. 130–53. Regarding
changes in forms of social integration, Habermas advances the explanation
(p. 148) that "the species learns not only in the dimension of technically
useful knowledge decisive for the development of productive forces, but
also in the dimension of moral-practical consciousness crucial for structures of interaction. The rules of communicative action, to be sure, evolve
in reaction to changes in the domain of instrumental and strategic behavior; but in doing so they follow *their own logic."*

34. Ibid., pp. 154–58. The introduction to *Zur Rekonstruktion des Historischen
Materialismus* contained further clarifications in both the ontogenetic and
phylogenetic domains. In the first domain the essay distinguished between
the sphere of the *epistemic ego,* comprising the maturation of cognitive,
linguistic, and interactive competences, and the sphere of the *practical
ego,* governing the formation of ego-identity. Establishing a parallel or
"homology" between ego- and group-identity, the paper indicated these
phylogenetic stages: neolithic societies; societies with state organization
(early civilizations); great empires (developed civilizations); and modernity. See "Historical Materialism and The Development of Normative
Structures," in *Communication and the Evolution of Society,* pp. 95–129.

35. Compare, for example, Joachim F. Wohlwill, *The Study of Behavioral Development* (New York: Academic Press, 1973); Edward O. Wilson, *Sociobiology: The New Synthesis* (Cambridge, Mass.: Belknap Press, 1975);
and Donald T. Campbell, "On The Conflicts between Biological and Social
Evolution and between Psychology and Moral Tradition," *American Psychologist,* vol. 30 (1975), pp. 1103–26.

36. Compare in this context Susan Buck-Morss, "Socio-Economic Bias in Piaget's Theory and Its Implications for Cross-Cultural Studies," *Human Development,* vol. 18 (1975), pp. 35–48; and Elizabeth Simpson, "Moral
Development Research: A Case of Scientific Cultural Bias," *Human Development,* vol. 17 (1974), pp. 81–106. Countering the view that modern
rationality structures derive entirely from a peculiar "Western spirit,"
Habermas at one point defends their universality, invoking Karl Jaspers'
notion of an axial age: "A more complex and (I think) more adequate explanation can be found by proceeding on the assumption that, far from being a peculiarity of occidental traditions, the universalistic potential is a

common feature of those world views which originated between 800–300 B.C. in China, India, Greece, and Israel. Those world views transcended mythical thought to the extent that they objectified the universe, differentiated natural from historical processes, developed the notion of abstract law, reduced the complexity of phenomena to principles, and replaced narrative by argumentative explanations." See Habermas, "Geschichte und Evolution," in *Zur Rekonstruktion des Historischen Materialismus*, pp. 241–42.

37. Habermas, *Communication and the Evolution of Society*, p. 106.

38. Ibid., p. 100.

39. Ibid., pp. 71–72 (translation slightly altered). He cites among other statements the following passage contained in Adorno's *Negative Dialectics* and referring to Kant's notion of the intelligible character (pp. 72–73): "According to the Kantian model subjects are free to the extent that they are conscious of, and identical with, themselves; and in such identity they are also unfree to the extent that they undergo and perpetuate its compulsion. As non-identical, diffuse nature they are unfree, and yet as such they are also free since in the impulses which overpower them they also escape from the compulsive character of identity." Habermas interprets the passage as "an aporetic delineation of the features of an ego-identity which renders freedom possible without demanding for it the price of unhappiness and of the violation of one's inner nature." However, instead of pondering further the *aporetic* quality, he prefers to resort to the "cruder tools of sociological action theory" in order to incorporate ego-autonomy into "empirical theories" amenable to "indirect testing"—although, on other occasions, he has repeatedly stressed the connection of empirical analysis with a "technical" cognitive interest in the "control" of objectified processes (that is, an interest far removed from the thrust of the cited passage).

40. Habermas, *Zur Rekonstruktion des Historischen Materialismus*, p. 95. Like Hegel, Habermas installs himself simultaneously in all perspectives; however, unlike Hegel, he fails to make clear the basis of this unification (e g , through reference to *absolute knowledge*). In a sense, intersubjectivity in Habermas' treatment is, as in Husserl's case, always simultaneously absent and present: present in a logical a priori fashion, and absent as a concrete (though intelligible) phenomenon. On the difficulties of the Hegelian approach to intersubjectivity see the section on French phenomenology in chapter 2.

41. See Habermas, *Communication and the Evolution of Society*, pp. 102, 121, and *Zur Rekonstruktion des Historischen Materialismus*, p. 96. On the assumption of a circular process, the absence of a corresponding social identity would jeopardize also the maintenance of ego-identity; for, Habermas adds, "as we have seen, an ego-identity can only be developed in the context of an overarching group identity."

42. In this respect one has to agree with Habermas' statement that "the very

concept of a developmental logic needs to be further pinpointed before we can specify formally what it means to describe the direction of development in ontogenesis and in the history of the species by means of such concepts as universalization, individuation, decentration (i.e., differentiation), autonomization, and growing reflexivity." See Habermas, *Communication and the Evolution of Society,* p. 117 (translation slightly altered).

43. Ibid., pp. 121, 140. The establishment of a yardstick for normal evolution is evident in a passage like the following (p. 141): "It is not the (actual) evolutionary processes which are *irreversible* but the structural sequences that a society must run through *if* and *to the extent that* it is involved in evolution."

44. See Habermas, *Zur Rekonstruktion des Historischen Materialismus,* p. 118; *Legitimation Crisis,* p. 141; *Communication and the Evolution of Society,* p. 148. The distinction between the epistemic and the practical ego does not seem to affect this status, especially since we are told (*Communication and the Evolution of Society,* p. 106) that the practical ego "secures the identity of the person within the epistemic structures of the ego in general." In the domain of language theory, Habermas likewise differentiates between propositional *logic* and discursive *pragmatics;* but the status of pragmatics seems to be on the whole *logical* in the traditional sense of the term. Compare, for instance, this passage in *Legitimation Crisis* (pp. 26–27): "The deep structures of a society are not logical structures in a narrow sense. Yet, propositional contents are always used in utterances. The logic that could justify speaking of 'social contradictions' would therefore have to be a *logic* of the employment of propositional contents in speech and action; it would have to apply to communicative relations between subjects capable of speaking and acting—and thus be universal pragmatics rather than logic." (Italics supplied.)

45. See Habermas, *Legitimation Crisis,* p. 95, and *Communication and the Evolution of Society,* p. 70.

46. See Lawrence Kohlberg, "From Is to Ought: How to Commit the Naturalistic Fallacy and Get Away With It in the Study of Moral Development," in Theodore Mischel, ed., *Cognitive Development and Epistemology* (New York: Academic Press, 1971), p. 223. Actually, Kohlberg's position is somewhat more complex on the issue. "To begin with," he writes (p. 222), "there are two forms of the 'naturalistic fallacy' we are not committing. The first is that of deriving moral judgements from psychological, cognitive-predictive judgements or pleasure-pain statements, as is done by naturalistic notions of moral judgement. . . . The second 'naturalistic fallacy' we are not committing is that of assuming that morality or moral maturity is part of man's biological nature, or that the biologically older is the better. The third form of the 'naturalistic fallacy' which we *are* committing is that of asserting that any conception of what moral judgement ought to be must rest on an adequate conception of what it is." He also notes (p. 223) that "science cannot prove or justify a morality,

because the rules of scientific discourse are not the rules of moral discourse." Nevertheless, he maintains (p. 224) that "while psychological theory and normative ethical theory are not reducible to each other, the two enterprises are isomorphic or *parallel*. In other words, an adequate psychological analysis of the structure of a moral judgement, and an adequate normative analysis of the judgement will be made in similar terms." With reference to Habermas, the danger of the naturalistic fallacy has been noted and criticized by Karl-Otto Apel, "Sprechakttheorie und transzendentale Sprachpragmatik zur Frage ethischer Normen," in Apel, ed., *Sprachpragmatik und Philosophie* (Frankfurt-Main: Suhrkamp, 1976), pp. 120–23.

47. See Klaus F. Riegel, "Dialectic Operations: The Final Period of Cognitive Development," *Human Development,* vol. 16 (1973), pp. 346–70, at pp. 348–50, 353, 364–66. Riegel's notion of dialectics is based both on Hegelian and Marxist thought; concerning the latter he notes (p. 367): "A theory integrating both interaction systems (i.e. psychological and cultural-historical) and, thus, regarding psychic activities and development in their joint interaction with both inner biological and outer cultural-historical conditions has been proposed by Rubinstein. . . . This theory has been based upon the historical and dialectic materialism of Marx, Engels, and Lenin which, in turn, has been derived from Hegel's dialectic idealism." Compare also his "Toward a Dialectical Theory of Development," *Human Development,* vol. 18 (1975), pp. 50–64; and Robert Hogan, "Dialectical Aspects of Moral Development," *Human Development,* vol. 17 (1974), pp. 107–17.

48. Habermas, *Communication and the Evolution of Society,* pp. 93–94 (translation slightly altered). As he adds (p. 94): "Autonomy which robs the ego of communicative access to its own inner nature also signals unfreedom. Ego-identity means a freedom which limits itself in the intention of reconciling, if not of identifying, dignity with happiness."

49. Habermas, *Legitimation Crisis,* p. 111. Compare in this context also these comments by Reid and Yanarella: "Rejecting an overly naturalistic conception of instinctual dynamics and needs (attributed to Marcuse) should not facilitate an uncritical appropriation of Habermas' concept of communicative action which tends to a notion of disembodied needs. . . . A truly dialectical theory must account for the 'element of otherness' in the needs-objects nexus in terms of a non-subjectivist theory of 'subjectivity,' i.e., the theory of the life-world and the material, concrete *apriori,* the latter constituting a central problematic of the 'historical matter' of social praxis." See Herbert G. Reid and Ernest J. Yanarella, "Critical Political Theory and Moral Development: On Kohlberg, Hampden-Turner, and Habermas," *Theory of Society,* vol. 4 (Winter, 1977–78), p. 533; also Vincent Di Norcia, "From Critical Theory to Critical Ecology," *Telos,* no. 22 (Winter, 1974–75), pp. 85–95.

50. See Habermas, *Communication and the Evolution of Society,* p. 116; *Legit-*

imation Crisis, p. 120; and *Zur Rekonstruktion des Historischen Material-ismus,* pp. 107, 118–19. Habermas does not elaborate how the "foundations of the new identity" differ from, or circumscribe, formal procedure. Regarding identity content, he lists as possible sources modern science (especially in its "popularized" form), philosophy, and art; but their contributions are purely optional. He also mentions (*Zur Rekonstruktion des Historischen Materialismus,* p. 121) the possibility of a "critical recollection (or remembrance) of tradition"—without, however, clarifying this intriguing notion.

51. Maurice Merleau-Ponty, *Phenomenology of Perception,* trans. Colin Smith (London: Routledge and Kegan Paul, 1962), p. 355. As he adds: "With the *cogito* begins that struggle between consciousnesses, each one of which, as Hegel says, seeks the death of the other. For the struggle ever to begin, and for each consciousness to be capable of suspecting the alien presences which it negates, all must necessarily have some common ground and be mindful of their peaceful co-existence in the world of childhood." For further criticisms of Piaget compare Merleau-Ponty's comments in *Bulletin de Psychologie,* no. 236 (November 1964), pp. 130–210.

52. Merleau-Ponty, *Phenomenology of Perception,* pp. 346–47 (translation slightly altered). Compare in this context also Derrida's comments: "What one must be suspicious of, I repeat, is the *metaphysical* concept of history. That is the concept of history seen as a history of meaning. . . . a meaning which is produced, develops, and reaches fulfillment, all this in linear fashion, either in a straight or circular line. This is why, incidentally, the 'end of metaphysics' cannot have the shape of a *line.*" See Jacques Derrida, *Positions* (Paris: Editions de Minuit, 1972), p. 77.

53. Maurice Merleau-Ponty, "From Mauss to Claude Lévi-Strauss," and "Everywhere and Nowhere," in *Signs,* trans. Richard C. McCleary (Evanston, Ill.: Northwestern University Press, 1964), pp. 120, 139. Compare also Hwa Yol Jung, *The Crisis of Political Understanding: A Phenomenological Perspective in the Conduct of Political Inquiry* (Pittsburgh: Duquesne University Press, 1979), pp. 82–83.

54. See Giambattista Vico, *The New Science,* trans. Thomas G. Bergin and Max H. Fisch (Garden City, N.Y.: Doubleday, 1961), paragraphs 326, 331, 378, 918, 973, 1038, 1106. The last point is expressed by Vico in these terms (paragraph 1108): "It is true that men have themselves made this world of nations (and we took this as the first incontestable principle of our Science, since we despaired of finding it from the philosophers and philologists), but this world without doubt has issued from a mind often diverse, at times quite contrary, and always superior to the particular ends that men had proposed themselves; which narrow ends, made means to serve wider ends, it has always employed to preserve the human race upon this earth." Regarding the status of Vico's own investigation compare Max Fisch's comments (p. xlix): "In devoting half the book to poetic wisdom, Vico exhibits scientific and philosophic wisdom seeking to know it-

self by recovering its own origins in vulgar or poetic or creative wisdom. In doing this, it becomes itself creative or re-creative. Doubtless all science is in some sense constructive, but the new science is so in a special way. For in *this* science, philosophic or scientific wisdom comprehends, though with the greatest difficulty, that vulgar or creative wisdom which is the origin and presupposition of all science and all philosophy."

55. See Theodor W. Adorno, "Die Idee der Naturgeschichte," in his *Philosophische Frühschriften* (*Gesammelte Schriften*, vol. 1), ed. Rolf Tiedemann (Frankfurt-Main: Suhrkamp, 1973), pp. 351–53. In regard to post-Husserlian phenomenology, Adorno criticized chiefly the neo-ontological conception of history as propounded by Max Scheler and, in part, by Heidegger.

56. Ibid., pp. 355–65.

57. See Max Horkheimer and Theodor W. Adorno, *Dialektik der Aufklärung: Philosophische Fragmente* (first published in Amsterdam, 1947; Frankfurt-Main: Fischer Verlag, 1969), trans. John Cumming under the title *Dialectic of Enlightenment* (New York: Herder and Herder, 1972). According to the authors (English version, p. xvi), the central thrust of the study was encapsulated in the counterpoint of these two theses: "that mythology points toward enlightenment, just as enlightenment tends to lapse into mythology." (In this and subsequent citations I have partially altered the translation for purposes of clarity.)

58. Ibid., pp. xi, xiii, xv. Turning against critics of modern culture like Aldous Huxley, Karl Jaspers, and José Ortega y Gasset, the study added (p. xv): "Enlightenment must reflect upon itself, if men are not to be wholly betrayed. What is at issue is not the conservation of the past, but the redemption of the hopes of the past. Today, however, the past persists as destruction of the past." The affinity with Vico was probably not accidental. In 1930 Horkheimer had written (as *Habilitationsschrift*) a monograph on the beginnings of the modern philosophy of history, a study culminating in a careful and sympathetic analysis of Vico's *New Science;* see Max Horkheimer, *Anfänge der bürgerlichen Geschichtsphilosophie* (Stuttgart: Kohlhammer, 1930).

59. Horkheimer and Adorno, *Dialectic of Enlightenment,* pp. 3–4, 7, 9, 14.

60. Ibid., pp. 12, 27.

61. Ibid., pp. 3, 13. Compare in this context also the statement (p. 32): "The essence of enlightenment is the alternative which is inescapably domination. Men have always had to choose between their subjection to nature or nature's subjection to human control. With the spreading of the bourgeois market economy, the dark horizon of myth is illumined by the sun of calculating reason beneath whose icy rays the seed of the new barbarism grows to fruition. Under the pressure of domination human labor has always tended to break away from myth—into whose spell it constantly returned under the impulse of domination."

62. Ibid., p. 36. Vico's portrayal is as follows: "But if the peoples are rotting

in that ultimate civil disease . . . , then providence for their extreme ill has its extreme remedy at hand. For such peoples, like so many beasts, have fallen into the custom of each man thinking only of his own private interests and have reached the extreme of delicacy, or better of pride, in which like wild animals they bristle and lash out at the slightest displeasure. Thus no matter how great the throng and press of their bodies, they live like wild beasts in a deep solitude of spirit and will, scarcely any two being able to agree since each follows his own pleasure or caprice. By reason of all this, providence decrees that, through obstinate factions and desperate civil wars, they shall turn their cities into forests and the forests into dens and lairs of men. In this way, through long centuries of barbarism, rust will consume the misbegotten subtleties of malicious wits that have turned them into beasts made more inhuman by the barbarism of reflection than the first men had been made by the barbarism of sense." *New Science,* paragraph 1106.

63. Horkheimer and Adorno, *Dialectic of Enlightenment,* pp. 17–18, 36, 39–40. Compare also the statement (p. 42): "As organ of adaptation or as a mere factory of instruments, enlightenment is as destructive as its romantic enemies have always charged. It comes into its own only by cancelling this consensus and by daring to renounce the false premise: the principle of blind domination."

64. Theodor W. Adorno, *Negative Dialectics,* trans. E. B. Ashton (New York: Seabury Press, 1973), pp. 317–18. (In this and subsequent citations I have partially altered the translation for purposes of clarity.) Compare also the comment (p. 320): "Worthy object of definition, the world spirit should be defined as permanent catastrophe. Under the sway of the all-powerful principle of identity, everything that eludes identity and the scheming designs of instrumental rationality turns into a source of fright—in retribution for the calamity inflicted by identity on the non-identical world. History permits hardly another type of philosophical interpretation—without succumbing to idealist mystification."

65. Ibid., pp. 320, 356–57.
66. Ibid., pp. 355–56, 359.

CHAPTER FIVE

1. W. D. Hudson, ed., *The Is-Ought Question: A Collection of Papers on the Central Problem in Moral Philosophy* (London: Macmillan, 1969), p. 11.
2. This is true of some versions of intuitionism and of radical existentialism (stressing the primacy and indeterminate character of human decision).
3. For a defense of the role of freedom in ethics and of the prescriptive character of norms see especially R. M. Hare, *Freedom and Reason* (Oxford: Oxford University Press, 1963). For a general discussion of descriptivism and prescriptivism in contemporary ethics compare William D. Hudson,

Modern Moral Philosophy (Garden City, N.Y.: Doubleday/Anchor, 1970).

4. For a recent attempt to translate the is-ought problem into a relationship of factual conditions see M. Zimmerman, "The 'Is-Ought': An Unnecessary Dualism," pp. 83–91, and Kenneth Hanly, "Zimmerman's 'Is-Is': A Schizophrenic Monism," pp. 92–94, both in Hudson, *The Is-Ought Question.*

5. Alan Gewirth, "The 'Is-Ought' Problem Resolved," *Proceedings and Addresses of the American Philosophical Association,* vol. 47 (Clinton, N.Y.: 1973–74), p. 37.

6. *The Meno,* 81C; see Plato, *Protagoras and Meno,* trans. W. K. C. Guthrie (Harmondsworth: Penguin Books, 1956), pp. 129–30.

7. *The Meno,* 89. As he adds (89B): "If they were, there would probably be experts among us who could recognize the naturally good at an early stage. They would point them out to us and we should take them and shut them away safely in the Acropolis, sealing them up more carefully than bullion to protect them from corruption and ensure that when they came to maturity they would be of use to the State."

8. See Stephen E. Toulmin, *An Examination of the Place of Reason in Ethics* (Cambridge: University Press, 1950), p. 193; also Kurt Baier, *The Moral Point of View, A Rational Basis of Ethics* (Ithaca, N.Y.: Cornell University Press, 1958).

9. John R. Searle, *Speech Acts: An Essay in the Philosophy of Language* (Cambridge: University Press, 1970), especially chapter 8. The argument was initially published under the title "How to Derive 'Ought' from 'Is,' " in *The Philosophical Review,* vol. 73 (1964), pp. 43–58; a condensed version of this article is contained in Hudson, *The Is-Ought Question,* pp. 120–34.

10. Searle, *Speech Acts,* pp. 4, 12, 16–18.

11. Ibid., pp. 33, 38, 51.

12. Ibid., pp. 132, 136, 148.

13. Ibid., pp. 177–81. In lieu of the stipulation of temporal simultaneity, the earlier version of the argument contained a number of *ceteris paribus* clauses which, as Searle notes (p. 180), "proved to be a standing invitation to various kinds of irrelevant objections."

14. Ibid., pp. 183, 185.

15. Ibid., pp. 186, note 1, and 198.

16. Ibid., pp. 176, 188–89.

17. Ibid., pp. 190, 192–93, 197.

18. Ibid., p. 4.

19. Thus, he writes at one point: "If you like then, we have shown that 'promise' is an evaluative word since we have shown that the notion of promising is logically tied to the evaluative notion of obligation, but since it also is purely 'descriptive' (because it is a matter of objective fact whether or not someone made a promise), we have really shown that the whole distinction needs to be re-examined." Ibid., p. 187. At other points, Searle down-

plays the significance of his entire argument by noting, for instance, that his derivation is "concerned with 'ought,' not 'morally ought,' " or by insisting on the distinction between committing oneself to the literal word-usage of *promising* and endorsing the institution "as a good or acceptable institution." Ibid., pp. 176, 194–95.

20. See R. M. Hare, "The Promising Game," in Hudson, *The Is-Ought Question,* pp. 147, 149, 154–55.

21. See Alan Gewirth, *Moral Rationality* (Lawrence, Kansas: University of Kansas, 1972), and "The 'Is-Ought' Problem Resolved," pp. 34–61. More recently Gewirth has provided a detailed account of his perspective in *Reason and Morality* (Chicago: University of Chicago Press, 1978).

22. Gewirth, "The 'Is-Ought' Problem Resolved," pp. 47–48. The term *categorial features* is used in Gewirth, *Moral Rationality,* p. 21.

23. Gewirth, "The 'Is-Ought' Problem Resolved," pp. 35–36.

24. While he speaks of *material* derivation in "The 'Is-Ought' Problem Resolved," p. 40, Gewirth refers to *inductive reasoning* in *Moral Rationality,* pp. 11, 15.

25. Gewirth, *Moral Rationality,* p. 12. A typical example of the means-ends model can be found in Max Black, "The Gap Between 'Is' and 'Should,' " in Hudson, *The Is-Ought Question,* pp. 99–113. Under the rubric of this model Gewirth also discusses the contractarian theory delineated in John Rawls, *A Theory of Justice* (Cambridge, Mass.: Harvard University Press, 1971). According to Gewirth, Rawls' argument—by invoking the noncontractual premises of the *original position* and the *veil of ignorance*—succumbs to circularity: "For the veil of ignorance, in addition to its obvious non-rational (because non-cognitive) features, is, like the assumption of original equality, a way of removing from the rational choosers' consideration certain factors, consisting in the actual empirical inequalities and dissimilarities which obtain among men, which, together with their self-interest, would strongly influence them to make inegalitarian choices." See *Moral Rationality,* p. 13. For the tension between contractual and noumenal ingredients in Rawls' study compare Robert Paul Wolff, *Understanding Rawls: A Reconstruction and Critique of* A Theory of Justice (Princeton, N.J.: Princeton University Press, 1977).

26. Gewirth, "The 'Is-Ought' Problem Resolved," pp. 44–45, and *Moral Rationality,* p. 12.

27. Gewirth, "The 'Is-Ought' Problem Resolved," p. 43.

28. Ibid., pp. 44–46, and *Moral Rationality,* pp. 4, 6.

29. Gewirth, "The 'Is-Ought' Problem Resolved," pp. 46–47, 49. In this lecture the method is characterized simply as dialectically necessary. *Moral Rationality,* on the other hand, speaks both of dialectical necessities and deductive inference. Commenting on the logical-methodological status of his assertions, Gewirth writes in the latter essay (pp. 19–20): "I shall interpret these assertions as conceptual or logical analyses of the concept of action, rather than as statements of the criteria of action or as inductive generalizations. I shall interpret the conceptual analyses, moreover, on the

model of deductive inference, such that the various components into which a complex concept is analyzed belong to it with logical necessity, so that it is contradictory to affirm that the complex concept applies and to deny that one of its component concepts applies."

30. Gewirth, "The 'Is-Ought' Problem Resolved," pp. 50–57. In *Moral Rationality* (p. 25) the maxim is called the principle of categorial consistency (PCC).

31. Gewirth, "The 'Is-Ought' Problem Resolved," pp. 50, 57–58.

32. Gewirth, *Moral Rationality,* p. 38.

33. Ibid., pp. 26, 29. Compare also his comment (p. 35) that "the analyticity of a moral rule or judgment essentially involves its normative, not its empirical content, its rightness or wrongness, not the empirical facts which enter into it."

34. Ibid., pp. 16–17.

35. Ibid., pp. 26–27. According to the second lecture, circularity is allegedly avoided because of the "necessary" status of the entailment. "The 'ought' which is derived within that context is prescriptive," we read; "but nevertheless the derivation is not circular, because the derived 'ought' reflects not a dispensable choice or commitment but rather a necessity which is not subject to any choice or decision on the part of the agent." Likewise, the "commitment in the premise is not one that the deriver has *chosen* or has *put into* the premise." See Gewirth, "The 'Is-Ought' Problem Resolved," pp. 60–61.

36. Gewirth, *Moral Rationality,* pp. 24–25, 28, 31–33. In his capacity of prospective agent, Gewirth states (pp. 24–25), it is "not the case" that the agent "cannot avoid participating voluntarily and purposively in transactions in which he is involved. For although it is necessarily true that insofar as he is an agent he participates voluntarily and purposively in the transactions he initiates, it is by no means necessarily true that his participation in all his future transactions will be voluntary and purposive, since his participation in them may not be as an agent at all." But obviously it is "necessarily true" that "insofar as he is an agent (in the future)" his participation in future transactions will be voluntary and purposive; alternatively, if agency is avoidable in the future, it seems equally avoidable in the present.

37. Fred M. Frohock, *Normative Political Theory* (Englewood Cliffs, N.J.: Prentice-Hall, 1974), pp. 9, 96.

38. Ibid., pp. 32–34, 75–76. Frohock also reviews the normative status of laws or legal systems construed as social institutions. While admitting (p. 53) that "the connection between physicalist facts and institutional facts is tighter" in legally defined situations, he reaches basically the same conclusion (p. 61): Since "it is possible without complication to move to the outside of any social arrangements with an evaluative question," so *"any* definition of law, by virtue of the fact that law is a social convention, must be vulnerable to the possibility of external evaluation."

39. Ibid., pp. 84, 106–09. Among consequences of universality, Frohock also

mentions that a moral polity will "emphasize the general qualities of social experience at the expense of its particular features" and that its outlook will be "nonheroic" since "the extraordinary man or action, in the public sphere, violates the public similarity which moral policy requires."

40. Thus, in reviewing natural law theory as articulated by Lon Fuller, he comments: "What Fuller appears to have offered us is a description of what it is for rules to be rational, not what it means for rules to be legal or moral." Similarly, in examining Hare's principle of universalizability, he notes: "We are left without any identifying feature of morality, though we have a cogent definition of rationality. Unfortunately, however, both doctors and murderers can be rational, each in their own way in their own systems, and only morality can separate them for judgment." It is at least doubtful that the substitution of universality for universalizability alters this conclusion. See ibid., pp. 60–61, 83.

41. Ibid., pp. 84–85. A similar disclaimer is attached to the outline of a moral polity (p. 109): "A set of concepts 'defining' morality has been used to describe a political society. If the account of morality is unacceptable, then so too will be the description of the moral polity, and in any case, nothing exhaustive or definitive is claimed for this exercise."

42. Ibid., pp. 35, 75–76, 110. A footnote attached to the latter comments (p. 110, note 19) refers chiefly to Noam Chomsky's "revival of rationalist philosophy through a theory of language" and to Maurice Natanson and Peter Winch as representatives of "phenomenology in social analysis."

43. Compare, for example, Willi Oelmüller, ed., *Transzendentalphilosophische Normenbegründungen* (Paderborn: F. Schöningh, 1978).

44. Karl-Otto Apel, "Sprechakttheorie und transzendentale Sprachpragmatik zur Frage ethischer Normen," in Apel, ed., *Sprachpragmatik und Philosophie* (Frankfurt-Main: Suhrkamp, 1976), p. 16. By concentrating on linguistic communication, he adds (p. 26), transcendental reflection seeks to uncover "the *subjective-intersubjective* conditions of possibility of all types of *intersubjectively valid* knowledge" (including intersubjectively justifiable norms).

45. Ibid., p. 55.

46. Ibid., pp. 65–66.

47. Ibid., pp. 73, 76, 78–79. Regarding the role of *understanding,* Apel (p. 79) credits Searle with having made "a contribution to the methodology of the social sciences conceived as hermeneutical disciplines, a contribution which corroborates Peter Winch's insight regarding the need of the social scientist to ascertain—through participation in the native language game—that he has correctly interpreted the rules followed by the members of the investigated group."

48. Ibid., pp. 79–80, 82–83.

49. Ibid., pp. 114, 120, 126. According to Apel, reliance on the transcendental premises of discourse does not involve a recourse to *ontic* facts (not even to metaphysically construed facts), but only to the process of rational re-

flection. In this respect he differentiates his outlook from the perspective of universal pragmatics as formulated by Jürgen Habermas, with its focus on positive-universal conditions of speech. "Ethics," he writes (pp. 121–22), "cannot be grounded in a *universal theory of reconstructive social science*— this would only amount to an updated version of the 'naturalistic fallacy'. . . . This consideration applies to the attempt to justify norms by means of a reconstruction of the factually always recognized norms implicit in the *fact* of 'communicative competence' (not to mention the attempt to provide such justification through a 'normative genesis' of social evolution or through a reconstruction of the development of moral consciousness in the manner of Piaget and Kohlberg)." For Habermas' position compare especially his "Was heisst Universalpragmatik?," ibid., pp. 174–272.

50. For the concept of a recollective interpretation or hermeneutics (formulated from a phenomenological perspective) see Paul Ricoeur, *Freud and Philosophy: An Essay on Interpretation,* trans. Denis Savage (New Haven: Yale University Press, 1970), especially pp. 28–32. In terms of Kantian philosophy the above-mentioned practice bears resemblance less to *practical reason* than to the domain of *judgment* discussed in the Third Critique where rational understanding is said to be "in the service of imagination rather than the other way around"; see Immanuel Kant, *Werke,* vol. 5; *Kritik der Urteilskraft* (Darmstadt: Wissenschaftliche Buchhandlung, 1966), p. 326. Regarding *poetic* or *vulgar wisdom* and especially *poetic morals* compare Giambattista Vico, *The New Science,* trans. Thomas G. Bergin and Max H. Fisch (Garden City, N.Y., Doubleday/Anchor, 1961), book 2, pp. 69–241.

51. Theodor W. Adorno, *Negative Dialektik* (Frankfurt-Main: Suhrkamp, 1966), pp. 228, 232, 251.

52. Ibid., pp. 219, 226, 279–80, 292. Adorno refers in this context (p. 292) to the "Jewish theologoumenon" according to which "in the redeemed state everything would only be slightly different from the present condition— although even the slightest detail cannot now be imagined as it would be."

53. Maurice Merleau-Ponty, *Phenomenology of Perception,* trans. Colin Smith (London: Routledge and Kegan Paul, 1962), pp. 438–39, 442 (translation slightly altered).

54. Ibid., pp. 440–41 (translation slightly altered). Compare also the attempt, partially inspired by Merleau-Ponty, to develop a contextual but non-contingent ethics in Bernhard Waldenfels, "Verhaltensnorm und Verhaltens-kontext," in Waldenfels and others, eds., *Phänomenologie und Marxismus,* vol. 2: *Praktische Philosophie* (Frankfurt-Main: Suhrkamp, 1977), pp. 134–57.

55. Martin Heidegger, *Über den Humanismus* (Frankfurt-Main: Klostermann, 1949), pp. 35, 39, 41–43. Compare also Jacques Derrida's comments: "Thought (or at least the precomprehension) of Being *conditions* . . . the *recognition* of the essence of the existent (for example someone, exis-

tent *as* other, *as* other self, etc.). It conditions the respect for the other *as what it is:* other. Without this acknowledgment, which is not a knowledge, or let us say without this 'letting-be' of an existent (other) as something existing outside me in the essence of what it is (first in its otherness), no ethics would be possible." See his *Writing and Difference,* trans. Alan Bass (Chicago: University of Chicago Press, 1978), pp. 137–38 (translation slightly altered).

INDEX